THE INTERPRETATION OF CULTURES

SELECTED ESSAYS

BY

Clifford Geertz

Basic Books, Inc., Publishers

NEW YORK

Copyright © 1973 by Basic Books, Inc.
Library of Congress Catalog Card Number: 73-81196
ISBN: 0-465-03425-X (cloth)
ISBN: 0-465-09719-7 (paper)
Printed in the United States of America
80 81   10 9 8 7 6 5 4

Contents

PART IV

PART V

Preface

When an anthropologist, urged on by an attentive publisher, begins to gather together certain of his essays for a kind of retrospective exhibition of what he has been doing, or trying to do, over the fifteen-year period since his release from graduate school, he is faced by two tearing decisions: what to include, and how reverently to treat what is included. All of us who write social science journal pieces have a nonbook in us, and more and more of us are publishing them; all of us imagine that anything our past self has done our present self could do better, and stand ready to perpetrate improvements upon our own work we would never stand for from any editor. To try to find the figure in the carpet of one's writings can be as chilling as trying to find it in one's life; to weave, *post facto,* a figure in—"this is what I *meant* to say"—is an intense temptation.

I have faced up to the first of these decisions by including in this collection only those of my essays which bear, directly and explicitly, on the concept of culture. The majority of the essays are, in fact, empirical studies rather than theoretical disquisitions, for I grow uncomfortable when I get too far away from the immediacies of social life. But all of them are basically concerned with pushing forward, instant case by instant case, a particular, some would say peculiar, view of what culture is, what role it plays in social life, and how it ought properly to be studied. Though this redefinition of culture has perhaps been my most persistent interest as an anthropologist, I have also worked with some extensiveness in the areas of economic development, social organization, comparative history, and cultural ecology—concerns which are, save tangentially, not reflected here. Thus, what is ostensibly a set of essays emerges, so I hope, somewhat as a treatise—a treatise in cultural theory as developed through a series of concrete analyses. Not just an "and then I wrote . . ." review of a somewhat vagrant professional career, this book has an argument to make.

The second decision has been a bit trickier to deal with. In general, I hold to a *stare decisis* view of published pieces, if only because if they need very much revision they probably ought not to be reprinted at all, but should be replaced with a wholly new article getting the damn thing right. Further, correcting one's misjudgments by writing changed views back into earlier works seems to me not wholly cricket, and it obscures the development of ideas that one is supposedly trying to demonstrate in collecting the essays in the first place.

However, for all that, there does seem justification for a certain amount of retroactive editing in cases where the substance of the argument is not seriously affected but to leave things exactly as originally written is either to purvey out-of-date information or undercut a still valid discussion by tying it too closely to a particular set of now faded events.

There are two places in the essays below where these considerations seemed to me relevant, and where I have therefore made some changes in what I originally wrote. The first is in the two essays of Part II on culture and biological evolution, where the fossil datings given in the original essays have been definitely superseded. The dates have, in general, been moved back in time, and as this change leaves my central arguments essentially intact, I see no harm in introducing the newer estimations. There seems little point in continuing to tell the world that Australopithecines go back a million years when archeologists are now finding fossils datable to four or five million years. The second is in connection with Chapter 10, in Part IV, "The Integrative Revolution," where the flow—if that is what it should be called—of new state history since the article was written in the early 1960s makes some of the passages read oddly. As Nasser is dead, Pakistan has split, Nigeria has been defederalized, and the Communist Party has disappeared from the Indonesian scene, to write as though these things had not occurred is to give a sense of unreality to the discussion, a discussion which, again, I regard as still valid, even if it is Nehru's daughter rather than Nehru who now leads India and the Republic of Malaya has expanded into the Federation of Malaysia. Thus, I have in that essay made two sorts of changes. First, I have changed tenses, introduced clauses, added a footnote or two, and so on, in the body of the text to make it read a little less as though the last ten years had not occurred. I have not, however, changed anything of substance so as to improve my argument. Second, I have added to each of the case histories—and clearly set off from them —a paragraph summary of relevant developments since the essay was written, so as to indicate that, if anything, those developments demonstrate the continued relevance of the issues the essay treats in terms of earlier events, and again to dissipate the Rip Van Winkle effect. Except for minor typographical and grammatical corrections (and changes in referencing style for the sake of consistency), the remainder of the book is essentially unaltered.

I have added, however, a new chapter, the first one, in an attempt to state my present position as generally as I can. As my views on the matters the chapters discuss have evolved over the fifteen years they span, there are indeed some differences in the way certain things are put in this introductory chapter and the way they are put in some of the reprinted ones. Some of my earlier concerns—with functionalism, for example—now are less prominent in my mind; some of my later ones —with semiotics, for example—are now more so. But the trend of thought in the essays—which are arranged in a lógical, not a chronological, order—seems to me relatively consistent, and the introductory chapter represents an effort to state more explicitly and systematically what that trend of thought is: an attempt, in fine, to say what I have been saying.

I have eliminated all the acknowledgments contained in the original essays. Those who have helped me know that they have and how very much they have. I can only hope that by now they know that I know it too. Rather than implicate them in my confusions once again, let me instead take the rather peculiar tack of thanking three remarkable academic institutions that have provided me with the kind of setting for scholarly work I am convinced could not be surpassed right now anywhere in the world: The Department of Social Relations of Harvard University, where I was trained; the Department of Anthropology of the University of Chicago, where I taught for a decade; and The Institute for Advanced Study in Princeton, where I now work. At a time when the American university system is under attack as irrelevant or worse, I can only say that it has been for me a redemptive gift.

C. G.

Princeton
1973

PART I

Chapter 1 / Thick Description: Toward an Interpretive Theory of Culture

I

In her book, *Philosophy in a New Key,* Susanne Langer remarks that certain ideas burst upon the intellectual landscape with a tremendous force. They resolve so many fundamental problems at once that they seem also to promise that they will resolve all fundamental problems, clarify all obscure issues. Everyone snaps them up as the open sesame of some new positive science, the conceptual center-point around which a comprehensive system of analysis can be built. The sudden vogue of such a *grande idée,* crowding out almost everything else for a while, is due, she says, "to the fact that all sensitive and active minds turn at once to exploiting it. We try it in every connection, for every purpose, experiment with possible stretches of its strict meaning, with generalizations and derivatives."

After we have become familiar with the new idea, however, after it has become part of our general stock of theoretical concepts, our expectations are brought more into balance with its actual uses, and its excessive popularity is ended. A few zealots persist in the old key-to-the-universe view of it; but less driven thinkers settle down after a while to the problems the idea has really generated. They try to apply it and extend it where it applies and where it is capable of extension; and they desist where it does not apply or cannot be extended. It becomes, if it was, in truth, a seminal idea in the first place, a permanent and enduring part of our intellectual armory. But it no longer has the grandiose, all-promising scope, the infinite versatility of apparent application, it once had. The second law of thermodynamics, or the principle of natural selection, or the notion of unconscious motivation, or the organization of the means of production does not explain everything, not even everything human, but it still explains something; and our attention shifts to isolating just what that something is, to disentangling ourselves from a lot of pseudoscience to which, in the first flush of its celebrity, it has also given rise.

Whether or not this is, in fact, the way all centrally important scientific concepts develop, I don't know. But certainly this pattern fits the concept of culture, around which the whole discipline of anthropology arose, and whose domination that discipline has been increasingly concerned to limit, specify, focus, and contain. It is to this cutting of the culture concept down to size, therefore actually insuring its continued importance rather than undermining it, that the essays below are all, in their several ways and from their several directions, dedicated. They all argue, sometimes explicitly, more often merely through the particular analysis they develop, for a narrowed, specialized, and, so I imagine, theoretically more powerful concept of culture to replace E. B. Tylor's famous "most complex whole," which, its originative power not denied, seems to me to have reached the point where it obscures a good deal more than it reveals.

The conceptual morass into which the Tylorean kind of *pot-au-feu* theorizing about culture can lead, is evident in what is still one of the better general introductions to anthropology, Clyde Kluckhohn's *Mirror for Man*. In some twenty-seven pages of his chapter on the concept, Kluckhohn managed to define culture in turn as: (1) "the total way of life of a people"; (2) "the social legacy the individual acquires from his group"; (3) "a way of thinking, feeling, and believing"; (4) "an abstraction from behavior"; (5) a theory on the part of the anthropologist about the way in which a group of people in fact behave; (6) a "store-

house of pooled learning"; (7) "a set of standardized orientations to recurrent problems"; (8) "learned behavior"; (9) a mechanism for the
normative regulation of behavior; (10) "a set of techniques for adjusting
both to the external environment and to other men"; (11) "a precipitate
of history"; and turning, perhaps in desperation, to similes, as a map, as
a sieve, and as a matrix. In the face of this sort of theoretical diffusion,
even a somewhat constricted and not entirely standard concept of culture, which is at least internally coherent and, more important, which
has a definable argument to make is (as, to be fair, Kluckhohn himself
keenly realized) an improvement. Eclecticism is self-defeating not because there is only one direction in which it is useful to move, but because there are so many: it is necessary to choose.

The concept of culture I espouse, and whose utility the essays below
attempt to demonstrate, is essentially a semiotic one. Believing, with
Max Weber, that man is an animal suspended in webs of significance he
himself has spun, I take culture to be those webs, and the analysis of it
to be therefore not an experimental science in search of law but an interpretive one in search of meaning. It is explication I am after,
construing social expressions on their surface enigmatical. But this pro-
nouncement, a doctrine in a clause, demands itself some explication.

II

Operationalism as a methodological dogma never made much sense so
far as the social sciences are concerned, and except for a few rather too
well-swept corners—Skinnerian behaviorism, intelligence testing, and
so on—it is largely dead now. But it had, for all that, an important
point to make, which, however we may feel about trying to define charisma or alienation in terms of operations, retains a certain force: if you
want to understand what a science is, you should look in the first instance not at its theories or its findings, and certainly not at what its
apologists say about it; you should look at what the practitioners of it
do.

In anthropology, or anyway social anthropology, what the practioners
do is ethnography. And it is in understanding what ethnography is, or
more exactly *what doing ethnography is,* that a start can be made to-

ward grasping what anthropological analysis amounts to as a form of knowledge. This, it must immediately be said, is not a matter of methods. From one point of view, that of the textbook, doing ethnography is establishing rapport, selecting informants, transcribing texts, taking genealogies, mapping fields, keeping a diary, and so on. But it is not these things, techniques and received procedures, that define the enterprise. What defines it is the kind of intellectual effort it is: an elaborate venture in, to borrow a notion from Gilbert Ryle, "thick description."

Ryle's discussion of "thick description" appears in two recent essays of his (now reprinted in the second volume of his *Collected Papers*) addressed to the general question of what, as he puts it, *"Le Penseur"* is doing: "Thinking and Reflecting" and "The Thinking of Thoughts." Consider, he says, two boys rapidly contracting the eyelids of their right eyes. In one, this is an involuntary twitch; in the other, a conspiratorial signal to a friend. The two movements are, as movements, identical; from an I-am-a-camera, "phenomenalistic" observation of them alone, one could not tell which was twitch and which was wink, or indeed whether both or either was twitch or wink. Yet the difference, however unphotographable, between a twitch and a wink is vast; as anyone unfortunate enough to have had the first taken for the second knows. The winker is communicating, and indeed communicating in a quite precise and special way: (1) deliberately, (2) to someone in particular, (3) to impart a particular message, (4) according to a socially established code, and (5) without cognizance of the rest of the company. As Ryle points out, the winker has not done two things, contracted his eyelids and winked, while the twitcher has done only one, contracted his eyelids. Contracting your eyelids on purpose when there exists a public code in which so doing counts as a conspiratorial signal *is* winking. That's all there is to it: a speck of behavior, a fleck of culture, and— *voilà!*—a gesture.

That, however, is just the beginning. Suppose, he continues, there is a third boy, who, "to give malicious amusement to his cronies," parodies the first boy's wink, as amateurish, clumsy, obvious, and so on. He, of course, does this in the same way the second boy winked and the first twitched: by contracting his right eyelids. Only this boy is neither winking nor twitching, he is parodying someone else's, as he takes it, laughable, attempt at winking. Here, too, a socially established code exists (he will "wink" laboriously, overobviously, perhaps adding a grimace—the usual artifices of the clown); and so also does a message. Only now it is not conspiracy but ridicule that is in the air. If the others think he is actually winking, his whole project misfires as completely, though with somewhat different results, as if they think he is twitching. One can go further: uncertain of his mimicking abilities, the would-be satirist may practice at home before the mirror, in which case he is not twitching, winking, or parodying, but rehearsing; though so far as what a camera, a radical behaviorist, or a believer in protocol sentences would record he is just rapidly contracting his right eyelids like all the others. Complexities are possible, if not practically without end, at least logically so. The original winker might, for example, actually have been fake-winking, say, to mislead outsiders into imagining there was a conspiracy afoot when there in fact was not, in which case our descriptions of what the parodist is parodying and the rehearser rehearsing of course shift accordingly. But the point is that between what Ryle calls the "thin description" of what the rehearser (parodist, winker, twitcher . . .) is doing ("rapidly contracting his right eyelids") and the "thick description" of what he is doing ("practicing a burlesque of a friend faking a wink to deceive an innocent into thinking a conspiracy is in motion") lies the object of ethnography: a stratified hierarchy of meaningful structures in terms of which twitches, winks, fake-winks, parodies, rehearsals of parodies are produced, perceived, and interpreted, and without which they would not (not even the zero-form twitches, which, *as a cultural category,* are as much nonwinks as winks are nontwitches) in fact exist, no matter what anyone did or didn't do with his eyelids.

Like so many of the little stories Oxford philosophers like to make up for themselves, all this winking, fake-winking, burlesque-fake-winking, rehearsed-burlesque-fake-winking, may seem a bit artificial. In way of adding a more empirical note, let me give, deliberately unpreceded by any prior explanatory comment at all, a not untypical excerpt from my own field journal to demonstrate that, however evened off for didactic purposes, Ryle's example presents an image only too exact of the sort of piled-up structures of inference and implication through which an ethnographer is continually trying to pick his way:

The French [the informant said] had only just arrived. They set up twenty or so small forts between here, the town, and the Marmusha area up in the middle of the mountains, placing them on promontories so they could survey the countryside. But for all this they couldn't guarantee safety, especially at night, so although the *mezrag,* trade-pact, system was supposed to be legally abolished it in fact continued as before.

One night, when Cohen (who speaks fluent Berber), was up there, at Marmusha, two other Jews who were traders to a neighboring tribe came by to purchase some goods from him. Some Berbers, from yet another neighboring tribe, tried to break into Cohen's place, but he fired his rifle in the air. (Traditionally, Jews were not allowed to carry weapons; but at this period things were so unsettled many did so anyway.) This attracted the attention of the French and the marauders fled.

The next night, however, they came back, one of them disguised as a woman who knocked on the door with some sort of a story. Cohen was suspicious and didn't want to let "her" in, but the other Jews said, "oh, it's all right, it's only a woman." So they opened the door and the whole lot came pouring in. They killed the two visiting Jews, but Cohen managed to barricade himself in an adjoining room. He heard the robbers planning to burn him alive in the shop after they removed his goods, and so he opened the door and, laying about him wildly with a club, managed to escape through a window.

He went up to the fort, then, to have his wounds dressed, and complained to the local commandant, one Captain Dumari, saying he wanted his 'ar—i.e., four or five times the value of the merchandise stolen from him. The robbers were from a tribe which had not yet submitted to French authority and were in open rebellion against it, and he wanted authorization to go with his *mezrag*-holder, the Marmusha tribal *sheikh,* to collect the indemnity that, under traditional rules, he had coming to him. Captain Dumari couldn't officially give him permission to do this, because of the French prohibition of the *mezrag* relationship, but he gave him verbal authorization, saying, "If you get killed, it's your problem."

So the *sheikh,* the Jew, and a small company of armed Marmushans went off ten or fifteen kilometers up into the rebellious area, where there were of course no French, and, sneaking up, captured the thief-tribe's shepherd and stole its herds. The other tribe soon came riding out on horses after them, armed with rifles and ready to attack. But when they saw who the "sheep thieves" were, they thought better of it and said, "all right, we'll talk." They couldn't really deny what had happened—that some of their men had robbed Cohen and killed the two visitors—and they weren't prepared to start the serious feud with the Marmusha a scuffle with the invading party would bring on. So the two groups talked, and talked, and talked, there on the plain amid the thousands of sheep, and decided finally on five-hundred-sheep damages. The two armed Berber groups then lined up on their horses at opposite ends of the plain, with the sheep herded between them, and Cohen, in his black gown, pillbox hat, and flapping slippers, went out alone among the sheep, picking out, one by one and at his own good speed, the best ones for his payment.

So Cohen got his sheep and drove them back to Marmusha. The French, up in their fort, heard them coming from some distance ("Ba, ba, ba" said Cohen, happily, recalling the image) and said, "What the hell is that?" And Cohen said, "That is my 'ar." The French couldn't believe he had actually done what he said he had done, and accused him of being a spy for the rebellious Berbers, put him in prison, and took his sheep. In the town, his family, not having heard from him in so long a time, thought he was dead. But after a while the French released him and he came back home, but without his sheep. He then went to the Colonel in the town, the Frenchman in charge of the whole region, to complain. But the Colonel said, "I can't do anything about the matter. It's not my problem."

Quoted raw, a note in a bottle, this passage conveys, as any similar one similarly presented would do, a fair sense of how much goes into ethnographic description of even the most elemental sort—how extraordinarily "thick" it is. In finished anthropological writings, including those collected here, this fact—that what we call our data are really our own constructions of other people's constructions of what they and their compatriots are up to—is obscured because most of what we need to comprehend a particular event, ritual, custom, idea, or whatever is insinuated as background information before the thing itself is directly examined. (Even to reveal that this little drama took place in the highlands of central Morocco in 1912—and was recounted there in 1968—is to determine much of our understanding of it.) There is nothing particularly wrong with this, and it is in any case inevitable. But it does lead to a view of anthropological research as rather more of an observational and rather less of an interpretive activity than it really is. Right down at the factual base, the hard rock, insofar as there is any, of the whole enterprise, we are already explicating: and worse, explicating explications. Winks upon winks upon winks.

Analysis, then, is sorting out the structures of signification—what Ryle called established codes, a somewhat misleading expression, for it makes the enterprise sound too much like that of the cipher clerk when it is much more like that of the literary critic—and determining their social ground and import. Here, in our text, such sorting would begin with distinguishing the three unlike frames of interpretation ingredient in the situation, Jewish, Berber, and French, and would then move on to show how (and why) at that time, in that place, their copresence produced a situation in which systematic misunderstanding reduced traditional form to social farce. What tripped Cohen up, and with him the whole, ancient pattern of social and economic relationships within which he functioned, was a confusion of tongues.

I shall come back to this too-compacted aphorism later, as well as to the details of the text itself. The point for now is only that ethnography

is thick description. What the ethnographer is in fact faced with—
except when (as, of course, he must do) he is pursuing the more auto-
matized routines of data collection—is a multiplicity of complex conceptual structures, many of them superimposed upon or knotted into
one another, which are at once strange, irregular, and inexplicit, and
which he must contrive somehow first to grasp and then to render. And
this is true at the most down-to-earth, jungle field work levels of his activity: interviewing informants, observing rituals, eliciting kin terms,
tracing property lines, censusing households . . . writing his journal.
Doing ethnography is like trying to read (in the sense of "construct a
reading of") a manuscript—foreign, faded, full of ellipses, incoher-
encies, suspicious emendations, and tendentious commentaries, but written
not in conventionalized graphs of sound but in transient examples of
shaped behavior.

III

Culture, this acted document, thus is public, like a burlesqued wink or a
mock sheep raid. Though ideational, it does not exist in someone's
head; though unphysical, it is not an occult entity. The interminable,
because unterminable, debate within anthropology as to whether culture
is "subjective" or "objective," together with the mutual exchange of intellectual insults ("idealist!"—"materialist!"; "mentalist!"—"behaviorist!"; "impressionist!"—"positivist!") which accompanies it, is
wholly misconceived. Once human behavior is seen as (most of the
time; there *are* true twitches) symbolic action—action which, like pho-
nation in speech, pigment in painting, line in writing, or sonance in
music, signifies—the question as to whether culture is patterned conduct or a frame of mind, or even the two somehow mixed together,
loses sense. The thing to ask about a burlesqued wink or a mock sheep
raid is not what their ontological status is. It is the same as that of
rocks on the one hand and dreams on the other—they are things of this
world. The thing to ask is what their import is: what it is, ridicule or
challenge, irony or anger, snobbery or pride, that, in their occurrence
and through their agency, is getting said.
    This may seem like an obvious truth, but there are a number of ways

to obscure it. One is to imagine that culture is a self-contained "super-organic" reality with forces and purposes of its own; that is, to reify it. Another is to claim that it consists in the brute pattern of behavioral events we observe in fact to occur in some identifiable community or other; that is, to reduce it. But though both these confusions still exist, and doubtless will be always with us, the main source of theoretical muddlement in contemporary anthropology is a view which developed in reaction to them and is right now very widely held—namely, that, to quote Ward Goodenough, perhaps its leading proponent, "culture [is located] in the minds and hearts of men."

Variously called ethnoscience, componential analysis, or cognitive anthropology (a terminological wavering which reflects a deeper uncertainty), this school of thought holds that culture is composed of psychological structures by means of which individuals or groups of individuals guide their behavior. "A society's culture," to quote Goodenough again, this time in a passage which has become the *locus classicus* of the whole movement, "consists of whatever it is one has to know or believe in order to operate in a manner acceptable to its members." And from this view of what culture is follows a view, equally assured, of what describing it is—the writing out of systematic rules, an ethnographic algorithm, which, if followed, would make it possible so to operate, to pass (physical appearance aside) for a native. In such a way, extreme subjectivism is married to extreme formalism, with the expected result: an explosion of debate as to whether particular analyses (which come in the form of taxonomies, paradigms, tables, trees, and other ingenuities) reflect what the natives "really" think or are merely clever simulations, logically equivalent but substantively different, of what they think.

As, on first glance, this approach may look close enough to the one being developed here to be mistaken for it, it is useful to be explicit as to what divides them. If, leaving our winks and sheep behind for the moment, we take, say, a Beethoven quartet as an, admittedly rather special but, for these purposes, nicely illustrative, sample of culture, no one would, I think, identify it with its score, with the skills and knowledge needed to play it, with the understanding of it possessed by its performers or auditors, nor, to take care, *en passant,* of the reductionists and reifiers, with a particular performance of it or with some mysterious entity transcending material existence. The "no one" is perhaps too strong here, for there are always incorrigibles. But that a Beethoven quartet is a temporally developed tonal structure, a coherent sequence of modeled sound—in a word, music—and not anybody's knowledge of or belief about anything, including how to play it, is a proposition to which most people are, upon reflection, likely to assent.

To play the violin it is necessary to possess certain habits, skills, knowledge, and talents, to be in the mood to play, and (as the old joke goes) to have a violin. But violin playing is neither the habits, skills, knowledge, and so on, nor the mood, nor (the notion believers in "material culture" apparently embrace) the violin. To make a trade pact in Morocco, you have to do certain things in certain ways (among others, cut, while chanting Quranic Arabic, the throat of a lamb before the assembled, undeformed, adult male members of your tribe) and to be possessed of certain psychological characteristics (among others, a desire for distant things). But a trade pact is neither the throat cutting nor the desire, though it is real enough, as seven kinsmen of our Marmusha sheikh discovered when, on an earlier occasion, they were executed by him following the theft of one mangy, essentially valueless sheepskin from Cohen.

Culture is public because meaning is. You can't wink (or burlesque one) without knowing what counts as winking or how, physically, to contract your eyelids, and you can't conduct a sheep raid (or mimic one) without knowing what it is to steal a sheep and how practically to go about it. But to draw from such truths the conclusion that knowing how to wink is winking and knowing how to steal a sheep is sheep raiding is to betray as deep a confusion as, taking thin descriptions for thick, to identify winking with eyelid contractions or sheep raiding with chasing woolly animals out of pastures. The cognitivist fallacy—that culture consists (to quote another spokesman for the movement, Stephen Tyler) of "mental phenomena which can [he means "should"] be analyzed by formal methods similar to those of mathematics and logic"—is as destructive of an effective use of the concept as are the behaviorist and idealist fallacies to which it is a misdrawn correction. Perhaps, as its errors are more sophisticated and its distortions subtler, it is even more so.

The generalized attack on privacy theories of meaning is, since early Husserl and late Wittgenstein, so much a part of modern thought that it need not be developed once more here. What is necessary is to see to it that the news of it reaches anthropology; and in particular that it is made clear that to say that culture consists of socially established structures of meaning in terms of which people do such things as signal conspiracies and join them or perceive insults and answer them, is no more to say that it is a psychological phenomenon, a characteristic of someone's mind, personality, cognitive structure, or whatever, than to say that Tantrism, genetics, the progressive form of the verb, the classification of wines, the Common Law, or the notion of "a conditional curse" (as Westermarck defined the concept of 'ar in terms of which Cohen pressed his claim to damages) is. What, in a place like Morocco, most prevents those of us who grew up winking other winks or attending other sheep from grasping what people are up to is not ignorance as to how cognition works (though, especially as, one assumes, it works the same among them as it does among us, it would greatly help to have less of that too) as a lack of familiarity with the imaginative universe within which their acts are signs. As Wittgenstein has been invoked, he may as well be quoted:

We . . . say of some people that they are transparent to us. It is, however, important as regards this observation that one human being can be a complete enigma to another. We learn this when we come into a strange country with entirely strange traditions; and, what is more, even given a mastery of the country's language. We do not *understand* the people. (And not because of not knowing what they are saying to themselves.) We cannot find our feet with them.

12/11

IV

Finding our feet, an unnerving business which never more than distantly succeeds, is what ethnographic research consists of as a personal experience; trying to formulate the basis on which one imagines, always excessively, one has found them is what anthropological writing consists of as a scientific endeavor. We are not, or at least I am not, seeking either to become natives (a compromised word in any case) or to mimic them. Only romantics or spies would seem to find point in that. We are seeking, in the widened sense of the term in which it encompasses very much more than talk, to converse with them, a matter a great deal more difficult, and not only with strangers, than is commonly recognized. "If speaking *for* someone else seems to be a mysterious process," Stanley Cavell has remarked, "that may be because speaking *to* someone does not seem mysterious enough."

Looked at in this way, the aim of anthropology is the enlargement of the universe of human discourse. That is not, of course, its only aim—instruction, amusement, practical counsel, moral advance, and the discovery of natural order in human behavior are others; nor is anthropology the only discipline which pursues it. But it is an aim to which a semiotic concept of culture is peculiarly well adapted. As interworked systems of construable signs (what, ignoring provincial usages, I would call symbols), culture is not a power, something to which social events, behaviors, institutions, or processes can be causally attributed; it is a context, something within which they can be intelligibly—that is, thickly—described.

The famous anthropological absorption with the (to us) exotic—Berber horsemen, Jewish peddlers, French Legionnaires—is, thus, essentially a device for displacing the dulling sense of familiarity with which the mysteriousness of our own ability to relate perceptively to one another is concealed from us. Looking at the ordinary in places where it takes unaccustomed forms brings out not, as has so often been claimed, the arbitrariness of human behavior (there is nothing especially arbitrary about taking sheep theft for insolence in Morocco), but the degree to which its meaning varies according to the pattern of life by which it is informed. Understanding a people's culture exposes their normalness without reducing their particularity. (The more I manage to follow what the Moroccans are up to, the more logical, and the more singular, they seem.) It renders them accessible: setting them in the frame of their own banalities, it dissolves their opacity.

It is this maneuver, usually too casually referred to as "seeing things from the actor's point of view," too bookishly as "the *verstehen* approach," or too technically as "emic analysis," that so often leads to the notion that anthropology is a variety of either long-distance mind reading or cannibal-isle fantasizing, and which, for someone anxious to navigate past the wrecks of a dozen sunken philosophies, must therefore be executed with a great deal of care. Nothing is more necessary to comprehending what anthropological interpretation is, and the degree to which it *is* interpretation, than an exact understanding of what it means —and what it does not mean—to say that our formulations of other peoples' symbol systems must be actor-oriented.[1]

[1] Not only other peoples': anthropology *can* be trained on the culture of which it is itself a part, and it increasingly is; a fact of profound importance, but which, as it raises a few tricky and rather special second order problems, I shall put to the side for the moment.

What it means is that descriptions of Berber, Jewish, or French culture must be cast in terms of the constructions we imagine Berbers, Jews, or Frenchmen to place upon what they live through, the formulae they use to define what happens to them. What it does not mean is that such descriptions are themselves Berber, Jewish, or French—that is, part of the reality they are ostensibly describing; they are anthropological—that is, part of a developing system of scientific analysis. They must be cast in terms of the interpretations to which persons of a particular denomination subject their experience, because that is what they profess to be descriptions of; they are anthropological because it is, in fact, anthropologists who profess them. Normally, it is not necessary to point out quite so laboriously that the object of study is one thing and the study of it another. It is clear enough that the physical world is not physics and *A Skeleton Key to Finnegan's Wake* not *Finnegan's Wake*. But, as, in the study of culture, analysis penetrates into the very body of the object—that is, *we begin with our own interpretations of what our informants are up to, or think they are up to, and then systematize those*—the line between (Moroccan) culture as a natural fact and (Moroccan) culture as a theoretical entity tends to get blurred. All the more so, as the latter is presented in the form of an actor's-eye description of (Moroccan) conceptions of everything from violence, honor, divinity, and justice, to tribe, property, patronage, and chiefship.

In short, anthropological writings are themselves interpretations, and second and third order ones to boot. (By definition, only a "native" makes first order ones: it's *his* culture.) [2] They are, thus, fictions; fictions, in the sense that they are "something made," "something fashioned"—the original meaning of *fictiō*—not that they are false, unfactual, or merely "as if" thought experiments. To construct actor-oriented descriptions of the involvements of a Berber chieftain, a Jewish merchant, and a French soldier with one another in 1912 Morocco is clearly an imaginative act, not all that different from constructing similar descriptions of, say, the involvements with one another of a provincial French doctor, his silly, adulterous wife, and her feckless lover in

[2] The order problem is, again, complex. Anthropological works based on other anthropological works (Lévi-Strauss', for example) may, of course, be fourth order or higher, and informants frequently, even habitually, make second order interpretations—what have come to be known as "native models." In literate cultures, where "native" interpretation can proceed to higher levels—in connection with the Maghreb, one has only to think of Ibn Khaldun; with the United States, Margaret Mead—these matters become intricate indeed.

nineteenth century France. In the latter case, the actors are represented as not having existed and the events as not having happened, while in the former they are represented as actual, or as having been so. This is a difference of no mean importance; indeed, precisely the one Madame Bovary had difficulty grasping. But the importance does not lie in the fact that her story was created while Cohen's was only noted. The conditions of their creation, and the point of it (to say nothing of the manner and the quality) differ. But the one is as much a *fictiō*—"a making"—as the other.

Anthropologists have not always been as aware as they might be of this fact, that although culture exists in the trading post, the hill fort, or the sheep run, anthropology exists in the book, the article, the lecture, the museum display, or, sometimes nowadays, the film. To become aware of it is to realize that the line between mode of representation and substantive content is as undrawable in cultural analysis as it is in painting; and that fact in turn seems to threaten the objective status of anthropological knowledge by suggesting that its source is not social reality but scholarly artifice.

It does threaten it, but the threat is hollow. The claim to attention of an ethnographic account does not rest on its author's ability to capture primitive facts in faraway places and carry them home like a mask or a carving, but on the degree to which he is able to clarify what goes on in such places, to reduce the puzzlement—what manner of men are these?—to which unfamiliar acts emerging out of unknown backgrounds naturally give rise. This raises some serious problems of verification, all right—or, if "verification" is too strong a word for so soft a science (I, myself, would prefer "appraisal"), of how you can tell a better account from a worse one. But that is precisely the virtue of it. If ethnography is thick description and ethnographers those who are doing the describing, then the determining question for any given example of it, whether a field journal squib or a Malinowski-sized monograph, is whether it sorts winks from twitches and real winks from mimicked ones. It is not against a body of uninterpreted data, radically thinned descriptions, that we must measure the cogency of our explications, but against the power of the scientific imagination to bring us into touch with the lives of strangers. It is not worth it, as Thoreau said, to go round the world to count the cats in Zanzibar.

V

Now, this proposition, that it is not in our interest to bleach human behavior of the very properties that interest us before we begin to examine it, has sometimes been escalated into a larger claim: namely, that as it is only those properties that interest us, we need not attend, save cursorily, to behavior at all. Culture is most effectively treated, the argument goes, purely as a symbolic system (the catch phrase is, "in its own terms"), by isolating its elements, specifying the internal relationships among those elements, and then characterizing the whole system in some general way—according to the core symbols around which it is organized, the underlying structures of which it is a surface expression, or the ideological principles upon which it is based. Though a distinct improvement over "learned behavior" and "mental phenomena" notions of what culture is, and the source of some of the most powerful theoretical ideas in contemporary anthropology, this hermetical approach to things seems to me to run the danger (and increasingly to have been overtaken by it) of locking cultural analysis away from its proper object, the informal logic of actual life. There is little profit in extricating a concept from the defects of psychologism only to plunge it immediately into those of schematicism.

Behavior must be attended to, and with some exactness, because it is through the flow of behavior—or, more precisely, social action—that cultural forms find articulation. They find it as well, of course, in various sorts of artifacts, and various states of consciousness; but these draw their meaning from the role they play (Wittgenstein would say their "use") in an ongoing pattern of life, not from any intrinsic relationships they bear to one another. It is what Cohen, the sheikh, and "Captain Dumari" were doing when they tripped over one another's purposes—pursuing trade, defending honor, establishing dominance— that created our pastoral drama, and that is what the drama is, therefore, "about." Whatever, or wherever, symbol systems "in their own terms" may be, we gain empirical access to them by inspecting events, not by arranging abstracted entities into unified patterns.

A further implication of this is that coherence cannot be the major test of validity for a cultural description. Cultural systems must have a minimal degree of coherence, else we would not call them systems; and, by observation, they normally have a great deal more. But there is nothing so coherent as a paranoid's delusion or a swindler's story. The force of our interpretations cannot rest, as they are now so often made to do, on the tightness with which they hold together, or the assurance with which they are argued. Nothing has done more, I think, to discredit cultural analysis than the construction of impeccable depictions of formal order in whose actual existence nobody can quite believe.

If anthropological interpretation is constructing a reading of what happens, then to divorce it from what happens—from what, in this time or that place, specific people say, what they do, what is done to them, from the whole vast business of the world—is to divorce it from its applications and render it vacant. A good interpretation of anything—a poem, a person, a history, a ritual, an institution, a society—takes us into the heart of that of which it is the interpretation. When it does not do that, but leads us instead somewhere else—into an admiration of its own elegance, of its author's cleverness, or of the beauties of Euclidean order—it may have its intrinsic charms; but it is something else than what the task at hand—figuring out what all that rigamarole with the sheep is about—calls for.

The rigamarole with the sheep—the sham theft of them, the reparative transfer of them, the political confiscation of them—is (or was) essentially a social discourse, even if, as I suggested earlier, one conducted in multiple tongues and as much in action as in words.

Claiming his 'ar, Cohen invoked the trade pact; recognizing the claim, the sheikh challenged the offenders' tribe; accepting responsibility, the offenders' tribe paid the indemnity; anxious to make clear to sheikhs and peddlers alike who was now in charge here, the French showed the imperial hand. As in any discourse, code does not determine conduct, and what was actually said need not have been. Cohen might not have, given its illegitimacy in Protectorate eyes, chosen to press his claim. The sheikh might, for similar reasons, have rejected it. The offenders' tribe, still resisting French authority, might have decided to regard the raid as "real" and fight rather than negotiate. The French, were they more *habile* and less *dur* (as, under Mareschal Lyautey's seigniorial tutelage, they later in fact became), might have permitted Cohen to keep his sheep, winking—as we say—at the continuance of the trade pattern and its limitation to their authority. And there are other possibilities: the Marmushans might have regarded the French action as too great an insult to bear and gone into dissidence themselves; the French might have attempted not just to clamp down on Cohen but to bring the sheikh himself more closely to heel; and Cohen might have concluded that between renegade Berbers and Beau Geste soldiers, driving trade in the Atlas highlands was no longer worth the candle and retired to the better-governed confines of the town. This, indeed, is more or less what happened, somewhat further along, as the Protectorate moved toward genuine sovereignty. But the point here is not to describe what did or did not take place in Morocco. (From this simple incident one can widen out into enormous complexities of social experience.) It is to demonstrate what a piece of anthropological interpretation consists in: tracing the curve of a social discourse; fixing it into an inspectable form.

The ethnographer "inscribes" social discourse; *he writes it down*. In so doing, he turns it from a passing event, which exists only in its own moment of occurrence, into an account, which exists in its inscriptions and can be reconsulted. The sheikh is long dead, killed in the process of being, as the French called it, "pacified"; "Captain Dumari," his pacifier, lives, retired to his souvenirs, in the south of France; and Cohen went last year, part refugee, part pilgrim, part dying patriarch, "home" to Israel. But what they, in my extended sense, "said" to one another on an Atlas plateau sixty years ago is—very far from perfectly—preserved for study. "What," Paul Ricoeur, from whom this whole idea of the inscription of action is borrowed and somewhat twisted, asks, "what does writing fix?"

Not the event of speaking, but the "said" of speaking, where we understand by the "said" of speaking that intentional exteriorization constitutive of the aim of discourse thanks to which the *sagen*—the saying—wants to become *Aus-sage*—the enunciation, the enunciated. In short, what we write is the *noema* ["thought," "content," "gist"] of the speaking. It is the meaning of the speech event, not the event as event.

This is not itself so very "said"—if Oxford philosophers run to little stories, phenomenological ones run to large sentences; but it brings us anyway to a more precise answer to our generative question, "What does the ethnographer do?"—he writes.[3] This, too, may seem a less than startling discovery, and to someone familiar with the current "liter-

---

[3] Or, again, more exactly, "inscribes." Most ethnography is in fact to be found in books and articles, rather than in films, records, museum displays, or whatever; but even in them there are, of course, photographs, drawings, diagrams, tables, and so on. Self-consciousness about modes of representation (not to speak of experiments with them) has been very lacking in anthropology.

ature," an implausible one. But as the standard answer to our question has been, "He observes, he records, he analyzes"—a kind of *veni, vidi, vici* conception of the matter—it may have more deep-going consequences than are at first apparent, not the least of which is that distinguishing these three phases of knowledge-seeking may not, as a matter of fact, normally be possible; and, indeed, as autonomous "operations" they may not in fact exist.

The situation is even more delicate, because, as already noted, what we inscribe (or try to) is not raw social discourse, to which, because, save very marginally or very specially, we are not actors, we do not have direct access, but only that small part of it which our informants can lead us into understanding.[4] This is not as fatal as it sounds, for, in fact, not all Cretans are liars, and it is not necessary to know everything in order to understand something. But it does make the view of anthropological analysis as the conceptual manipulation of discovered facts, a logical reconstruction of a mere reality, seem rather lame. To set forth symmetrical crystals of significance, purified of the material complexity in which they were located, and then attribute their existence to autogenous principles of order, universal properties of the human mind, or vast, a priori *weltanschauungen,* is to pretend a science that does not exist and imagine a reality that cannot be found. Cultural analysis is (or should be) guessing at meanings, assessing the guesses, and drawing explanatory conclusions from the better guesses, not discovering the Continent of Meaning and mapping out its bodiless landscape.

VI

So, there are three characteristics of ethnographic description: it is interpretive; what it is interpretive of is the flow of social discourse; and the interpreting involved consists in trying to rescue the "said" of such discourse from its perishing occasions and fix it in perusable terms. The *kula* is gone or altered; but, for better or worse, *The Argonauts of the*

---

[4] So far as it has reinforced the anthropologist's impulse to engage himself with his informants as persons rather than as objects, the notion of "participant observation" has been a valuable one. But, to the degree it has lead the anthropologist to block from his view the very special, culturally bracketed nature of his own role and to imagine himself something more than an interested (in both senses of that word) sojourner, it has been our most powerful source of bad faith.

Western Pacific remains. But there is, in addition, a fourth characteristic of such description, at least as I practice it: it is microscopic.

This is not to say that there are no large-scale anthropological interpretations of whole societies, civilizations, world events, and so on. Indeed, it is such extension of our analyses to wider contexts that, along with their theoretical implications, recommends them to general attention and justifies our constructing them. No one really cares anymore, not even Cohen (well . . . maybe, Cohen), about those sheep as such. History may have its unobtrusive turning points, "great noises in a little room"; but this little go-round was surely not one of them.

It is merely to say that the anthropologist characteristically approaches such broader interpretations and more abstract analyses from the direction of exceedingly extended acquaintances with extremely small matters. He confronts the same grand realities that others—historians, economists, political scientists, sociologists—confront in more fateful settings: Power, Change, Faith, Oppression, Work, Passion, Authority, Beauty, Violence, Love, Prestige; but he confronts them in contexts obscure enough—places like Marmusha and lives like Cohen's—to take the capital letters off them. These all-too-human constancies, "those big words that make us all afraid," take a homely form in such homely contexts. But that is exactly the advantage. There are enough profundities in the world already.

Yet, the problem of how to get from a collection of ethnographic miniatures on the order of our sheep story—an assortment of remarks and anecdotes—to wall-sized culturescapes of the nation, the epoch, the continent, or the civilization is not so easily passed over with vague allusions to the virtues of concreteness and the down-to-earth mind. For a science born in Indian tribes, Pacific islands, and African lineages and subsequently seized with grander ambitions, this has come to be a major methodological problem, and for the most part a badly handled one. The models that anthropologists have themselves worked out to justify their moving from local truths to general visions have been, in fact, as responsible for undermining the effort as anything their critics—sociologists obsessed with sample sizes, psychologists with measures, or economists with aggregates—have been able to devise against them.

Of these, the two main ones have been: the Jonesville-is-the-USA "microcosmic" model; and the Easter-Island-is-a-testing-case "natural experiment" model. Either heaven in a grain of sand, or the farther shores of possibility.

The Jonesville-is-America writ small (or America-is-Jonesville writ large) fallacy is so obviously one that the only thing that needs explanation is how people have managed to believe it and expected others to believe it. The notion that one can find the essence of national societies, civilizations, great religions, or whatever summed up and simplified in so-called "typical" small towns and villages is palpable nonsense. What one finds in small towns and villages is (alas) small-town or village life. If localized, microscopic studies were really dependent for their greater relevance upon such a premise—that they captured the great world in the little—they wouldn't have any relevance.

But, of course, they are not. The locus of study is not the object of study. Anthropologists don't study villages (tribes, towns, neighborhoods . . .); they study *in* villages. You can study different things in different places, and some things—for example, what colonial domination does to established frames of moral expectation—you can best study in confined localities. But that doesn't make the place what it is you are studying. In the remoter provinces of Morocco and Indonesia I have wrestled with the same questions other social scientists have wrestled with in more central locations—for example, how comes it that men's most importunate claims to humanity are cast in the accents of group pride?—and with about the same conclusiveness. One can add a dimension—one much needed in the present climate of size-up-and-solve social science; but that is all. There is a certain value, if you are going to run on about the exploitation of the masses in having seen a Javanese sharecropper turning earth in a tropical downpour or a Moroccan tailor embroidering kaftans by the light of a twenty-watt bulb. But the notion that this gives you the thing entire (and elevates you to some moral vantage ground from which you can look down upon the ethically less privileged) is an idea which only someone too long in the bush could possibly entertain.

The "natural laboratory" notion has been equally pernicious, not only because the analogy is false—what kind of a laboratory is it where *none* of the parameters are manipulable?—but because it leads to a notion that the data derived from ethnographic studies are purer, or more fundamental, or more solid, or less conditioned (the most favored word is "elementary") than those derived from other sorts of social inquiry. The great natural variation of cultural forms is, of course, not only anthropology's great (and wasting) resource, but the ground of its deepest theoretical dilemma: how is such variation to be squared with the biological unity of the human species? But it is not, even metaphorically, experimental variation, because the context in which it occurs varies along with it, and it is not possible (though there are those who try) to isolate the y's from x's to write a proper function.

The famous studies purporting to show that the Oedipus complex was backwards in the Trobriands, sex roles were upside down in Tchambuli, and the Pueblo Indians lacked aggression (it is characteristic that they were all negative—"but not in the South"), are, whatever their empirical validity may or may not be, not "scientifically tested and approved" hypotheses. They are interpretations, or misinterpretations, like any others, arrived at in the same way as any others, and as inherently inconclusive as any others, and the attempt to invest them with the authority of physical experimentation is but methodological sleight of hand. Ethnographic findings are not privileged, just particular: another country heard from. To regard them as anything more (*or anything less*) than that distorts both them and their implications, which are far profounder than mere primitivity, for social theory.

Another country heard from: the reason that protracted descriptions of distant sheep raids (and a really good ethnographer would have gone into what kind of sheep they were) have general relevance is that they present the sociological mind with bodied stuff on which to feed. The important thing about the anthropologist's findings is their complex specificness, their circumstantiality. It is with the kind of material produced by long-term, mainly (though not exclusively) qualitative, highly participative, and almost obsessively fine-comb field study in confined contexts that the mega-concepts with which contemporary social science is afflicted—legitimacy, modernization, integration, conflict, charisma, structure, . . . meaning—can be given the sort of sensible actuality that makes it possible to think not only realistically and concretely *about* them, but, what is more important, creatively and imaginatively *with* them.

(The methodological problem which the microscopic nature of ethnography presents is both real and critical.) But it is not to be resolved by regarding a remote locality as the world in a teacup or as the sociological equivalent of a cloud chamber. It is to be resolved—or, anyway, decently kept at bay—by realizing that social actions are comments on more than themselves; that where an interpretation comes from does not determine where it can be impelled to go. Small facts speak to large issues, winks to epistemology, or sheep raids to revolution, because they are made to.

VII

Which brings us, finally, to theory. The besetting sin of interpretive approaches to anything—literature, dreams, symptoms, culture—is that they tend to resist, or to be permitted to resist, conceptual articulation and thus to escape systematic modes of assessment. You either grasp an interpretation or you do not, see the point of it or you do not, accept it or you do not. Imprisoned in the immediacy of its own detail, it is presented as self-validating, or, worse, as validated by the supposedly developed sensitivities of the person who presents it; any attempt to cast what it says in terms other than its own is regarded as a travesty—as, the anthropologist's severest term of moral abuse, ethnocentric.

For a field of study which, however timidly (though I, myself, am not timid about the matter at all), asserts itself to be a science, this just will not do. There is no reason why the conceptual structure of a cultural interpretation should be any less formulable, and thus less susceptible to explicit canons of appraisal, than that of, say, a biological observation or a physical experiment—no reason except that the terms in which such formulations can be cast are, if not wholly nonexistent, very nearly so. We are reduced to insinuating theories because we lack the power to state them.

At the same time, it must be admitted that there are a number of characteristics of cultural interpretation which make the theoretical development of it more than usually difficult. The first is the need for theory to stay rather closer to the ground than tends to be the case in sciences more able to give themselves over to imaginative abstraction. Only short flights of ratiocination tend to be effective in anthropology; longer ones tend to drift off into logical dreams, academic bemusements with formal symmetry. The whole point of a semiotic approach to culture is, as I have said, to aid us in gaining access to the conceptual world in which our subjects live so that we can, in some extended sense of the term, converse with them. The tension between the pull of this need to penetrate an unfamiliar universe of symbolic action and the requirements of technical advance in the theory of culture, between the need to grasp and the need to analyze, is, as a result, both necessarily great and essentially irremovable. Indeed, the further theoretical development goes, the deeper the tension gets. This is the first condition for cultural theory: it is not its own master. As it is unseverable from the immediacies thick description presents, its freedom to shape itself in terms of its internal logic is rather limited. What generality it contrives to achieve grows out of the delicacy of its distinctions, not the sweep of its abstractions.

And from this follows a peculiarity in the way, as a simple matter of empirical fact, our knowledge of culture . . . cultures . . . a culture . . . grows: in spurts. Rather than following a rising curve of cumulative findings, cultural analysis breaks up into a disconnected yet coherent sequence of bolder and bolder sorties. Studies do build on other studies, not in the sense that they take up where the others leave off, but in the sense that, better informed and better conceptualized, they plunge more deeply into the same things. Every serious cultural analysis starts from a sheer beginning and ends where it manages to get before exhausting its intellectual impulse. Previously discovered facts are mobilized, previously developed concepts used, previously formulated hypotheses tried out; but the movement is not from already proven theorems to newly proven ones, it is from an awkward fumbling for the most elementary understanding to a supported claim that one has achieved that and surpassed it. A study is an advance if it is more incisive—whatever that may mean—than those that preceded it; but it less stands on their shoulders than, challenged and challenging, runs by their side.

It is for this reason, among others, that the essay, whether of thirty pages or three hundred, has seemed the natural genre in which to present cultural interpretations and the theories sustaining them, and why, if one looks for systematic treatises in the field, one is so soon disappointed, the more so if one finds any. Even inventory articles are rare here, and anyway of hardly more than bibliographical interest. The major theoretical contributions not only lie in specific studies—that is true in almost any field—but they are very difficult to abstract from such studies and integrate into anything one might call "culture theory" as such. Theoretical formulations hover so low over the interpretations they govern that they don't make much sense or hold much interest apart from them. This is so, not because they are not general (if they are not general, they are not theoretical), but because, stated independently of their applications, they seem either commonplace or vacant. One can, and this in fact is how the field progresses conceptually, take a line of theoretical attack developed in connection with one exercise in ethnographic interpretation and employ it in another, pushing it forward to greater precision and broader relevance; but one cannot write a "General Theory of Cultural Interpretation." Or, rather, one can, but there appears to be little profit in it, because the essential task of theory building here is not to codify abstract regularities but to make thick description possible, not to generalize across cases but to generalize within them.

To generalize within cases is usually called, at least in medicine and depth psychology, clinical inference. Rather than beginning with a set of observations and attempting to subsume them under a governing law, such inference begins with a set of (presumptive) signifiers and attempts to place them within an intelligible frame. Measures are matched to the-oretical predictions, but symptoms (even when they are measured) are scanned for theoretical peculiarities—that is, they are diagnosed. In the study of culture the signifiers are not symptoms or clusters of symptoms, but symbolic acts or clusters of symbolic acts, and the aim is not therapy but the analysis of social discourse. But the way in which theory is used—to ferret out the unapparent import of things—is the same.

Thus we are lead to the second condition of cultural theory: it is not, at least in the strict meaning of the term, predictive. The diagnostician doesn't predict measles; he decides that someone has them, or at the very most *anticipates* that someone is rather likely shortly to get them. But this limitation, which is real enough, has commonly been both mis-understood and exaggerated, because it has been taken to mean that cul-tural interpretation is merely post facto: that, like the peasant in the old story, we first shoot the holes in the fence and then paint the bull's-eyes around them. It is hardly to be denied that there is a good deal of that sort of thing around, some of it in prominent places. It is to be denied, however, that it is the inevitable outcome of a clinical approach to the use of theory.

It is true that in the clinical style of theoretical formulation, concep-tualization is directed toward the task of generating interpretations of matters already in hand, not toward projecting outcomes of experimen-tal manipulations or deducing future states of a determined system. But that does not mean that theory has only to fit (or, more carefully, to generate cogent interpretations of) realities past; it has also to survive —intellectually survive—realities to come. Although we formulate our interpretation of an outburst of winking or an instance of sheep-raiding after its occurrence, sometimes long after, the theoretical framework in terms of which such an interpretation is made must be capable of continuing to yield defensible interpretations as new social phenomena swim into view. Although one starts any effort at thick description, beyond the obvious and superficial, from a state of general bewilderment as to what the devil is going on—trying to find one's feet—one does not start (or ought not) intellectually empty-handed. Theoretical ideas are not created wholly anew in each study; as I have said, they are adopted from other, related studies, and, refined in the process, applied to new interpretive problems. If they cease being useful with respect to such problems, they tend to stop being used and are more or less abandoned. If they continue being useful, throwing up new understandings, they are further elaborated and go on being used.[5]

Such a view of how theory functions in an interpretive science suggests that the distinction, relative in any case, that appears in the experimental or observational sciences between "description" and "explanation" appears here as one, even more relative, between "inscription" ("thick description") and "specification" ("diagnosis")—between setting down the meaning particular social actions have for the actors whose actions they are, and stating, as explicitly as we can manage, what the knowledge thus attained demonstrates about the society in which it is found and, beyond that, about social life as such. Our double task is to uncover the conceptual structures that inform our subjects' acts, the "said" of social discourse, and to construct a system of analysis in whose terms what is generic to those structures, what belongs to them because they are what they are, will stand out against the other determinants of human behavior. In ethnography, the office of theory is to provide a vocabulary in which what symbolic action has to say about itself —that is, about the role of culture in human life—can be expressed.

Aside from a couple of orienting pieces concerned with more foundational matters, it is in such a manner that theory operates in the

[5] Admittedly, this is something of an idealization. Because theories are seldom if ever decisively disproved in clinical use but merely grow increasingly awkward, unproductive, strained, or vacuous, they often persist long after all but a handful of people (though *they* are often most passionate) have lost much interest in them. Indeed, so far as anthropology is concerned, it is almost more of a problem to get exhausted ideas out of the literature than it is to get productive ones in, and so a great deal more of theoretical discussion than one would prefer is critical rather than constructive, and whole careers have been devoted to hastening the demise of moribund notions. As the field advances one would hope that this sort of intellectual weed control would become a less prominent part of our activities. But, for the moment, it remains true that old theories tend less to die than to go into second editions.

essays collected here. A repertoire of very general, made-in-the-academy concepts and systems of concepts—"integration," "rationalization," "symbol," "ideology," "ethos," "revolution," "identity," "metaphor," "structure," "ritual," "world view," "actor," "function," "sacred," and, of course, "culture" itself—is woven into the body of thick-description ethnography in the hope of rendering mere occurrences scientifically eloquent.[6] The aim is to draw large conclusions from small, but very densely textured facts; to support broad assertions about the role of culture in the construction of collective life by engaging them exactly with complex specifics.

Thus it is not only interpretation that goes all the way down to the most immediate observational level: the theory upon which such interpretation conceptually depends does so also. My interest in Cohen's story, like Ryle's in winks, grew out of some very general notions indeed. The "confusion of tongues" model—the view that social conflict is not something that happens when, out of weakness, indefiniteness, obsolescence, or neglect, cultural forms cease to operate, but rather something which happens when, like burlesqued winks, such forms are pressed by unusual situations or unusual intentions to operate in unusual ways—is not an idea I got from Cohen's story. It is one, instructed by colleagues, students, and predecessors, I brought to it.

Our innocent-looking "note in a bottle" is more than a portrayal of the frames of meaning of Jewish peddlers, Berber warriors, and French proconsuls, or even of their mutual interference. It is an argument that to rework the pattern of social relationships is to rearrange the coordinates of the experienced world. Society's forms are culture's substance.

VIII

There is an Indian story—at least I heard it as an Indian story—about an Englishman who, having been told that the world rested on a platform which rested on the back of an elephant which rested in turn on

[6] The overwhelming bulk of the following chapters concern Indonesia rather than Morocco, for I have just begun to face up to the demands of my North African material which, for the most part, was gathered more recently. Field work in Indonesia was carried out in 1952–1954, 1957–1958, and 1971; in Morocco in 1964, 1965–1966, 1968–1969, and 1972.

the back of a turtle, asked (perhaps he was an ethnographer; it is the way they behave), what did the turtle rest on? Another turtle. And that turtle? "Ah, Sahib, after that it is turtles all the way down."

Such, indeed, is the condition of things. I do not know how long it would be profitable to meditate on the encounter of Cohen, the sheikh, and "Dumari" (the period has perhaps already been exceeded); but I do know that however long I did so I would not get anywhere near to the bottom of it. Nor have I ever gotten anywhere near to the bottom of anything I have ever written about, either in the essays below or elsewhere. Cultural analysis is intrinsically incomplete. And, worse than that, the more deeply it goes the less complete it is. It is a strange science whose most telling assertions are its most tremulously based, in which to get somewhere with the matter at hand is to intensify the suspicion, both your own and that of others, that you are not quite getting it right. But that, along with plaguing subtle people with obtuse questions, is what being an ethnographer is like.

There are a number of ways to escape this—turning culture into folklore and collecting it, turning it into traits and counting it, turning it into institutions and classifying it, turning it into structures and toying with it. But they *are* escapes. The fact is that to commit oneself to a semiotic concept of culture and an interpretive approach to the study of it is to commit oneself to a view of ethnographic assertion as, to borrow W. B. Gallie's by now famous phrase, "essentially contestable." Anthropology, or at least interpretive anthropology, is a science whose progress is marked less by a perfection of consensus than by a refinement of debate. What gets better is the precision with which we vex each other.

This is very difficult to see when one's attention is being monopolized by a single party to the argument. Monologues are of little value here, because there are no conclusions to be reported; there is merely a discussion to be sustained. Insofar as the essays here collected have any importance, it is less in what they say than what they are witness to: an enormous increase in interest, not only in anthropology, but in social studies generally, in the role of symbolic forms in human life. Meaning, that elusive and ill-defined pseudoentity we were once more than content to leave philosophers and literary critics to fumble with, has now come back into the heart of our discipline. Even Marxists are quoting Cassirer; even positivists, Kenneth Burke.

My own position in the midst of all this has been to try to resist subjectivism on the one hand and cabbalism on the other, to try to keep the analysis of symbolic forms as closely tied as I could to concrete social events and occasions, the public world of common life, and to organize it in such a way that the connections between theoretical formulations and descriptive interpretations were unobscured by appeals to dark sciences. I have never been impressed by the argument that, as complete objectivity is impossible in these matters (as, of course, it is), one might as well let one's sentiments run loose. As Robert Solow has remarked, that is like saying that as a perfectly aseptic environment is impossible, one might as well conduct surgery in a sewer. Nor, on the other hand, have I been impressed with claims that structural linguistics, computer engineering, or some other advanced form of thought is going to enable us to understand men without knowing them. Nothing will discredit a semiotic approach to culture more quickly than allowing it to drift into a combination of intuitionism and alchemy, no matter how elegantly the intuitions are expressed or how modern the alchemy is made to look.

The danger that cultural analysis, in search of all-too-deep-lying turtles, will lose touch with the hard surfaces of life—with the political, economic, stratificatory realities within which men are everywhere contained—and with the biological and physical necessities on which those surfaces rest, is an ever-present one. The only defense against it, and against, thus, turning cultural analysis into a kind of sociological aestheticism, is to train such analysis on such realities and such necessities in the first place. It is thus that I have written about nationalism, about violence, about identity, about human nature, about legitimacy, about revolution, about ethnicity, about urbanization, about status, about death, about time, and most of all about particular attempts by particular peoples to place these things in some sort of comprehensible, meaningful frame.

To look at the symbolic dimensions of social action—art, religion, ideology, science, law, morality, common sense—is not to turn away from the existential dilemmas of life for some empyrean realm of de-emotionalized forms; it is to plunge into the midst of them. The essential vocation of interpretive anthropology is not to answer our deepest questions, but to make available to us answers that others, guarding other sheep in other valleys, have given, and thus to include them in the consultable record of what man has said.

PART II

Chapter 2 / The Impact of the Concept of Culture on the Concept of Man

I

Toward the end of his recent study of the ideas used by tribal peoples, *La Pensée Sauvage,* the French anthropologist Lévi-Strauss remarks that scientific explanation does not consist, as we have been led to imagine, in the reduction of the complex to the simple. Rather, it consists, he says, in a substitution of a complexity more intelligible for one which is less. So far as the study of man is concerned, one may go even further, I think, and argue that explanation often consists of substituting complex pictures for simple ones while striving somehow to retain the persuasive clarity that went with the simple ones.

Elegance remains, I suppose, a general scientific ideal; but in the social sciences, it is very often in departures from that ideal that truly creative developments occur. Scientific advancement commonly consists in a progressive complication of what once seemed a beautifully simple set of notions but now seems an unbearably simplistic one. It is after this sort of disenchantment occurs that intelligibility, and thus explanatory power, comes to rest on the possibility of substituting the involved but comprehensible for the involved but incomprehensible to which

Lévi-Strauss refers. Whitehead once offered to the natural sciences the maxim "Seek simplicity and distrust it"; to the social sciences he might well have offered "Seek complexity and order it."

Certainly the study of culture has developed as though this maxim were being followed. The rise of a scientific concept of culture amounted to, or at least was connected with, the overthrow of the view of human nature dominant in the Enlightenment—a view that, whatever else may be said for or against it, was both clear and simple—and its replacement by a view not only more complicated but enormously less clear. The attempt to clarify it, to reconstruct an intelligible account of what man is, has underlain scientific thinking about culture ever since. Having sought complexity and, on a scale grander than they ever imagined, found it, anthropologists became entangled in a tortuous effort to order it. And the end is not yet in sight.

The Enlightenment view of man was, of course, that he was wholly of a piece with nature and shared in the general uniformity of composition which natural science, under Bacon's urging and Newton's guidance, had discovered there. There is, in brief, a human nature as regularly organized, as thoroughly invariant, and as marvelously simple as Newton's universe. Perhaps some of its laws are different, but there *are* laws; perhaps some of its immutability is obscured by the trappings of local fashion, but it *is* immutable.

A quotation that Lovejoy (whose magisterial analysis I am following here) gives from an Enlightenment historian, Mascou, presents the position with the useful bluntness one often finds in a minor writer:

The stage setting [in different times and places] is, indeed, altered, the actors change their garb and their appearance; but their inward motions arise from the same desires and passions of men, and produce their effects in the vicissitudes of kingdoms and peoples.[1]

Now, this view is hardly one to be despised; nor, despite my easy references a moment ago to "overthrow," can it be said to have disappeared from contemporary anthropological thought. The notion that men are men under whatever guise and against whatever backdrop has not been replaced by "other mores, other beasts."

Yet, cast as it was, the Enlightenment concept of the nature of human nature had some much less acceptable implications, the main one being that, to quote Lovejoy himself this time, "anything of which the intelli-

---

[1] A. O. Lovejoy, *Essays in the History of Ideas* (New York, 1960), p. 173.

gibility, verifiability, or actual affirmation is limited to men of a special age, race, temperament, tradition or condition is [in and of itself] without truth or value, or at all events without importance to a reasonable man." [2] The great, vast variety of differences among men, in beliefs and values, in customs and institutions, both over time and from place to place, is essentially without significance in defining his nature. It consists of mere accretions, distortions even, overlaying and obscuring what is truly human—the constant, the general, the universal—in man.

Thus, in a passage now notorious, Dr. Johnson saw Shakespeare's genius to lie in the fact that "his characters are not modified by the customs of particular places, unpractised by the rest of the world; by the peculiarities of studies or professions, which can operate upon but small numbers; or by the accidents of transient fashions or temporary opinions." [3] And Racine regarded the success of his plays on classical themes as proof that "the taste of Paris . . . conforms to that of Athens; my spectators have been moved by the same things which, in other times, brought tears to the eyes of the most cultivated classes of Greece." [4]

The trouble with this kind of view, aside from the fact that it sounds comic coming from someone as profoundly English as Johnson or as French as Racine, is that the image of a constant human nature independent of time, place, and circumstance, of studies and professions, transient fashions and temporary opinions, may be an illusion, that what man is may be so entangled with where he is, who he is, and what he believes that it is inseparable from them. It is precisely the consideration of such a possibility that led to the rise of the concept of culture and the decline of the uniformitarian view of man. Whatever else modern anthropology asserts—and it seems to have asserted almost everything at one time or another—it is firm in the conviction that men unmodified by the customs of particular places do not in fact exist, have never existed, and most important, could not in the very nature of the case exist. There is, there can be, no backstage where we can go to catch a glimpse of Mascou's actors as "real persons" lounging about in street clothes, disengaged from their profession, displaying with artless candor their spontaneous desires and unprompted passions. They may

[2] Ibid., p. 80.

[3] "Preface to Shakespeare," *Johnson on Shakespeare* (London, 1931), pp. 11–12.

[4] From the Preface to *Iphigénie*.

change their roles, their styles of acting, even the dramas in which they play; but—as Shakespeare himself of course remarked—they are always performing.

This circumstance makes the drawing of a line between what is natural, universal, and constant in man and what is conventional, local, and variable extraordinarily difficult. In fact, it suggests that to draw such a line is to falsify the human situation, or at least to misrender it seriously.

Consider Balinese trance. The Balinese fall into extreme dissociated states in which they perform all sorts of spectacular activities—biting off the heads of living chickens, stabbing themselves with daggers, throwing themselves wildly about, speaking with tongues, performing miraculous feats of equilibration, mimicking sexual intercourse, eating feces, and so on—rather more easily and much more suddenly than most of us fall asleep. Trance states are a crucial part of every ceremony. In some, fifty or sixty people may fall, one after the other ("like a string of firecrackers going off," as one observer puts it), emerging anywhere from five minutes to several hours later, totally unaware of what they have been doing and convinced, despite the amnesia, that they have had the most extraordinary and deeply satisfying experience a man can have. What does one learn about human nature from this sort of thing and from the thousand similarly peculiar things anthropologists discover, investigate, and describe? That the Balinese are peculiar sorts of beings, South Sea Martians? That they are just the same as we at base, but with some peculiar, but really incidental, customs we do not happen to have gone in for? That they are innately gifted or even instinctively driven in certain directions rather than others? Or that human nature does not exist and men are pure and simply what their culture makes them?

It is among such interpretations as these, all unsatisfactory, that anthropology has attempted to find its way to a more viable concept of man, one in which culture, and the variability of culture, would be taken into account rather than written off as caprice and prejudice, and yet, at the same time, one in which the governing principle of the field, "the basic unity of mankind," would not be turned into an empty phrase. To take the giant step away from the uniformitarian view of human nature is, so far as the study of man is concerned, to leave the Garden. To entertain the idea that the diversity of custom across time and over space is not a mere matter of garb and appearance, of stage settings and comedic masques, is to entertain also the idea that humanity is as various in its essence as it is in its expression. And with that reflection some well-fastened philosophical moorings are loosed and an uneasy drifting into perilous waters begins.

Perilous, because if one discards the notion that Man with a capital "M," is to be looked for "behind," "under," or "beyond" his customs and replaces it with the notion that man, uncapitalized, is to be looked for "in" them, one is in some danger of losing sight of him altogether. Either he dissolves, without residue, into his time and place, a child and a perfect captive of his age, or he becomes a conscripted soldier in a vast Tolstoian army, engulfed in one or another of the terrible historical determinisms with which we have been plagued from Hegel forward. We have had, and to some extent still have, both of these aberrations in the social sciences—one marching under the banner of cultural relativism, the other under that of cultural evolution. But we also have had, and more commonly, attempts to avoid them by seeking in culture patterns themselves the defining elements of a human existence which, although not constant in expression, are yet distinctive in character.

II

Attempts to locate man amid the body of his customs have taken several directions, adopted diverse tactics; but they have all, or virtually all, proceeded in terms of a single overall intellectual strategy: what I will call, so as to have a stick to beat it with, the "stratigraphic" conception of the relations between biological, psychological, social, and cultural factors in human life. In this conception, man is a composite of "levels," each superimposed upon those beneath it and underpinning those above it. As one analyzes man, one peels off layer after layer, each such layer being complete and irreducible in itself, revealing another, quite different sort of layer underneath. Strip off the motley forms of culture and one finds the structural and functional regularities of social organization. Peel off these in turn and one finds the underlying psychological factors—"basic needs" or what-have-you—that support and make them possible. Peel off psychological factors and one is left with the biological foundations—anatomical, physiological, neurological—of the whole edifice of human life.

The attraction of this sort of conceptualization, aside from the fact that it guaranteed the established academic disciplines their independence and sovereignty, was that it seemed to make it possible to have one's cake and eat it. One did not have to assert that man's culture was all there was to him in order to claim that it was, nonetheless, an essential and irreducible, even a paramount ingredient in his nature. Cultural facts could be interpreted against the background of noncultural facts without dissolving them into that background or dissolving that background into them. Man was a hierarchically stratified animal, a sort of evolutionary deposit, in whose definition each level—organic, psychological, social, and cultural—had an assigned and incontestable place. To see what he really was, we had to superimpose findings from the various relevant sciences—anthropology, sociology, psychology, biology —upon one another like so many patterns in a *moiré;* and when that was done, the cardinal importance of the cultural level, the only one distinctive to man, would naturally appear, as would what it had to tell us, in its own right, about what he really was. For the eighteenth century image of man as the naked reasoner that appeared when he took his cultural costumes off, the anthropology of the late nineteenth and early twentieth centuries substituted the image of man as the transfigured animal that appeared when he put them on.

At the level of concrete research and specific analysis, this grand strategy came down, first, to a hunt for universals in culture, for empirical uniformities that, in the face of the diversity of customs around the world and over time, could be found everywhere in about the same form, and, second, to an effort to relate such universals, once found, to the established constants of human biology, psychology, and social organization. If some customs could be ferreted out of the cluttered catalogue of world culture as common to all local variants of it, and if these could then be connected in a determinate manner with certain invariant points of reference on the subcultural levels, then at least some progress might be made toward specifying which cultural traits are essential to human existence and which merely adventitious, peripheral, or ornamental. In such a way, anthropology could determine cultural dimensions of a concept of man commensurate with the dimensions provided, in a similar way, by biology, psychology, or sociology.

In essence, this is not altogether a new idea. The notion of a *consensus gentium* (a consensus of all mankind)—the notion that there are some things that all men will be found to agree upon as right, real, just, or attractive and that these things are, therefore, in fact right, real, just, or attractive—was present in the Enlightenment and probably has been present in some form or another in all ages and climes. It is one of those ideas that occur to almost anyone sooner or later. Its development in modern anthropology, however—beginning with Clark Wissler's elaboration in the 1920s of what he called "the universal cultural pattern," through Bronislaw Malinowski's presentation of a list of "universal institutional types" in the early forties, up to G. P. Murdock's elaboration of a set of "common-denominators of culture" during and since World War II—added something new. It added the notion that, to quote Clyde Kluckhohn, perhaps the most persuasive of the *consensus gentium* theorists, "some aspects of culture take their specific forms solely as a result of historical accidents; others are tailored by forces which can properly be designated as universal." [5] With this, man's cultural life is split in two: part of it is, like Mascou's actors' garb, independent of men's Newtonian "inward motions"; part is an emanation of those motions themselves. The question that then arises is: Can this halfway house between the eighteenth and twentieth centuries really stand?

Whether it can or not depends on whether the dualism between empirically universal aspects of culture rooted in subcultural realities and empirically variable aspects not so rooted can be established and sustained. And this, in turn, demands (1) that the universals proposed be substantial ones and not empty categories; (2) that they be specifically grounded in particular biological, psychological, or sociological processes, not just vaguely associated with "underlying realities"; and (3) that they can convincingly be defended as core elements in a definition of humanity in comparison with which the much more numerous cultural particularities are of clearly secondary importance. On all three of these counts it seems to me that the *consensus gentium* approach fails; rather than moving toward the essentials of the human situation it moves away from them.

The reason the first of these requirements—that the proposed universals be substantial ones and not empty or near-empty categories—has not been met is that it cannot be. There is a logical conflict between asserting that, say, "religion," "marriage," or "property" are empirical universals and giving them very much in the way of specific content, for to say that they are empirical universals is to say that they have the same content, and to say they have the same content is to fly in the face

5 A. L. Kroeber, ed., *Anthropology Today* (Chicago, 1953), p. 516.

of the undeniable fact that they do not. If one defines religion generally and indeterminately—as man's most fundamental orientation to reality, for example—then one cannot at the same time assign to that orientation a highly circumstantial content; for clearly what composes the most fundamental orientation to reality among the transported Aztecs, lifting pulsing hearts torn live from the chests of human sacrifices toward the heavens, is not what comprises it among the stolid Zuñi, dancing their great mass supplications to the benevolent gods of rain. The obsessive ritualism and unbuttoned polytheism of the Hindus express a rather different view of what the "really real" is really like from the uncompromising monotheism and austere legalism of Sunni Islam. Even if one does try to get down to less abstract levels and assert, as Kluckhohn did, that a concept of the afterlife is universal, or as Malinowski did, that a sense of Providence is universal, the same contradiction haunts one. To make the generalization about an afterlife stand up alike for the Confucians and the Calvinists, the Zen Buddhists and the Tibetan Buddhists, one has to define it in most general terms, indeed—so general, in fact, that whatever force it seems to have virtually evaporates. So, too, with any notion of a sense of Providence, which can include under its wing both Navajo notions about the relations of gods to men and Trobriand ones. And as with religion, so with "marriage," "trade," and all the rest of what A. L. Kroeber aptly called "fake universals," down to so seemingly tangible a matter as "shelter." That everywhere people mate and produce children, have some sense of mine and thine, and protect themselves in one fashion or another from rain and sun are neither false nor, from some points of view, unimportant; but they are hardly very much help in drawing a portrait of man that will be a true and honest likeness and not an unteneted "John Q. Public" sort of cartoon.

My point, which should be clear and I hope will become even clearer in a moment, is not that there are no generalizations that can be made about man as man, save that he is a most various animal, or that the study of culture has nothing to contribute toward the uncovering of such generalizations. My point is that such generalizations are not to be discovered through a Baconian search for cultural universals, a kind of public-opinion polling of the world's peoples in search of a *consensus gentium* that does not in fact exist, and, further, that the attempt to do so leads to precisely the sort of relativism the whole approach was expressly designed to avoid. "Zuñi culture prizes restraint," Kluckhohn writes; "Kwakiutl culture encourages exhibitionism on the part of the individual. These are contrasting values, but in adhering to them the Zuñi and Kwakiutl show their allegiance to a universal value; the prizing of the distinctive norms of one's culture." [6] This is sheer evasion, but it is only more apparent, not more evasive, than discussions of cultural universals in general. What, after all, does it avail us to say, with Herskovits, that "morality is a universal, and so is enjoyment of beauty, and some standard for truth," if we are forced in the very next sentence, as he is, to add that "the many forms these concepts take are but products of the particular historical experience of the societies that manifest them"? [7] Once one abandons uniformitarianism, even if, like the *consensus gentium* theorists, only partially and uncertainly, relativism is a genuine danger; but it can be warded off only by facing directly and fully the diversities of human culture, the Zuñi's restraint and the Kwakiutl's exhibitionism, and embracing them within the body of one's concept of man, not by gliding past them with vague tautologies and forceless banalities.

Of course, the difficulty of stating cultural universals which are at the same time substantial also hinders fulfillment of the second requirement facing the *consensus gentium* approach, that of grounding such universals in particular biological, psychological, or sociological processes. But there is more to it than that: the "stratigraphic" conceptualization of the relationships between cultural and noncultural factors hinders such a grounding even more effectively. Once culture, psyche, society, and organism have been converted into separate scientific "levels," complete and autonomous in themselves, it is very hard to bring them back together again.

The most common way of trying to do so is through the utilization of what are called "invariant points of reference." These points are to be found, to quote one of the most famous statements of this strategy—the "Toward a Common Language for the Areas of the Social Sciences" memorandum produced by Talcott Parsons, Kluckhohn, O. H. Taylor, and others in the early forties—

in the nature of social systems, in the biological and psychological nature of the component individuals, in the external situations in which they live and act, in the necessity of coordination in social systems. In [culture] . . .

[6] C. Kluckhohn, *Culture and Behavior* (New York, 1962), p. 280.
[7] M. J. Herskovits, *Cultural Anthropology* (New York, 1955), p. 364.

these "foci" of structure are never ignored. They must in some way be "adapted to" or "taken account of."

Cultural universals are conceived to be crystallized responses to these unevadable realities, institutionalized ways of coming to terms with them.

Analysis consists, then, of matching assumed universals to postulated underlying necessities, attempting to show there is some goodness of fit between the two. On the social level, reference is made to such irrefragable facts as that all societies, in order to persist, must reproduce their membership or allocate goods and services, hence the universality of some form of family or some form of trade. On the psychological level, recourse is had to basic needs like personal growth—hence the ubiquity of educational institutions—or to panhuman problems, like the Oedipal predicament—hence the ubiquity of punishing gods and nurturant goddesses. Biologically, there is metabolism and health; culturally, dining customs and curing procedures. And so on. The tack is to look at underlying human requirements of some sort or other and then to try to show that those aspects of culture that are universal are, to use Kluckhohn's figure again, "tailored" by these requirements.

The problem here is, again, not so much whether in a general way this sort of congruence exists, but whether it is more than a loose and indeterminate one. It is not difficult to relate some human institutions to what science (or common sense) tells us are requirements for human existence, but it is very much more difficult to state this relationship in an unequivocal form. Not only does almost any institution serve a multiplicity of social, psychological, and organic needs (so that to say marriage is a mere reflex of the social need to reproduce, or that dining customs are a reflex of metabolic necessities, is to court parody), but there is no way to state in any precise and testable way the interlevel relationships that are conceived to hold. Despite first appearances, there is no serious attempt here to apply the concepts and theories of biology, psychology, or even sociology to the analysis of culture (and, of course, not even a suggestion of the reverse exchange) but merely a placing of supposed facts from the cultural and subcultural levels side by side so as to induce a vague sense that some kind of relationship between them —an obscure sort of "tailoring"—obtains. There is no theoretical integration here at all but a mere correlation, and that intuitive, of separate findings. With the levels approach, we can never, even by invoking "in-

variant points of reference," construct genuine functional interconnections between cultural and noncultural factors, only more or less persuasive analogies, parallelisms, suggestions, and affinities.

However, even if I am wrong (as, admittedly, many anthropologists
would hold) in claiming that the *consensus gentium* approach can produce neither substantial universals nor specific connections between cultural and noncultural phenomena to explain them, the question still remains whether such universals should be taken as the central elements
in the definition of man, whether a lowest-common-denominator view of
humanity is what we want anyway. This is, of course, now a philosophical question, not as such a scientific one; but the notion that the essence
of what it means to be human is most clearly revealed in those features
of human culture that are universal rather than in those that are distinctive to this people or that is a prejudice we are not necessarily obliged
to share. Is it in grasping such general facts—that man has everywhere
some sort of "religion"—or in grasping the richness of this religious
phenomenon or that—Balinese trance or Indian ritualism, Aztec human
sacrifice or Zuñi rain-dancing—that we grasp him? Is the fact that
"marriage" is universal (if it is) as penetrating a comment on what we
are as the facts concerning Himalayan polyandry, or those fantastic
Australian marriage rules, or the elaborate bride-price systems of Bantu
Africa? The comment that Cromwell was the most typical Englishman
of his time precisely in that he was the oddest may be relevant in this
connection, too: it may be in the cultural particularities of people—in
their oddities—that some of the most instructive revelations of what it
is to be generically human are to be found; and the main contribution
of the science of anthropology to the construction—or reconstruction
—of a concept of man may then lie in showing us how to find them.

III

The major reason why anthropologists have shied away from cultural
particularities when it came to a question of defining man and have
taken refuge instead in bloodless universals is that, faced as they are
with the enormous variation in human behavior, they are haunted by a
fear of historicism, of becoming lost in a whirl of cultural relativism so

convulsive as to deprive them of any fixed bearings at all. Nor has there not been some occasion for such a fear: Ruth Benedict's *Patterns of Culture,* probably the most popular book in anthropology ever published in this country, with its strange conclusion that anything one group of people is inclined toward doing is worthy of respect by another, is perhaps only the most outstanding example of the awkward positions one can get into by giving oneself over rather too completely to what Marc Bloch called "the thrill of learning singular things." Yet the fear is a bogey. The notion that unless a cultural phenomenon is empirically universal it cannot reflect anything about the nature of man is about as logical as the notion that because sickle-cell anemia is, fortunately, not universal, it cannot tell us anything about human genetic processes. It is not whether phenomena are empirically common that is critical in science—else why should Becquerel have been so interested in the peculiar behavior of uranium?—but whether they can be made to reveal the enduring natural processes that underly them. Seeing heaven in a grain of sand is not a trick only poets can accomplish.

In short, we need to look for systematic relationships among diverse phenomena, not for substantive identities among similar ones. And to do that with any effectiveness, we need to replace the "stratigraphic" conception of the relations between the various aspects of human existence with a synthetic one; that is, one in which biological, psychological, sociological, and cultural factors can be treated as variables within unitary systems of analysis. The establishment of a common language in the social sciences is not a matter of mere coordination of terminologies or, worse yet, of coining artificial new ones; nor is it a matter of imposing a single set of categories upon the area as a whole. It is a matter of integrating different types of theories and concepts in such a way that one can formulate meaningful propositions embodying findings now sequestered in separate fields of study.

In attempting to launch such an integration from the anthropological side and to reach, thereby, a more exact image of man, I want to propose two ideas. The first of these is that culture is best seen not as complexes of concrete behavior patterns—customs, usages, traditions, habit clusters—as has, by and large, been the case up to now, but as a set of control mechanisms—plans, recipes, rules, instructions (what computer engineers call "programs")—for the governing of behavior. The second idea is that man is precisely the animal most desperately dependent upon such extragenetic, outside-the-skin control mechanisms, such cultural programs, for ordering his behavior.

Neither of these ideas is entirely new, but a number of recent developments, both within anthropology and in other sciences (cybernetics, information theory, neurology, molecular genetics) have made them susceptible of more precise statement as well as lending them a degree of empirical support they did not previously have. And out of such reformulations of the concept of culture and of the role of culture in human life comes, in turn, a definition of man stressing not so much the empirical commonalities in his behavior, from place to place and time to time, but rather the mechanisms by whose agency the breadth and indeterminateness of his inherent capacities are reduced to the narrowness and specificity of his actual accomplishments. One of the most significant facts about us may finally be that we all begin with the natural equipment to live a thousand kinds of life but end in the end having lived only one.

The "control mechanism" view of culture begins with the assumption that human thought is basically both social and public—that its natural habitat is the house yard, the marketplace, and the town square. Thinking consists not of "happenings in the head" (though happenings there and elsewhere are necessary for it to occur) but of a traffic in what have been called, by G. H. Mead and others, significant symbols—words for the most part but also gestures, drawings, musical sounds, mechanical devices like clocks, or natural objects like jewels—anything, in fact, that is disengaged from its mere actuality and used to impose meaning upon experience. From the point of view of any particular individual, such symbols are largely given. He finds them already current in the community when he is born, and they remain, with some additions, subtractions, and partial alterations he may or may not have had a hand in, in circulation after he dies. While he lives he uses them, or some of them, sometimes deliberately and with care, most often spontaneously and with ease, but always with the same end in view: to put a construction upon the events through which he lives, to orient himself within "the ongoing course of experienced things," to adopt a vivid phrase of John Dewey's.

Man is so in need of such symbolic sources of illumination to find his bearings in the world because the nonsymbolic sort that are constitutionally ingrained in his body cast so diffused a light. The behavior patterns of lower animals are, at least to a much greater extent, given to them with their physical structure; genetic sources of information order their actions within much narrower ranges of variation, the narrower and more thoroughgoing the lower the animal. For man, what are innately given are extremely general response capacities, which, although they make possible far greater plasticity, complexity, and, on the scattered occasions when everything works as it should, effectiveness of behavior, leave it much less precisely regulated. This, then, is the second face of our argument: Undirected by culture patterns—organized systems of significant symbols—man's behavior would be virtually ungovernable, a mere chaos of pointless acts and exploding emotions, his experience virtually shapeless. Culture, the accumulated totality of such patterns, is not just an ornament of human existence but—the principal basis of its specificity—an essential condition for it.

Within anthropology some of the most telling evidence in support of such a position comes from recent advances in our understanding of what used to be called the descent of man: the emergence of *Homo sapiens* out of his general primate background. Of these advances three are of critical importance: (1) the discarding of a sequential view of the relations between the physical evolution and the cultural development of man in favor of an overlap or interactive view; (2) the discovery that the bulk of the biological changes that produced modern man out of his most immediate progenitors took place in the central nervous system and most especially in the brain; (3) the realization that man is, in physical terms, an incomplete, an unfinished, animal; that what sets him off most graphically from nonmen is less his sheer ability to learn (great as that is) than how much and what particular sorts of things he *has* to learn before he is able to function at all. Let me take each of these points in turn.

The traditional view of the relations between the biological and the cultural advance of man was that the former, the biological, was for all intents and purposes completed before the latter, the cultural, began. That is to say, it was again stratigraphic: Man's physical being evolved, through the usual mechanisms of genetic variation and natural selection, up to the point where his anatomical structure had arrived at more or less the status at which we find it today; then cultural development got under way. At some particular stage in his phylogenetic history, a marginal genetic change of some sort rendered him capable of producing and carrying culture, and thenceforth his form of adaptive response to environmental pressures was almost exclusively cultural rather than genetic. As he spread over the globe, he wore furs in cold climates and loin cloths (or nothing at all) in warm ones; he didn't alter his innate mode of response to environmental temperature. He made weapons to extend his inherited predatory powers and cooked foods to render a wider range of them digestible. Man became man, the story continues, when, having crossed some mental Rubicon, he became able to transmit "knowledge, belief, law, morals, custom" (to quote the items of Sir Edward Tylor's classical definition of culture) to his descendants and his neighbors through teaching and to acquire them from his ancestors and his neighbors through learning. After that magical moment, the advance of the hominids depended almost entirely on cultural accumulation, on the slow growth of conventional practices, rather than, as it had for ages past, on physical organic change.

The only trouble is that such a moment does not seem to have existed. By the most recent estimates the transition to the cultural mode of life took the genus *Homo* several million years to accomplish; and stretched out in such a manner, it involved not one or a handful of marginal genetic changes but a long, complex, and closely ordered sequence of them.

In the current view, the evolution of *Homo sapiens*—modern man— out of his immediate pre*sapiens* background got definitely under way nearly four million years ago with the appearance of the now famous Australopithecines—the so-called ape men of southern and eastern Africa—and culminated with the emergence of *sapiens* himself only some one to two or three hundred thousand years ago. Thus, as at least elemental forms of cultural, or if you wish protocultural, activity (simple toolmaking, hunting, and so on) seem to have been present among some of the Australopithecines, there was an overlap of, as I say, well over a million years between the beginning of culture and the appearance of man as we know him today. The precise dates—which are tentative and which further research may later alter in one direction or another—are not critical; what is critical is that there was an overlap and that it was a very extended one. The final phases (final to date, at any rate) of the phylogenetic history of man took place in the same grand geological era—the so-called Ice Age—as the initial phases of his cultural history. Men have birthdays, but man does not.

What this means is that culture, rather than being added on, so to speak, to a finished or virtually finished animal, was ingredient, and centrally ingredient, in the production of that animal itself. The slow, steady, almost glacial growth of culture through the Ice Age altered the balance of selection pressures for the evolving *Homo* in such a way as to play a major directive role in his evolution. The perfection of tools, the adoption of organized hunting and gathering practices, the beginnings of true family organization, the discovery of fire, and, most critically, though it is as yet extremely difficult to trace it out in any detail, the increasing reliance upon systems of significant symbols (language, art, myth, ritual) for orientation, communication, and self-control all created for man a new environment to which he was then obliged to adapt. As culture, step by infinitesimal step, accumulated and developed, a selective advantage was given to those individuals in the population most able to take advantage of it—the effective hunter, the persistent gatherer, the adept toolmaker, the resourceful leader—until what had been a small-brained, protohuman *Australopithecus* became the large-brained fully human *Homo sapiens*. Between the cultural pattern, the body, and the brain, a positive feedback system was created in which each shaped the progress of the other, a system in which the interaction among increasing tool use, the changing anatomy of the hand, and the expanding representation of the thumb on the cortex is only one of the more graphic examples. By submitting himself to governance by symbolically mediated programs for producing artifacts, organizing social life, or expressing emotions, man determined, if unwittingly, the culminating stages of his own biological destiny. Quite literally, though quite inadvertently, he created himself.

Though, as I mentioned, there were a number of important changes in the gross anatomy of genus *Homo* during this period of his crystallization—in skull shape, dentition, thumb size, and so on—by far the most important and dramatic were those that evidently took place in the central nervous system; for this was the period when the human brain, and most particularly the forebrain, ballooned into its present top-heavy proportions. The technical problems are complicated and controversial here; but the main point is that though the Australopithecines had a torso and arm configuration not drastically different from our own, and a pelvis and leg formation at least well-launched toward our own, they had cranial capacities hardly larger than those of the living apes—that is to say, about a third to a half of our own. What sets true men off most distinctly from protomen is apparently not over-all bodily form but complexity of nervous organization. The overlap period of cultural and biological change seems to have consisted in an intense concentration on neural development and perhaps associated refinements of various behaviors—of the hands, bipedal locomotion, and so on—for which the basic anatomical foundations—mobile shoulders and wrists, a broadened ilium, and so on—had already been securely laid. In itself, this is perhaps not altogether startling; but, combined with what I have already said, it suggests some conclusions about what sort of animal man is that are, I think, rather far not only from those of the eighteenth century but from those of the anthropology of only ten or fifteen years ago.

Most bluntly, it suggests that there is no such thing as a human nature independent of culture. Men without culture would not be the clever savages of Golding's *Lord of the Flies* thrown back upon the cruel wisdom of their animal instincts; nor would they be the nature's noblemen of Enlightenment primitivism or even, as classical anthropological theory would imply, intrinsically talented apes who had somehow failed to find themselves. They would be unworkable monstrosities with very few useful instincts, fewer recognizable sentiments, and no intellect: mental basket cases. As our central nervous system—and most particularly its crowning curse and glory, the neocortex—grew up in great part in interaction with culture, it is incapable of directing our behavior or organizing our experience without the guidance provided by systems of significant symbols. What happened to us in the Ice Age is that we were obliged to abandon the regularity and precision of detailed genetic control over our conduct for the flexibility and adaptability of a more generalized, though of course no less real, genetic control over it. To supply the additional information necessary to be able to act, we were forced, in turn, to rely more and more heavily on cultural sources—the accumulated fund of significant symbols. Such symbols are thus not mere expressions, instrumentalities, or correlates of our biological, psychological, and social existence; they are prerequisites of it. Without men, no culture, certainly; but equally, and more significantly, without culture, no men.

We are, in sum, incomplete or unfinished animals who complete or finish ourselves through culture—and not through culture in general but through highly particular forms of it: Dobuan and Javanese, Hopi and Italian, upper-class and lower-class, academic and commercial. Man's great capacity for learning, his plasticity, has often been remarked, but what is even more critical is his extreme dependence upon a certain sort of learning: the attainment of concepts, the apprehension and application of specific systems of symbolic meaning. Beavers build dams, birds build nests, bees locate food, baboons organize social groups, and mice mate on the basis of forms of learning that rest predominantly on the instructions encoded in their genes and evoked by appropriate patterns of external stimuli: physical keys inserted into organic locks. But men build dams or shelters, locate food, organize their social groups, or find sexual partners under the guidance of instructions encoded in flow charts and blueprints, hunting lore, moral systems and aesthetic judgments: conceptual structures molding formless talents.

We live, as one writer has neatly put it, in an "information gap." Between what our body tells us and what we have to know in order to function, there is a vacuum we must fill ourselves, and we fill it with information (or misinformation) provided by our culture. The boundary between what is innately controlled and what is culturally controlled in human behavior is an ill-defined and wavering one. Some things are, for all intents and purposes, entirely controlled intrinsically: we need no more cultural guidance to learn how to breathe than a fish needs to learn how to swim. Others are almost certainly largely cultural; we do not attempt to explain on a genetic basis why some men put their trust in centralized planning and others in the free market, though it might be an amusing exercise. Almost all complex human behavior is, of course, the interactive, nonadditive outcome of the two. Our capacity to speak is surely innate; our capacity to speak English is surely cultural. Smiling at pleasing stimuli and frowning at unpleasing ones are surely in some degree genetically determined (even apes screw up their faces at noxious odors); but sardonic smiling and burlesque frowning are equally surely predominantly cultural, as is perhaps demonstrated by the Balinese definition of a madman as someone who, like an American, smiles when there is nothing to laugh at. Between the basic ground plans for our life that our genes lay down—the capacity to speak or to smile—and the precise behavior we in fact execute—speaking English in a certain tone of voice, smiling enigmatically in a delicate social situation—lies a complex set of significant symbols under whose direction we transform the first into the second, the ground plans into the activity.

Our ideas, our values, our acts, even our emotions, are, like our nervous system itself, cultural products—products manufactured, indeed, out of tendencies, capacities, and dispositions with which we were born, but manufactured nonetheless. Chartres is made of stone and glass. But it is not just stone and glass; it is a cathedral, and not only a cathedral, but a particular cathedral built at a particular time by certain members of a particular society. To understand what it means, to perceive it for what it is, you need to know rather more than the generic properties of stone and glass and rather more than what is common to all cathedrals. You need to understand also—and, in my opinion, most critically—the specific concepts of the relations among God, man, and architecture that, since they have governed its creation, it consequently embodies. It is no different with men: they, too, every last one of them, are cultural artifacts.

IV

Whatever differences they may show, the approaches to the definition of human nature adopted by the Enlightenment and by classical anthropology have one thing in common: they are both basically typological. They endeavor to construct an image of man as a model, an archetype, a Platonic idea or an Aristotelian form, with respect to which actual men—you, me, Churchill, Hitler, and the Bornean headhunter—are but reflections, distortions, approximations. In the Enlightenment case, the elements of this essential type were to be uncovered by stripping the trappings of culture away from actual men and seeing what then was left—natural man. In classical anthropology, it was to be uncovered by factoring out the commonalities in culture and seeing what then appeared —consensual man. In either case, the result is the same as that which tends to emerge in all typological approaches to scientific problems generally: the differences among individuals and among groups of individuals are rendered secondary. Individuality comes to be seen as eccentricity, distinctiveness as accidental deviation from the only legitimate object of study for the true scientist: the underlying, unchanging, normative type. In such an approach, however elaborately formulated and resourcefully defended, living detail is drowned in dead stereotype: we are in quest of a metaphysical entity, Man with a capital "M," in the interests of which we sacrifice the empirical entity we in fact encounter, man with a small "m."

The sacrifice is, however, as unnecessary as it is unavailing. There is no opposition between general theoretical understanding and circumstantial understanding, between synoptic vision and a fine eye for detail. It is, in fact, by its power to draw general propositions out of particular phenomena that a scientific theory—indeed, science itself—is to be judged. If we want to discover what man amounts to, we can only find it in what men are: and what men are, above all other things, is various. It is in understanding that variousness—its range, its nature, its basis, and its implications—that we shall come to construct a concept of human nature that, more than a statistical shadow and less than a primitivist dream, has both substance and truth.

It is here, to come round finally to my title, that the concept of culture has its impact on the concept of man. When seen as a set of symbolic devices for controlling behavior, extrasomatic sources of information, culture provides the link between what men are intrinsically capable of becoming and what they actually, one by one, in fact become. Becoming human is becoming individual, and we become individual under the guidance of cultural patterns, historically created systems of meaning in terms of which we give form, order, point, and direction to our lives. And the cultural patterns involved are not general but specific—not just "marriage" but a particular set of notions about what men and women are like, how spouses should treat one another, or who should properly marry whom; not just "religion" but belief in the wheel of karma, the observance of a month of fasting, or the practice of cattle sacrifice. Man is to be defined neither by his innate capacities alone, as the Enlightenment sought to do, nor by his actual behaviors alone, as much of contemporary social science seeks to do, but rather by the link between them, by the way in which the first is transformed into the second, his generic potentialities focused into his specific performances. It is in man's *career,* in its characteristic course, that we can discern, however dimly, his nature, and though culture is but one element in determining that course, it is hardly the least important. As culture shaped us as a single species—and is no doubt still shaping us—so too it shapes us as separate individuals. This, neither an unchanging subcultural self nor an established cross-cultural consensus, is what we really have in common.

Oddly enough—though on second thought, perhaps not so oddly— many of our subjects seem to realize this more clearly than we anthropologists ourselves. In Java, for example, where I have done much of my work, the people quite flatly say, "To be human is to be Javanese." Small children, boors, simpletons, the insane, the flagrantly immoral, are said to be *ndurung djawa,* "not yet Javanese." A "normal" adult capable of acting in terms of the highly elaborate system of etiquette, possessed of the delicate aesthetic perceptions associated with music, dance, drama, and textile design, responsive to the subtle promptings of the divine residing in the stillnesses of each individual's inward-turning consciousness, is *sampun djawa,* "already Javanese," that is, already human. To be human is not just to breathe; it is to control one's breathing, by yogalike techniques, so as to hear in inhalation and exhalation the literal voice of God pronouncing His own name—"hu Allah." It is not just to talk, it is to utter the appropriate words and phrases in the appropriate social situations in the appropriate tone of voice and with the appropriate evasive indirection. It is not just to eat; it is to prefer certain foods cooked in certain ways and to follow a rigid table etiquette in consuming them. It is not even just to feel but to feel certain quite distinctively Javanese (and essentially untranslatable) emotions—"patience," "detachment," "resignation," "respect."

To be human here is thus not to be Everyman; it is to be a particular kind of man, and of course men differ: "Other fields," the Javanese say, "other grasshoppers." Within the society, differences are recognized, too—the way a rice peasant becomes human and Javanese differs from the way a civil servant does. This is not a matter of tolerance and ethical relativism, for not all ways of being human are regarded as equally admirable by far; the way the local Chinese go about it is, for example, intensely dispraised. The point is that there are different ways; and to shift to the anthropologist's perspective now, it is in a systematic review and analysis of these—of the Plains Indian's bravura, the Hindu's obsessiveness, the Frenchman's rationalism, the Berber's anarchism, the American's optimism (to list a series of tags I should not like to have to defend as such)—that we shall find out what it is, or can be, to be a man.

We must, in short, descend into detail, past the misleading tags, past the metaphysical types, past the empty similarities to grasp firmly the essential character of not only the various cultures but the various sorts of individuals within each culture, if we wish to encounter humanity face to face. In this area, the road to the general, to the revelatory simplicities of science, lies through a concern with the particular, the circumstantial, the concrete, but a concern organized and directed in terms of the sort of theoretical analyses that I have touched upon—analyses of physical evolution, of the functioning of the nervous system, of social organization, of psychological process, of cultural patterning, and so on —and, most especially, in terms of the interplay among them. That is to say, the road lies, like any genuine Quest, through a terrifying complexity.

"Leave him alone for a moment or two," Robert Lowell writes, not as one might suspect of the anthropologist but of that other eccentric inquirer into the nature of man, Nathaniel Hawthorne.

> Leave him alone for a moment or two,
> and you'll see him with his head
> bent down, brooding, brooding,
> eyes fixed on some chip,
> some stone, some common plant,
> the commonest thing,
> as if it were the clue.
> The disturbed eyes rise,
> furtive, foiled, dissatisfied
> from meditation on the true
> and insignificant.[8]

Bent over his own chips, stones, and common plants, the anthropologist broods, too, upon the true and insignificant, glimpsing in it, or so he thinks, fleetingly and insecurely, the disturbing, changeful image of himself.

---

[8] Reprinted with permission of Farrar, Straus & Giroux, Inc., and Faber & Faber, Ltd., from "Hawthorne," in *For the Union Dead,* p. 39. Copyright © 1964 by Robert Lowell.

Chapter 3/The Growth of Culture and the Evolution of Mind

The statement "the mind is its own place," as theorists might construe it, is not true, for the mind is not even a metaphorical "place." On the contrary, the chessboard, the platform, the scholar's desk, the judge's bench, the lorry-driver's seat, the studio and the football field are among its places. These are where people work and play stupidly or intelligently. "Mind" is not the name of another person, working or frolicking behind an impenetrable screen; it is not the name of another place where work is done or games are played; and it is not the name of another tool with which work is done, or another appliance with which games are played.

GILBERT RYLE

I

In the intellectual history of the behavioral sciences the concept of "mind" has played a curious double role. Those who have regarded the development of such sciences as involving a rectilinear extension of the methods of physical science into the realm of the organic have used it as a devil word, the referent of which was all those methods and theories which failed to measure up to a rather heroic ideal of "objectivism." Terms such as insight, understanding, conceptual thinking, image, idea, feeling, reflection, fantasy, and so on, have been stigmatized as mentalistic, "i.e., contaminated with the subjectivity of consciousness," and the appeal to them castigated as a lamentable failure of scientific nerve.[1] But those who have, on the contrary, regarded the move from a physical to an organic, and most especially to a human, subject matter as implying far-reaching revisions in theoretical approach and research procedure have tended to use "mind" as a cautionary concept, one intended more to point to defects in understanding than to repair them, more to stress the limits of positive science than to extend them. For such thinkers its main function has been to give a vaguely defined but intuitively valid expression to their settled conviction that human experience has important dimensions of order which physical theory (and, *pari passu,* psychological and social theories modeled on physical theory) omits to consider. Sherrington's image of "naked mind"—"all that counts in life. Desire, zest, truth, love, knowledge, values"—going "in our spatial world more ghostly than a ghost," serves as an epitome of this position, as Pavlov's reported practice of levying fines on any of his students who so much as uttered mentalistic words in his laboratory does of the opposite.[2]

In fact, with some exceptions, the term "mind" has not functioned as a scientific concept at all but as a rhetorical device, even when its use has been forbidden. More exactly, it has acted to communicate—and sometimes to exploit—a fear rather than to define a process, a fear of subjectivism on the one hand and of mechanism on the other. "Even when fully aware of the nature of anthropomorphic subjectivism and its dangers," Clark Hull warns us solemnly, "the most careful and experienced thinker is likely to find himself a victim to its seductions," and urges as a "prophylaxis" the strategy of viewing all behavior as if it were produced by a dog, an albino rat, or, safest of all, a robot.[3] While, for the opposition, Gordon Allport professes to see a threat to human dignity in such an approach, complaining that "the models we have been following lack the long-range orientation which is the essence of morality . . . . An addiction to machines, rats, or infants leads us to overplay those features of human behavior that are peripheral, signal-oriented, or genetic [and] to underplay those features that are central,

[1] M. Scheerer, "Cognitive Theory," in *Handbook of Social Psychology* (Reading, Mass., 1954).
[2] C. Sherrington, *Man on His Nature,* 2nd ed. (New York, 1953), p. 161; L. S. Kubie, "Psychiatric and Psychoanalytic Considerations of the Problem of Consciousness," in *Brain Mechanisms and Consciousness,* ed. E. Adrian et al. (Oxford, England, 1954), pp. 444–467.
[3] C. L. Hull, *Principles of Behavior* (New York, 1943).

future-oriented, or symbolic." [4] In the face of such contradictory descriptions of the specter that is haunting the study of man, it is small wonder that a recent group of psychologists, torn between their wish to present a convincing analysis of the directional aspects of human behavior and to meet scientific canons of objectivity, found themselves tempted by the rather desperate stratagem of referring to themselves as "subjective behaviorists." [5]

So far as the concept of mind is concerned, this state of affairs is extremely unfortunate because an extraordinarily useful notion and one for which there is no precise equivalent, save perhaps the archaism "psyche," is turned into a shibboleth. It is even more unfortunate because the fears which have so crippled the term are largely baseless, the dying echoes of the great mock civil war between materialism and dualism generated by the Newtonian revolution. Mechanism, as Ryle has said, is a bogey, because the fear of it rests on the assumption that it is somehow contradictory to say that one and the same occurrence is governed by mechanical laws and moral principles, as though a golfer cannot at once conform to the laws of ballistics, obey the rules of golf, and play with elegance.[6] But subjectivism is a bogey too, for the fear of it rests on the equally peculiar assumption that because I cannot know what you dreamed of last night, thought of while memorizing a string of nonsense syllables, or feel about the doctrine of infant damnation unless you choose to tell me, any theorizing I may do about the role such mental facts play in your behavior must be based on a false "anthropomorphic" analogy from what I know or think I know, about the role they play in mine. Lashley's tart comment that "metaphysicians and theologians have spent so many years weaving fairy tales about [mind] that they have come to believe one another's phantasies," is inaccurate only in that it neglects to note that a great many behavioral scientists have been engaged in the same sort of collective autism.[7]

One of the most frequently suggested methods for rehabilitating mind as a useful scientific concept is to transform it into a verb or participle, "Mind is minding, the reaction of an organism as a whole as a coherent

[4] G. W. Allport, "Scientific Models and Human Morals," *Psychol. Rev.* 54 (1947):182–192.

[5] G. A. Miller, E. H. Galanter, and K. H. Pribram, *Plans and the Structure of Behavior* (New York, 1960).

[6] G. Ryle, *The Concept of Mind* (New York, 1949).

[7] K. S. Lashley, "Cerebral Organization and Behavior," in *The Brain and Human Behavior*, ed. H. Solomon et al. (Baltimore, 1958).

unit . . . [a view which] releases us from the verbal bondage of a sterile and paralyzing metaphysics, and sets us free to sow and reap in a field what will bear fruit." [8] But this "cure" involves falling in with the school bench story that "a noun is a word that names a person, place, or thing," which was not true in the first place. The use of nouns as dispositional terms—i.e., words denoting capacities and propensities rather than entities or activities—is actually a standard and indispensable practice in English, both natural and scientific.[9] If "mind" is to go, "faith," "hope," and "charity" will have to go with it, as well as "cause," "force," and "gravitation" and "motive," "role," and "culture." "Mind is minding" may be all right, "science is sciencing" at least bearable.[10] But "superego is superegoing" is a little awkward. Even more important, although it is true that part of the fog of confusion which has arisen around the concept of mind is a result of a false analogy with nouns which do name persons, places, or things, it mainly springs from much deeper sources than the merely linguistic. Consequently, making it into a verb is no real protection at all against "a sterile and paralyzing metaphysics." Like mechanists, subjectivists are men of infinite resource, and an occult activity may simply be substituted for an occult entity, as in the case, for example, of "introspecting."

From the scientific point of view, to identify mind with behavior, "the reaction of the organism as a whole," is to render it as uselessly redundant as to identify it with an entity "more ghostly than a ghost." The notion that it is more defensible to transform a reality into another reality than to transform it into an unreality is not correct: a rabbit disappears just as completely when he is magically changed into a horse as he does when he is changed into a centaur. "Mind" is a term denoting a class of skills, propensities, capacities, tendencies, habits; it refers in Dewey's phrase to an "active and eager background which lies in wait and engages whatever comes its way." [11] And, as such, it is neither an action nor a thing, but an organized system of dispositions which finds its manifestation in some actions and some things. As Ryle has pointed out, if a clumsy man trips accidentally, we do not regard it proper to ascribe his actions to the workings of his mind, but if a clown trips on purpose, we do feel it proper to say this:

[8] L. A. White, *The Science of Culture* (New York, 1949).
[9] Ryle, *The Concept of Mind*.
[10] White, *The Science of Culture*.
[11] J. Dewey, *Art as Experience* (New York, 1934).

The cleverness of the clown may be exhibited in his tripping and tumbling. He trips and tumbles just as clumsy people do, except that he trips and tumbles on purpose and after much rehearsal and at the golden moment and where the children can see him and so as not to hurt himself. The spectators applaud his skill at seeming clumsy, but what they applaud is not some extra hidden performance executed "in his head." It is his visible performance that they admire, but they admire it not for being an effect of any hidden internal causes but for being an exercise of skill. Now a skill is not an act. It is therefore neither a witnessable nor an unwitnessable act. To recognize that a performance is an exercise of a skill is indeed to appreciate it in the light of a factor which could not be separately recorded by a camera. But the reason why the skill exercised in a performance cannot be separately recorded by a camera is not that it is an occult or ghostly happening, but that it is not a happening at all. It is a disposition, or complex of dispositions, and a disposition is a factor of the wrong logical type to be seen or unseen, recorded or unrecorded. Just as the habit of talking loudly is not itself loud or quiet, since it is not the sort of term of which "loud" or "quiet" can be predicated, or just as a susceptibility to headaches is for the same reason not itself unendurable or endurable, so the skills, tastes, and bents which are exercised in overt or internal operations are not themselves overt or internal, witnessable or unwitnessable.[12]

A similar argument applies to objects; we would not refer, save in a metaphorical way, to the legendary burned pig the Chinese produced by accidentally setting fire to his house as "cooked," even though he ate it, because it did not result from the exercise of a mental capability called "knowledge of cooking." But we would so refer to the second such pig the now-educated Chinese produced by deliberately burning down his house again, because it did result from such a capability, no matter how crude. Such judgments, being empirical, may be wrong; a man may have really tripped when we thought he was only clowning, or a pig really been cooked when we thought it merely burned. But the point is that when we attribute mind to an organism, we are talking about neither the organism's actions nor its products per se, but about its capacity and its proneness, its disposition, to perform certain kinds of actions and produce certain kinds of products, a capacity and a proneness we of course infer from the fact that he does sometimes perform such actions and produce such products. There is nothing extramundane about this; it merely indicates that a language lacking dispositional terms would make the scientific description and analysis of human behavior extraordi-

---

[12] Ryle, *The Concept of Mind*, p. 33. Quoted by permission of Barnes & Noble Books and Hutchinson Publishing Group Ltd.

narily difficult, and severely cripple its conceptual development, in the same way that a language, such as the Arapesh, in which you must enumerate by saying "one, two, two and one, one dog (i.e., 'four'), one dog and one, one dog and two, one dog and two and one, two dogs, . . . etc.," cripples mathematical development by making counting so troublesome that people find it such an effort to go beyond two dogs and two dogs and two dogs (i.e., "twenty-four") that they refer to all larger quantities as "a lot." [13]

Further, within such a general conceptual framework it is possible to discuss the biological, psychological, sociological, and cultural determinants of man's mental life concurrently without making any reductionist hypotheses at all. This is because a capacity for something, or a proneness to do something, not being an entity or a performance, is simply not susceptible to reduction. In the case of Ryle's clown, I could say, no doubt incorrectly, that his tumbling was reducible to a chain of conditioned reflexes, but I could not say that his skill was so reducible, because by his skill I only mean to say that he can tumble. For "the clown can tumble," it is possible, if simplistic, to write "(this organism) can (produce the described reflex series)," but it is possible to get the "can" out of the sentence only by replacing it with "is able to," "has the capacity to," etc., which is not a reduction but merely an immaterial shift from a verbal to an adjectival or nounal form. All one can do in the analysis of skills is to show the way in which they are (or are not) dependent upon various factors such as nervous system complexity, repressed desires to exhibit, the existence of social institutions such as circuses, or the presence of a cultural tradition of mimicking clumsiness for the purposes of satire. Once dispositional predicates are admitted into scientific description they are not eliminated by shifts in the "level" of description employed. And, with the recognition of this fact, a whole range of pseudoproblems, false issues, and unrealistic fears can simply be set aside.

In perhaps no area of inquiry is such an avoidance of manufactured paradoxes more useful than that of the study of mental evolution. Burdened in the past by almost all the classic anthropological fallacies— ethnocentrism, an overconcern with human uniqueness, imaginatively reconstructed history, a superorganic concept of culture, a priori stages of evolutionary change—the whole search for the origins of human

[13] M. Mead, "Comment," in *Discussions in Child Development*, ed. J. Tanner and B. Inhelder (New York, n.d.), 1:480–503.

mentality has tended to fall into disrepute, or at any rate to be neglected. But legitimate questions—and how man came to have his mind is a legitimate question—are not invalidated by misconceived answers. So far as anthropology is concerned, at least, one of the most important advantages of a dispositional answer to the question, "What is mind?" is that it permits us to reopen a classic issue without reviving classic controversies.

II

Over the past half century, two views of the evolution of the human mind, both inadequate, have been current. The first is the thesis that the sort of human thought processes Freud called "primary"—substitution, reversal, condensation, and so on—are phylogenetically prior to those he called "secondary"—directed, logically ordered, reasoning, and so on.[14] Within the confines of anthropology, this thesis has been based on the assumption that it is possible simply to identify patterns of culture and modes of thought.[15] On such an assumption, groups of people lacking the cultural resources of modern science which have been, at least in certain contexts, so effectively employed in directive reasoning in the West are considered ipso facto to lack the very capacity for intellection these resources serve; as though the confinement of the Arapesh to combinations of "one," "two," and "dog" were a result rather than a cause of their lack of mathematical facility. If one then adds to this argument the invalid empirical generalization that tribal peoples employ whatever meager culture resources they do have for intellection less frequently, less persistently, and less circumspectly than do Western peoples, the proposition that primary process thinking proceeds secondary process thinking phylogenetically needs only the final mistake of viewing tribal peoples as primitive forms of humanity, "living fossils," to complete it.[16]

---

[14] S. Freud, "The Interpretation of Dreams," trans. in *The Basic Writings of Sigmund Freud,* ed. A. A. Brill (New York, 1938), pp. 179–548; S. Freud, "Formulations Regarding Two Principles in Mental Functioning," in *Collected Papers of Sigmund Freud* (London, 1946), 4:13–27.

[15] L. Levy-Bruhl, *Primitive Mentality* (London, 1923).

[16] In addition, this proposition has been supported, as Hallowell (A. I. Hallowell, "The Recapitulation Theory and Culture," reprinted in *Culture and Experi-*

It was in reaction to this tissue of errors that the second view of human mental evolution arose, namely, that not only is the existence of the human mind in essentially its modern form a prerequisite for the acquisition of culture, but the growth of culture in itself has been without any significance for mental evolution:

The bird gave up a pair of walking limbs to acquire wings. It added a new faculty by transforming part of an old one. . . . The airplane, on the contrary, gave men a new faculty without diminishing or even impairing any of those they had previously possessed. It led to no visible bodily changes, no alterations of mental capacity.[17]

But, in turn, this argument implies two corollaries, one of which, the doctrine of the psychic unity of mankind, has found increasing empirical substantiation as anthropological research has proceeded, but the other of which, the "critical point" theory of the appearance of culture, has become increasingly tenuous. The doctrine of the psychic unity of mankind, which so far as I am aware, is today not seriously questioned by any reputable anthropologist, is but the direct contradictory of the primitive mentality argument; it asserts that there are no essential differences in the fundamental nature of the thought process among the various living races of man. If the existence of a modern type of mind is held to be prerequisite to the acquisition of culture, the universal possession of culture by all contemporary human groups, of course, makes of the psychic unity doctrine a simple tautology; but whether genuinely tautological or not, it is a proposition for whose empirical validity the ethnographic and psychological evidence is altogether overwhelming.[18]

As for the critical point theory of the appearance of culture, it postulates that the development of the capacity for acquiring culture was a sudden, all-or-none type of occurrence in the phylogeny of the pri-

ence, by A. I. Hallowell [Philadelphia, 1939], pp. 14–31) has pointed out, by an uncritical application of Haeckel's now rejected "law of recapitulation," in which presumed parallels in the thought of children, psychotics, and savages were used as evidence of the phylogenetic priority of autism. For suggestions that primary processes are not even ontogenetically prior to secondary ones, see: H. Hartmann, "Ego Psychology and the Problem of Adaptation," trans. and abridged in Organization and Pathology of Thought, ed. D. Rappaport (New York, 1951), pp. 362–396; and H. Hartmann, E. Kris, and R. Lowenstein, "Comments on the Formation of Psychic Structure," in The Psychoanalytic Study of the Child (New York, 1946), 2:11–38.

[17] A. L. Kroeber, Anthropology (New York, 1948).

[18] C. Kluckhohn, "Universal Categories of Culture," in Anthropology Today, ed. A. L. Kroeber (Chicago, 1953), pp. 507–523; see also, Kroeber, Anthropology, p. 573.

mates.[19] At some specific moment in the new unrecoverable history of hominidization a portentous, but in genic or anatomical terms probably quite minor, organic alteration took place—presumably in cortical structure—in which an animal whose parents had not been disposed "to communicate, to learn and to teach, to generalize from the endless chain of discrete feelings and attitudes" was so disposed and "therewith he began to be able to act as a receiver and transmitter and begin the accumulation that is culture." [20] With him culture was born, and, once born, set on its own course so as to grow wholly independently of the further organic evolution of man. The whole process of the creation of modern man's capacity for producing and using culture, his most distinctive mental attribute, is conceptualized as one of a marginal quantitative change giving rise to a radical qualitative difference, as when water, reduced degree by degree without any loss of fluidity suddenly freezes at 0°C., or when a taxiing plane gains sufficient speed to launch itself into flight.[21]

But we are talking of neither water nor airplanes, and the question is can the sharp line between enculturated man and nonenculturated nonman that this view implies in fact be drawn, or, if we must have analogies, would not a more historical one, such as the unbroken gradual rise of modern out of medieval England, be more apt. Within the physical branch of anthropology, the doubt that one can talk about the appearance of man "as if he had suddenly been promoted from colonel to brigadier general, and had a date of rank" has grown with increasing rapidity as the Australopithecine fossils originally of South Africa but now quite widely found, have come to be placed more and more in the hominid line.[22] These fossils, which date from the upper Pliocene and lower Pleistocene periods of three or four million years ago, show a striking mosaic of primitive and advanced morphological characteristics, in which the most outstanding features are a pelvis and leg formation strikingly similar to that of modern man and a cranial capacity hardly larger than that of living apes.[23] Although the initial tendency

[19] Kroeber, *Anthropology*, pp. 71–72.
[20] Ibid.
[21] Ibid; White, *The Science of Culture*, p. 33.
[22] W. W. Howells, "Concluding Remarks of the Chairman," in *Cold Spring Harbor Symposia on Quantitative Biology* 15 (1950):79–86.
[23] On the original discoveries of Australopithecines, see R. A. Dart, *Adventures with the Missing Link* (New York, 1959); for a recent review, see P. V. Tobias, "The Taxonomy and Phylogeny of the Australopithecines," in *Taxonomy*

was to regard this conjunction of a "manlike" bipedal locomotive system and an "apelike" brain as indicating that the Australopithecines represented an aberrant and ill-fated line of development separate from both hominids and pongids, the contemporary consensus follows Howells' conclusion that "the first hominids were small-brained, newly bipedal, protoaustralopith hominoids, and that what we have always meant by 'man' represents later forms of this group with secondary adaptations in the direction of large brains and modified skeletons of the same form." [24]

Now, these more-or-less erect, small-brained hominids, their hands freed from locomotion, manufactured tools and probably hunted small animals. But that they could have had a developed culture comparable to that of, say, the Australian aborigine or possessed language in the modern sense of the term with 500 cubic centimeters of brain is unlikely.[25] In the Australopithecines we seem to have, therefore, an odd sort of "man" who evidently was capable of acquiring some elements of culture—simple toolmaking, sporadic "hunting," and perhaps some system of communication more advanced than that of contemporary apes and less advanced than that of true speech—but not others, a state of affairs which casts fairly serious doubt on the viability of the "critical point" theory.[26] In fact, as the *Homo sapiens* brain is about three times as large as that of the Australopithecines, the greater part of human cortical expansion has followed, not preceded, the "beginning" of culture, a rather inexplicable circumstance if the capacity for culture is considered to have been the unitary outcome of a quantitatively slight

---

and *Phylogeny of Old World Primates with Reference to the Origin of Man,* ed. B. Chiarelli (Turin, 1968), pp. 277–315.

[24] By "hominoid" is meant the superfamily of animals, living and extinct, to which both man and the pongid apes (gorilla, orang, chimpanzee, and gibbon) belong, and by "hominid," the family of animals, living and extinct, to which man belongs, but not the apes. For the "aberrant" view, see E. Hooton, *Up From the Ape,* rev. ed. (New York, 1949); for the consensus, Howells, "Concluding Remarks of the Chairman." The statement that the Australopithecines were the *"first* hominids" would now, I think, have to be modified.

[25] For a general review, see A. I. Hallowell, "Self, Society and Culture in Phylogenetic Perspective," in *The Evolution of Man,* ed. S. Tax (Chicago, 1960), pp. 309–372. In the past decade, the whole discussion has proceeded with accelerating speed and increasing precision. For a series of references, see the inventory article by R. L. Holloway and Elizabeth Szinyei-Merse, "Human Biology: a Catholic Review," in *Biennial Review of Anthropology, 1971,* ed. B. J. Siegel (Stanford, 1972), pp. 83–166.

[26] For a general discussion of "critical point" theory in light of recent anthropological work, see C. Geertz, "The Transition to Humanity," in *Horizons of Anthropology,* ed. S. Tax (Chicago, 1964), pp. 37–48.

but qualitatively metastatic change of the freezing-of-water sort.[27] Not only has it now become misleading to employ the appointment of rank image for the appearance of man, but "it is equally doubtful whether we should any longer talk in terms of the 'appearance of culture,' as if culture, too, along with 'man,' had suddenly leaped into existence." [28]

As paradox is a sign of antecedent error, the fact that one of its corollaries seems to be valid while the other does not suggests that the thesis which holds mental evolution and cultural accumulation to be two wholly separate processes, the first having been essentially completed before the second began, is itself incorrect. And if this is the case, it becomes necessary to find some way in which we can rid ourselves of such a thesis without at the same time undermining the doctrine of psychic unity, in whose absence "we should have to consign most of history, anthropology and sociology to the scrap heap and begin over again with a psychosomatic genetic interpretation of man and his varieties." [29] We need to be able both to deny any significant relationship between (group) cultural achievement and innate mental capacity in the present, and to affirm such a relationship in the past.

The means by which to accomplish this oddly two-headed task lies in what may appear to be a simple technical trick, but is actually an important methodological reorientation, the choice of a more finely graduated time scale in terms of which to discriminate the stages of evolutionary change which have produced *Homo sapiens* out of an Eocene protohominoid. Whether one sees the appearance of the capacity for culture as a more-or-less abrupt, instantaneous occurrence, or a slowly moving, continuous development, obviously depends, at least in part, on the size of the elementary units in one's time scale; for a geologist, measuring by eons, the whole evolution of the primates may look like an undifferentiated qualitative burst. In fact, the argument against the critical point theory might be more precisely phrased in terms of a complaint that it derives from an inappropriate choice of time scale, a time scale whose basal intervals are too large for a refined analysis of recent evolutionary history, in the same way as a biologist foolish enough to

[27] S. L. Washburn, "Speculations on the Interrelations of Tools and Biological Evolution," in *The Evolution of Man's Capacity for Culture*, ed. J. M. Spuhler (Detroit, 1959), pp. 21–31.

[28] A. I. Hallowell, "Culture, Personality and Society," in *Anthropology Today*, ed. A. L. Kroeber (Chicago, 1953), pp. 597–620. Cf. A. I. Hallowell, "Behavioral Evolution and the Emergence of the Self," in *Evolution and Anthropology: A Centennial Appraisal*, ed. B. J. Meggers (Washington, D.C., 1959), pp. 36–60.

[29] Kroeber, *Anthropology*, p. 573.

study human maturation with decades as his interval would see adulthood as a sudden transformation of childhood and miss adolescence altogether.

A good example of such a cavalier approach to temporal considerations is implicit in what is probably the most frequent kind of scientific data invoked in support of the "difference in kind rather than difference in degree" view of human culture; the comparison of man with his closest living relatives, the pongids, and particularly the chimpanzee. Man can talk, can symbolize, can acquire culture, this argument goes, but the chimpanzee (and, by extension, all less-endowed animals) cannot. Therefore, man is unique in this regard, and insofar as mentality is concerned "we are confronted by a series of leaps, not an ascending continuum." [30] But this overlooks the fact that, although the pongids may be man's closest relatives, "close" is an elastic term and, given a realistic time scale from the evolutionary point of view, they are really not so close at all, last common ancestor being at the very least an upper Pliocene (and at the very most an upper Oligocene) ape and phyletic differentiation having proceeded with ever-increasing rapidity since that time. The fact that chimpanzees do not talk is both interesting and important, but to draw from that fact the conclusion that speech is an all-or-nothing-at-all phenomenon is to collapse anywhere from one to forty million years into a single instant of time and lose the whole pre-*sapiens* hominid line as surely as our biologist lost adolescence. Interspecific comparison of living animals is, if handled with care, a legitimate and, in fact, indispensable device for deducing general evolutionary trends; but in the same way that the finite wave length of light limits the discrimination possible in physical measurements, so the fact that the closest living relatives of man are at best pretty far removed cousins (*not* ancestors) limits the degree of refinement in the measure of evolutionary change in the hominoid line when one confines oneself entirely to contrasts between extant forms. [31]

If, on the contrary, we spread hominid phylogeny out along a more appropriate time scale, training our attention on what seems to have happened in the "human" line since the radiation of the hominoids, and

[30] L. A. White, "Four Stages in the Evolution of Minding," in *The Evolution of Man*, ed. S. Tax (Chicago, 1960), pp. 239–253; the argument is very common.

[31] For a general discussion of the dangers involved in an uncritical use of comparisons among contemporaneous forms to generate historical hypotheses, see G. Simpson, "Some Principles of Historical Biology Bearing on Human Organisms," in *Cold Spring Harbor Symposia on Quantitative Biology* 15 (1950):55–66.

in particular since the emergence of *Australopithecus* toward the end of the Pliocene, a subtler analysis of the evolutionary growth of mind is made possible. Most crucially, it then becomes apparent that not only was cultural accumulation under way well before organic development ceased, but that such accumulation very likely played an active role in shaping the final stages of that development. Though it is apparently true enough that the invention of the airplane led to no visible bodily changes, no alterations of (innate) mental capacity, this was not necessarily the case for the pebble tool or the crude chopper, in whose wake seems to have come not only more erect stature, reduced dentition, and a more thumb-dominated hand, but the expansion of the human brain to its present size.[32] Because tool manufacture puts a premium on manual skill and foresight, its introduction must have acted to shift selection pressures so as to favor the rapid growth of the forebrain as, in all likelihood, did the advances in social organization, communication, and moral regulation which there is reason to believe also occurred during this period of overlap between cultural and biological change. Nor were such nervous system changes merely quantitative; alterations in the interconnections among neurons and their manner of functioning may have been of even greater importance than the simple increase in their number. Details aside, however—and the bulk of them remain to be determined—the point is that the innate, generic constitution of modern man (what used, in a simpler day, to be called "human nature") now appears to be both a cultural and a biological product in that "it is probably more correct to think of much of our structure as a result of culture rather than to think of men anatomically like ourselves slowly discovering culture."[33]

The Pleistocene period, with its rapid and radical variations in climate, land formations, and vegetation, has long been recognized to be a period in which conditions were ideal for the speedy and efficient evolutionary development of man; now it seems also to have been a period in which a cultural environment increasingly supplemented the natural environment in the selection process so as to further accelerate the rate of hominid evolution to an unprecedented speed. The Ice Age appears not to have been merely a time of receding brow ridges and shrinking jaws, but a time in which were forged nearly all those characteristics of man's existence which are most graphically human: his thoroughly encephe-

[32] Washburn, "Speculations on the Interrelations."
[33] Ibid.

lated nervous system, his incest-taboo-based social structure, and his capacity to create and use symbols. The fact that these distinctive features of humanity emerged together in complex interaction with one another rather than serially as for so long supposed is of exceptional importance in the interpretation of human mentality, because it suggests that man's nervous system does not merely enable him to acquire culture, it positively demands that he do so if it is going to function at all. Rather than culture acting only to supplement, develop, and extend organically based capacities logically and genetically prior to it, it would seem to be ingredient to those capacities themselves. A cultureless human being would probably turn out to be not an intrinsically talented though unfulfilled ape, but a wholly mindless and consequently unworkable monstrosity. Like the cabbage it so much resembles, the *Homo sapiens* brain, having arisen within the framework of human culture, would not be viable outside of it.[34]

In fact, this type of reciprocally creative relationship between somatic and extrasomatic phenomena seems to have been of crucial significance during the whole of the primate advance. That any (living or extinct) infrahominid primates can be said to possess true culture—in the narrowed sense of "an ordered system of meaning and symbols . . . in terms of which individuals define their world, express their feelings and make their judgments"—is, of course, extremely doubtful.[35] But that apes and monkeys are such through-and-through social creatures as to be unable to achieve emotional maturity in isolation, to acquire a great many of their most important performance capacities through imitative learning, and to develop distinctive, intraspecifically variable collective social traditions which are transmitted as a nonbiological heritage from generation to generation is now well established.[36] As DeVore remarks in summary of the available material, "Primates literally have a 'social brain'." [37] Thus, well before it was influenced by cultural forces as such,

---

[34] As for "wolf-children" and other feral fantasies, see K. Lorenz, "Comment," in *Discussions on Child Development,* ed. J. Tanner and B. Inhelder (New York, n.d.), 1:95–96.
[35] See Chapter 6 in this book, p. 145.
[36] On isolation, see H. Harlow, "Basic Social Capacity of Primates," in *The Evolution of Man's Capacity for Culture,* ed. J. Spuhler (Detroit, 1959), pp. 40–52; on imitative learning, H. W. Nissen, "Problems of Mental Evolution in the Primates," in *The Non-Human Primates and Human Evolution,* ed. J. Gavan (Detroit, 1955), pp. 99–109.
[37] B. I. DeVore, "Primate Behavior and Social Evolution" (unpublished, n.d.).

the evolution of what eventually developed into the human nervous system was positively shaped by social ones.[38]

On the other hand, however, a denial of a simple independence of sociocultural and biological processes in pre-*Homo sapiens* man does not imply a rejection of the doctrine of psychic unity, because phyletic differentiation within the hominid line effectively ceased with the terminal Pleistocene spread of *Homo sapiens* over nearly the whole world and the extinction of whatever other *Homo* species may have been in existence at that time. Thus, although some minor evolutionary changes have no doubt occurred since the rise of modern man, all living peoples form part of a single polytypical species and, as such, vary anatomically and physiologically within a very narrow range.[39] The combination of weakened mechanisms of reproductive isolation, an extended period of individual sexual immaturity, and the accumulation of culture to the point where its importance as an adaptive factor almost wholly dominated its role as a selective one, produced such an extreme deceleration of the hominid rate of evolution that the development of any significant variation in innate mental capacity among human subgroups seems to have been precluded. With the unequivocal triumph of *Homo sapiens* and the cessation of the glaciations, the link between organic and cultural change was, if not severed, at least greatly weakened. Since that time organic evolution in the human line has slowed to a walk, while the growth of culture had continued to proceed with ever-increasing rapidity. It is, therefore, unnecessary to postulate either a discontinuous, "difference-in-kind" pattern of human evolution or a nonselective role for culture during all phases of hominid development in order to preserve the empirically established generalization that "as far as their [inborn] capacity to learn, maintain, transmit, and transform culture is concerned, different groups of *Homo sapiens* must be regarded as equally competent." [40] Psychic unity may no longer be a tautology, but it is still a fact.

[38] Some subprimate mammals also follow a definitely social mode of life, so that this whole process probably predates primates altogether. The social behavior of some birds and insects is of less immediate relevance, however, because these orders are tangential to the human developmental line.

[39] M. F. A. Montagu, "A Consideration of the Concept of Race," in *Cold Spring Harbor Symposia on Quantitative Biology* 15 (1950):315–334.

[40] M. Mead, "Cultural Determinants of Behavior," in *Culture and Behavior*, ed. A. Roe and G. Simpson (New Haven, 1958).

III

One of the more encouraging—if strangely delayed—developments in the behavioral sciences is the current attempt of physiological psychology to arouse itself from its long enthrallment with the wonders of the reflex arc. The conventional picture of a sensory impulse making its way through a maze of synapses to a motor nerve culmination is coming to be revised, a quarter century after its most illustrious proponent pointed out that it was inadequate to explain the integrative aspects of the behavior of a sparrow or a sheep dog, much less that of a man.[41] Sherrington's solution was a spectral mind to pull things together (as Hull's was a no less mysterious automatic switchboard).[42] But today the stress is upon a more verifiable construct: the concept of rhythmic, spontaneous, centrally proceeding pattern of nervous activity upon which peripheral stimulus configurations are superimposed and out of which authoritative effector commands emerge. Advancing under the banner of "an active organism," and supported by the closed circuit anatomizing of Cayal and de Nó,[43] this new persuasion emphasizes the way in which the ongoing processes both of the brain and subordinate neuronal aggregates select precepts, fix experiences, and order responses so as to produce a delicately modulated pattern of behavior:

The working of the central nervous system is a hierarchic affair in which functions at the higher levels do not deal directly with the ultimate structural units, such as neurons or motor units, but operate by activating lower patterns that have their own relatively autonomous structural unity. The same is true for the sensory input, which does not project itself down to the last final path of motor neurons, but operates by affecting, distorting, and somehow modifying the pre-existing, preformed patterns of central coordination, which, in turn, then confer their distortions upon the lower patterns of effection and so on. The final output is then the outcome of this hierarchical passing down of distortions and modifications of intrinsically performed pat-

---

[41] C. Sherrington, *Man*.
[42] C. L. Hull, *Principles*.
[43] L. de Nó, "Cerebral Cortex Architecture," in *The Physiology of the Nervous System*, ed. J. F. Fulton (New York, 1943); J. S. Bruner, "Neural Mechanisms in Perception," in *The Brain and Human Behavior*, ed. H. Solomon et al. (Baltimore, 1958), pp. 118–143; R. W. Gerard, "Becoming: The Residue of Change," in *The Evolution of Man*, ed. S. Tax (Chicago, 1960), pp. 255–268; K. S. Lashley, "The Problem of Serial Order in Behavior," in *Cerebral Mechanisms and Behavior*, ed. L. Jeffress (New York, 1951), pp. 112–136.

terns of excitation which are in no way replicas of the input. The structure of the input does not produce the structure of the output, but merely modifies intrinsic nervous activities that have a structural organization of their own.[44]

Further development of this theory of an autonomously excited, hierarchically organized central nervous system not only promises to make the brisk competence of Sherrington's sheep dog as it collects its scattered flock from the hillside less of a physiological mystery, but it should also prove valuable in providing a credible neurological underpinning for the complex of skills and propensities which constitute the human mind; the ability to follow a logic proof or a tendency to become flustered when called upon to speak demand more than a reflex arc, conditioned or otherwise, to support them biologically. And, as Hebb has pointed out, the very notion of "higher" and "lower" evolutionary levels of mentality seems in itself to imply a comparable gradation in degree of central nervous system autonomy:

I hope I do not shock biological scientists by saying that one feature of the phylogenetic development is an increasing evidence of what is known in some circles as free will; in my student days also referred to as the Harvard Law, which asserts that any well-trained experimental animal, on controlled stimulation, will do as he damn well pleases. A more scholarly formulation is that the higher animal is less stimulus-bound. Brain action is less fully controlled by afferent input, behavior therefore less fully predictable from the situation in which the animal is put. A greater role of ideational activity is recognizable in the animal's ability to "hold" a variety of stimulations for some time before acting on them and in the phenomenon of purposive behavior. There is more autonomous activity in the higher brain, and more selectivity as to *which* afferent activity will be integrated with the "stream of thought," the dominant, ongoing activity in control of behavior. Traditionally, we say that the subject is "interested" in this part of the environment, not interested in that; in these terms, the higher animal has a wider variety of interests and the interest of the moment plays a greater part in behavior, which means a greater unpredictability as to what stimulus will be responded to and as to the form of the response.[45]

These overall evolutionary trends—increasing ability to focus attention, delay response, vary interest, sustain purpose, and, in general, deal

[44] P. Weiss, "Comment on Dr. Lashley's Paper," in *Cerebral Mechanisms in Behavior*, ed. L. A. Jeffress (New York, 1951), pp. 140–142.
[45] D. O. Hebb, "The Problem of Consciousness and Introspection," in *Brain Mechanics and Consciousness*, ed. E. Adrian et al. (Oxford, 1954), pp. 402–417. References omitted.

positively with the complexities of present stimulation—culminate in man to make of him the most active of active organisms, as well as the most unpredictable. The extreme intricacy, flexibility, and comprehensiveness of what Kluckhohn and Murray have aptly called regnant processes in the human brain—the processes which make these abilities physically possible—are but the outcome of a definable phylogenetic development which is traceable back at least to the coelenterates.[46] Though they lack a central nervous concentration—a brain—and therefore the various parts of the animal operate in relative independence, each possessing its own set of sensory, neural, and motor elements, these humble jellyfish, sea anemones, and the like nevertheless show a surprising degree of intrinsic modulation of nervous activity: a strong stimulus received in the daytime may be followed by locomotion during the following night; certain corals experimentally subjected to excessive stimulation luminesce for several minutes afterward with a spontaneous frenzy which suggests "beserking"; and regularized stimulation may lead, through some still obscure form of "memory" to a coordination of activity in different muscles and to a patterned recurrence of activity over time.[47] In the higher invertebrates (crustaceans, etc.) multiple pathways, graded synaptic potentials, and triggered responses all appear, permitting precise pacemaker control of internal functions as in the lobster heart, while with the arrival of the lower vertebrates both peripheral sensory and effector elements and neuronal conduction between them—i.e., the celebrated reflex arc—are essentially perfected.[48] And, finally, the bulk of the fundamental innovations in the design of nervous circuits—i.e., closed loops, the superposition of higher level loops on lower ones, and so on—probably were accomplished with the arrival of the mammals, at which time at least the basic differentiations of the forebrain were also achieved.[49] In functional terms, the whole process seems to be one of a relatively steady expansion and diversification of endogenous nervous activity and the consequent increasing centraliza-

[46] C. Kluckhohn and H. Murray, eds., *Personality in Nature, Society and Culture* (New York, 1948); T. H. Bullock, "Evolution of Neurophysiological Mechanisms," in *Behavior and Evolution*, ed. A. Roe and G. Simpson (New Haven, 1958), pp. 165–177.

[47] Bullock, "Evolution."

[48] Ibid.; Gerard, "Becoming."

[49] Bullock, "Evolution"; K. H. Pribram, "Comparative Neurology and the Evolution of Behavior," in *Behavior and Evolution*, ed. A. Roe and G. Simpson (New Haven, 1958), pp. 140–164.

tion of what were previously more isolated, independently acting part-processes.

What sort of neural evolution has taken place during the phyletic differentiation of the mammals—i.e., in particular, during the advance of the primates and hominids—is evidently rather less clear and more controversial, however. On the one hand, Gerard has argued that the changes have been almost entirely quantitative, a growth in the sheer number of neurons, as reflected in the rapid expansion of the brain size:

The further gains in capacity, seen most strikingly in the primate line and culminating in man are due to simple increase in numbers rather than to improvement in units or patterns. The increasing brain size parallels richer performance, even for particular regions and functions (e.g., tongue motor area and speech), is a commonplace; how this operates is less clear. Sheer increase in number, without secondary specification (which does also occur), might seem unable to generate new capacities but only to intensify old ones, but this is not the case. . . . In the brain, an increase in the anatomical neurone population raises the limit on the physiological neurone reserve and so allows greater variety of selection and greater richness of analysis and combination expressed in modifiable and insightful behavior.[50]

But Bullock, though agreeing that the nervous systems of the higher animals and man show no important differences in terms of known neurophysiological mechanisms or architecture, sharply questions this point of view, and argues that there is a pressing need to search for yet undiscovered parameters of nervous functioning, "emergent levels of physiological relations between neurons in masses," to account for the subtleties of behavior in advanced organisms:

Though we cannot point to fundamentally new elements in the neuronal mechanisms of the higher centers, still it is difficult to assume that their greatly enlarged accomplishments are solely attributable to the great increase in numbers and interconnections between them, unless this in itself brings on new properties and mechanisms. Many apparently assume as a first approximation that the main factor in increasing behavioral complexity in evolution is the number of neurons—even invoking a kind of critical mass which permits new levels of behavior . . . [but] it seems clear that the number of neurons correlates with behavioral complexity so poorly as to explain little unless we add as the really essential part that certain kinds of neurons, not now definable, or—what is the same thing—certain kinds of newer properties of consequences or neuronal architecture, are the impor-

[50] Gerard, "Becoming"; see also R. W. Gerard, "Brains and Behavior," in *The Evolution of Man's Capacity for Culture*, ed. J. Spuhler (Detroit, 1959), pp. 14–20.

tant substratum of advance. . . . I do not believe that our present physiology of neurons, extrapolated, can account for behavior. The main factor in evolutionary advance is not just numbers of cells and connections. . . . Our hope lies in the discovery of new parameters of neuronal systems.[51]

To an outsider, perhaps the most striking aspect of this controversy is the degree to which both parties seem somewhat uneasy and vaguely dissatisfied with the unalloyed versions of their own argument, the degree to which it seems not to be entirely plausible even to themselves. On the one side there is an admission that the precise nature of the relation between brain size and behavioral complexity is indeed unclear and some *sotto voce* reservations about "secondary specification"; on the other, a frank puzzlement concerning the apparent absence of novel mechanisms in advanced nervous systems and a hopeful murmuring about "emergent properties." There is actually something of an agreement that the attribution of the secular increase in mammalian mental capacity solely and simply to a gross increase in neuron population taxes credulity. The difference is that in one case doubts are quieted by a stress on the fact that a parallelism between increasing brain size and richer performance does, anyhow, obtain; while, on the other, doubts are accentuated by a stress on the fact that something seems to be missing to make this parallelism satisfactorily explicable.

This issue may eventually be clarified as Gerard suggests, by advances in work with computer circuits where performance does improve with a simple multiplication of identical units; or, as Bullock suggests, by further refinements in the analysis of chemical differences between nerve cells.[52] But it is even more likely that the main avenue to its resolution lies in the abandonment of the wholly nativistic conceptualization of nervous functioning in the higher mammals which seems to be implicit in both these approaches. The synchronic emergence in primates of an expanded forebrain, developed forms of social organization, and, at least after Australopithecines got their hands on tools, institutionalized patterns of culture indicates that the standard procedure of treating biological, social, and cultural parameters serially—the first being taken as primary to the second, and the second to the third —is ill-advised. On the contrary, these so-called levels should be seen as reciprocally interrelated and considered conjointly. And if this is done, the sort of novel properties we shall search for within the central

[51] Bullock, "Evolution."
[52] R. W. Gerard, "Brains and Behavior"; Bullock, "Evolution."

nervous system to serve as a physical basis for the striking development of autonomous fields of recurrent neural excitation in primates generally, and in man particularly, will differ radically from the sort of properties we would seek were we to regard those fields as "logically and genetically prior" to society and culture, and therefore requiring a full determination in terms of intrinsic physiological parameters alone. Perhaps we have been asking too much of neurons; or, if not too much, at least the wrong things.

In fact, so far as man is concerned, one of the most striking characteristics of his central nervous system is the relative incompleteness with which, acting within the confines of autogenous parameters alone, it is able to specify behavior. By and large, the lower an animal, the more it tends to respond to a "threatening" stimulus with an intrinsically connected series of performed activities which taken together comprise a comparatively stereotyped—which is *not* to say unlearned—"flight" or "fight" response.[53] Man's intrinsic response to such a stimulus tends to consist, however, of a diffuse, variably intense, "fear" or "rage" excitability accompanied by few, if any, automatically preset, well-defined behavioral sequences.[54] Like a frightened animal, a frightened man may run, hide, bluster, dissemble, placate, or, desperate with panic, attack; but in his case the precise patterning of such overt acts is guided predominantly by cultural rather than genetic templates. In the always diagnostic area of sex, where control of behavior proceeds phylogenetically from gonadal, to pituitary, to central nervous system prepotency, a similar evolutionary trend away from fixed activity sequences toward generalized arousal and "increasing flexibility and modifiability of sexual patterns" is apparent; a trend of which the justly famous cultural

[53] K. Lorenz, *King Solomon's Ring* (London, 1952).
[54] D. O. Hebb and W. R. Thompson, "The Social Significance of Animal Studies," in *Handbook of Psychology* (Reading, Mass., 1954), pp. 532–561. The uncritical use of the term "instinct" so as to confuse three separate (but not unrelated) contrasts—that between behavior patterns which rest on learning and those which do not; that between behavior patterns which are innate (i.e., an outcome of genetically programmed physical processes) and those which are not (i.e., an outcome of extragenetically programmed physical processes); and that between behavior patterns which are inflexible (stereotyped) and those which are flexible (variable)—has led to an incorrect assumption that to say a behavior pattern is innate is to say that it is inflexible in its expression. (See K. H. Pribram, "Comparative Neurology and Evolution"; and F. A. Beach, "The De-scent of Instinct," *Psychol. Rev.* 62 [1955]:401–410.) Here, the term "intrinsic," as against "extrinsic," is used to characterize behavior which, on comparative grounds, seems to rest largely, or at least preponderantly, on innate dispositions, independently of questions of learning or flexibility as such.

variation in the sexual practices of man would seem to represent a logical extension.[55] Thus, in apparent paradox, an increasing autonomy,
hierarchical complexity, and regnancy of ongoing central nervous system activity seem to go hand in hand with a less fully detailed determination of such activity by the structure of the central nervous system in
and of itself; i.e., intrinsically. All of which suggests that some of the
more important developments in neural evolution which occurred during the period of overlap between biological and sociocultural change
may turn out to consist of the appearance of properties which improve
the performance capacity of the central nervous system but reduce its
functional self-sufficiency.

From this standpoint, the accepted view that mental functioning is essentially an intracerebral process, which can only be secondarily assisted or amplified by the various artificial devices which that process
has enabled man to invent, appears to be quite wrong. On the contrary,
a fully specified, adaptively sufficient definition of regnant neural processes in terms of intrinsic parameters being impossible, the human
brain is thoroughly dependent upon cultural resources for its very operation; and those resources are, consequently, not adjuncts to, but constituents of, mental activity. In fact, thinking as an overt, public act, involving the purposeful manipulation of objective materials, is probably
fundamental to human beings; and thinking as a covert, private act, and
without recourse to such materials, a derived, though not unuseful, capability. As the observation of how school children learn to calculate
shows, adding numbers in your head is actually a more sophisticated
mental accomplishment than adding them with a paper and pencil,
through an arrangement of tally sticks, or by counting, piggy-fashion,
one's fingers and toes. Reading aloud is a more elementary achievement

---

55 F. A. Beach, "Evolutionary Aspects of Psycho-Endocrinology," in *Culture*
and Behavior, ed. A. Roe and G. Simpson (New Haven, 1958), pp. 81–102; C. S.
Ford and F. A. Beach, *Patterns of Sexual Behavior* (New York, 1951). But,
again, this general trend appears already well established in the subhuman primates: "Some [male] chimpanzees have to learn to copulate. It has been noted
that sexually mature but inexperienced males placed with the receptive female
show signs of marked sexual excitement, but the resulting attempts to accomplish
copulation are usually unsuccessful. The naive male appears incapable of carrying
out his part of the mating act, and it has been suggested that a great deal of
practice and learning is essential to biologically effective coition in this species.
Adult male rodents which have been reared in isolation copulate normally the
first time they are offered an estrous female." [F. A. Beach, "Evolutionary
Changes in the Physiological Control of Mating Behavior in Mammals," *Psychol.*
Rev. 54 (1947):293–315.] For some vivid descriptions of generalized fear and
rage in chimpanzees, see Hebb and Thompson, "Social Significance."

than reading to oneself, the latter ability having only arisen, as a matter of fact, in the Middle Ages.[56] And a similar point about speech has often been made; except in our less naive moments, we are all like Forester's little old lady—we don't know what we think until we see what we say.

It has sometimes been argued against this last point that "the comparative evidence, as well as the literature on aphasia, clearly makes thought prior to speech, not conditional on it." [57] But, though true enough in itself, this does not undermine the general position taken here—namely, that human culture is an ingredient not supplementary to human thought—for several reasons. First, the fact that subhuman animals learn to reason with sometimes startling effectiveness, without learning to speak, does not prove that men can do so, any more than the fact that a rat can copulate without the mediation of imitative learning or practice proves that a chimpanzee can do so. Second, aphasics are people who have learned to speak and to interiorize speech, and then lost (or, more usually, partially lost) the former capacity, not people who have never learned to speak at all. Third, and most important, speech in the specific sense of vocalized talk is far from being the sole public instrumentality available to individuals projected into a pre-existing cultural milieu. Such phenomena as Helen Keller learning to think through a combination of the manipulation of such cultural objects as mugs and water taps and the purposeful patterning (by Miss Sullivan) of tactile sensations on her hand, or a prespeech child developing the concept of ordinal number through the setting up of two parallel lines of matched blocks, demonstrate that what is essential is the existence of an overt symbol system of any sort.[58] For man, in particular, to conceive of thinking as essentially a private process is to overlook almost completely what people actually do when they go about reasoning:

Imaginal thinking is neither more nor less than constructing an image of the environment, running the model faster than the environment, and predicting that the environment will behave as the model does. . . . The first step in the solution of a problem consists in the construction of a model or image

[56] Ryle, The Concept of Mind, p. 27.
[57] Hebb, "Problem of Consciousness and Introspection."
[58] On ordinal numbers, see K. S. Lashley, "Persistent Problems in the Evolution of Mind," Quart. Rev. 24 (1949):28–42. It is perhaps advisable also to point out explicitly that the view that humans normally learn to talk intelligently aloud and with others before they learn to "talk" to themselves, in silence, does not involve either a motor theory of thought or an argument that all covert mentation takes place in terms of imagined words.

of the "relevant features" of the [environment]. These models can be constructed from many things, including parts of the organic tissue of the body and, by man, paper and pencil or actual artifacts. Once a model has been constructed it can be manipulated under various hypothetical conditions and constraints. The organism is then able to "observe" the outcome of these manipulations, and to project them onto the environment so that prediction is possible. According to this view, an aeronautical engineer is thinking when he manipulates a model of a new airplane in a wind tunnel. The motorist is thinking when he runs his finger over a line on a map, the finger serving as a model of the relevant aspects of the automobile, the map as a model of the road. External models of this kind are often used in thinking about complex [environments]. Images used in covert thinking depend upon the availability of the physico-chemical events of the organism which must be used to form models.[59]

It is a further implication of this view of reflective thought as consisting not of happenings in the head but of a matching of the states and processes of symbolic models against the states and processes of the wider world, that it is stimulus deficit which initiates mental activity and stimulus "discovery" which terminates it.[60] The motorist running his finger over a road map is doing so because he lacks information about how to get where he is going, and he will cease doing so when he has acquired that information. The engineer performs his experiments in the wind tunnel in order to find out how his model airplane behaves under various artificially produced aerodynamic conditions, and he will quit performing it if and when he indeed finds out. A man searching for a coin in his pocket does so because he lacks a coin in hand, and he stops searching when he gets hold of one—or, of course, when he comes to the conclusion that the whole project is bootless, because it happens that there is no coin in his pocket, or that it is uneconomical, because the effort involved is such that the search "costs more than it comes to." [61] Motivational problems (which involve another sense of "because") aside, directive reasoning begins in puzzlement and ends in either the abandonment of inquiry or the resolution of puzzlement: "The function of reflective thought is . . . to transform a situation in which there is experienced obscurity . . . of some sort, into a situation that is clear, coherent, settled, harmonious." [62]

[59] E. Galanter and M. Gerstenhaber, "On Thought: The Extrinsic Theory," *Psychol. Rev.* 63 (1956):218–227.
[60] J. A. Deutsch, "A New Type of Behavior Theory," *British Journal of Psychology* 44 (1953):304–317.
[61] Ibid.
[62] J. Dewey, *Intelligence and the Modern World*, ed. J. Ratner (New York, 1939), p. 851.

In sum, human intellection, in the specific sense of directive reasoning, depends upon the manipulation of certain kinds of cultural resources in such a manner as to produce (discover, select) environmental stimuli needed—for whatever purpose—by the organism; it is a search for information. And this search is the more pressing because of the high degree of generality of the information intrinsically available to the organism from genetic sources. The lower an animal, the less it needs to find out in detail from the environment prior to behavioral performance; birds need not build wind tunnels to test aerodynamic principles before learning to fly—those they already "know." The "uniqueness" of man has often been expressed in terms of how much and how many different sorts of things he is capable of learning. Although monkeys, pigeons, and even octopuses may now and then disconcert us with the rather "human" things they prove capable of learning to do, in a general way this is true enough. But it is of perhaps even more fundamental theoretical importance to stress how much and how many things man *has* to learn. That, "fetalized," "domesticated," and generally unhardy as he is, man would be a physically unviable animal independently of culture has often been pointed out.[63] That he would be mentally unviable as well has been rather less frequently noted.[64]

All this is no less true for the affective side of human thought than it is for the intellective. In a series of books and papers, Hebb has developed the intriguing theory that the human nervous system (and to a correspondingly lesser extent, that of lower animals) demands a relatively continuous stream of optimally existing environmental stimuli as a precondition to competent performance.[65] On the one hand, man's brain is "not like a calculating machine operated by an electric motor, which can lie idle, without input, for indefinite periods; instead it must be kept warmed up and working by a constantly varied input during the waking period at least, if it is to function effectively." [66] On the other hand, given the tremendous intrinsic emotional susceptibility of man, such input cannot be too intense, too varied, too disturbing, because then

---

[63] For example, W. La Barre, *The Human Animal* (Chicago, 1954).

[64] But see J. Dewey, "The Need for a Social Psychology," *Psychol. Rev.* 24 (1917):266–277; A. I. Hallowell, "Culture, Personality and Society."

[65] D. O. Hebb, "Emotion in Man and Animal: An Analysis of the Intuitive Process of Recognition," *Psychol. Rev.* 53 (1946):88–106; D. O. Hebb, *The Organization of Behavior* (New York, 1949); D. O. Hebb, "Problem of Consciousness and Introspection"; D. O. Hebb and W. R. Thompson, "Social Significance of Animal Studies."

[66] D. O. Hebb, "Problem of Consciousness and Introspection."

emotional collapse and a complete breakdown of the thought process
ensue. Both boredom and hysteria are enemies of reason.[67]

Thus, as "man is the most emotional as well as the most rational animal," a very careful cultural control of frightening, enraging, suggestive,
etc., stimuli—through taboos, homogenization of behavior, rapid "rationalization" of strange stimuli in terms of familiar concepts, and so on
—is necessary to prevent continual affective instability, a constant oscillation between the extremes of passion.[68] But, as man cannot
perform efficiently in the absence of a fairly high degree of reasonably
persistent emotional activation, cultural mechanisms assuring the ready
availability of the continually varying sort of sensory experience that
can sustain such activities are equally essential. Institutionalized regula-
tions against the open display of corpses outside of well-defined contexts (funerals, etc.) protect a peculiarly high-strung animal against the
fears aroused by death and bodily destruction; watching or participating
in automobile races (not all of which take place at tracks) deliciously
stimulates the same fears. Prize fighting arouses hostile feelings; a firmly
institutionalized interpersonal affability moderates them. Erotic impulses are titillated by a series of devious artifices of which there is, evidently, no end; but they are kept from running riot by an insistence on
the private performance of explicitly sexual activities.

But, contrary to what these rather simplistic examples suggest, the
achievement of a workable, well-ordered, clearly articulated emotional
life in man is not a simple matter of ingenious instrumental control, a
kind of clever hydraulic engineering of affect. Rather, it is a matter of
giving specific, explicit, determinate form to the general, diffuse, ongoing flow of bodily sensation; of imposing upon the continual shifts in
sentience to which we are inherently subject a recognizable, meaningful
order, so that we may not only feel but know what we feel and act accordingly:

[It is] mental activity . . . [that] chiefly determines the way a person
meets his surrounding world. Pure sensation—now pain, now pleasure—
would have no unity, and would change the receptivity of the body for future pains and pleasures only in rudimentary ways. It is sensation, remembered and anticipated, feared or sought, or even imagined and eschewed that

[67] P. Solomon et al., "Sensory Deprivation: A Review," *American Journal of
Psychiatry,* 114 (1957):357–363; L. F. Chapman, "Highest Integrative Functions
of Man During Stress," in *The Brain and Human Behavior,* ed. H. Solomon
(Baltimore, 1958), pp. 491–534.

[68] D. O. Hebb and W. R. Thompson, "Social Significance of Animal Studies."

is important in human life. It is perception molded by imagination that gives us the outward world that we know. And it is the continuity of thought that systematizes our emotional reactions into attitudes with distinct feeling tones, and sets a certain scope for the individual's passions. In other words: by virtue of our thought and imagination we have not only feelings, but a *life of feeling*.[69]

In this context our mental task shifts from a gathering of information about the pattern of events in the external world per se toward a determining of the affective significance, the emotional import of that pattern of events. We are concerned not with solving problems, but with clarifying feelings. Nevertheless, the existence of cultural resources, of an adequate system of public symbols, is just as essential to this sort of process as it is to that of directive reasoning. And therefore, the development, maintenance, and dissolution of "moods," "attitudes," "sentiments," and so on—which are "feelings" in the sense of states or conditions, not sensations or motives—constitute no more a basically private activity in human beings than does directive "thinking." The use of a road map enables us to make our way from San Francisco to New York with precision; the reading of Kafka's novels enables us to form a distinct and well-defined attitude toward modern bureaucracy. We acquire the ability to design flying planes in wind tunnels; we develop the capacity to feel true awe in church. A child counts on his fingers before he counts "in his head"; he feels love on his skin before he feels it "in his heart." Not only ideas, but emotions too, are cultural artifacts in man.[70]

Given the lack of specificity of intrinsic affect in man, the attainment of an optimal flow of stimulation to his nervous system is a much more complicated operation than a prudent steering between the extremes of "too much" and "too little." Rather, it involves a very delicate qualitative regulation of what comes in through the sensory apparatus; a matter, here again, more of an active seeking for required stimuli than a mere watchful waiting for them. Neurologically, this regulation is achieved by efferent impulses from the central nervous system which

[69] S. Langer, *Feeling and Form* (New York, 1953), p. 372; italics in original.

[70] The kind of cultural symbols that serve the intellective and affective sides of human mentality tend to differ—discursive language, experimental routines, mathematics, and so on, on the one hand; myth, ritual, and art on the other. But this contrast should not be drawn too sharply: mathematics has its affective uses, poetry its intellectual; and the difference in any case is only functional, not substantial.

modify receptor activity.[71] Psychologically, the same process may be phrased in terms of the attitudinal control of perception.[72] But the point is that in man neither regnant fields nor mental sets can be formed with sufficient precision in the absence of guidance from symbolic models of emotion. In order to make up our minds we must know how we feel about things; and to know how we feel about things we need the public images of sentiment that only ritual, myth, and art can provide.

IV

The term "mind" refers to a certain set of dispositions of an organism. The ability to count is a mental characteristic; so is chronic cheerfulness; so also—though it has not been possible to discuss the problem of motivation here—is greed. The problem of the evolution of mind is, therefore, neither a false issue generated by a misconceived metaphysic, nor one of discovering at which point in the history of life an invisible anima was superadded to organic material. It is a matter of tracing the development of certain sorts of abilities, capacities, tendencies, and propensities in organisms and delineating the factors or types of factors upon which the existence of such characteristics depends.

Recent research in anthropology suggests that the prevailing view that the mental dispositions of man are genetically prior to culture and that his actual capabilities represent the amplification or extension of these pre-existent dispositions by cultural means is incorrect.[73] The apparent fact that the final stages of the biological evolution of man oc-

[71] R. Granit, *Receptors and Sensory Perception* (New Haven, 1955).
[72] J. S. Bruner and L. Postman, "Emotional Selectivity in Perception and Reaction," *J. Personality* 16 (1947):69–77.
[73] In using such variably employed terms as "mind" and "culture," the decision of how far down the phylogenetic ladder to extend them—i.e., how broadly to define them—is in great part but a matter of custom, policy, and taste. Here, perhaps somewhat inconsistently, but in line with what seems to be common usage, opposite choices have been made for mind and culture: mind has been defined broadly to include the learned capacities of monkeys to communicate or rats to solve T-mazes; culture has been defined narrowly to include only post-toolmaking symbolic patterns. For an argument that culture should be defined as "a learned pattern of the meaning of signals and signs" and extended through the whole world of living organisms, see T. Parsons, "An Approach to Psychological Theory in Terms of the Theory of Action," in *Psychology: A Study of a Science*, ed. S. Koch (New York, 1959), 3:612–711.

curred after the initial stages of the growth of culture implies that "basic," "pure," or "unconditioned," human nature, in the sense of the innate constitution of man, is so functionally incomplete as to be unworkable. Tools, hunting, family organization, and, later, art, religion, and "science" molded man somatically; and they are, therefore, necessary not merely to his survival but to his existential realization.

The application of this revised view of human evolution leads to the hypothesis that cultural resources are ingredient, not accessory, to human thought. As one moves from lower to higher animals phylogenetically, behavior is characterized by increasing active unpredictability with reference to present stimuli, a trend apparently supported physiologically by an increasing complexity and regnancy of centrally proceeding patterns of nervous activity. Up to the level of the lower mammals, at least the major part of this growth of autonomous central fields can be accounted for in terms of the development of novel neural mechanisms. But in the higher mammals such novel mechanisms have as yet not been found. Although, conceivably, mere increase in numbers of neurons may in itself prove able fully to account for the florescence of mental capacity in man, the fact that the large human brain and human culture emerged synchronically, not serially, indicates that the most recent developments in the evolution of nervous structure consist in the appearance of mechanisms which both permit the maintenance of more complex regnant fields and make the full determination of these fields in terms of intrinsic (innate) parameters increasingly impossible. The human nervous system relies, inescapably, on the accessibility of public symbolic structures to build up its own autonomous, ongoing pattern of activity.

This, in turn, implies that human thinking is primarily an overt act conducted in terms of the objective materials of the common culture, and only secondarily a private matter. In the sense both of directive reasoning and the formulation of sentiment, as well as the integration of these into motives, man's mental processes indeed take place at the scholar's desk or the football field, in the studio or lorry-driver's seat, on the platform, the chessboard, or the judge's bench. Isolationist claims for the closed-system substantiality of culture, social organization, individual behavior, or nervous physiology to the contrary notwithstanding, progress in the scientific analysis of the human mind demands a joint attack from virtually all of the behavioral sciences, in which the findings of each will force continual theoretical reassessments upon all of the others.

PART III

Chapter 4/Religion

As a Cultural System

Any attempt to speak without speaking any particular
language is not more hopeless than the attempt to have
a religion that shall be no religion in particular
. . . . Thus every living and healthy religion has a
marked idiosyncrasy. Its power consists in its special
and surprising message and in the bias which that revelation gives to life. The vistas it opens and the mysteries
it propounds are another world to live in; and another
world to live in—whether we expect ever to pass wholly
over into it or no—is what we mean by having a religion.

SANTAYANA, *Reason in Religion*

I

Two characteristics of anthropological work on religion accomplished
since the second world war strike me as curious when such work is
placed against that carried out just before and just after the first. One is
that it has made no theoretical advances of major importance. It is living off the conceptual capital of its ancestors, adding very little, save a
certain empirical enrichment, to it. The second is that it draws what
concepts it does use from a very narrowly defined intellectual tradition.
There is Durkheim, Weber, Freud, or Malinowski, and in any particular
work the approach of one or two of these transcendent figures is followed, with but a few marginal corrections necessitated by the natural
tendency to excess of seminal minds or by the expanded body of reliable descriptive data. But virtually no one even thinks of looking
elsewhere—to philosophy, history, law, literature, or the "harder"

sciences—as these men themselves looked, for analytical ideas. And it occurs to me, also, that these two curious characteristics are not unrelated.

If the anthropological study of religion is in fact in a state of general stagnation, I doubt that it will be set going again by producing more minor variations on classical theoretical themes. Yet one more meticulous case in point for such well-established propositions as that ancestor worship supports the jural authority of elders, that initiation rites are means for the establishment of sexual identity and adult status, that ritual groupings reflect political oppositions, or that myths provide charters for social institutions and rationalizations of social privilege, may well finally convince a great many people, both inside the profession and out, that anthropologists are, like theologians, firmly dedicated to proving the indubitable. In art, this solemn reduplication of the achievements of accepted masters is called academicism; and I think this is the proper name for our malady also. Only if we abandon, in a phrase of Leo Steinberg's, that sweet sense of accomplishment which comes from parading habitual skills and address ourselves to problems sufficiently unclarified as to make discovery possible, can we hope to achieve work which will not just reincarnate that of the great men of the first quarter of this century, but match it.[1]

The way to do this is not to abandon the established traditions of social anthropology in this field, but to widen them. At least four of the contributions of the men who, as I say, dominate our thought to the point of parochializing it—Durkheim's discussion of the nature of the sacred, Weber's *Verstehenden* methodology, Freud's parallel between personal rituals and collective ones, and Malinowski's exploration of the distinction between religion and common sense—seem to me inevitable starting-points for any useful anthropological theory of religion. But they are starting-points only. To move beyond them we must place them in a much broader context of contemporary thought than they, in and of themselves, encompass. The dangers of such a procedure are obvious: arbitrary eclecticism, superficial theory-mongering, and sheer intellectual confusion. But I, at least, can see no other road of escape from what, referring to anthropology more generally, Janowitz has called the dead hand of competence.[2]

[1] L. Steinberg, "The Eye Is Part of the Mind," *Partisan Review* 70 (1953): 194–212.
[2] M. Janowitz, "Anthropology and the Social Sciences," *Current Anthropology* 4 (1963):139, 146–154.

In working toward such an expansion of the conceptual envelope in which our studies take place, one can, of course, move in a great number of directions; and perhaps the most important initial problem is to avoid setting out, like Stephen Leacock's mounted policeman, in all of them at once. For my part, I shall confine my effort to developing what, following Parsons and Shils, I refer to as the cultural dimension of religious analysis.[3] The term "culture" has by now acquired a certain aura of ill-repute in social anthropological circles because of the multiplicity of its referents and the studied vagueness with which it has all too often been invoked. (Though why it should suffer more for these reasons than "social structure" or "personality" is something I do not entirely understand.) In any case, the culture concept to which I adhere has neither multiple referents nor, so far as I can see, any unusual ambiguity: it denotes an historically transmitted pattern of meanings embodied in symbols, a system of inherited conceptions expressed in symbolic forms by means of which men communicate, perpetuate, and develop their knowledge about and attitudes toward life. Of course, terms such as "meaning," "symbol," and "conception" cry out for explication. But that is precisely where the widening, the broadening, and the expanding come in. If Langer is right that "the concept of meaning, in all its varieties, is the dominant philosophical concept of our time," that "sign, symbol, denotation, signification, communication . . . are our [intellectual] stock in trade," it is perhaps time that social anthropology, and particularly that part of it concerned with the study of religion, became aware of the fact.[4]

II

As we are to deal with meaning, let us begin with a paradigm: viz., that sacred symbols function to synthesize a people's ethos—the tone, character, and quality of their life, its moral and aesthetic style and mood —and their world view—the picture they have of the way things in sheer actuality are, their most comprehensive ideas of order. In religious belief and practice a group's ethos is rendered intellectually rea-

[3] T. Parsons and E. Shils, *Toward a General Theory of Action* (Cambridge, Mass., 1951).

[4] S. Langer, *Philosophical Sketches* (Baltimore, 1962).

sonable by being shown to represent a way of life ideally adapted to the actual state of affairs the world view describes, while the world view is rendered emotionally convincing by being presented as an image of an actual state of affairs peculiarly well-arranged to accommodate such a way of life. This confrontation and mutual confirmation has two fundamental effects. On the one hand, it objectivizes moral and aesthetic preferences by depicting them as the imposed conditions of life implicit in a world with a particular structure, as mere common sense given the unalterable shape of reality. On the other, it supports these received beliefs about the world's body by invoking deeply felt moral and aesthetic sentiments as experiential evidence for their truth. Religious symbols formulate a basic congruence between a particular style of life and a specific (if, most often, implicit) metaphysic, and in so doing sustain each with the borrowed authority of the other.

Phrasing aside, this much may perhaps be granted. The notion that religion tunes human actions to an envisaged cosmic order and projects images of cosmic order onto the plane of human experience is hardly novel. But it is hardly investigated either, so that we have very little idea of how, in empirical terms, this particular miracle is accomplished. We just know that it is done, annually, weekly, daily, for some people almost hourly; and we have an enormous ethnographic literature to demonstrate it. But the theoretical framework which would enable us to provide an analytic account of it, an account of the sort we can provide for lineage segmentation, political succession, labor exchange, or the socialization of the child, does not exist.

Let us, therefore, reduce our paradigm to a definition, for, although it is notorious that definitions establish nothing, in themselves they do, if they are carefully enough constructed, provide a useful orientation, or reorientation, of thought, such that an extended unpacking of them can be an effective way of developing and controlling a novel line of inquiry. They have the useful virtue of explicitness: they commit themselves in a way discursive prose, which, in this field especially, is always liable to substitute rhetoric for argument, does not. Without further ado, then, a *religion* is:

(1) a system of symbols which acts to (2) establish powerful, pervasive, and long-lasting moods and motivations in men by (3) formulating conceptions of a general order of existence and (4) clothing these conceptions with such an aura of factuality that (5) the moods and motivations seem uniquely realistic.

a system of symbols which acts to . . .

Such a tremendous weight is being put on the term "symbol" here that our first move must be to decide with some precision what we are going to mean by it. This is no easy task, for, rather like "culture," "symbol" has been used to refer to a great variety of things, often a number of them at the same time.

In some hands it is used for anything which signifies something else to someone: dark clouds are the symbolic precursors of an on-coming rain. In others it is used only for explicitly conventional signs of one sort or another: a red flag is a symbol of danger, a white of surrender. In others it is confined to something which expresses in an oblique and figurative manner that which cannot be stated in a direct and literal one, so that there are symbols in poetry but not in science, and symbolic logic is misnamed. In yet others, however, it is used for any object, act, event, quality, or relation which serves as a vehicle for a conception— the conception is the symbol's "meaning"—and that is the approach I shall follow here.[5] The number 6, written, imagined, laid out as a row of stones, or even punched into the program tapes of a computer, is a symbol. But so also is the Cross, talked about, visualized, shaped worriedly in air or fondly fingered at the neck, the expanse of painted canvas called "Guernica" or the bit of painted stone called a churinga, the word "reality," or even the morpheme "-ing." They are all symbols, or at least symbolic elements, because they are tangible formulations of notions, abstractions from experience fixed in perceptible forms, concrete embodiments of ideas, attitudes, judgments, longings, or beliefs. To undertake the study of cultural activity—activity in which symbolism forms the positive content—is thus not to abandon social analysis for a Platonic cave of shadows, to enter into a mentalistic world of introspective psychology or, worse, speculative philosophy, and wander there forever in a haze of "Cognitions," "Affections," "Conations," and other elusive entities. Cultural acts, the construction, apprehension, and utilization of symbolic forms, are social events like any other; they are as public as marriage and as observable as agriculture.

They are not, however, exactly the same thing; or, more precisely, the symbolic dimension of social events is, like the psychological, itself theoretically abstractable from those events as empirical totalities. There is still, to paraphrase a remark of Kenneth Burke's, a difference

[5] S. Langer, *Philosophy in a New Key*, 4th ed. (Cambridge. Mass., 1960).

between building a house and drawing up a plan for building a house, and reading a poem about having children by marriage is not quite the same thing as having children by marriage.[6] Even though the building of the house may proceed under the guidance of the plan or—a less likely occurrence—the having of children may be motivated by a reading of the poem, there is something to be said for not confusing our traffic with symbols with our traffic with objects or human beings, for these latter are not in themselves symbols, however often they may function as such.[7] No matter how deeply interfused the cultural, the social, and the psychological may be in the everyday life of houses, farms, poems, and marriages, it is useful to distinguish them in analysis, and, so doing, to isolate the generic traits of each against the normalized background of the other two. → BASIC

So far as culture patterns, that is, systems or complexes of symbols, are concerned, the generic trait which is of first importance for us here is that they are extrinsic sources of information. By "extrinsic," I mean only that—unlike genes, for example—they lie outside the boundaries of the individual organism as such in that intersubjective world of common understandings into which all human individuals are born, in which they pursue their separate careers, and which they leave persisting behind them after they die. By "sources of information," I mean only that—like genes—they provide a blueprint or template in terms of which processes external to themselves can be given a definite form. As the order of bases in a strand of DNA forms a coded program, a set of instructions, or a recipe, for the synthesis of the structurally complex proteins which shape organic functioning, so culture patterns provide such programs for the institution of the social and psychological processes which shape public behavior. Though the sort of information and the mode of its transmission are vastly different in the two cases, this comparison of gene and symbol is more than a strained analogy of the familiar "social heredity" sort. It is actually a substantial relationship, for it is precisely because of the fact that genetically programmed processes are so highly generalized in men, as compared with lower ani-

[6] K. Burke, *The Philosophy of Literary Form* (Baton Rouge, La.: Louisiana State University Press, 1941), p. 9.
[7] The reverse mistake, especially common among neo-Kantians such as Cassirer, of taking symbols to be identical with, or "constitutive of," their referents is equally pernicious. [Cf. E. Cassirer, *The Philosophy of Symbolic Forms* (New Haven: 1953–1957), 3 vols.] "One can point to the moon with one's finger," some, probably well-invented, Zen Master is supposed to have said, "but to take one's finger for the moon is to be a fool."

mals, that culturally programmed ones are so important; only because human behavior is so loosely determined by intrinsic sources of information that extrinsic sources are so vital. To build a dam a beaver needs only an appropriate site and the proper materials—his mode of procedure is shaped by his physiology. But man, whose genes are silent on the building trades, needs also a conception of what it is to build a dam, a conception he can get only from some symbolic source—a blueprint, a textbook, or a string of speech by someone who already knows how dams are built—or, of course, from manipulating graphic or linguistic elements in such a way as to attain for himself a conception of what dams are and how they are built.

This point is sometimes put in the form of an argument that cultural patterns are "models," that they are sets of symbols whose relations to one another "model" relations among entities, processes or what-have-you in physical, organic, social, or psychological systems by "paralleling," "imitating," or "simulating" them.[8] The term "model" has, however, two senses—an "of" sense and a "for" sense—and though these are but aspects of the same basic concept they are very much worth distinguishing for analytic purposes. In the first, what is stressed is the manipulation of symbol structures so as to bring them, more or less closely, into parallel with the pre-established nonsymbolic system, as when we grasp how dams work by developing a theory of hydraulics or constructing a flow chart. The theory or chart models physical relationships in such a way—that is, by expressing their structure in synoptic form—as to render them apprehensible; it is a model *of* "reality." In the second, what is stressed is the manipulation of the nonsymbolic systems in terms of the relationships expressed in the symbolic, as when we construct a dam according to the specifications implied in an hydraulic theory or the conclusions drawn from a flow chart. Here, the theory is a model under whose guidance physical relationships are organized: it is a model *for* "reality." For psychological and social systems, and for cultural models that we would not ordinarily refer to as "theories," but rather as "doctrines," "melodies," or "rites," the case is in no way different. Unlike genes, and other nonsymbolic information sources, which are only models *for,* not models *of,* culture patterns have an intrinsic double aspect: they give meaning, that is, objective conceptual form, to social and psychological reality both by shaping themselves to it and by shaping it to themselves.

[8] K. Craik, *The Nature of Explanation* (Cambridge, 1952).

It is, in fact, this double aspect which sets true symbols off from other sorts of significative forms. Models *for* are found, as the gene example suggests, through the whole order of nature; for wherever there is a communication of pattern, such programs are, in simple logic, required. Among animals, imprint learning is perhaps the most striking example, because what such learning involves is the automatic presentation of an appropriate sequence of behavior by a model animal in the presence of a learning animal which serves, equally automatically, to call out and stabilize a certain set of responses genetically built into the learning animal.[9] The communicative dance of two bees, one of which has found nectar and the other of which seeks it, is another, somewhat different, more complexly coded, example.[10] Craik has even suggested that the thin trickle of water which first finds its way down from a mountain spring to the sea and smooths a little channel for the greater volume of water that follows after it plays a sort of model *for* function.[11] But models *of*—linguistic, graphic, mechanical, natural, etc., processes which function not to provide sources of information in terms of which other processes can be patterned, but to represent those patterned processes as such, to express their structure in an alternative medium—are much rarer and may perhaps be confined, among living animals, to man. The perception of the structural congruence between one set of processes, activities, relations, entities, and so on, and another set for which it acts as a program, so that the program can be taken as a representation, or conception—a symbol—of the programmed, is the essence of human thought. The intertransposability of models *for* and models *of* which symbolic formulation makes possible is the distinctive characteristic of our mentality.

> . . . to establish powerful, pervasive, and long-lasting moods
> and motivations in men by . . .

So far as religious symbols and symbol systems are concerned this intertransposability is clear. The endurance, courage, independence, perseverance, and passionate willfulness in which the vision quest practices the Plains Indian are the same flamboyant virtues by which he attempts

[9] K. Lorenz, *King Solomon's Ring* (London, 1952).
[10] K. von Frisch, "Dialects in the Language of the Bees," *Scientific American*, August 1962.
[11] Craik, *Nature of Explanation*.

to live: while achieving a sense of revelation he stabilizes a sense of direction.[12] The consciousness of defaulted obligation, secreted guilt, and, when a confession is obtained, public shame in which Manus' séance rehearses him are the same sentiments that underlie the sort of duty ethic by which his property-conscious society is maintained: the gaining of an absolution involves the forging of a conscience.[13] And the same self-discipline which rewards a Javanese mystic staring fixedly into the flame of a lamp with what he takes to be an intimation of divinity drills him in that rigorous control of emotional expression which is necessary to a man who would follow a quietistic style of life.[14] Whether one sees the conception of a personal guardian spirit, a family tutelary, or an immanent God as synoptic formulations of the character of reality or as templates for producing reality with such a character seems largely arbitrary, a matter of which aspect, the model *of* or model *for,* one wants for the moment to bring into focus. The concrete symbols involved—one or another mythological figure materializing in the wilderness, the skull of the deceased household head hanging censoriously in the rafters, or a disembodied "voice in the stillness" soundlessly chanting enigmatic classical poetry—point in either direction. They both express the world's climate and shape it.

They shape it by inducing in the worshipper a certain distinctive set of dispositions (tendencies, capacities, propensities, skills, habits, liabilities, pronenesses) which lend a chronic character to the flow of his activity and the quality of his experience. A disposition describes not an activity or an occurrence but a probability of an activity being performed or an occurrence occurring in certain circumstances: "When a cow is said to be a ruminant, or a man is said to be a cigarette-smoker, it is not being said that the cow is ruminating now or that the man is smoking a cigarette now. To be a ruminant is to tend to ruminate from time to time, and to be a cigarette-smoker is to be in the habit of smoking cigarettes." [15] Similarly, to be pious is not to be performing something we would call an act of piety, but to be liable to perform such acts. So, too, with the Plains Indian's bravura, the Manus' compunctiousness, or the Javanese's quietism, which, in their contexts, form the substance of piety. The virtue of this sort of view of what are usually

[12] R. H. Lowie, *Primitive Religion* (New York, 1924).
[13] R. F. Fortune, *Manus Religion* (Philadelphia, 1935).
[14] C. Geertz, *The Religion of Java* (Glencoe, Ill., 1960).
[15] G. Ryle, *The Concept of Mind* (London and New York, 1949).

called "mental traits" or, if the Cartesianism is unavowed, "psychological forces" (both unobjectionable enough terms in themselves) is that it gets them out of any dim and inaccessible realm of private sensation into that same well-lit world of observables in which reside the brittleness of glass, the inflammability of paper, and, to return to the metaphor, the dampness of England.

So far as religious activities are concerned (and learning a myth by heart is as much a religious activity as detaching one's finger at the knuckle), two somewhat different sorts of disposition are induced by them: moods and motivations.

A motivation is a persisting tendency, a chronic inclination to perform certain sorts of acts and experience certain sorts of feeling in certain sorts of situations, the "sorts" being commonly very heterogenous and rather ill-defined classes in all three cases:

> On hearing that a man is vain [i.e., motivated by vanity] we expect him to behave in certain ways, namely to talk a lot about himself, to cleave to the society of the eminent, to reject criticisms, to seek the footlights and to disengage himself from conversations about the merits of others. We expect him to indulge in roseate daydreams about his own successes, to avoid recalling past failures and to plan for his own advancement. To be vain is to tend to act in these and innumerable other kindred ways. Certainly we also expect the vain man to feel certain pangs and flutters in certain situations; we expect him to have an acute sinking feeling when an eminent person forgets his name, and to feel buoyant of heart and light of toe on hearing of the misfortunes of his rivals. But feelings of pique and buoyancy are not more directly indicative of vanity than are public acts of boasting or private acts of daydreaming.[16]

Similarly for any motivations. As a motive, "flamboyant courage" consists in such enduring propensities as to fast in the wilderness, to conduct solitary raids on enemy camps, and to thrill to the thought of counting coup. "Moral circumspection" consists in such ingrained tendencies as to honor onerous promises, to confess secret sins in the face of severe public disapproval, and to feel guilty when vague and generalized accusations are made at seances. And "dispassionate tranquility" consists in such persistent inclinations as to maintain one's poise come hell or high water, to experience distaste in the presence of even moderate emotional displays, and to indulge in contentless contemplations of featureless objects. Motives are thus neither acts (that is, intentional be-

[16] Ibid., p. 86. Quoted by permission of Barnes & Noble Books and Hutchinson Publishing Group Ltd.

haviors) nor feelings, but liabilities to perform particular classes of act or have particular classes of feeling. And when we say that a man is religious, that is, motivated by religion, this is at least part—though only part—of what we mean.

Another part of what we mean is that he has, when properly stimulated, a susceptibility to fall into certain moods, moods we sometimes lump together under such covering terms as "reverential," "solemn," or "worshipful." Such generalized rubrics actually conceal, however, the enormous empirical variousness of the dispositions involved, and, in fact, tend to assimilate them to the unusually grave tone of most of our own religious life. The moods that sacred symbols induce, at different times and in different places, range from exultation to melancholy, from self-confidence to self-pity, from an incorrigible playfulness to a bland listlessness—to say nothing of the erogenous power of so many of the world's myths and rituals. No more than there is a single sort of motivation one can call piety is there a single sort of mood one can call worshipful.

The major difference between moods and motivations is that where the latter are, so to speak, vectorial qualities, the former are merely scalar. Motives have a directional cast, they describe a certain overall course, gravitate toward certain, usually temporary, consummations. But moods vary only as to intensity: they go nowhere. They spring from certain circumstances but they are responsive to no ends. Like fogs, they just settle and lift; like scents, suffuse and evaporate. When present they are totalistic: if one is sad everything and everybody seems dreary; if one is gay, everything and everybody seems splendid. Thus, though a man can be vain, brave, willful, and independent at the same time, he can't very well be playful and listless, or exultant and melancholy, at the same time.[17] Further, where motives persist for more or less extended periods of time, moods merely recur with greater or lesser frequency, coming and going for what are often quite unfathomable reasons. But perhaps the most important difference, so far as we are concerned, between moods and motivations is that motivations are "made meaningful" with reference to the ends toward which they are conceived to conduce, whereas moods are "made meaningful" with reference to the conditions from which they are conceived to spring. We interpret motives in terms of their consummations, but we interpret moods in terms of their sources. We say that a person is industrious be-

[17] Ibid., p. 99.

cause he wishes to succeed; we say that a person is worried because he is conscious of the hanging threat of nuclear holocaust. And this is no less the case when the interpretations are ultimate. Charity becomes Christian charity when it is enclosed in a conception of God's purposes; optimism is Christian optimism when it is grounded in a particular conception of God's nature. The assiduity of the Navaho finds its rationale in a belief that, since "reality" operates mechanically, it is coercible; their chronic fearfulness finds its rationale in a conviction that, however "reality" operates, it is both enormously powerful and terribly dangerous.[18]

*. . . by formulating conceptions of a general order
of existence and . . .*

That the symbols or symbol systems which induce and define dispositions we set off as religious and those which place those dispositions in a cosmic framework are the same symbols ought to occasion no surprise. For what else do we mean by saying that a particular mood of awe is religious and not secular, except that it springs from entertaining a conception of all-pervading vitality like mana and not from a visit to the Grand Canyon? Or that a particular case of asceticism is an example of a religious motivation, except that it is directed toward the achievement of an unconditioned end like nirvana and not a conditioned one like weight-reduction? If sacred symbols did not at one and the same time induce dispositions in human beings and formulate, however obliquely, inarticulately, or unsystematically, general ideas of order, then the empirical differentia of religious activity or religious experience would not exist. A man can indeed be said to be "religious" about golf, but not merely if he pursues it with passion and plays it on Sundays: he must also see it as symbolic of some transcendent truths. And the pubescent boy gazing soulfully into the eyes of the pubescent girl in a William Steig cartoon and murmuring, "There is something about you, Ethel, which gives me a sort of religious feeling," is, like most adolescents, confused. What any particular religion affirms about the fundamental nature of reality may be obscure, shallow, or, all too often, perverse; but it must, if it is not to consist of the mere collection of re-

[18] C. Kluckhohn, "The Philosophy of the Navaho Indians," in *Ideological Differences and World Order,* ed. F. S. C. Northrop (New Haven, 1949), pp. 356–384.

ceived practices and conventional sentiments we usually refer to as moralism, affirm something. If one were to essay a minimal definition of
religion today, it would perhaps not be Tylor's famous "belief in spiritual beings," to which Goody, wearied of theoretical subtleties, has
lately urged us to return, but rather what Salvador de Madariaga has
called "the relatively modest dogma that God is not mad." [19]

Usually, of course, religions affirm very much more than this: we believe, as James remarked, all that we can and would believe everything
if we only could.[20] The thing we seem least able to tolerate is a threat to
our powers of conception, a suggestion that our ability to create, grasp,
and use symbols may fail us, for were this to happen, we would be
more helpless, as I have already pointed out, than the beavers. The extreme generality, diffuseness, and variability of man's innate (that is, genetically programmed) response capacities means that without the assistance of cultural patterns he would be functionally incomplete, not
merely a talented ape who had, like some underprivileged child, unfortunately been prevented from realizing his full potentialities, but a kind
of formless monster with neither sense of direction nor power of self-
control, a chaos of spasmodic impulses and vague emotions. Man depends upon symbols and symbol systems with a dependence so great as
to be decisive for his creatural viability and, as a result, his sensitivity
to even the remotest indication that they may prove unable to cope with
one or another aspect of experience raises within him the gravest sort of
anxiety:

[Man] can adapt himself somehow to anything his imagination can cope
with; but he cannot deal with Chaos. Because his characteristic function and
highest asset is conception, his greatest fright is to meet what he cannot
construe—the "uncanny," as it is popularly called. It need not be a new object; we do meet new things, and "understand" them promptly, if tenta-
tively, by the nearest analogy, when our minds are functioning freely; but
under mental stress even perfectly familiar things may become suddenly disorganized and give us the horrors. Therefore our most important assets are
always the symbols of our general *orientation* in nature, on the earth, in society, and in what we are doing: the symbols of our *Weltanschauung* and
Lebensanschauung. Consequently, in a primitive society, a daily ritual is incorporated in common activities, in eating, washing, fire-making, etc., as
well as in pure ceremonial; because the need of reasserting the tribal morale
and recognizing its cosmic conditions is constantly felt. In Christian Europe

[19] J. Goody, "Religion and Ritual: The Definition Problem," *British Journal of
Psychology* 12 (1961):143–164.
[20] W. James, *The Principles of Psychology*, 2 vols. (New York, 1904).

the Church brought men daily (in some orders even hourly) to their knees, to enact if not to contemplate their assent to the ultimate concepts.[21]

There are at least three points where chaos—a tumult of events which lack not just interpretations but *interpretability*—threatens to break in upon man: at the limits of his analytic capacities, at the limits of his powers of endurance, and at the limits of his moral insight. Bafflement, suffering, and a sense of intractable ethical paradox are all, if they become intense enough or are sustained long enough, radical challenges to the proposition that life is comprehensible and that we can, by taking thought, orient ourselves effectively within it—challenges with which any religion, however "primitive," which hopes to persist must attempt somehow to cope.

Of the three issues, it is the first which has been least investigated by modern social anthropologists (though Evans-Pritchard's classic discussion of why granaries fall on some Azande and not on others, is a notable exception).[22] Even to consider people's religious beliefs as attempts to bring anomalous events or experiences—death, dreams, mental fugues, volcanic eruptions, or marital infidelity—within the circle of the at least potentially explicable seems to smack of Tyloreanism or worse. But it does appear to be a fact that at least some men—in all probability, most men—are unable to leave unclarified problems of analysis merely unclarified, just to look at the stranger features of the world's landscape in dumb astonishment or bland apathy without trying to develop, however fantastic, inconsistent, or simple-minded, some notions as to how such features might be reconciled with the more ordinary deliverances of experience. Any chronic failure of one's explanatory apparatus, the complex of received culture patterns (common sense, science, philosophical speculation, myth) one has for mapping the empirical world, to explain things which cry out for explanation tends to lead to a deep disquiet—a tendency rather more widespread and a disquiet rather deeper than we have sometimes supposed since the pseudoscience view of religious belief was, quite rightfully, deposed. After all, even that high priest of heroic atheism, Lord Russell, once remarked that although the problem of the existence of God had never bothered him, the ambiguity of certain mathematical axioms had threatened to unhinge his mind. And Einstein's profound dissatisfaction with quantum me-

[21] Langer, *Philosophy in a New Key*, p. 287. Italics in original.
[22] E. Evans-Pritchard, *Witchcraft, Oracles and Magic Among the Azande* (Oxford, 1937).

chanics was based on a—surely religious—inability to believe that, as he put it, God plays dice with the universe.

But this quest for lucidity and the rush of metaphysical anxiety that occurs when empirical phenomena threaten to remain intransigently opaque is found on much humbler intellectual levels. Certainly, I was struck in my own work, much more than I had at all expected to be, by the degree to which my more animistically inclined informants behaved like true Tyloreans. They seemed to be constantly using their beliefs to "explain" phenomena: or, more accurately, to convince themselves that the phenomena were explainable within the accepted scheme of things, for they commonly had only a minimal attachment to the particular soul possession, emotional disequilibrium, taboo infringement, or bewitchment hypothesis they advanced and were all too ready to abandon it for some other, in the same genre, which struck them as more plausible given the facts of the case. What they were *not* ready to do was abandon it for no other hypothesis at all; to leave events to themselves.

And what is more, they adopted this nervous cognitive stance with respect to phenomena which had no immediate practical bearing on their own lives, or for that matter on anyone's. When a peculiarly shaped, rather large toadstool grew up in a carpenter's house in the short space of a few days (or, some said, a few hours), people came from miles around to see it, and everyone had some sort of explanation—some animist, some animatist, some not quite either—for it. Yet it would be hard to argue that the toadstool had any social value in Radcliffe-Brown's sense, or was connected in any way with anything which did and for which it could have been standing proxy, like the Andaman cicada.[23] Toadstools play about the same role in Javanese life as they do in ours, and in the ordinary course of things Javanese have about as much interest in them as we do. It was just that this one was "odd," "strange," "uncanny"—*aneh*. And the odd, strange, and uncanny simply must be accounted for—or, again, the conviction that it *could be accounted for* sustained. One does not shrug off a toadstool which grows five times as fast as a toadstool has any right to grow. In the broadest sense the "strange" toadstool did have implications, and critical ones, for those who heard about it. It threatened their most general ability to understand the world, raised the uncomfortable question of whether the beliefs which they held about nature were workable, the standards of truth they used valid.

[23] A. R. Radcliffe-Brown, *Structure and Function in Primitive Society* (Glencoe, Ill., 1952).

Nor is this to argue that it is only, or even mainly, sudden eruptions of extraordinary events which engender in man the disquieting sense that his cognitive resources may prove unavailing or that this intuition appears only in its acute form. More commonly it is a persistent, constantly re-experienced difficulty in grasping certain aspects of nature, self, and society, in bringing certain elusive phenomena within the sphere of culturally formulatable fact, which renders man chronically uneasy and toward which a more equable flow of diagnostic symbols is consequently directed. It is what lies beyond a relatively fixed frontier of accredited knowledge that, looming as a constant background to the daily round of practical life, sets ordinary human experience in a permanent context of metaphysical concern and raises the dim, back-of-the-mind suspicions that one may be adrift in an absurd world:

Another subject which is matter for this characteristic intellectual enquiry [among the Iatmul] is the nature of ripples and waves on the surface of water. It is said secretly that men, pigs, trees, grass—all the objects in the world—are only patterns of waves. Indeed there seems to be some agreement about this, although it perhaps conflicts with the theory of reincarnation, according to which the ghost of the dead is blown as a mist by the East Wind up the river and into the womb of the deceased's son's wife. Be that as it may—there is still the question of how ripples and waves are caused. The clan which claims the East Wind as a totem is clear enough about this: the Wind with her mosquito fan causes the waves. But other clans have personified the waves and say that they are a person (Kontummali) independent of the wind. Other clans, again, have other theories. On one occasion I took some Iatmul natives down to the coast and found one of them sitting by himself gazing with rapt attention at the sea. It was a windless day, but a slow swell was breaking on the beach. Among the totemic ancestors of his clan he counted a personified slit gong who had floated down the river to the sea and who was believed to cause the waves. He was gazing at the waves which were heaving and breaking when no wind was blowing, demonstrating the truth of his clan myth.[24]

[24] G. Bateson, *Naven,* 2nd ed. (Stanford, 1958). That the chronic and acute forms of this sort of cognitive concern are closely interrelated, and that responses to the more unusual occasions of it are patterned on responses established in coping with the more usual is also clear from Bateson's description, however, as he goes on to say: "On another occasion I invited one of my informants to witness the development of photographic plates. I first desensitized the plates and then developed them in an open dish in moderate light, so that my informant was able to see the gradual appearance of the images. He was much interested, and some days later made me promise never to show this process to members of other clans. Kontum-mali was one of his ancestors, and he saw in the process of photographic development the actual embodiment of ripples into images, and regarded this as a demonstration of the clan's secret."

The second experiential challenge in whose face the meaningfulness of a particular pattern of life threatens to dissolve into a chaos of thingless names and nameless things—the problem of suffering—has been rather more investigated, or at least described, mainly because of the great amount of attention given in works on tribal religion to what are perhaps its two main loci: illness and mourning. Yet for all the fascinated interest in the emotional aura that surrounds these extreme situations, there has been, with a few exceptions such as Lienhardt's recent discussion of Dinka divining, little conceptual advance over the sort of crude confidence-type theory set forth by Malinowski: viz., that religion helps one to endure "situations of emotional stress" by "open [ing] up escapes from such situations and such impasses as offer no empirical way out except by ritual and belief into the domain of the supernatural." [25] The inadequacy of this "theology of optimism," as Nadel rather dryly called it, is, of course, radical.[26] Over its career religion has probably disturbed men as much as it has cheered them; forced them into a head-on, unblinking confrontation of the fact that they are born to trouble as often as it has enabled them to avoid such a confrontation by projecting them into sort of infantile fairy-tale worlds where —Malinowski again—"hope cannot fail nor desire deceive." [27] With the possible exception of Christian Science, there are few if any religious traditions, "great" or "little," in which the proposition that life hurts is not strenuously affirmed, and in some it is virtually glorified:

She was an old [Ba-Ila] woman of a family with a long genealogy. Leza, "the Besetting One", stretched out his hand against the family. He slew her mother and father while she was yet a child, and in the course of years all connected with her perished. She said to herself, "Surely I shall keep those who sit on my thighs." But no, even they, the children of her children, were taken from her. . . . Then came into her heart a desperate resolution to find God and to ask the meaning of it all. . . . So she began to travel, going through country after country, always with the thought in her mind: "I shall come to where the earth ends and there I shall find a road to God and I shall ask him: 'What have I done to thee that thou afflictest me in this manner?' " She never found where the earth ends, but though disappointed she did not give up her search, and as she passed through the different countries they asked her, "What have you come for, old woman?" And the

[25] G. Lienhardt, *Divinity and Experience* (Oxford, 1961), p. 151ff; B. Malinowski, *Magic, Science and Religion* (Boston, 1948), p. 67.
[26] S. F. Nadel, "Malinowski on Magic and Religion," in *Man and Culture*, ed. R. Firth (London, 1957), pp. 189–208.
[27] Malinowski, *Magic, Science and Religion* (Boston, 1948), p. 67.

answer would be, "I am seeking Leza." "Seeking Leza! For what?" "My brothers, you ask me! Here in the nations is there one who suffers as I have suffered?" And they would ask again, "How have you suffered?" "In this way. I am alone. As you see me, a solitary old woman; that is how I am!" And they answered, "Yes, we see. That is how you are! Bereaved of friends and husband? In what do you differ from others? The Besetting-One sits on the back of every one of us and we cannot shake him off." She never obtained her desire; she died of a broken heart.[28]

As a religious problem, the problem of suffering is, paradoxically, not how to avoid suffering but how to suffer, how to make of physical pain, personal loss, wordly defeat, or the helpless contemplation of others' agony something bearable, supportable—something, as we say, sufferable. It was in this effort that the Ba-Ila woman—perhaps necessarily, perhaps not—failed and, literally not knowing how to feel about what had happened to her, how to suffer, perished in confusion and despair. Where the more intellective aspects of what Weber called the Problem of Meaning are a matter affirming the ultimate explicability of experience, the more affective aspects are a matter of affirming its ultimate sufferableness. As religion on one side anchors the power of our symbolic resources for formulating analytic ideas in an authoritative conception of the overall shape of reality, so on another side it anchors the power of our, also symbolic, resources for expressing emotions— moods, sentiments, passions, affections, feelings—in a similar conception of its pervasive tenor, its inherent tone and temper. For those able to embrace them, and for so long as they are able to embrace them, religious symbols provide a cosmic guarantee not only for their ability to comprehend the world, but also, comprehending it, to give a precision to their feeling, a definition to their emotions which enables them, morosely or joyfully, grimly or cavalierly, to endure it.

Consider in this light the well-known Navaho curing rites usually referred to as "sings." [29] A sing—the Navaho have about sixty different ones for different purposes, but virtually all of them are dedicated to removing some sort of physical or mental illness—is a kind of religious psychodrama in which there are three main actors: the "singer" or curer, the patient, and, as a kind of antiphonal chorus, the patient's family and friends. The structure of all the sings, the drama's plot, is

    [28] C. W. Smith and A. M. Dale, *The Ila-Speaking Peoples of Northern Rhodesia* (London, 1920), p. 197ff.; quoted in P. Radin, *Primitive Man as a Philosopher* (New York, 1957), pp. 100–101.
    [29] C. Kluckhohn and D. Leighton, *The Navaho* (Cambridge, Mass., 1946); G. Reichard, *Navaho Religion,* 2 vols. (New York, 1950).

quite similar. There are three main acts: a purification of the patient and audience; a statement, by means of repetitive chants and ritual manipulations, of the wish to restore well-being ("harmony") in the patient; an identification of the patient with the Holy People and his consequent "cure." The purification rites involve forced sweating, induced vomiting, and so on, to expel the sickness from the patient physically. The chants, which are numberless, consist mainly of simple optative phrases ("may the patient be well," "I am getting better all over," etc.). And, finally, the identification of the patient with the Holy People, and thus with cosmic order generally, is accomplished through the agency of a sand painting depicting the Holy People in one or another appropriate mythic setting. The singer places the patient on the painting, touching the feet, hands, knees, shoulders, breast, back, and head of the divine figures and then the corresponding parts of the patient, performing thus what is essentially a bodily identification of the human and the divine.[30] This is the climax of the sing: the whole curing process may be likened, Reichard says, to a spiritual osmosis in which the illness in man and the power of the deity penetrate the ceremonial membrane in both directions, the former being neutralized by the latter. Sickness seeps out in the sweat, vomit, and other purification rites; health seeps in as the Navaho patient touches, through the medium of the singer, the sacred sand painting. Clearly, the symbolism of the sing focuses upon the problem of human suffering and attempts to cope with it by placing it in a meaningful context, providing a mode of action through which it can be expressed, being expressed understood, and being understood, endured. The sustaining effect of the sing (and since the commonest disease is tuberculosis, it can in most cases be only sustaining), rests ultimately on its ability to give the stricken person a vocabulary in terms of which to grasp the nature of his distress and relate it to the wider world. Like a calvary, a recitation of Buddha's emergence from his father's palace, or a performance of *Oedipus Tyrannos* in other religious traditions, a sing is mainly concerned with the presentation of a specific and concrete image of truly human, and so endurable, suffering powerful enough to resist the challenge of emotional meaninglessness raised by the existence of intense and unremovable brute pain.

The problem of suffering passes easily into the problem of evil, for if suffering is severe enough it usually, though not always, seems morally undeserved as well, at least to the sufferer. But they are not, however, exactly the same thing—a fact I think Weber, too influenced by the

[30] Reichard, *Navaho Religion.*

biases of a monotheistic tradition in which, as the various aspects of human experience must be conceived to proceed from a single, voluntaristic source, man's pain reflects directly on God's goodness, did not fully recognize in his generalization of the dilemmas of Christian theodicy Eastward. For where the problem of suffering is concerned with threats to our ability to put our "undisciplined squads of emotion" into some sort of soldierly order, the problem of evil is concerned with threats to our ability to make sound moral judgments. What is involved in the problem of evil is not the adequacy of our symbolic resources to govern our affective life, but the adequacy of those resources to provide a workable set of ethical criteria, normative guides to govern our action. The vexation here is the gap between things as they are and as they ought to be if our conceptions of right and wrong make sense, the gap between what we deem various individuals deserve and what we see that they get—a phenomenon summed up in that profound quatrain:

> The rain falls on the just
> And on the unjust fella;
> But mainly upon the just,
> Because the unjust has the just's umbrella.

Or if this seems too flippant an expression of an issue that, in somewhat different form, animates the Book of Job and the *Baghavad Gita,* the following classical Javanese poem, known, sung, and repeatedly quoted in Java by virtually everyone over the age of six, puts the point —the discrepancy between moral prescriptions and material rewards, the seeming inconsistency of "is" and "ought"—rather more elegantly:

> We have lived to see a time without order
> In which everyone is confused in his mind.
> One cannot bear to join in the madness,
> But if he does not do so
> He will not share in the spoils,
> And will starve as a result.
> Yes, God; wrong is wrong:
> Happy are those who forget,
> Happier yet those who remember and have deep insight.

Nor is it necessary to be theologically self-conscious to be religiously sophisticated. The concern with intractable ethical paradox, the disquieting sense that one's moral insight is inadequate to one's moral experience, is as alive on the level of so-called primitive religion as it is on that of the so-called civilized. The set of notions about "division in the world" that Lienhardt describes for the Dinka is a useful case in point.[31] Like so many peoples, the Dinka believe that the sky, where "Divinity" is located, and earth, where man dwells, were at one time contiguous, the sky lying just above the earth and being connected to it by a rope, so that men could move at will between the two realms. There was no death and the first man and woman were permitted but a single grain of millet a day, which was all that they at that time required. One day, the woman—of course—decided, out of greed, to plant more than the permitted grain of millet, and in her avid haste and industry accidentally struck Divinity with the handle of the hoe. Offended, he severed the rope, withdrew into the distant sky of today, and left man to labor for his food, to suffer sickness and death, and to experience separation from the source of his being, his Creator. Yet the meaning of this strangely familiar story to the Dinka is, as indeed is Genesis to Jews and Christians, not homiletic but descriptive:

Those [Dinka] who have commented on these stories have sometimes made it clear that their sympathies lie with Man in his plight, and draw attention to the smallness of the fault for which Divinity withdrew the benefits of his closeness. The image of striking Divinity with a hoe . . . often evokes a certain amusement, almost as though the story were indulgently being treated as too childish to explain the consequences attributed to the event. But it is clear that the point of the story of Divinity's withdrawal from men is not to suggest an improving moral judgment on human behaviour. It is to represent a total situation known to the Dinka today. Men now are—as the first man and woman then became—active, self-assertive, inquiring, acquisitive. Yet they are also subject to suffering and death, ineffective, ignorant and poor. Life is insecure; human calculations often prove erroneous, and men must often learn by experience that the consequences of their acts are quite other than they may have anticipated or consider equitable. Divinity's withdrawal from Man as the result of a comparatively trifling offence, by human standards, presents the contrast between equitable human judgments and the action of the Power which are held ultimately to control what happens in Dinka life. . . . To the Dinka, the moral order is ultimately constituted according to principles which often elude men, which experience and tradition in part reveal, and which human action cannot change. . . . The myth of Divinity's withdrawal then reflects the facts of existence as they are known. The Dinka are in a universe which is largely beyond their control, and where events may contradict the most reasonable human expectations.[32]

Thus the problem of evil, or perhaps one should say the problem *about* evil, is in essence the same sort of problem of or about bafflement and the problem of or about suffering. The strange opacity of certain

---

[31] Ibid., pp. 28–55.
[32] Ibid.

empirical events, the dumb senselessness of intense or inexorable pain, and the enigmatic unaccountability of gross iniquity all raise the uncomfortable suspicion that perhaps the world, and hence man's life in the world, has no genuine order at all—no empirical regularity, no emotional form, no moral coherence. And the religious response to this suspicion is in each case the same: the formulation, by means of symbols, of an image of such a genuine order of the world which will account for, and even celebrate, the perceived ambiguities, puzzles, and paradoxes in human experience. The effort is not to deny the undeniable— that there are unexplained events, that life hurts, or that rain falls upon the just—but to deny that there are inexplicable events, that life is unendurable, and that justice is a mirage. The principles which constitute the moral order may indeed often elude men, as Lienhardt puts it, in the same way as fully satisfactory explanations of anomalous events or effective forms for the expression of feeling often elude them. What is important, to a religious man at least, is that this elusiveness be accounted for, that it be not the result of the fact that there are no such principles, explanations, or forms, that life is absurd and the attempt to make moral, intellectual, or emotional sense out of experience is bootless. The Dinka can admit, in fact insist upon, the moral ambiguities and contradictions of life as they live it because these ambiguities and contradictions are seen not as ultimate, but as the "rational," "natural," "logical" (one may choose one's own adjective here, for none of them is truly adequate) outcome of the moral structure of reality which the myth of the withdrawn "Divinity" depicts, or as Lienhardt says, "images."

The Problem of Meaning in each of its intergrading aspects (how these aspects in fact intergrade in each particular case, what sort of interplay there is between the sense of analytic, emotional, and moral impotence, seems to me one of the outstanding, and except for Weber untouched, problems for comparative research in this whole field) is a matter of affirming, or at least recognizing, the inescapability of ignorance, pain, and injustice on the human plane while simultaneously denying that these irrationalities are characteristic of the world as a whole. And it is in terms of religious symbolism, a symbolism relating man's sphere of existence to a wider sphere within which it is conceived to rest, that both the affirmation and the denial are made.[33]

---

[33] This is *not*, however, to say that everyone in every society does this; for as the immortal Don Marquis once remarked, you don't have to have a soul unless

> . . . and clothing those conceptions with such an aura of
> factuality that . . .

There arises here, however, a more profound question: how is it that this denial comes to be believed? How is it that the religious man moves from a troubled perception of experienced disorder to a more or less settled conviction of fundamental order? Just what does "belief" mean in a religious context? Of all the problems surrounding attempts to conduct anthropological analysis of religion this is the one that has perhaps been most troublesome and therefore the most often avoided, usually by relegating it to psychology, that raffish outcast discipline to which social anthropologists are forever consigning phenomena they are unable to deal with within the framework of a denatured Durkheimianism. But the problem will not go away, it is not "merely" psychological (nothing social is), and no anthropological theory of religion which fails to attack it is worthy of the name. We have been trying to stage Hamlet without the Prince quite long enough.

It seems to me that it is best to begin any approach to this issue with frank recognition that religious belief involves not a Baconian induction from everyday experience—for then we should all be agnostics—but rather a prior acceptance of authority which transforms that experience. The existence of bafflement, pain, and moral paradox—of The Problem of Meaning—is one of the things that drives men toward belief in gods, devils, spirits, totemic principles, or the spiritual efficacy of cannibalism (an enfolding sense of beauty or a dazzling perception of power are others), but it is not the basis upon which those beliefs rest, but rather their most important field of application:

We point to the state of the world as illustrative of doctrine, but never as evidence for it. So Belsen illustrates a world of original sin, but original sin is not an hypothesis to account for happenings like Belsen. We justify a particular religious belief by showing its place in the total religious conception; we justify a religious belief as a whole by referring to authority. We accept authority because we discover it at some point in the world at which we

---

you really want one. The oft-heard generalization that religion is a human universal embodies a confusion between the probably true (though on present evidence unprovable) proposition that there is no human society in which cultural patterns that we can, under the present definition or one like it, call religious are totally lacking, and the surely untrue proposition that all men in all societies are, in any meaningful sense of the term, religious. But if the anthropological study of religious commitment is underdeveloped, the anthropological study of religious noncommitment is nonexistent. The anthropology of religion will have come of age when some more subtle Malinowski writes a book called "Belief and Unbelief (or even "Faith and Hypocrisy") in a Savage Society."

worship, at which we accept the lordship of something not ourselves. We do not worship authority, but we accept authority as defining the worshipful. So someone may discover the possibility of worship in the life of the Reformed Churches and accept the Bible as authoritative; or in the Roman Church and accept papal authority.[34]

This is, of course, a Christian statement of the matter; but it is not to be despised on that account. In tribal religions authority lies in the persuasive power of traditional imagery; in mystical ones in the apodictic force of supersensible experience; in charismatic ones in the hypnotic attraction of an extraordinary personality. But the priority of the acceptance of an authoritative criterion in religious matters over the revelation which is conceived to flow from that acceptance is not less complete than in scriptural or hieratic ones. The basic axiom underlying what we may perhaps call "the religious perspective" is everywhere the same: he who would know must first believe.

But to speak of "the religious perspective" is, by implication, to speak of one perspective among others. A perspective is a mode of seeing, in that extended sense of "see" in which it means "discern," "apprehend," "understand," or "grasp." It is a particular way of looking at life, a particular manner of construing the world, as when we speak of an historical perspective, a scientific perspective, an aesthetic perspective, a common-sense perspective, or even the bizarre perspective embodied in dreams and in hallucinations.[35] The question then comes down to, first, what is "the religious perspective" generically considered, as differentiated from other perspectives; and second, how do men come to adopt it.

[34] A. MacIntyre, "The Logical Status of Religious Belief," in Metaphysical Beliefs, ed. A. MacIntyre (London, 1957), pp. 167–211.

[35] The term "attitude" as in "aesthetic attitude" or "natural attitude" is another, perhaps more common term for what I have here called "perspective." [For the first, see C. Bell, Art, London, 1914; for the second, though the phrase is originally Husserl's, see A. Schutz, The Problem of Social Reality, vol. 1 of Collected Papers (The Hague, 1962).] But I have avoided it because of its strong subjectivist connotations, its tendency to place the stress upon a supposed inner state of an actor rather than on a certain sort of relation—a symbolically mediated one—between an actor and a situation. This is not to say, of course, that a phenomenological analysis of religious experience, if cast in intersubjective, nontranscendental, genuinely scientific terms [e.g., W. Percy, "Symbol, Consciousness and Intersubjectivity," Journal of Philosophy 15 (1958):631–641] is not essential to a full understanding of religious belief, but merely that that is not the focus of my concern here. "Outlook," "frame of reference," "frame of mind," "orientation," "stance," "mental set," and so on, are other terms sometimes employed, depending upon whether the analyst wishes to stress the social, psychological, or cultural aspects of the matter.

   If we place the religious perspective against the background of three
of the other major perspectives in terms of which men construe the
world—the common-sensical, the scientific, and the aesthetic—its special character emerges more sharply. What distinguishes common sense
as a mode of "seeing" is, as Schutz has pointed out, a simple acceptance
of the world, its objects, and its processes as being just what they seem
to be—what is sometimes called naive realism—and the pragmatic motive, the wish to act upon that world so as to bend it to one's practical
purposes, to master it, or so far as that proves impossible, to adjust to
it.[36] The world of everyday life, itself, of course, a cultural product,
for it is framed in terms of the symbolic conceptions of "stubborn fact"
handed down from generation to generation, is the established scene
and given object of our actions. Like Mt. Everest it is just there, and
the thing to do with it, if one feels the need to do anything with it at all,
is to climb it. In the scientific perspective it is precisely this givenness
which disappears.[37] Deliberate doubt and systematic inquiry, the suspension of the pragmatic motive in favor of disinterested observation,
the attempt to analyze the world in terms of formal concepts whose relationship to the informal conceptions of common sense become increasingly problematic—there are the hallmarks of the attempt to grasp
the world scientifically. And as for the aesthetic perspective, which
under the rubric of "the aesthetic attitude" has been perhaps most exquisitely examined, it involves a different sort of suspension of naive
realism and practical interest, in that instead of questioning the credentials of everyday experience, one merely ignores that experience in
favor of an eager dwelling upon appearances, an engrossment in surfaces, an absorption in things, as we say, "in themselves": "The function of artistic illusion is not 'make-believe'. . . but the very opposite,
disengagement from belief—the contemplation of sensory qualities
without their usual meanings of 'here's that chair', 'that's my
telephone'. . . etc. The knowledge that what is before us has no practical significance in the world is what enables us to give attention to its
appearance as such."[38] And like the common sensical and the scientific (or the historical, the philosophical, and the artistic), this perspective, this "way of seeing" is not the product of some mysterious Carte-
sian chemistry, but is induced, mediated, and in fact created by means

[36] Schutz, *The Problem of Social Reality.*
[37] Ibid.
[38] S. Langer, *Feeling and Form* (New York, 1953), p. 49.

of curious quasi objects—poems, dramas, sculptures, symphonies—
which, dissociating themselves from the solid world of common sense,
take on the special sort of eloquence only sheer appearances can
achieve.

The religious perspective differs from the common-sensical in that, as
already pointed out, it moves beyond the realities of everyday life to
wider ones which correct and complete them, and its defining concern is
not action upon those wider realities but acceptance of them, faith in
them. It differs from the scientific perspective in that it questions the
realities of everyday life not out of an institutionalized scepticism which
dissolves the world's givenness into a swirl of probabilistic hypotheses,
but in terms of what it takes to be wider, nonhypothetical truths. Rather
than detachment, its watchword is commitment; rather than analysis,
encounter. And it differs from art in that instead of effecting a disengagement from the whole question of factuality, deliberately manufac-
turing an air of semblance and illusion, it deepens the concern with fact
and seeks to create an aura of utter actuality. It is this sense of the
"really real" upon which the religious perspective rests and which the
symbolic activities of religion as a cultural system are devoted to producing, intensifying, and, so far as possible, rendering inviolable by the
discordant revelations of secular experience. It is, again, the imbuing of
a certain specific complex of symbols—of the metaphysic they formulate and the style of life they recommend—with a persuasive authority
which, from an analytic point of view, is the essence of religious action.

Which brings us, at length, to ritual. For it is in ritual—that is, consecrated behavior—that this conviction that religious conceptions are
veridical and that religious directives are sound is somehow generated.
It is in some sort of ceremonial form—even if that form be hardly
more than the recitation of a myth, the consultation of an oracle, or the
decoration of a grave—that the moods and motivations which sacred
symbols induce in men and the general conceptions of the order of existence which they formulate for men meet and reinforce one another. In
a ritual, the world as lived and the world as imagined, fused under the
agency of a single set of symbolic forms, turn out to be the same world,
producing thus that idiosyncratic transformation in one's sense of reality
to which Santayana refers in my epigraph. Whatever role divine intervention may or may not play in the creation of faith—and it is not the
business of the scientist to pronounce upon such matters one way or the
other—it is, primarily at least, out of the context of concrete acts of re-

ligious observance that religious conviction emerges on the human plane.

However, though any religious ritual, no matter how apparently automatic or conventional (if it is truly automatic or merely conventional it is not religious), involves this symbolic fusion of ethos and world view, it is mainly certain more elaborate and usually more public ones, ones in which a broad range of moods and motivations on the one hand and of metaphysical conceptions on the other are caught up, which shape the spiritual consciousness of a people. Employing a useful term introduced by Singer, we may call these full-blown ceremonies "cultural performances" and note that they represent not only the point at which the dispositional and conceptual aspects of religious life converge for the believer, but also the point at which the interaction between them can be most readily examined by the detached observer:

Whenever Madrasi Brahmans (and non-Brahmans, too, for that matter) wished to exhibit to me some feature of Hinduism, they always referred to, or invited me to see, a particular rite or ceremony in the life cycle, in a temple festival, or in the general sphere of religious and cultural performances. Reflecting on this in the course of my interviews and observations I found that the more abstract generalizations about Hinduism (my own as well as those I heard) could generally be checked, directly or indirectly, against these observable performances.[39]

Of course, all cultural performances are not religious performances, and the line between those that are and artistic, or even political, ones is often not so easy to draw in practice, for, like social forms, symbolic forms can serve multiple purposes. But the point is that, paraphrasing slightly, Indians—"and perhaps all peoples"—seem to think of their religion "as encapsulated in these discrete performances which they [can] exhibit to visitors and to themselves."[40] The mode of exhibition is however radically different for the two sorts of witness, a fact seemingly overlooked by those who would argue that "religion is a form of human art."[41] Where for "visitors" religious performances can, in the nature of the case, only be presentations of a particular religious perspective, and thus aesthetically appreciated or scientifically dissected,

[39] M. Singer, "The Cultural Pattern of Indian Civilization," *Far Eastern Quarterly* 15 (1955):23–26.

[40] M. Singer, "The Great Tradition in a Metropolitan Center: Madras," in *Traditional India,* ed. M. Singer (Philadelphia, 1958), pp. 140–182.

[41] R. Firth, *Elements of Social Organization* (London and New York, 1951), p. 250.

for participants they are in addition enactments, materializations, realizations of it—not only models of what they believe, but also models *for* the believing of it. In these plastic dramas men attain their faith as they portray it.

As a case in point, let me take a spectacularly theatrical cultural performance from Bali—that in which a terrible witch called Rangda engages in a ritual combat with an endearing monster called Barong.[42] Usually, but not inevitably presented on the occasion of a death temple celebration, the drama consists of a masked dance in which the witch —depicted as a wasted old widow, prostitute, and eater of infants— comes to spread plague and death upon the land and is opposed by the monster—depicted as a kind of cross between a clumsy bear, a silly puppy, and a strutting Chinese dragon. Rangda, danced by a single male, is a hideous figure. Her eyes bulge from her forehead like swollen boils. Her teeth become tusks curving up over her cheeks and fangs protruding down over her chin. Her yellowed hair falls down around her in a matted tangle. Her breasts are dry and pendulous dugs edged with hair, between which hang, like so many sausages, strings of colored entrails. Her long red tongue is a stream of fire. And as she dances she splays her dead-white hands, from which protrude ten-inch claw-like fingernails, out in front of her and utters unnerving shrieks of metallic laughter. Barong, danced by two men fore-and-aft in vaudeville horse fashion, is another matter. His shaggy sheepdog coat is hung with gold and mica ornaments that glitter in the half-light. He is adorned with flowers, sashes, feathers, mirrors, and a comical beard made from human hair. And though a demon too, his eyes also pop and he snaps his fanged jaws with seemly fierceness when faced with Rangda or other affronts to his dignity; the cluster of tinkling bells which hang from his absurdly arching tail somehow contrives to take most of the edge off his fearfulness. If Rangda is a satanic image, Barong is a farcical one, and their clash is a clash (an inconclusive one) between the malignant and the ludicrous.

---

[42] The Rangda–Barong complex has been extensively described and analyzed by a series of unusually gifted ethnographers and I shall make no attempt to present it here in more than schematic form. [See, for example, J. Belo, *Bali: Rangda and Barong* (New York, 1949); J. Belo, *Trance in Bali* (New York, 1960); B. DeZoete and W. Spies, *Dance and Drama in Bali* (London, 1938); G. Bateson and M. Mead, *Balinese Character* (New York, 1942); M. Covarrubias, *The Island of Bali* (New York, 1937).] Much of my interpretation of the complex rests on personal observations made in Bali during 1957–1958.

This odd counterpoint of implacable malice and low comedy pervades the whole performance. Rangda, clutching her magical white cloth, moves around in a slow stagger, now pausing immobile in thought or uncertainty, now lurching suddenly forward. The moment of her entry (one sees those terrible long-nailed hands first as she emerges through the split gateway at the top of a short flight of stone stairs) is one of terrific tension when it seems, to a "visitor" at least, that everyone is about to break and run in panic. She herself seems insane with fear and hatred as she screams deprecations at Barong amid the wild clanging of the gamelan. She may in fact go amok. I have myself seen Rangdas hurl themselves headlong into the gamelan or run frantically about in total confusion, being subdued and reoriented only by the combined force of a half-dozen spectators; and one hears many tales of amok Rangdas holding a whole village in terror for hours and of impersonators becoming permanently deranged by their experiences. But Barong, though he is charged with the same mana-like sacred power (*sakti* in Balinese) as Rangda, and his impersonators are also entranced, seems to have very great difficulty in being serious. He frolics with his retinue of demons (who add to the gaiety by indelicate pranks of their own), lies down on a metallaphone while it is being played or beats on a drum with his legs, moves in one direction in his front half and another in his rear or bends his segmented body into foolish contortions, brushes flies from his body or sniffs aromas in the air, and generally prances about in paroxysms of narcissistic vanity. The contrast is not absolute, for Rangda is sometimes momentarily comic as when she pretends to polish the mirrors on Barong's coat, and Barong becomes rather more serious after Rangda appears, nervously clacking his jaws at her and ultimately attacking her directly. Nor are the humorous and the horrible always kept rigidly separated, as in that strange scene in one section of the cycle in which several minor witches (disciples of Rangda) toss the corpse of a stillborn child around to the wild amusement of the audience; or another, no less strange, in which the sight of a pregnant woman alternating hysterically between tears and laughter while being knocked about by a group of gravediggers, seems for some reason excruciatingly funny. The twin themes of horror and hilarity find their purest expression in the two protagonists and their endless, indecisive struggle for dominance, but they are woven with deliberate intricacy through the whole texture of the drama. They—or rather the relations between them—are what it is about.

It is unnecessary to attempt a thoroughgoing description of a Rangda–Barong performance here. Such performances vary widely in detail, consist of several not too closely integrated parts, and in any case are so complex in structure as to defy easy summary. For our purposes, the main point to be stressed is that the drama is, for the Balinese, not merely a spectacle to be watched but a ritual to be enacted. There is no aesthetic distance here separating actors from audience and placing the depicted events in an unenterable world of illusion, and by the time a full-scale Rangda–Barong encounter has been concluded a majority, often nearly all, of the members of the group sponsoring it will have become caught up in it not just imaginatively but bodily. In one of Belo's examples I count upwards of seventy-five people—men, women, and children—taking part in the activity at some point or other, and thirty to forty participants is in no way unusual. As a performance, the drama is like a high mass, not like a presentation of *Murder in the Cathedral:* it is a drawing near, not a standing back.

In part, this entry into the body of the ritual takes place through the agency of the various supporting roles contained in it—minor witches, demons, various sorts of legendary and mythical figures—which selected villagers enact. But mostly it takes place through the agency of an extraordinarily developed capacity for psychological dissociation on the part of a very large segment of the population. A Rangda–Barong struggle is inevitably marked by anywhere from three or four to several dozen spectators becoming possessed by one or another demon, falling into violent trances "like firecrackers going off one after the other," [43] and, snatching up krisses, rushing to join the fray. Mass trance, spreading like a panic, projects the individual Balinese out of the commonplace world in which he usually lives into that most uncommonplace one in which Rangda and Barong live. To become entranced is, for the Balinese, to cross a threshold into another order of existence—the word for trance is *nadi,* from *dadi,* often translated "to become" but which might be even more simply rendered as "to be." And even those who, for whatever reasons, do not make this spiritual crossing are caught up in the proceedings, for it is they who must keep the frenzied activities of the entranced from getting out of hand by the application of physical restraint if they are ordinary men, by the sprinkling of holy water and the chanting of spells if they are priests. At its height a Rangda–Barong rite hovers, or at least seems to hover, on the brink of mass amok with

[43] Belo, *Trance in Bali.*

the diminishing band of the unentranced striving desperately (and, it seems, almost always successfully) to control the growing band of the entranced.

In its standard form—if it can be said to have a standard form—the performance begins with an appearance of Barong, prancing and preening, as a general prophylactic against what is to follow. Then may come various mythic scenes relating the story—not always precisely the same ones—upon which the performance is based, until finally Barong and then Rangda appear. Their battle begins. Barong drives Rangda back toward the gate of the death temple. But he has not the power to expel her completely, and he is in turn driven back toward the village. At length, when it seems as though Rangda will finally prevail, a number of entranced men rise, krisses in hand, and rush to support Barong. But as they approach Rangda (who has turned her back in meditation), she wheels upon them and, waving her *sakti* white cloth, leaves them comatose on the ground. Rangda then hastily retires (or is carried) to the temple, where she herself collapses, hidden from the aroused crowd which, my informants said, would kill her were it to see her in a helpless state. The Barong moves among the kris dancers and wakens them by snapping his jaws at them or nuzzling them with his beard. As they return, still entranced, to "consciousness," they are enraged by the disappearance of Rangda, and unable to attack her they turn their krisses (harmlessly because they are entranced) against their own chests in frustration. Usually sheer pandemonium breaks out at this point with members of the crowd, of both sexes, falling into trance all around the courtyard and rushing out to stab themselves, wrestle with one another, devour live chicks or excrement, wallow convulsively in the mud, and so on, while the nonentranced attempt to relieve them of their krisses and keep them at least minimally in order. In time, the trancers sink, one by one, into coma, from which they are aroused by the priests' holy water and the great battle is over—once more a complete stand-off. Rangda has not been conquered, but neither has she conquered.

One place to search for the meaning of this ritual is in the collection of myths, tales, and explicit beliefs which it supposedly enacts. However, not only are these various and variable—for some people Rangda is an incarnation of Durga, Siva's malignant consort; for others she is Queen Mahendradatta, a figure from a court legend set in eleventh century Java; for yet others, the spiritual leader of witches as the Brahmana Priest is the spiritual leader of men. Notions of who (or "what")

Barong is are equally diverse and even vaguer—but they seem to play only a secondary role in the Balinese' perception of the drama. It is in the direct encounter with the two figures in the context of the actual performance that the villager comes to know them as, so far as he is concerned, genuine realities. They are, then, not representations of anything, but presences. And when the villagers go into trance they become—*nadi*—themselves part of the realm in which those presences exist. To ask, as I once did, a man who has *been* Rangda whether he thinks she is real is to leave oneself open to the suspicion of idiocy.

The acceptance of authority that underlies the religious perspective that the ritual embodies thus flows from the enactment of the ritual itself. By inducing a set of moods and motivations—an ethos—and defining an image of cosmic order—a world view—by means of a single set of symbols, the performance makes the model *for* and model *of* aspects of religious belief mere transpositions of one another. Rangda evokes fear (as well as hatred, disgust, cruelty, horror, and, though I have not been able to treat the sexual aspects of the performance here, lust); but she also depicts it:

The fascination which the figure of the Witch holds for the Balinese imagination can only be explained when it is recognized that the Witch is not only a fear inspiring figure, but that she is Fear. Her hands with their long menacing finger-nails do not clutch and claw at her victims, although children who play at being witches do curl their hands in such gestures. But the Witch herself spreads her arms with palms out and her finger flexed backward, in the gesture the Balinese call *kapar,* a term which they apply to the sudden startled reaction of a man who falls from a tree. . . . Only when we see the Witch as herself afraid, as well as frightening, is it possible to explain her appeal, and the pathos which surrounds her as she dances, hairy, forbidding, tusked and alone, giving her occasional high eerie laugh.[44]

And on his side Barong not only induces laughter, he incarnates the Balinese version of the comic spirit—a distinctive combination of playfulness, exhibitionism, and extravagant love of elegance, which, along with fear, is perhaps the dominant motive in their life. The constantly recurring struggle of Rangda and Barong to an inevitable draw is thus—for the believing Balinese—both the formulation of a general religious conception and the authoritative experience which justifies, even compels, its acceptance.

[44] G. Bateson and M. Mead, *Balinese Character,* p. 36.

. . . that the moods and motivations seem uniquely realistic

But no one, not even a saint, lives in the world religious symbols formulate all of the time, and the majority of men live in it only at moments. The everyday world of common-sense objects and practical acts is, as Schutz says, the paramount reality in human experience—paramount in the sense that it is the world in which we are most solidly rooted, whose inherent actuality we can hardly question (however much we may question certain portions of it), and from whose pressures and requirements we can least escape.[45] A man, even large groups of men, may be aesthetically insensitive, religiously unconcerned, and unequipped to pursue formal scientific analysis, but he cannot be completely lacking in common sense and survive. The dispositions which religious rituals induce thus have their most important impact—from a human point of view—outside the boundaries of the ritual itself as they reflect back to color the individual's conception of the established world of bare fact. The peculiar tone that marks the Plains vision quest, the Manus confession, or the Javanese mystical exercise pervades areas of the life of these peoples far beyond the immediately religious, impressing upon them a distinctive style in the sense both of a dominant mood and a characteristic movement. The interweaving of the malignant and the comic, which the Rangda–Barong combat depicts, animates a very wide range of everyday Balinese behavior, much of which, like the ritual itself, has an air of candid fear narrowly contained by obsessive playfulness. Religion is sociologically interesting not because, as vulgar positivism would have it, it describes the social order (which, in so far as it does, it does not only very obliquely but very incompletely), but because, like environment, political power, wealth, jural obligation, personal affection, and a sense of beauty, it shapes it.

The movement back and forth between the religious perspective and the common-sense perspective is actually one of the more obvious empirical occurrences on the social scene, though, again, one of the most neglected by social anthropologists, virtually all of whom have seen it happen countless times. Religious belief has usually been presented as a homogeneous characteristic of an individual, like his place of residence, his occupational role, his kinship position, and so on. But religious belief in the midst of ritual, where it engulfs the total person, transporting

[45] Schutz, *The Problem of Social Reality,* p. 226ff.

him, so far as he is concerned, into another mode of existence, and religious belief as the pale, remembered reflection of that experience in the midst of everyday life are not precisely the same thing, and the failure to realize this has led to some confusion, most especially in connection with the so-called primitive-mentality problem. Much of the difficulty between Lévy-Bruhl and Malinowski on the nature of "native thought," for example, arises from a lack of full recognition of this distinction; for where the French philosopher was concerned with the view of reality savages adopted when taking a specifically religious perspective, the Polish-English ethnographer was concerned with that which they adopted when taking a strictly common-sense one.[46] Both perhaps vaguely sensed that they were not talking about exactly the same thing, but where they went astray was in failing to give a specific accounting of the way in which these two forms of "thought"—or, as I would rather say, these two modes of symbolic formulations—interacted, so that where Lévy-Bruhl's savages tended to live, despite his postludial disclaimers, in a world composed entirely of mystical encounters, Malinowski's tended to live, despite his stress on the functional importance of religion, in a world composed entirely of practical actions. They became reductionists (an idealist is as much of a reductionist as a materialist) in spite of themselves because they failed to see man as moving more or less easily, and very frequently, between radically contrasting ways of looking at the world, ways which are not continuous with one another but separated by cultural gaps across which Kierkegaardian leaps must be made in both directions:

There are as many innumerable kinds of different shock experiences as there are different finite provinces of meaning upon which I may bestow the accent of reality. Some instances are: the shock of falling asleep as the leap into the world of dreams; the inner transformation we endure if the curtain in the theatre rises as the transition to the world of the stageplay; the radical change in our attitude if, before a painting, we permit our visual field to be limited by what is within the frame as the passage into the pictorial world; our quandary relaxing into laughter, if, in listening to a joke, we are for a short time ready to accept the fictitious world of the jest as a reality in relation to which the world of our daily life takes on the character of foolishness; the child's turning toward his toy as the transition into the play-world; and so on. But also the religious experiences in all their varieties—for instance, Kierkegaard's experience of the "instant" as the leap into the religious sphere—are examples of such a shock, as well as the decision of the

[46] Malinowski, *Magic, Science and Religion*; L. Lévy-Bruhl, *How Natives Think* (New York, 1926).

scientist to replace all passionate participation in the affairs of "this world" by a disinterested [analytical] attitude.[47]

The recognition and exploration of the qualitative difference—an empirical, not a transcendental difference—between religion pure and religion applied, between an encounter with the supposedly "really real" and a viewing of ordinary experience in light of what that encounter seems to reveal, will, therefore, take us further toward an understanding of what a Bororo means when he says "I am a parakeet," or a Christian when he says "I am a sinner," than either a theory of primitive mysticism in which the commonplace world disappears into a cloud of curious ideas or of a primitive pragmatism in which religion disintegrates into a collection of useful fictions. The parakeet example, which I take from Percy, is a good one.[48] For, as he points out, it is unsatisfactory to say either that the Bororo thinks he is literally a parakeet (for he does not try to mate with other parakeets), that his statement is false or nonsense (for, clearly, he is not offering—or at least not only offering— the sort of class-membership argument which can be confirmed or refuted as, say, "I am a Bororo" can be confirmed or refuted), or yet again that it is false scientifically but true mythically (because that leads immediately to the pragmatic fiction notion which, as it denies the accolade of truth to "myth" in the very act of bestowing it, is internally self-contradictory). More coherently it would seem to be necessary to see the sentence as having a different sense in the context of the "finite province of meaning" which makes up the religious perspective and of that which makes up the common-sensical. In the religious, our Bororo is "really" a "parakeet," and given the proper ritual context might well "mate" with other "parakeets"—with metaphysical ones like himself, not commonplace ones such as those which fly bodily about in ordinary trees. In the common-sensical perspective he is a parakeet in the sense —I assume—that he belongs to a clan whose members regard the parakeet as their totem, a membership from which, given the fundamental nature of reality as the religious perspective reveals it, certain moral and practical consequences flow. A man who says he is a parakeet is, if he says it in normal conversation, saying that, as myth and ritual demonstrate, he is shot through with parakeetness and that this religious fact has some crucial social implications—we parakeets must stick to-

[47] Schutz, *The Problem of Social Reality,* p. 231.
[48] W. Percy, "The Symbolic Structure of Interpersonal Process," *Psychiatry* 24 (1961): 39–52.

gether, not marry one another, not eat mundane parakeets, and so on, for to do otherwise is to act against the grain of the whole universe. It is this placing of proximate acts in ultimate contexts that makes religion, frequently at least, socially so powerful. It alters, often radically, the whole landscape presented to common sense, alters it in such a way that the moods and motivations induced by religious practice seem themselves supremely practical, the only sensible ones to adopt given the way things "really" are.

Having ritually "lept" (the image is perhaps a bit too athletic for the actual facts—"slipped" might be more accurate) into the framework of meaning which religious conceptions define, and the ritual ended, returned again to the common-sense world, a man is—unless, as sometimes happens, the experience fails to register—changed. And as he is changed, so also is the common-sense world, for it is now seen as but the partial form of a wider reality which corrects and completes it.

But this correction and completion is not, as some students of "comparative religion" would have it, everywhere the same in content. The nature of the bias religion gives to ordinary life varies with the religion involved, with the particular dispositions induced in the believer by the specific conceptions of cosmic order he has come to accept. On the level of the "great" religions, organic distinctiveness is usually recognized, at times insisted upon to the point of zealotry. But even at its simplest folk and tribal levels—where the individuality of religious traditions has so often been dissolved into such desiccated types as "animism," "animatism," "totemism," "shamanism," "ancestor worship," and all the other insipid categories by means of which ethnographers of religion devitalize their data—the idiosyncratic character of how various groups of men behave because of what they believe they have experienced is clear. A tranquil Javanese would be no more at home in guilt-ridden Manus than an activist Crow would be in passionless Java. And for all the witches and ritual clowns in the world, Rangda and Barong are not generalized but thoroughly singular figurations of fear and gaiety. What men believe is as various as what they are—a proposition that holds with equal force when it is inverted.

It is this particularity of the impact of religious systems upon social systems (and upon personality systems) which renders general assessments of the value of religion in either moral or functional terms impossible. The sorts of moods and motivations which characterize a man who has just come from an Aztec human sacrifice are rather different from those of one who has just put off his Kachina mask. Even within the same society, what one "learns" about the essential pattern of life from a sorcery rite and from a commensal meal will have rather diverse effects on social and psychological functioning. One of the main methodological problems in writing about religion scientifically is to put aside at once the tone of the village atheist and that of the village preacher, as well as their more sophisticated equivalents, so that the social and psychological implications of particular religious beliefs can emerge in a clear and neutral light. And when that is done, overall questions about whether religion is "good" or "bad," "functional" or "dysfunctional," "ego strengthening" or "anxiety producing," disappear like the chimeras they are, and one is left with particular evaluations, assessments, and diagnoses in particular cases. There remains, of course, the hardly unimportant questions of whether this or that religious assertion is true, this or that religious experience genuine, or whether true religious assertions and genuine religious experiences are possible at all. But such questions cannot even be asked, much less answered, within the self-imposed limitations of the scientific perspective.

III

For an anthropologist, the importance of religion lies in its capacity to serve, for an individual or for a group, as a source of general, yet distinctive, conceptions of the world, the self, and the relations between them, on the one hand—its model *of* aspect—and of rooted, no less distinctive "mental" dispositions—its model *for* aspect—on the other. From these cultural functions flow, in turn, its social and psychological ones.

Religious concepts spread beyond their specifically metaphysical contexts to provide a framework of general ideas in terms of which a wide range of experience—intellectual, emotional, moral—can be given meaningful form. The Christian sees the Nazi movement against the background of The Fall which, though it does not, in a causal sense, explain it, places it in a moral, a cognitive, even an affective sense. An Azande sees the collapse of a granary upon a friend or relative against the background of a concrete and rather special notion of witchcraft and thus avoids the philosophical dilemmas as well as the psychological stress of indeterminism. A Javanese finds in the borrowed and reworked concept of *rasa* ("sense-taste-feeling-meaning") a means by which to "see" choreographic, gustatory, emotional, and political phenomena in a new light. A synopsis of cosmic order, a set of religious beliefs, is also a gloss upon the mundane world of social relationships and psychological events. It renders them graspable.

But more than gloss, such beliefs are also a template. They do not merely interpret social and psychological processes in cosmic terms—in which case they would be philosophical, not religious—but they shape them. In the doctrine of original sin is embedded also a recommended attitude toward life, a recurring mood, and a persisting set of motivations. The Azande learns from witchcraft conceptions not just to understand apparent "accidents" as not accidents at all, but to react to these spurious accidents with hatred for the agent who caused them and to proceed against him with appropriate resolution. *Rasa,* in addition to being a concept of truth, beauty, and goodness, is also a preferred mode of experiencing, a kind of affectless detachment, a variety of bland aloofness, an unshakable calm. The moods and motivations a religious orientation produces cast a derivative, lunar light over the solid features of a people's secular life.

The tracing of the social and psychological role of religion is thus not so much a matter of finding correlations between specific ritual acts and specific secular social ties—though these correlations do, of course, exist and are very worth continued investigation, especially if we can contrive something novel to say about them. More, it is a matter of understanding how it is that men's notions, however implicit, of the "really real" and the dispositions these notions induce in them, color their sense of the reasonable, the practical, the humane, and the moral. How far they do so (for in many societies religion's effects seem quite circumscribed, in others completely pervasive), how deeply they do so (for some men, and groups of men, seem to wear their religion lightly so far as the secular world goes, while others seem to apply their faith to each occasion, no matter how trivial), and how effectively they do so (for the width of the gap between what religion recommends and what people actually do is most variable cross-culturally)—all these are crucial issues in the comparative sociology and psychology of religion. Even the degree to which religious systems themselves are developed seems to vary extremely widely, and not merely on a simple evolutionary basis. In one society, the level of elaboration of symbolic formulations of ultimate actuality may reach extraordinary degrees of complexity and systematic articulation; in another, no less developed socially, such formulations may remain primitive in the true sense, hardly more than congeries of fragmentary by-beliefs and isolated images, of sacred reflexes and spiritual pictographs. One need only think of the Australians and the Bushmen, the Toradja and the Alorese, the Hopi and the Apache, the Hindus and the Romans, or even the Italians and the Poles, to see that degree of religious articulateness is not a constant even as between societies of similar complexity.

The anthropological study of religion is therefore a two-stage operation: first, an analysis of the system of meanings embodied in the symbols which make up the religion proper, and, second, the relating of these systems to social-structural and psychological processes. My dissatisfaction with so much of contemporary social anthropological work in religion is not that it concerns itself with the second stage, but that it neglects the first, and in so doing takes for granted what most needs to be elucidated. To discuss the role of ancestor worship in regulating political succession, of sacrificial feasts in defining kinship obligations, of spirit worship in scheduling agricultural practices, of divination in reinforcing social control, or of initiation rites in propelling personality maturation, are in no sense unimportant endeavors, and I am not recommending they be abandoned for the kind of jejune cabalism into which symbolic analysis of exotic faiths can so easily fall. But to attempt them with but the most general, common-sense view of what ancestor worship, animal sacrifice, spirit worship, divination, or initiation rites are as religious patterns seems to me not particularly promising. Only when we have a theoretical analysis of symbolic action comparable in sophistication to that we now have for social and psychological action, will we be able to cope effectively with those aspects of social and psychological life in which religion (or art, or science, or ideology) plays a determinant role.

Chapter 5 / Ethos,
World View, and the
Analysis of Sacred Symbols

꧁꧂

I

Religion is never merely metaphysics. For all peoples the forms, vehicles, and objects of worship are suffused with an aura of deep moral seriousness. The holy bears within it everywhere a sense of intrinsic obligation: it not only encourages devotion, it demands it; it not only induces intellectual assent, it enforces emotional commitment. Whether it be formulated as *mana,* as *Brahma,* or as the Holy Trinity, that which is set apart as more than mundane is inevitably considered to have far-reaching implications for the direction of human conduct. Never merely metaphysics, religion is never merely ethics either. The source of its moral vitality is conceived to lie in the fidelity with which it expresses the fundamental nature of reality. The powerfully coercive "ought" is felt to grow out of a comprehensive factual "is," and in such a way religion grounds the most specific requirements of human action in the most general contexts of human existence.

In recent anthropological discussion, the moral (and aesthetic) aspects of a given culture, the evaluative elements, have commonly been summed up in the term "ethos," while the cognitive, existential aspects have been designated by the term "world view." A people's ethos is the tone, character, and quality of their life, its moral and aesthetic style and mood; it is the underlying attitude toward themselves and their world that life reflects. Their world view is their picture of the way things in sheer actuality are, their concept of nature, of self, of society. It contains their most comprehensive ideas of order. Religious belief and ritual confront and mutually confirm one another; the ethos is made intellectually reasonable by being shown to represent a way of life implied by the actual state of affairs which the world view describes, and the world view is made emotionally acceptable by being presented as an image of an actual state of affairs of which such a way of life is an authentic expression. This demonstration of a meaningful relation between the values a people holds and the general order of existence within which it finds itself is an essential element in all religions, however those values or that order be conceived. Whatever else religion may be, it is in part an attempt (of an implicit and directly felt rather than explicit and consciously thought-about sort) to conserve the fund of general meanings in terms of which each individual interprets his experience and organizes his conduct.

But meanings can only be "stored" in symbols: a cross, a crescent, or a feathered serpent. Such religious symbols, dramatized in rituals or related in myths, are felt somehow to sum up, for those for whom they are resonant, what is known about the way the world is, the quality of the emotional life it supports, and the way one ought to behave while in it. Sacred symbols thus relate an ontology and a cosmology to an aesthetics and a morality: their peculiar power comes from their presumed ability to identify fact with value at the most fundamental level, to give to what is otherwise merely actual, a comprehensive normative import. The number of such synthesizing symbols is limited in any culture, and though in theory we might think that a people could construct a wholly autonomous value system independent of any metaphysical referent, an ethics without ontology, we do not in fact seem to have found such a people. The tendency to synthesize world view and ethos at some level, if not logically necessary, is at least empirically coercive; if it is not philosophically justified, it is at least pragmatically universal.

Let me give as an example of this fusion of the existential and the normative a quotation from one of James Walker's Oglala (Sioux) informants, which I find in Paul Radin's neglected classic, *Primitive Man as a Philosopher:*

The Oglala believe the circle to be sacred because the great spirit caused everything in nature to be round except stone. Stone is the implement of destruction. The sun and the sky, the earth and the moon are round like a shield, though the sky is deep like a bowl. Everything that breathes is round like the stem of a plant. Since the great spirit has caused everything to be round mankind should look upon the circle as sacred, for it is the symbol of all things in nature except stone. It is also the symbol of the circle that makes the edge of the world and therefore of the four winds that travel there. Consequently it is also the symbol of the year. The day, the night, and the moon go in a circle above the sky. Therefore the circle is a symbol of these divisions of time and hence the symbol of all time.

For these reasons the Oglala make their *tipis* circular, their camp-circle circular, and sit in a circle at all ceremonies. The circle is also the symbol of the *tipi* and of shelter. If one makes a circle for an ornament and it is not divided in any way, it should be understood as the symbol of the world and of time.[1]

Here is a subtle formulation of the relation between good and evil, and of their grounding in the very nature of reality. Circle and eccentric form, sun and stone, shelter and war are segregated into pairs of disjunct classes whose significance is aesthetic, moral, and ontological. The reasoned articulateness of this statement is atypical: for most Oglala the circle, whether found in nature, painted on a buffalo skin, or enacted in a sun dance, is but an unexamined luminous symbol whose meaning is intuitively sensed, not consciously interpreted. But the power of the symbol, analyzed or not, clearly rests on its comprehensiveness, on its fruitfulness in ordering experience. Again and again the idea of a sacred circle, a natural form with a moral import, yields, when applied to the world within which the Oglala lives, new meanings; continually it connects together elements within their experience which would otherwise seem wholly disparate and, wholly disparate, incomprehensible.

The common roundness of a human body and plant stem, of a moon and a shield, of a *tipi* and a camp-circle, give them a vaguely conceived but intensely felt significance. And this meaningful common element, once abstracted, can then be employed for ritual purposes—as when in a peace ceremony the pipe, the symbol of social solidarity, moves deliberately in a perfect circle from one smoker to the next, the purity of the form evoking the beneficence of the spirits—or to construe mythologically the peculiar paradoxes and anomalies of moral experience, as when one sees in a round stone the shaping power of good over evil.

[1] P. Radin, *Primitive Man as a Philosopher* (New York, 1957), p. 227.

II

It is a cluster of sacred symbols, woven into some sort of ordered whole, which makes up a religious system. For those who are committed to it, such a religious system seems to mediate genuine knowledge, knowledge of the essential conditions in terms of which life must, of necessity, be lived. Particularly where these symbols are uncriticized, historically or philosophically, as they are in most of the world's cultures, individuals who ignore the moral-aesthetic norms the symbols formulate, who follow a discordant style of life, are regarded not so much as evil as stupid, insensitive, unlearned, or in the case of extreme dereliction, mad. In Java, where I have done field work, small children, simpletons, boors, the insane, and the flagrantly immoral are all said to be "not yet Javanese," and, not yet Javanese, not yet human. Unethical behavior is referred to as "uncustomary," the more serious crimes (incest, sorcery, murder) are commonly accounted for by an assumed lapse of reason, the less serious ones by a comment that the culprit "does not know order," and the word for "religion" and that for "science" are the same. Morality has thus the air of simple realism, of practical wisdom; religion supports proper conduct by picturing a world in which such conduct is only common sense.

It is only common sense because between ethos and world view, between the approved style of life and the assumed structure of reality, there is conceived to be a simple and fundamental congruence such that they complete one another and lend one another meaning. In Java, for example, this view is summed up in a concept one hears continually invoked, that of *tjotjog*. *Tjotjog* means to fit, as a key does in a lock, as an efficacious medicine does to a disease, as a solution does to an arithmetic problem, as a man does with the woman he marries (if he does not, they will divorce). If your opinion agrees with mine we *tjotjog;* if the meaning of my name fits my character (and if it brings me luck), it is said to be *tjotjog*. Tasty food, correct theories, good manners, comfortable surroundings, gratifying outcomes are all *tjotjog*. In the broadest and most abstract sense, two items *tjotjog* when their coincidence forms a coherent pattern which gives to each a significance and a value it does not in itself have. There is implied here a contrapuntal view of the universe in which that which is important is what natural relationship the separate elements have to one another, how they must be arranged to strike a chord and to avoid a dissonance. And, as in harmony, the ultimately correct relationships are fixed, determinate, and knowable, so religion, like harmony, is ultimately a kind of practical science, producing value out of fact as music is produced out of sound. In its specificity, *tjotjog* is a peculiarly Javanese idea, but the notion that life takes on its true import when human actions are tuned to cosmic conditions is widespread.

The sort of counterpoint between style of life and fundamental reality which the sacred symbols formulate varies from culture to culture. For the Navaho, an ethic prizing calm deliberateness, untiring persistence, and dignified caution complements an image of nature as tremendously powerful, mechanically regular, and highly dangerous. For the French, a logical legalism is a response to the notion that reality is rationally structured, that first principles are clear, precise, and unalterable and so need only be discerned, memorized, and deductively applied to concrete cases. For the Hindus, a transcendental moral determinism in which one's social and spiritual status in a future incarnation is an automatic outcome of the nature of one's action in the present, is completed by a ritualistic duty-ethic bound to caste. In itself, either side, the normative or the metaphysical, is arbitrary, but taken together they form a gestalt with a peculiar kind of inevitability; a French ethic in a Navaho world, or a Hindu one in a French world would seem only quixotic, for it would lack the air of naturalness and simple factuality which it has in its own context. It is this air of the factual, of describing, after all, the genuinely reasonable way to live which, given the facts of life, is the primary source of such an ethic's authoritativeness. What all sacred symbols assert is that the good for man is to live realistically; where they differ is in the vision of reality they construct.

However, it is not only positive values that sacred symbols dramatize, but negative ones as well. They point not only toward the existence of good but also of evil, and toward the conflict between them. The so-called problem of evil is a matter of formulating in world-view terms the actual nature of the destructive forces within the self and outside of it, of interpreting murder, crop failure, sickness, earthquakes, poverty, and oppression in such a way that it is possible to come to some sort of terms with them. Declaring evil fundamentally unreal—as in Indian religions and some versions of Christianity—is but one, rather uncommon, solution to the problem; more often, the reality of evil is accepted and characterized positively, and an attitude toward it—resignation, active opposition, hedonistic escape, self-recrimination and repentance, or a humble plea for mercy—is enjoined as reasonable and proper, given its nature. Among the African Azande, where all natural misfortune (death, illness, crop failure) is seen as caused by the hatred of one man for another acting mechanically through witchcraft, the attitude toward evil is a straightforward and practical one: it is to be dealt with by means of reliably established divination in order to discover the witch, and proven methods of social pressure to force him to abandon his attack, or failing this, by effective vengeance-magic to kill him. Among the Melanesian Manus, the conception that illness, death, or financial failure are the result of a secret sin (adultery, stealing, lying) which has offended the moral sensibilities of the household spirit is coupled with an emphasis on public confession and repentance as the rational way to cope with evil. For the Javanese, evil results from unregulated passion and is resisted by detachment and self-control. Thus, both what a people prizes and what it fears and hates are depicted in its world view, symbolized in its religion, and in turn expressed in the whole quality of its life. Its ethos is distinctive not merely in terms of the sort of nobility it celebrates, but also in terms of the sort of baseness it condemns; its vices are as stylized as its virtues.

The force of a religion in supporting social values rests, then, on the ability of its symbols to formulate a world in which those values, as well as the forces opposing their realization, are fundamental ingredients. It represents the power of the human imagination to construct an image of reality in which, to quote Max Weber, "events are not just there and happen, but they have a meaning and happen because of that meaning." The need for such a metaphysical grounding for values seems to vary quite widely in intensity from culture to culture and from individual to individual, but the tendency to desire some sort of factual basis for one's commitments seems practically universal; mere conventionalism satisfies few people in any culture. However its role may differ at various times, for various individuals, and in various cultures, religion, by fusing ethos and world view, gives to a set of social values what they perhaps most need to be coercive: an appearance of objectivity. In sacred rituals and myths values are portrayed not as subjective human preferences but as the imposed conditions for life implicit in a world with a particular structure.

III

The sort of symbols (or symbol complexes) regarded by a people as sacred varies very widely. Elaborate initiation rites, as among the Australians; complex philosophical tales, as among the Maori; dramatic shamanistic exhibitions, as among the Eskimo; cruel human sacrifice rites, as among the Aztecs; obsessive curing ceremonies, as among the Navaho; large communal feasts, as among various Polynesian groups—all these patterns and many more seem to one people or another to sum up most powerfully what it knows about living. Nor is there commonly but one such complex: Malinowski's famous Trobrianders seem equally concerned with the rituals of gardening and those of trade. In a complex civilization such as that of the Javanese—in which Hinduistic, Islamic, and pagan influences all remain very strong—one could choose any of several symbol complexes as revealing one or another aspect of the integration of ethos and world view. But perhaps the clearest and most direct insight into the relation between Javanese values and Javanese metaphysics can be gained through a brief analysis of one of the most deeply rooted and highly developed of their art forms which is at the same time a religious rite: the shadow-puppet play, or *wajang.*

The shadow play is called so because the puppets, which are flat cutouts of leather, painted in golds, reds, blues, and blacks, are made to cast large shadows on a white screen. The *dalang,* as the puppeteer is called, sits on a mat in front of the screen, with a *gamelan* percussion orchestra behind him, an oil lamp hanging over his head. A banana tree trunk lies horizontally in front of him into which the puppets, each of them fastened to a tortoiseshell handle, are stuck. A performance lasts a whole night. As the play progresses, the *dalang* takes and replaces characters from the tree trunk as he needs them, holding them up in either hand over his head and interposing them between the light and the screen. From the *dalang's* side of the screen—where traditionally only the men were permitted to sit—one sees the puppets themselves, their shadows rising up dominant on the screen behind them; from the reverse side of the screen—where the women and children sit—one sees their shadows only.

The stories dramatized are mostly episodes taken from the Indian epic Mahabarata, somewhat adapted and placed in a Javanese setting.

(Stories from the Ramayana are sometimes dramatized, but they are less popular.) In this cycle there are three major groups of characters. First, there are the gods and goddesses, headed by Siva and his wife Durga. As in the Greek epics, the gods are far from uniformly righteous, are marked by human frailties and human passions, and seem peculiarly interested in the things of this world. Second, there are the kings and nobles, who are, in theory, the ancestors of the present-day Javanese. The two most important groups of these nobles are the Pendawas and the Korawas. The Pendawas are the famous five hero brothers—Yudistira, Bima, Arjuna, and the identical twins, Nakula and Sadéwa—who are usually accompanied, as a general advisor and protector, by Krisna, an incarnation of Visnu. The Korawas, of whom there are a hundred, are cousins of the Pendawas. They have usurped the kingdom of Ngastina from them, and it is the struggle over this disputed country which provides the major theme of the *wajang;* a struggle which culminates in the great Bratajuda war of kinsmen, as related in the Bhagavad Gita, in which the Korawas are defeated by the Pendawas. And, third, there are those Javanese additions to the original Hindu cast of characters, the great low clowns—Semar, Petruk, and Garèng, constant companions of the Pendawas, at once their servants and their protectors. Semar, the father of the other two, is actually a god in all-too-human form, a brother to Siva, king of the gods. The guardian spirit of all Javanese from their first appearance until the end of time, this gross and clumsy fool is perhaps the most important figure in the whole *wajang* mythology.

The types of action characteristic of the *wajang* also are three: there are the "talking" episodes in which two groups of opposed nobles confront one another and discuss (the *dalang* imitates all the voices) the issues between them; there are the fighting episodes, in which diplomacy having failed, the two groups of nobles fight (the *dalang* knocks the puppets together and kicks a clapper with his foot to symbolize the sounds of war); and there are the slapstick comic scenes, in which the clowns mock the nobles, each other, and, if the *dalang* is clever, members of the audience or the local powers-that-be. Generally, the three sorts of episodes are differentially distributed over the course of the evening. The declamatory scenes are mostly toward the beginning, the comic ones toward the middle, and the war toward the end. From nine until midnight, the political leaders of the various kingdoms confront one another and state the framework of the story—a *wajang* hero wishes to marry the daughter of a neighboring king, a subjugated country wants its freedom, or whatever. From midnight until three o'clock or so difficulties of some sort set in—someone else is bidding for the daughter's hand, the imperialist country refuses freedom to its colony. And, finally, these difficulties are resolved in the last section, ending at dawn, inevitably, by a war in which the heroes triumph—an action followed by a brief celebration of the accomplished marriage or the achieved freedom. Western-educated Javanese intellectuals often compare the *wajang* to a sonata; it opens with an exposition of a theme, follows with a development and complication of it, and ends with its resolution and recapitulation.

Another comparison which, offhand, strikes the Western observer is with Shakespeare's chronicle plays. The long formal scenes in the courts with the messengers coming and going, interspersed with short, breathless transitional scenes in the woods or along the road, the double plot, the clowns speaking a rough common language full of worldly-wise ethics, caricaturing the forms of action of the great nobles, who speak an elevated language full of apostrophes to honor, justice, and duty, the final war, which, like those at Shrewsbury and Agincourt, leaves the vanquished beaten but still noble—all these suggest Shakespeare's historical dramas. But the world view the *wajang* expresses, despite the surface similarities in the two feudal codes, is hardly Elizabethan at base. It is not the external world of principalities and powers which provides the main setting for human action, but the internal one of sentiments and desires. Reality is looked for not outside the self, but within it; consequently what the *wajang* dramatizes is not a philosophical politics but a metaphysical psychology.

For the Javanese (or at least for those of them in whose thought the influence of Java's Hindu-Buddhist period from the second to the fifteenth centuries still is dominant), the flow of subjective experience, taken in all its phenomenological immediacy, presents a microcosm of the universe generally; in the depths of the fluid interior world of thought-and-emotion they see reflected ultimate reality itself. This inward-looking sort of world view is best expressed in a concept the Javanese have also borrowed from India and also peculiarly reinterpreted: *rasa*. *Rasa* has two primary meanings: "feeling" and "meaning." As "feeling" it is one of the traditional Javanese five senses—seeing, hearing, talking, smelling, and feeling, and it includes within itself three aspects of "feeling" that our view of the five senses separates: taste on the tongue, touch on the body, and emotional "feeling" within the "heart" like sadness and happiness. The taste of a banana is its *rasa;* a hunch is a *rasa;* a pain is a *rasa;* and so is a passion. As "meaning," *rasa* is applied to the words in a letter, in a poem, or even in common speech to indicate the between-the-lines type of indirection and allusive suggestion that is so important in Javanese communication and social intercourse. And it is given the same application to behavioral acts generally: to indicate the implicit import, the connotative "feeling" of dance movements, polite gestures, and so forth. But in this second, semantic sense, it also means "ultimate significance"—the deepest meaning at which one arrives by dint of mystical effort and whose clarification resolves all the ambiguities of mundane existence. *Rasa,* said one of my most articulate informants, is the same as life; whatever lives has *rasa* and whatever has *rasa* lives. To translate such a sentence one could only render it twice: whatever lives feels and whatever feels lives; or: whatever lives has meaning and whatever has meaning lives.

By taking *rasa* to mean both "feeling" and "meaning," the more speculatively inclined among the Javanese have been able to develop a highly sophisticated phenomenological analysis of subjective experience to which everything else can be tied. Because fundamentally "feeling" and "meaning" are one, and therefore the ultimate religious experience taken *subjectively* is also the ultimate religious truth taken *objectively,* an empirical analysis of inward perception yields at the same time a metaphysical analysis of outward reality. This being granted— and the actual discriminations, categorizations, and connections made are often both subtle and detailed—then the characteristic way in which human action comes to be considered, from either a moral or an aesthetic point of view, is in terms of the emotional life of the individual who experiences it. This is true whether this action is seen from within as one's own behavior or from without as that of someone else: the more refined one's feelings, then the more profound one's understanding, the more elevated one's moral character, and the more beautiful one's external aspect, in clothes, movements, speech, and so on. The management of the individual's emotional economy becomes, therefore, his primary concern, in terms of which all else is ultimately rationalized. The spiritually enlightened man guards well his psychological equilibrium and makes a constant effort to maintain its placid stability. His inner life must be, in a simile repeatedly employed, like a still pool of clear water to the bottom of which one can easily see. The individual's proximate aim is, thus, emotional quiescence, for passion is crude feeling, fit for children, animals, madmen, primitives, and foreigners. But his ultimate aim, which this quiescence makes possible, is gnosis—the direct comprehension of the ultimate *rasa*.

Javanese religion (or at least this variant of it) is consequently mystical: God is found by means of spiritual discipline, in the depths of the self as pure *rasa*. And Javanese ethics (and aesthetics) are, correspondingly, affect-centered without being hedonistic: emotional equanimity, a certain flatness of affect, a strange inner stillness, is the prized psychological state, the mark of a truly noble character. One must attempt to get beyond the emotions of everyday life to the genuine feeling-meaning which lies within us all. Happiness and unhappiness are, after all, just the same. You shed tears when you laugh and also when you cry. And, besides, they imply one another: happy now, unhappy later; unhappy now, happy later. The reasonable, prudent, "wise" man strives not for happiness, but for a tranquil detachment which frees him from his endless oscillation between gratification and frustration. Similarly, Javanese etiquette, which comprises almost the whole of this morality, focuses around the injunction not to disturb the equilibrium of another by sudden gestures, loud speech, or startling, erratic actions of any sort, mainly because so doing will cause the other in turn to act erratically and so upset one's own balance. On the world-view side, there are yoga-like mystical techniques (meditation, staring at candles, repeating set words or phrases) and highly involved speculative theories of the emotions and their relations to sickness, natural objects, social institutions, and so on. On the ethos side, there is a moral stress on subdued dress, speech, and gesture, on refined sensitivity to small changes in the emotional state both of oneself and of others, and on a stable, highly regularized predictability of behavior. "If you start off north, go north," a Javanese proverb says, "don't turn east, west, or south." Both religion and ethics, both mysticism and politesse, thus point to the same end: a detached tranquility which is proof against disturbance from either within or without.

But, unlike India, this tranquillity is not to be gained by a retreat from the world and from society, but must be achieved while in it. It is a this-worldly, even practical, mysticism, as expressed in the following composite quotation from two Javanese petty traders who are members of a mystical society:

He said that the society was concerned with teaching you not to pay too much attention to worldly things, not to care too much about the things of everyday life. He said this is very difficult to do. His wife, he said, was not yet able to do it much, and she agreed with him, e.g., she still likes to ride in motorcars while he doesn't care; he can take them or leave them alone. It takes much long study and meditation. For example, you have to get so that if someone comes to buy cloth you don't care if he buys it or not . . . and you don't get your emotions really involved in the problems of commerce, but just think of God. The society wants to turn people toward God and avoids any strong attachments to everyday life.

. . . Why did he meditate? He said it was only to make the heart peaceful, to make you calm inside, so you will not be easily upset. For example, if you're selling cloth and are upset you may sell a piece of cloth for forty rupiah when it cost you sixty. If a person comes here and my mind is not calm, well then I can't sell him anything. . . . I said, well, why do you have a meeting, why not meditate at home? And he said, well, in the first place you are not supposed to achieve peace by withdrawing from society; you are supposed to stay in society and mix with people, only with peace in your heart.

This fusion between a mystical-phenomenological world view and an etiquette-centered ethos is expressed in the *wajang* in various ways. First, it appears most directly in terms of an explicit iconography. The five Pendawas are commonly interpreted as standing for the five senses which the individual must unite into one undivided psychological force in order to achieve gnosis. Meditation demands a "cooperation" among the senses as close as that among the hero brothers, who act as one in all they do. Or the shadows of the puppets are identified with the outward behavior of man, the puppets themselves with his inward self, so that in him as in them the visible pattern of conduct is a direct outcome of an underlying psychological reality. The very design of the puppets has explicit symbolic significance: in Bima's red, white, and black sarong, the red is usually taken to indicate courage, the white purity, the black fixity of will. The various tunes played on the accompanying *gamelan* orchestra each symbolize a certain emotion; similarly with the poems the *dalang* sings at various points in the play, and so on. Second, the fusion often appears as parable, as in the story of Bima's quest for the "clear water." After slaying many monsters in his wanderings in search of this water which he has been told will make him invulnerable, he meets a god as big as his little finger who is an exact replica of himself. Entering through the mouth of this mirror-image midget, he sees inside the god's body the whole world, complete in every detail, and upon emerging he is told by the god that there is no "clear water" as such, that the source of his own strength is within himself, after which he goes off to meditate. And third, the moral content of the play is sometimes interpreted analogically: the *dalang*'s absolute control over the puppets is said to parallel God's over men; or the alternation of polite speeches and violent wars is said to parallel modern international relationships, where so long as diplomats continue talking, peace prevails, but when talks break down, war follows.

But neither icons, parables, nor moral analogies are the main means by which the Javanese synthesis is expressed in the *wajang;* for the play as a whole is commonly perceived to be but a dramatization of individual subjective experience in terms at once moral and factual:

He [an elementary schoolteacher] said that the main purpose of the *wajang* was to draw a picture of inner thought and feeling, to give an external form to internal feeling. He said that more specifically it pictured the eternal conflict in the individual between what he wanted to do and what he felt he ought to do. Suppose you want to steal something. Well, at the same time something inside you tells you not to do it, restrains you, controls you. That which wants to do it is called the will; that which restrains is called the ego. All such tendencies threaten every day to ruin the individual, to destroy his thought and upset his behavior. These tendencies are called *goda,* which means something which plagues or teases someone or something. For example, you go to a coffee-shop where people are eating. They invite you to join them, and so you have a struggle within—should I eat with them . . . no, I've already eaten and I will be over full . . . but the food looks good . . . etc. . . . etc.

Well, in the *wajang* the various plagues, wishes, etc.—the *godas*—are represented by the hundred Korawas, and the ability to control oneself is represented by their cousins, the five Pendawas and by Krisna. The stories are ostensibly about a struggle over land. The reason for this is so the stories will seem real to the onlookers, so the abstract elements in the *rasa* can be represented in concrete external elements which will attract the audience and seem real to them and still communicate its inner message. For example, the *wajang* is full of war and this war, which occurs and reoccurs, is really supposed to represent the inner war which goes on continually in every person's subjective life between his base and his refined impulses.

Once again, this formulation is more self-conscious than most; the average man "enjoys" the *wajang* without explicitly interpreting its meaning. Yet, in the same way as the circle organizes Oglala experience, whether the individual Sioux is able to explicate its significance, or indeed has any interest in doing so, so the sacred symbols of the *wajang*—the music, characters, the action itself—give form to the ordinary Javanese experience.

For example, each of the three older Pendawas are commonly held to display a different sort of emotional-moral dilemma, centering around one or another of the central Javanese virtues. Yudistira, the eldest, is too compassionate. He is unable to rule his country effectively because when someone asks him for his land, his wealth, his food, he simply gives it out of pity, leaving himself powerless, poor, or starving. His enemies continually take advantage of his mercifulness to deceive him and to escape his justice. Bima, on the other hand, is single-minded, steadfast. Once he forms an intention, he follows it out straight to its conclusion; he doesn't look aside, doesn't turn off or idle along the way—he "goes north." As a result, he is often rash, and blunders into difficulties he could as well have avoided. Arjuna, the third brother, is perfectly just. His goodness comes from the fact that he opposes evil, that he shelters people from injustice, that he is coolly courageous in fighting for the right. But he lacks a sense of mercy, of sympathy for wrongdoers. He applies a divine moral code to human activity, and so he is often cold, cruel, or brutal in the name of justice. The resolution of these three dilemmas of virtue is the same: mystical insight. With a genuine comprehension of the realities of the human situation, a true perception of the ultimate *rasa,* comes the ability to combine Yudistira's compassion, Bima's will to action, and Arjuna's sense of justice into a truly moral outlook, an outlook which brings an emotional detachment and an inner peace in the midst of the world of flux, yet permits and demands a struggle for order and justice within such a world. And it is such a unification that the unshakable solidarity among the Pendawas in the play, continually rescuing one another from the defects of their virtues, clearly demonstrates.

But what, finally, of Semar, in whom so many oppositions seem to meet—the figure who is both god and clown, man's guardian spirit and his servant, the most spiritually refined inwardly and the most rough-looking outwardly? Again one thinks of the chronicle plays and of, in this case, Falstaff. Like Falstaff, Semar is a symbolic father to the play's heroes. Like Falstaff, he is fat, funny, and worldly-wise; and, like Falstaff, he seems to provide in his vigorous amoralism a general criticism of the very values the drama affirms. Both figures, perhaps, provide a reminder-that, despite overproud assertions to the contrary by religious fanatics and moral absolutists, no completely adequate and comprehensive human world view is possible, and behind all the pretense to absolute and ultimate knowledge, the sense for the irrationality of human life, for the fact that it is unlimitable, remains. Semar reminds the noble and refined Pendawas of their own humble, animal origins.

He resists any attempt to turn human beings into gods and to end the world of natural contingency by a flight to the divine world of absolute order, a final stilling of the eternal psychological–metaphysical struggle.

In one *wajang* story, Siva comes down to earth incarnated as a mystical teacher in an attempt to bring the Pendawas and Korawas together, to arrange a negotiated peace between them. He is succeeding quite well, opposed only by Semar. Arjuna is therefore instructed by Siva to kill Semar so that the Pendawas and Korawas will be able to get together and end their eternal struggle. Arjuna does not want to kill Semar, whom he loves, but he wishes a just solution to the differences between the two groups of cousins and so goes to Semar to murder him. Semar says: so this is how you treat me after I have followed you everywhere, served you loyally, and loved you. This is the most poignant point in the play and Arjuna is deeply ashamed; but true to his idea of justice, he persists in his duty. Semar says: all right, I will burn myself. He builds a bonfire and stands in it. But instead of dying, he is transformed into his godly form and defeats Siva in combat. Then the war between the Korawas and the Pendawas begins again.

Not all people have, perhaps, so well developed a sense for the necessary note of irrationality in any world view, and thus for the essential insolubility of the problem of evil. But whether in the form of a trickster, a clown, a belief in witchcraft, or a concept of original sin, the presence of such a symbolic reminder of the hollowness of human pretensions to religious or moral infallibility is perhaps the surest sign of spiritual maturity.

IV

The view of man as a symbolizing, conceptualizing, meaning-seeking animal, which has become increasingly popular both in the social sciences and in philosophy over the past several years, opens up a whole new approach not only to the analysis of religion as such, but to the understanding of the relations between religion and values. The drive to make sense out of experience, to give it form and order, is evidently as real and as pressing as the more familiar biological needs. And, this being so, it seems unnecessary to continue to interpret symbolic activities—religion, art, ideology—as nothing but thinly disguised expressions of something other than what they seem to be: attempts to provide orientation for an organism which cannot live in a world it is unable to understand. If symbols, to adapt a phrase of Kenneth Burke's, are strategies for encompassing situations, then we need to give more attention to how people define situations and how they go about coming to terms with them. Such a stress does not imply a removal of beliefs and values from their psychobiological and social contexts into a realm of "pure meaning," but it does imply a greater emphasis on the analysis of such beliefs and values in terms of concepts explicitly designed to deal with symbolic material.

The concepts used here, ethos and world view, are vague and imprecise; they are a kind of prototheory, forerunners, it is to be hoped, of a more adequate analytical framework. But even with them, anthropologists are beginning to develop an approach to the study of values which can clarify rather than obscure the essential processes involved in the normative regulation of behavior. One almost certain result of such an empirically oriented, theoretically sophisticated, symbol-stressing approach to the study of values is the decline of analyses which attempt to describe moral, aesthetic, and other normative activities in terms of theories based not on the observation of such activities but on logical considerations alone. Like bees who fly despite theories of aeronautics which deny them the right to do so, probably the overwhelming majority of mankind are continually drawing normative conclusions from factual premises (and factual conclusions from normative premises, for the relation between ethos and world view is circular) despite refined, and in their own terms impeccable, reflections by professional philosophers on the "naturalistic fallacy." An approach to a theory of value which looks toward the behavior of actual people in actual societies living in terms of actual cultures for both its stimulus and its validation will turn us away from abstract and rather scholastic arguments in which a limited number of classical positions are stated again and again with little that is new to recommend them, to a process of ever-increasing insight into both what values are and how they work. Once this enterprise in the scientific analysis of values is well launched, the philosophical discussions of ethics are likely to take on more point. The process is not that of replacing moral philosophy by descriptive ethics, but of providing moral philosophy with an empirical base and a conceptual framework which is somewhat advanced over that available to Aristotle, Spinoza, or G. E. Moore. The role of such a special science as anthropology in the analysis of values is not to replace philosophical investigation, but to make it relevant.

Chapter 6 / Ritual

and Social Change:

A Javanese Example

As in so many areas of anthropological concern, functionalism, either of the sociological sort associated with the name of Radcliffe-Brown or of the social-psychological sort associated with Malinowski, has tended to dominate recent theoretical discussions of the role of religion in society. Stemming originally from Durkheim's *The Elementary Forms of the Religious Life* and Robertson-Smith's *Lectures on the Religion of the Semites,* the sociological approach (or, as the British anthropologists prefer to call it, the social anthropological approach) emphasizes the manner in which belief and particularly ritual reinforce the traditional social ties between individuals; it stresses the way in which the social structure of a group is strengthened and perpetuated through the ritualistic or mythic symbolization of the underlying social values upon which it rests.[1] The social-psychological approach, of which Frazer and Tylor were perhaps the pioneers but which found its clearest statement in Malinowski's classic *Magic, Science and Religion,* emphasizes what religion does for the individual—how it satisfies both his cognitive and

[1] E. Durkheim, *The Elementary Forms of the Religious Life* (Glencoe, Ill., 1947); W. Robertson-Smith, *Lectures on the Religion of the Semites* (Edinburgh, 1894).

affective demands for a stable, comprehensible, and coercible world, and how it enables him to maintain an inner security in the face of natural contingency.[2] Together, the two approaches have given us an increasingly detailed understanding of the social and psychological "functions" of religion in a wide range of societies.

Where the functional approach has been least impressive, however, is in dealing with social change. As has been noted by several writers, the emphasis on systems in balance, on social homeostasis, and on timeless structural pictures, leads to a bias in favor of "well-integrated" societies in a stable equilibrium and to a tendency to emphasize the functional aspects of a people's social usages and customs rather than their dysfunctional implications.[3] In analyses of religion this static, ahistorical approach has led to a somewhat overconservative view of the role of ritual and belief in social life. Despite cautionary comments by Kluckhohn[4] and others on the "gain and cost" of various religious practices such as witchcraft, the tendency has been consistently to stress the harmonizing, integrating, and psychologically supportive aspects of religious patterns rather than the disruptive, disintegrative, and psychologically disturbing aspects; to demonstrate the manner in which religion preserves social and psychological structure rather than the manner in which it destroys or transforms it. Where change has been treated, as in Redfield's work on Yucatan, it has largely been in terms of progressive disintegration: "The changes in culture that in Yucatan appear to 'go along with' lessening isolation and homogeneity are seen to be chiefly three: disorganization of the culture, secularization and individualization." [5] Yet even a passing knowledge of our own religious history makes us hesitate to affirm such a simply "positive" role for religion generally.

It is the thesis of this chapter that one of the major reasons for the inability of functional theory to cope with change lies in its failure to treat sociological and cultural processes on equal terms; almost inevitably one of the two either is ignored or is sacrificed to become but a simple reflex, a "mirror image," of the other. Either culture is regarded as

[2] B. Malinowski, *Magic, Science and Religion* (Boston, 1948).

[3] See, for example, E. R. Leach, *Political Systems of Highland Burma* (Cambridge, Mass., 1954); and R. Merton, *Social Theory and Social Structure* (Glencoe, Ill., 1949).

[4] See C. Kluckhohn, *Navaho Witchcraft,* Peabody Museum Papers, No. 22 (Cambridge, Mass., 1944).

[5] R. Redfield, *The Folk Culture of Yucatan* (Chicago, 1941), p. 339.

wholly derivative from the forms of social organization—the approach characteristic of the British structuralists as well as many American sociologists; or the forms of social organization are regarded as behavioral embodiments of cultural patterns—the approach of Malinowski and many American anthropologists. In either case, the lesser term tends to drop out as a dynamic factor, and we are left either with an omnibus concept of culture ("that complex whole . . .") or else with a completely comprehensive concept of social structure ("social structure is not an aspect of culture but the entire culture of a given people handled in a special frame of theory").[6] In such a situation, the dynamic elements in social change that arise from the failure of cultural patterns to be perfectly congruent with the forms of social organization are largely incapable of formulation. "We functionalists," E. R. Leach has recently remarked, "are not really 'antihistorical' by principle; it is simply that we do not know how to fit historical materials into our framework of concepts."[7]

A revision of the concepts of functional theory so as to make them capable of dealing more effectively with "historical materials" might well begin with an attempt to distinguish analytically between the cultural and social aspects of human life, and to treat them as independently variable yet mutually interdependent factors. Though separable only conceptually, culture and social structure will then be seen to be capable of a wide range of modes of integration with one another, of which the simple isomorphic mode is but a limiting case—a case common only in societies which have been stable over such an extended time as to make possible a close adjustment between social and cultural aspects. In most societies, where change is a characteristic rather than an abnormal occurrence, we shall expect to find more or less radical discontinuities between the two. I would argue that it is in these very discontinuities that we shall find some of the primary driving forces in change.

One of the more useful ways—but far from the only one—of distinguishing between culture and social system is to see the former as an ordered system of meaning and of symbols, in terms of which social interaction takes place; and to see the latter as the pattern of social interaction itself.[8] On the one level there is the framework of beliefs, ex-

    [6] M. Fortes, "The Structure of Unilineal Descent Groups," *American Anthropologist,* 55 (1953): 17–41.

    [7] Leach, *Political Systems of Highland Burma,* p. 282.

    [8] T. Parsons and E. Shils, *Toward a General Theory of Action* (Cambridge, Mass., 1951).

pressive symbols, and values in terms of which individuals define their world, express their feelings, and make their judgments; on the other level there is the ongoing process of interactive behavior, whose persistent form we call social structure. Culture is the fabric of meaning in terms of which human beings interpret their experience and guide their action; social structure is the form that action takes, the actually existing network of social relations. Culture and social structure are then but different abstractions from the same phenomena. The one considers social action in respect to its meaning for those who carry it out, the other considers it in terms of its contribution to the functioning of some social system.

The nature of the distinction between culture and social system is brought out more clearly when one considers the contrasting sorts of integration characteristic of each of them. This contrast is between what Sorokin has called "logico-meaningful integration" and what he has called "causal-functional integration." [9] By logico-meaningful integration, characteristic of culture, is meant the sort of integration one finds in a Bach fugue, in Catholic dogma, or in the general theory of relativity; it is a unity of style, of logical implication, of meaning and value. By causal-functional integration, characteristic of the social system, is meant the kind of integration one finds in an organism, where all the parts are united in a single causal web; each part is an element in a reverberating causal ring which "keeps the system going." And because these two types of integration are not identical, because the particular form one of them takes does not directly imply the form the other will take, there is an inherent incongruity and tension between the two and between both of them and a third element, the pattern of motivational integration within the individual which we usually call personality structure:

Thus conceived, a social system is only one of three aspects of the structuring of a completely concrete system of social action. The other two are the personality systems of the individual actors and the cultural system which is built into their action. Each of the three must be considered to be an independent focus of the organization of the elements of the action system in the sense that no one of them is theoretically reducible to terms of one or a combination of the other two. Each is indispensable to the other two in the sense that without personalities and culture there would be no social system and so on around the roster of logical possibilities. But this interdependence and interpenetration is a very different matter from reducibility, which would mean that the important properties and processes of one class of sys-

[9] P. Sorokin, *Social and Cultural Dynamics*, 3 vols. (New York, 1937).

tem could be theoretically *derived* from our theoretical knowledge of one or both of the other two. The action frame of reference is common to all three and this fact makes certain "transformations" between them possible. But on the level of theory here attempted they do not constitute a single system, however this might turn out to be on some other theoretical level.[10]

I shall attempt to demonstrate the utility of this more dynamic functionalist approach by applying it to a particular case of a ritual which failed to function properly. I shall try to show how an approach which does not distinguish the "logico-meaningful" cultural aspects of the ritual pattern from the "causal-functional" social structural aspects is unable to account adequately for this ritual failure, and how an approach which does so distinguish them is able to analyze more explicitly the cause of the trouble. It will further be argued that such an approach is able to avoid the simplistic view of the functional role of religion in society which sees that role merely as structure-conserving, and to substitute for it a more complex conception of the relations between religious belief and practice and secular social life. Historical materials can be fitted into such a conception, and the functional analysis of religion can therefore be widened to deal more adequately with processes of change.

The Setting

The case to be described is that of a funeral held in Modjokuto, a small town in eastern Central Java. A young boy, about ten years of age, who was living with his uncle and aunt, died very suddenly. His death, instead of being followed by the usual hurried, subdued, yet methodically efficient Javanese funeral ceremony and burial routine, brought on an extended period of pronounced social strain and severe psychological tension. The complex of beliefs and rituals which had for generations brought countless Javanese safely through the difficult postmortem period suddenly failed to work with its accustomed effectiveness. To understand why it failed demands knowledge and understanding of a whole range of social and cultural changes which have taken place in Java since the first decades of this century. This disrupted funeral was in fact but a microscopic example of the broader conflicts, structural

[10] T. Parsons, *The Social System* (Glencoe, Ill., 1951), p. 6.

dissolutions, and attempted reintegrations which, in one form or another, are characteristic of contemporary Indonesian society.

The religious tradition of Java, particularly of the peasantry, is a composite of Indian, Islamic, and indigenous Southeast Asian elements. The rise of large, militaristic kingdoms in the inland rice basins in the early centuries of the Christian era was associated with the diffusion of Hinduist and Buddhist culture patterns to the island; the expansion of international maritime trade in the port cities of the northern coast in the fifteenth and sixteenth centuries was associated with the diffusion of Islamic patterns. Working their way into the peasant mass, these two world religions became fused with the underlying animistic traditions characteristic of the whole Malaysian culture area. The result was a balanced syncretism of myth and ritual in which Hindu gods and goddesses, Moslem prophets and saints, and local spirits and demons all found a proper place.

The central ritual form in this syncretism is a communal feast, called the *slametan*. Slametans, which are given with only slight variations in form and content on almost all occasions of religious significance—at passage points in the life cycle, on calendrical holidays, at certain stages of the crop cycle, on changing one's residence, and so on—are intended to be both offerings to the spirits and commensal mechanisms of social integration for the living. The meal, which consists of specially prepared dishes, each symbolic of a particular religious concept, is cooked by the female members of one nuclear family household and set out on mats in the middle of the living room. The male head of the household invites the male heads of the eight or ten contiguous households to attend; no closer neighbor is ignored in favor of one farther away. After a speech by the host explaining the spiritual purpose of the feast and a short Arabic chant, each man takes a few hurried, almost furtive, gulps of food, wraps the remainder of the meal in a banana-leaf basket, and returns home to share it with his family. It is said that the spirits draw their sustenance from the odor of the food, the incense which is burned, and the Moslem prayer; the human participants draw theirs from the material substance of the food and from their social interaction. The result of this quiet, undramatic little ritual is twofold: the spirits are appeased and neighborhood solidarity is strengthened.

The ordinary canons of functional theory are quite adequate for the analysis of such a pattern. It can rather easily be shown that the slametan is well designed both to "tune up the ultimate value attitudes" necessary to the effective integration of a territorially based social structure, and to fulfill the psychological needs for intellectual coherence and emotional stability characteristic of a peasant population. The Javanese village (once or twice a year, villagewide slametans are held) is essentially a set of geographically contiguous, but rather self-consciously autonomous, nuclear-family households whose economic and political interdependence is of roughly the same circumscribed and explicitly defined sort as that demonstrated in the slametan. The demands of the labor-intensive rice and dry-crop agricultural process require the perpetuation of specific modes of technical cooperation and enforce a sense of community on the otherwise rather self-contained families—a sense of community which the slametan clearly reinforces. And when we consider the manner in which various conceptual and behavioral elements from Hindu-Buddhism, Islam, and "animism" are reinterpreted and balanced to form a distinctive and nearly homogeneous religious style, the close functional adjustment between the communal feast pattern and the conditions of Javanese rural life is even more readily apparent.

But the fact is that in all but the most isolated parts of Java, both the simple territorial basis of village social integration and the syncretic basis of its cultural homogeneity have been progressively undermined over the past fifty years. Population growth, urbanization, monetization, occupational differentiation, and the like, have combined to weaken the traditional ties of peasant social structure; and the winds of doctrine which have accompanied the appearance of these structural changes have disturbed the simple uniformity of religious belief and practice characteristic of an earlier period. The rise of nationalism, Marxism, and Islamic reform as ideologies, which resulted in part from the increasing complexity of Javanese society, has affected not only the large cities where these creeds first appeared and have always had their greatest strength, but has had a heavy impact on the smaller towns and villages as well. In fact, much of recent Javanese social change is perhaps most aptly characterized as a shift from a situation in which the primary integrative ties between individuals (or between families) are phrased in terms of geographical proximity to one in which they are phrased in terms of ideological like-mindedness.

In the villages and small towns these major ideological changes appeared largely in the guise of a widening split between those who emphasized the Islamic aspects of the indigenous religious syncretism and those who emphasized the Hinduist and animistic elements. It is true that some difference between these variant subtraditions has been present since the arrival of Islam; some individuals have always been particularly skilled in Arabic chanting or particularly learned in Moslem law, while others have been adept at more Hinduistic mystical practices or specialists in local curing techniques. But these contrasts were softened by the easy tolerance of the Javanese for a wide range of religious concepts, so long as basic ritual patterns—that is, slametans—were faithfully supported; whatever social divisiveness they stimulated was largely obscured by the overriding commonalities of rural and small-town life.

However, the appearance after 1910 of Islamic modernism (as well as vigorous conservative reactions against it) and religious nationalism among the economically and politically sophisticated trading classes of the larger cities strengthened the feeling for Islam as an exclusivist, antisyncretic creed among the more orthodox element of the mass of the population. Similarly, secular nationalism and Marxism, appearing among the civil servants and the expanding proletariat of these cities, strengthened the pre-Islamic (that is, Hinduist-animist) elements of the syncretic pattern, which these groups tended to prize as a counterweight to puristic Islam and which some of them adopted as a general religious framework in which to set their more specifically political ideas. On the one hand, there arose a more self-conscious Moslem, basing his religious beliefs and practices more explicitly on the international and universalistic doctrines of Mohammed; on the other hand there arose a more self-conscious "nativist," attempting to evolve a generalized religious system out of the material—muting the more Islamic elements—of his inherited religious tradition. And the contrast between the first kind of man, called a *santri,* and the second, called an *abangan,* grew steadily more acute, until today it forms the major cultural distinction in the whole of the Modjokuto area.

It is especially in the town that this contrast has come to play a crucial role. The absence of pressures toward interfamilial cooperation exerted by the technical requirements of wet-rice growing, as well as lessened effectiveness of the traditional forms of village government in the face of the complexities of urban living, severely weaken the social supports of the syncretic village pattern. When each man makes his living —as chauffeur, trader, clerk, or laborer—more or less independently of how his neighbors make theirs, his sense of the importance of the neighborhood community naturally diminishes. A more differentiated class system, more bureaucratic and impersonal forms of government, greater heterogeneity of social background, all tend to lead to the same result: the de-emphasis of strictly geographical ties in favor of diffusely ideological ones. For the townsman, the distinction between santri and abangan becomes even sharper, for it emerges as his primary point of social reference; it becomes a symbol of his social identity, rather than a mere contrast in belief. The sort of friends he will have, the sort of organizations he will join, the sort of political leadership he will follow, the sort of person he or his son will marry, will all be strongly influenced by the side of this ideological bifurcation which he adopts as his own.

There is thus emerging in the town—though not only in the town—a new pattern of social living organized in terms of an altered framework of cultural classification. Among the elite this new pattern has already become rather highly developed, but among the mass of the townspeople it is still in the process of formation. Particularly in the *kampongs,* the off-the-street neighborhoods in which the common Javanese townsmen live crowded together in a helter-skelter profusion of little bamboo houses, one finds a transitional society in which the traditional forms of rural living are being steadily dissolved and new forms steadily reconstructed. In these enclaves of peasants-come-to-town (or of sons and grandsons of peasants-come-to-town), Redfield's folk culture is being constantly converted into his urban culture, though this latter is not accurately characterized by such negative and residual terms as "secular," "individualized," and "culturally disorganized." What is occurring in the kampongs is not so much a destruction of traditional ways of life, as a construction of a new one; the sharp social conflict characteristic of these lower-class neighborhoods is not simply indicative of a loss of cultural consensus, but rather is indicative of a search, not yet entirely successful, for new, more generalized, and flexible patterns of belief and value.

In Modjokuto, as in most of Indonesia, this search is taking place largely within the social context of the mass political parties, as well as in the women's clubs, youth organizations, labor unions, and other sodalities formally or informally linked with them. There are several of these parties (though the recent [1955] general election severely reduced their number), each led by educated urban elites—civil servants, teachers, traders, students, and the like—and each competing with the others for the political allegiance of both the half-rural, half-urban kampong dwellers and of the mass of the peasantry. And almost without exception, they appeal to one or another side of the santri–abangan split. Of this complex of political parties and sodalities, only two are of immediate concern to us here: Masjumi, a huge, Islam-based political party; and Permai, a vigorously anti-Moslem politico-religious cult.

Masjumi is the more or less direct descendant of the prewar Islamic reform movement. Led, at least in Modjokuto, by modernist santri intellectuals, it stands for a socially conscious, antischolastic, and somewhat puritanical version of back-to-the-Koran Islam. In company with the other Moslem parties, it also supports the institution of an "Islamic State" in Indonesia in place of the present secular republic. However, the meaning of this ideal is not entirely clear. Masjumi's enemies accuse it of pressing for an intolerant, medievalist theocracy in which abangans and non-Moslems will be persecuted and forced to follow exactly the prescripts of the Moslem law, while Masjumi's leaders claim that Islam is intrinsically tolerant and that they only desire a government explicitly based on the Moslem creed, one whose laws will be in consonance with the teachings of the Koran and Hadith. In any case, Masjumi, the country's largest Moslem party, is one of the major spokesmen on both the national and the local levels for the values and aspirations of the santri community.

Permai is not so impressive on a national scale. Though it is a nationwide party, it is a fairly small one, having strength only in a few fairly circumscribed regions. In the Modjokuto area, however, it happened to be of some importance, and what it lacked in national scope it made up in local intensity. Essentially, Permai is a fusion of Marxist politics with abangan religious patterns. It combines a fairly explicit anti-Westernism, anticapitalism, and anti-imperialism with an attempt to formalize and generalize some of the more characteristic diffuse themes of the peasant religious syncretism. Permai meetings follow both the slametan pattern, complete with incense and symbolic food (but without Islamic chants), and modern parliamentary procedure; Permai pamphlets contain calendrical and numerological divinatory systems and mystical teachings as well as analyses of class conflict; and Permai speeches are concerned with elaborating both religious and political concepts. In Modjokuto, Permai is also a curing cult, with its own special medical practices and spells, a secret password, and cabalistic interpretations of passages in the leaders' social and political writings.

But Permai's most notable characteristic is its strong anti-Moslem stand. Charging that Islam is a foreign import, unsuited to the needs and values of the Javanese, the cult urges a return to "pure" and "original" Javanese beliefs, by which they seem to mean to the indigenous syncretism with the more Islamic elements removed. In line with this, the cult-party has initiated a drive, on both national and local levels, for secular (that is, non-Islamic) marriage and funeral rites. As the situation stands now, all but Christians and Balinese Hindus must have their marriages legitimatized by means of the Moslem ritual.[11] Funeral rites are an individual concern but, because of the long history of syncretism, they are so deeply involved with Islamic customs that a genuinely non-Islamic funeral tends to be a practical impossibility.

Permai's action on the local level in pursuit of non-Islamic marriage and funeral ceremonies took two forms. One was heavy pressure on local government officials to permit such practices, and the other was heavy pressure on its own members to follow, voluntarily, rituals purified of Islamic elements. In the case of marriage, success was more or less precluded because the local officials' hands were tied by Central Government ordinances, and even highly ideologized members of the cult would not dare an openly "illegitimate" marriage. Without a change in the law, Permai had little chance to alter marriage forms, though a few abortive attempts were made to conduct civil ceremonies under the aegis of abangan-minded village chiefs.

The case of funerals was somewhat different, for a matter of custom rather than law was involved. During the period I was in the field (1952–1954), the tension between Permai and Masjumi increased very sharply. This was due in part to the imminence of Indonesia's first general elections, and in part to the effects of the cold war. It was also influenced by various special occurrences—such as a report that the national head of Permai had publicly called Mohammed a false prophet; a speech in the nearby regional capital by a Masjumi leader in which he accused Permai of intending to raise a generation of bastards in Indonesia; and a bitter village-chief election largely fought out on santri vs. abangan grounds. As a result, the local subdistrict officer, a worried bureaucrat trapped in the middle, called a meeting of all the village

---

[11] Actually, there are two parts to Javanese marriage rites. One, which is part of the general syncretism, is held at the bride's home and involves a slametan and an elaborate ceremonial "meeting" between bride and groom. The other, which is the official ceremony in the eyes of the Government, follows the Moslem law and takes place at the office of the subdistrict religious officer, or Naib. See C. Geertz, The Religion of Java (Glencoe, Ill., 1960), pp. 51–61, 203.

religious officials, or Modins. Among many other duties, a Modin is traditionally responsible for conducting funerals. He directs the whole ritual, instructs the mourners in the technical details of burial, leads the Koran chanting, and reads a set speech to the deceased at the graveside. The subdistrict officer instructed the Modins—the majority of whom were village Masjumi leaders—that in the case of the death of a member of Permai, they were merely to note the name and age of the deceased and return home; they were not to participate in the ritual. He warned that if they did not do as he advised, they would be responsible if trouble started and he would not come to their support.

This was the situation on July 17, 1954, when Paidjan, nephew of Karman, an active and ardent member of Permai, died suddenly in the Modjokuto kampong in which I was living.

The Funeral

The mood of a Javanese funeral is not one of hysterical bereavement, unrestrained sobbing, or even of formalized cries of grief for the deceased's departure. Rather, it is a calm, undemonstrative, almost languid letting go, a brief ritualized relinquishment of a relationship no longer possible. Tears are not approved of and certainly not encouraged; the effort is to get the job done, not to linger over the pleasures of grief. The detailed busy-work of the funeral, the politely formal social intercourse with the neighbors pressing in from all sides, the series of commemorative slametans stretched out at intervals for almost three years—the whole momentum of the Javanese ritual system is supposed to carry one through grief without severe emotional disturbance. For the mourner, the funeral and postfuneral ritual is said to produce a feeling of *iklas,* a kind of willed affectlessness, a detached and static state of "not caring"; for the neighborhood group it is said to produce *rukun,* "communal harmony."

The actual service is in essence simply another version of the slametan, adapted to the special requirements of interment. When the news of a death is broadcast through the area, everyone in the neighborhood must drop what he is doing and go immediately to the home of the survivors. The women bring bowls of rice, which is cooked up into a slametan; the men begin to cut wooden grave markers and to dig a grave. Soon the Modin arrives and begins to direct activities. The corpse is washed in ceremonially prepared water by the relatives (who unflinchingly hold the body on their laps to demonstrate their affection for the deceased as well as their self-control); then it is wrapped in muslin. About a dozen santris, under the leadership of the Modin, chant Arabic prayers over the body for five or ten minutes; after this it is carried, amid various ritual acts, in a ceremonial procession to the graveyard, where it is interred in prescribed ways. The Modin reads a graveside speech to the deceased, reminding him of his duties as a believing Moslem; and the funeral is over, usually only two or three hours after death. The funeral proper is followed by commemorative slametans in the home of the survivors at three, seven, forty, and one hundred days after death; on the first and second anniversary of death; and, finally, on the thousandth day, when the corpse is considered to have turned to dust and the gap between the living and the dead to have become absolute.

This was the ritual pattern which was called into play when Paidjan died. As soon as dawn broke (death occurred in the early hours of the morning), Karman, the uncle, dispatched a telegram to the boy's parents in a nearby city, telling them in characteristic Javanese fashion that their son was ill. This evasion was intended to soften the impact of death by allowing them to become aware of it more gradually. Javanese feel that emotional damage results not from the severity of a frustration but from the suddenness with which it comes, the degree to which it "surprises" one unprepared for it. It is "shock," not suffering itself, which is feared. Next, in the expectation that the parents would arrive within a few hours, Karman sent for the Modin to begin the ceremony. This was done on the theory that by the time the parents had come little would be left to do but inter the body, and they would thus once more be spared unnecessary stress. By ten o'clock at the very latest it should all be over; a saddening incident, but a ritually muted one.

But when the Modin, as he later told me, arrived at Karman's house and saw the poster displaying Permai's political symbol, he told Karman that he could not perform the ritual. After all, Karman belonged to "another religion," and he, the Modin, did not know the correct burial rituals for it; all he knew was Islam. "I don't want to insult your religion," he said piously. "On the contrary, I hold it in the utmost regard, for there is no intolerance in Islam. But I don't know your ritual. The Christians have their own ritual and their own specialist (the local preacher), but what does Permai do? Do they burn the corpse or what?" (This is a sly allusion to Hindu burial practices; evidently the Modin enjoyed himself hugely in this interchange.) Karman was, the Modin told me, rather upset at all this and evidently surprised, for although he was an active member of Permai, he was a fairly unsophisticated one. It had evidently never occurred to him that the anti-Moslem-funeral agitation of the party would ever appear as a concrete problem, or that the Modin would actually refuse to officiate. Karman was actually not a bad fellow, the Modin concluded; he was but a dupe of his leaders.

After leaving the now highly agitated Karman, the Modin went directly to the subdistrict officer to ask if he had acted properly. The officer was morally bound to say that he had, and thus fortified the Modin returned home to find Karman and the village policeman, to whom Karman had gone in desperation, waiting for him. The policeman, a personal friend of Karman's, told the Modin that according to time-honored custom he was supposed to bury everyone with impartiality, never mind whether he happened to agree with their politics. But the Modin, having now been personally supported by the subdistrict officer, insisted that it was no longer his responsibility. However, he suggested, if Karman wished, he could go to the village chief's office and sign a public statement, sealed with the Government stamp and countersigned by the village chief in the presence of two witnesses, declaring that he, Karman, was a true believing Moslem and that he wished the Modin to bury the boy according to Islamic custom. At this suggestion that he officially abandon his religious beliefs, Karman exploded into a rage and stormed from the house, rather uncharacteristic behavior for a Javanese. By the time he arrived home again, at his wit's end about what to do next, he found to his dismay that the news of the boy's death had been broadcast and the entire neighborhood was already gathering for the ceremony.

Like most of the kampongs in the town of Modjokuto, the one in which I lived consisted both of pious santris and ardent abangans (as well as a number of less intense adherents of either side), mixed together in a more or less random manner. In the town, people are forced to live where they can and take whomever they find for neighbors, in contrast to the rural areas where whole neighborhoods, even whole villages, still tend to be made up almost entirely of either abangans or santris. The majority of the santris in the kampong were members of Masjumi, and most of the abangans were followers of Permai, and in daily life, social interaction between the two groups was minimal. The abangans, most of whom were either petty artisans or manual laborers, gathered each late afternoon at Karman's roadside coffee shop for the idle twilight conversations which are typical of small-town and village life in Java; the santris—tailors, traders, and storekeepers for the most part —usually gathered in one or another of the santri-run shops for the same purpose. But despite this lack of close social ties, the demonstration of territorial unity at a funeral was still felt by both groups to be an unavoidable duty; of all the Javanese rituals, the funeral probably carries the greatest obligation on attendance. Everyone who lives within a certain roughly defined radius of the survivors' home is expected to come to the ceremony; and on this occasion everyone did.

With this as background, it is not surprising that when I arrived at Karman's house about eight o'clock, I found two separate clusters of sullen men squatting disconsolately on either side of the yard, a nervous group of whispering women sitting idly inside the house near the still-clothed body, and a general air of doubt and uneasiness in place of the usual quiet busyness of slametan preparing, body washing, and guest greeting. The abangans were grouped near the house, where Karman was crouched, staring blankly off into space, and where Sudjoko and Sastro, the town Chairman and Secretary of Permai (the only nonresidents of the kampong present) sat on chairs, looking vaguely out of place. The santris were crowded together under the narrow shadow of a coconut palm about thirty yards away, chatting quietly to one another about everything but the problem at hand. The almost motionless scene suggested an unlooked-for intermission in a familiar drama, as when a motion picture stops in mid-action.

After a half hour or so, a few of the abangans began to chip half-heartedly away at pieces of wood to make grave markers and a few women began to construct small flower offerings for want of anything better to do; but it was clear that the ritual was arrested and that no one quite knew what to do next. Tension slowly rose. People nervously watched the sun rise higher and higher in the sky, or glanced at the impassive Karman. Mutterings about the sorry state of affairs began to appear ("everything these days is a political problem," an old, traditionalistic man of about eighty grumbled to me, "you can't even die any more but what it becomes a political problem"). Finally, about 9:30, a young santri tailor named Abu decided to try to do something about the situation before it deteriorated entirely: he stood up and gestured to Karman, the first serious instrumental act which had occurred all morning. And Karman, roused from his meditation, crossed the no man's land to talk to him.

As a matter of fact, Abu occupied a rather special position in the kampong. Although he was a pious santri and a loyal Masjumi member, he had more contact with the Permai group because his tailor shop was located directly behind Karman's coffee shop. Though Abu, who stuck to his sewing machine night and day, was not properly a member of this group, he would often exchange comments with them from his work bench about twenty feet away. True, a certain amount of tension existed between him and the Permai people over religious issues. Once, when I was inquiring about their eschatological beliefs, they referred me sarcastically to Abu, saying he was an expert, and they teased him quite openly about what they considered the wholly ridiculous Islamic theories of the afterlife. Nevertheless, he had something of a social bond with them, and it was perhaps reasonable that he should be the one to try to break the deadlock.

"It is already nearly noon," Abu said. "Things can't go straight on like this." He suggested that he send Umar, another of the santris, to see if the Modin could now be induced to come; perhaps things were cooler with him now. Meanwhile, he could get the washing and wrapping of the corpse started himself. Karman replied that he would think about it, and returned to the other side of the yard for a discussion with the two Permai leaders. After a few minutes of vigorous gesturing and nodding, Karman returned and said simply, "All right, that way." "I know how you feel," Abu said; "I'll just do what is absolutely necessary and keep the Islam out as much as possible." He gathered the santris together and they entered the house.

The first requisite was stripping the corpse (which was still lying on the floor, because no one could bring himself to move it). But by now the body was rigid, making it necessary to cut the clothes off with a knife, an unusual procedure which deeply disturbed everyone, especially the women clustered around. The santris finally managed to get the body outside and set up the bathing enclosure. Abu asked for volunteers for the washing; he reminded them that God would consider such an act a good work. But the relatives, who normally would be expected to undertake this task, were by now so deeply shaken and confused that they were unable to bring themselves to hold the boy on their laps in the customary fashion. There was another wait while people looked hopelessly at each other. Finally, Pak Sura, a member of Karman's group but no relative, took the boy on his lap, although he was clearly frightened and kept whispering a protective spell. One reason the Javanese give for their custom of rapid burial is that it is dangerous to have the spirit of the deceased hovering around the house.

Before the washing could begin, however, someone raised the question as to whether one person was enough—wasn't it usually three? No one was quite sure, including Abu; some thought that although it was customary to have three people it was not obligatory, and some thought three a necessary number. After about ten minutes of anxious discussion, a male cousin of the boy and a carpenter, unrelated to him, managed to work up the courage to join Pak Sura. Abu, attempting to act the Modin's role as best he could, sprinkled a few drops of water on the corpse and then it was washed, rather haphazardly and in unsacralized water. When this was finished, however, the procedure was again stalled, for no one knew exactly how to arrange the small cotton pads which, under Moslem law, should plug the body orifices. Karman's wife, sister of the deceased's mother, could evidently take no more, for she broke into a loud, unrestrained wailing, the only demonstration of this sort I witnessed among the dozen or so Javanese funerals I attended. Everyone was further upset by this development, and most of the kampong women made a frantic but unavailing effort to comfort her. Most of the men remained seated in the yard, outwardly calm and inexpressive, but the embarrassed uneasiness which had been present since the beginning seemed to be turning toward fearful desperation. "It is not nice for her to cry that way," several men said to me, "it isn't proper." At this point, the Modin arrived.

However, he was still adamant. Further, he warned Abu that he was courting eternal damnation by his actions. "You will have to answer to God on Judgment Day," he said, "if you make mistakes in the ritual. It will be your responsibility. For a Moslem, burial is a serious matter and must be carried out according to the Law by someone who knows what the Law is, not according to the will of the individual." He then suggested to Sudjoko and Sastro, the Permai leaders, that they take charge of the funeral, for as party "intellectuals" they must certainly know what kind of funeral customs Permai followed. The two leaders, who had not moved from their chairs, considered this as everyone watched expectantly, but they finally refused, with some chagrin, saying they really did not know how to go about it. The Modin shrugged and turned away. One of the bystanders, a friend of Karman's, then suggested that they just take the body out and bury it and forget about the whole ritual; it was extremely dangerous to leave things as they were much longer. I don't know whether this remarkable suggestion would have been followed, for at this juncture the mother and father of the dead child entered the kampong.

They seemed quite composed. They were not unaware of the death, for the father later told me he had suspected as much when he got the telegram; he and his wife had prepared themselves for the worst and were more or less resigned by the time they arrived. When they approached the kampong and saw the whole neighborhood gathered, they knew that their fears were well founded. When Karman's wife, whose weeping had subsided slightly, saw the dead boy's mother come into the yard, she burst free of those who were comforting her and with a shriek rushed to embrace her sister. In what seemed a split second, both women had dissolved into wild hysterics and the crowd had rushed in and pulled them apart, dragging them to houses at opposite sides of the kampong. Their wailing continued in undiminished volume, and nervous comments arose to the effect that they ought to get on with the burial in one fashion or another, before the boy's spirit possessed someone.

But the mother now insisted on seeing the body of her child before it was wrapped. The father at first forbade it, angrily ordering her to stop crying—didn't she know that such behavior would darken the boy's pathway to the other world? But she persisted and so they brought her, stumbling, to where he lay in Karman's house. The women tried to keep her from drawing too close, but she broke loose and began to kiss the boy about the genitals. She was snatched away almost immediately by her husband and the women, though she screamed that she had not yet finished; and they pulled her into the back room where she subsided into a daze. After a while—the body was finally being wrapped, the Modin having unbent enough to point out where the cotton pads went —she seemed to lose her bearings entirely and began to move about the yard shaking hands with everyone, all strangers to her, and saying, "Forgive me my faults, forgive me my faults." Again she was forcibly restrained; people said, "Calm yourself; think of your other children— do you want to follow your son to the grave?"

The corpse was now wrapped, and new suggestions were made that it be taken off immediately to the graveyard. At this point, Abu approached the father, who, he evidently felt, had now displaced Karman as the man legally responsible for the proceedings. Abu explained that the Modin, being a Government official, did not feel free to approach the father himself, but he would like to know: how did he wish the boy to be buried—the Islamic way or what? The father, somewhat bewildered, said, "Of course, the Islamic way. I don't have much of any religion, but I'm not a Christian, and when it comes to death the burial should be the Islamic way. Completely Islamic." Abu explained again that the Modin could not approach the father directly, but that he, being "free," could do as he pleased. He said that he had tried to help as best he could but that he had been careful to do nothing Islamic before the father came. It was too bad, he apologized, about all the tension that was in the air, that political differences had to make so much trouble. But after all, everything had to be "clear" and "legal" about the funeral. It was important for the boy's soul. The santris, somewhat gleefully, now chanted their prayers over the corpse, and it was carried to the grave and buried in the usual manner. The Modin gave the usual graveyard speech, as amended for children, and the funeral was finally completed. None of the relatives or the women went to the graveyard; but when we returned to the house—it was now well after noon—the slametan was finally served, and Paidjan's spirit presumably left the kampong to begin its journey to the other world.

Three days later, in the evening, the first of the commemorative slametans was held, but it turned out that not only were no santris present but that it was as much a Permai political and religious cult meeting as a mourning ritual. Karman started off in the traditional fashion by announcing in high Javanese that this was a slametan in remembrance of the death of Paidjan. Sudjoko, the Permai leader, immediately burst in saying, "No, no, that is wrong. At a third day slametan you just eat and give a long Islamic chant for the dead, and we are certainly not going to do that." He then launched into a long, rambling speech. Everyone, he said, must know the philosophical-religious basis of the country. "Suppose this American [he pointed to me; he was not at all pleased by my presence] came up and asked you: what is the spiritual basis of the country? and you didn't know—wouldn't you be ashamed?"

He went on in this vein, building up a whole rationale for the present national political structure on the basis of a mystical interpretation of President Sukarno's "Five Points" (Monotheism, Social Justice, Humanitarianism, Democracy, and Nationalism) which are the official ideological foundation of the new republic. Aided by Karman and others, he worked out a micro-macrocosm correspondence theory in which the individual is seen to be but a small replica of the state, and the state but an enlarged image of the individual. If the state is to be ordered, then the individual must also be ordered; each implies the other. As the President's Five Points are at the basis of the state, so the five senses are at the basis of an individual. The process of harmonizing both are the same, and it is this we must be sure we know. The discussion continued for nearly half an hour, ranging widely through religious, philosophical, and political issues (including, evidently for my benefit, a discussion of the Rosenbergs' execution).

We paused for coffee and as Sudjoko was about to begin again, Paidjan's father, who had been sitting quietly and expressionless, began suddenly to talk, softly and with a curiously mechanical tonelessness, almost as if he were reasoning with himself, but without much hope of success. "I am sorry for my rough city accent," he said, "but I very much want to say something." He hoped they would forgive him; they could continue their discussion in a moment. "I have been trying to be *iklas* ['detached,' 'resigned'] about Paidjan's death. I'm convinced that everything that could have been done for him was done and that his death was just an event which simply happened." He said he was still in Modjokuto because he could not yet face the people where he lived, couldn't face having to tell each one of them what had occurred. His wife, he said, was a little more *iklas* now too. It was hard, though. He kept telling himself it was just the will of God, but it was so hard, for nowadays people didn't agree on things any more; one person tells you one thing and others tell you another. It's hard to know which is right, to know what to believe. He said he appreciated all the Modjokuto people coming to the funeral, and he was sorry it had been all mixed up. "I'm not very religious myself. I'm not Masjumi and I'm not Permai. But I wanted the boy to be buried in the old way. I hope no one's feelings were hurt." He said again he was trying to be *iklas,* to tell himself it was just the will of God, but it was hard, for things were so confused these days. It was hard to see why the boy should have died.

This sort of public expression of one's feelings is extremely unusual —in my experience unique—among Javanese, and in the formalized traditional slametan pattern there is simply no place for it (nor for philosophical or political discussion). Everyone present was rather shaken by the father's talk, and there was a painful silence. Sudjoko finally began to talk again, but this time he described in detail the boy's death. How Paidjan had first gotten a fever and Karman had called him, Sudjoko, to come and say a Permai spell. But the boy did not respond. They finally took him to a male nurse in the hospital, where he was given an injection. But still he worsened. He vomited blood and went into convulsions, which Sudjoko described rather graphically, and then he died. "I don't know why the Permai spell didn't work," he said; "it has worked before. This time it didn't. I don't know why; that sort of thing can't be explained no matter how much you think about it. Sometimes it just works and sometimes it just doesn't." There was another silence and then, after about ten minutes more of political discussion, we disbanded. The father returned the next day to his home and I was not invited to any of the later slametans. When I left the field about four months later, Karman's wife had still not entirely recovered from the experience, the tension between the santris and the abangans in the kampong had increased, and everyone wondered what would happen the next time a death occurred in a Permai family.

Analysis

"Of all the sources of religion," wrote Malinowski, "the supreme and final crisis of life—death—is of the greatest importance." [12] Death, he argued, provokes in the survivors a dual response of love and loathing, a deep-going emotional ambivalence of fascination and fear which threatens both the psychological and social foundations of human existence. The survivors are drawn toward the deceased by their affection for him, repelled from him by the dreadful transformation wrought by death. Funeral rites, and the mourning practices which follow them, focus around this paradoxical desire both to maintain the tie in the face of death and to break the bond immediately and utterly, and to insure the domination of the will to live over the tendency to despair. Mortuary rituals maintain the continuity of human life by preventing the survivors from yielding either to the impulse to flee panic-stricken from the scene or to the contrary impulse to follow the deceased into the grave:

[12] Malinowski, *Magic, Science and Religion*, p. 29.

And here into this play of emotional forces, into this supreme dilemma of life and final death, religion steps in, selecting the positive creed, the comforting view, the culturally valuable belief in immortality, in the spirit independent of the body, and in the continuance of life after death. In the various ceremonies at death, in commemoration and communion with the departed, and worship of ancestral ghosts, religion gives body and form to the saving beliefs. . . . Exactly the same function it fulfills also with regard to the whole group. The ceremonial of death, which ties the survivors to the body and rivets them to the place of death, the beliefs in the existence of the spirit, in its beneficent influences or malevolent intentions, in the duties of a series of commemorative or sacrificial ceremonies—in all this religion counteracts the centrifugal forces of fear, dismay, demoralization, and provides the most powerful means of reintegration of the group's shaken solidarity and of the re-establishment of its morale. In short, religion here assures the victory of tradition over the mere negative response of thwarted instinct.[13]

To this sort of theory, a case such as that described above clearly poses some difficult problems. Not only was the victory of tradition and culture over "thwarted instinct" a narrow one at best, but it seemed as if the ritual were tearing the society apart rather than integrating it, were disorganizing personalities rather than healing them. To this the functionalist has a ready answer, which takes one of two forms depending upon whether he follows the Durkheim or the Malinowski tradition: social disintegration or cultural demoralization. Rapid social change has disrupted Javanese society and this is reflected in a disintegrated culture; as the unified state of traditional village society was mirrored in the unified slametan, so the broken society of the kampong is mirrored in the broken slametan of the funeral ritual we have just witnessed. Or, in the alternate phraseology, cultural decay has led to social fragmentation; loss of a vigorous folk tradition has weakened the moral ties between individuals.

It seems to me that there are two things wrong with this argument, no matter in which of the two vocabularies it is stated: it identifies social (or cultural) conflict with social (or cultural) disintegration; it denies independent roles to both culture and social structure, regarding one of the two as a mere epiphenomenon of the other.

In the first place, kampong life is not simply anomic. Though it is marked by vigorous social conflicts, as is our own society, it nevertheless proceeds fairly effectively in most areas. If governmental, economic, familial, stratificatory, and social control institutions functioned

[13] Ibid., pp. 33–35.

as poorly as did Paidjan's funeral, a kampong would indeed be an uncomfortable place in which to live. But though some of the typical
symptoms of urban upheaval—such as increased gambling, petty thiev-
ery, and prostitution—are to some degree present, kampong social life
is clearly not on the verge of collapse; everyday social interaction does
not limp along with the suppressed bitterness and deep uncertainty we
have seen focused around burial. For most of its members most of the
time, a semiurban neighborhood in Modjokuto offers a viable way of
life, despite its material disadvantages and its transitional character; and
for all the sentimentality which has been lavished on descriptions of
rural life in Java, this is probably as much as one could say for the village. As a matter of fact, it is around religious beliefs and practices—
slametans, holidays, curing, sorcery, cult groups, and so on—that the
most seriously disruptive events seem to cluster. Religion here is somehow the center and source of stress, not merely the reflection of stress
elsewhere in the society.

Yet it is not a source of stress because commitment to the inherited
patterns of belief and ritual has been weakened. The conflict around
Paidjan's death took place simply because all the kampong residents did
share a common, highly integrated, cultural tradition concerning funerals. There was no argument over whether the slametan pattern was the
correct ritual, whether the neighbors were obligated to attend, or
whether the supernatural concepts upon which the ritual is based were
valid ones. For both santris and abangans in the kampongs, the slametan maintains its force as a genuine sacred symbol; it still provides a
meaningful framework for facing death—for most people the only
meaningful framework. We cannot attribute the failure of the ritual to
secularization, to a growth in skepticism, or to a disinterest in the traditional "saving beliefs," any more than we can attribute it to anomie.

We must rather, I think, ascribe it to a discontinuity between the
form of integration existing in the social structural ("causal-functional")
dimension and the form of integration existing in the cultural ("logico-
meaningful") dimension—a discontinuity which leads not to social and
cultural disintegration, but to social and cultural conflict. In more concrete, if somewhat aphoristic terms, the difficulty lies in the fact that socially kampong people are urbanites, while culturally they are still folk.

I have already pointed out that the Javanese kampong represents a
transitional sort of society, that its members stand "in between" the
more or less fully urbanized elite and the more or less traditionally organized peasantry. The social structural forms in which they participate

are for the most part urban ones. The emergence of a highly differentiated occupational structure in place of the almost entirely agricultural one of the countryside; the virtual disappearance of the semihereditary, traditional village government as a personalistic buffer between the individual and the rationalized central government bureaucracy, and its replacement by the more flexible forms of modern parliamentary democracy; the evolution of a multiclass society in which the kampong, unlike the village, is not even a potentially self-sufficient entity, but is only one dependent subpart—all this means that the kampong man lives in a very urban world. Socially, his is a *Gesellschaft* existence.

But on the cultural level—the level of meaning—there is much less of a contrast between the kampong dweller and the villager; much more between him and a member of the urban elite. The patterns of belief, expression, and value to which the kampong man is committed—his world view, ethos, ethic, or whatever—differ only slightly from those followed by the villager. Amid a radically more complex social environment, he clings noticeably to the symbols which guided him or his parents through life in rural society. And it is this fact which gave rise to the psychological and social tension surrounding Paidjan's funeral.

The disorganization of the ritual resulted from a basic ambiguity in the meaning of the rite for those who participated in it. Most simply stated, this ambiguity lay in the fact that the symbols which compose the slametan had both religious and political significance, were charged with both sacred and profane import. The people who came into Karman's yard, including Karman himself, were not sure whether they were engaged in a sacralized consideration of first and last things or in a secular struggle for power. This is why the old man (he was a graveyard keeper, as a matter of fact) complained to me that dying was nowadays a political problem; why the village policeman accused the Modin not of religious but of political bias for refusing to bury Paidjan; why the unsophisticated Karman was astonished when his ideological commitments suddenly loomed as obstacles to his religious practices; why Abu was torn between his willingness to submerge political differences in the interest of a harmonious funeral and his unwillingness to trifle with his religious beliefs in the interest of his own salvation; why the commemorative rite oscillated between political diatribe and a poignant search for an adequate explanation of what had happened—why, in sum, the slametan religious pattern stumbled when it attempted to "step in" with the "positive creed" and "the culturally valuable belief."

As emphasized earlier, the present severity of the contrast between santri and abangan is in great part due to the rise of nationalist social movements in twentieth century Indonesia. In the larger cities where these movements were born, they were originally of various sorts: tradesmen's societies to fight Chinese competition; unions of workers to resist plantation exploitation; religious groups trying to redefine ultimate concepts; philosophical discussion clubs attempting to clarify Indonesian metaphysical and moral notions; school associations striving to revivify Indonesian education; cooperative societies trying to work out new forms of economic organization; cultural groups moving toward a renaissance of Indonesian artistic life; and, of course, political parties working to build up effective opposition to Dutch rule. As time wore on, however, the struggle for independence absorbed more and more the energies of all these essentially elite groups. Whatever the distinctive aim of each of them—economic reconstruction, religious reform, artistic renaissance—it became submerged in a diffuse political ideology; all the groups were increasingly concerned with one end as the prerequisite of all further social and cultural progress—freedom. By the time the revolution began in 1945, reformulation of ideas outside the political sphere had noticeably slackened and most aspects of life had become intensely ideologized, a tendency which has continued into the postwar period.

In the villages and small-town kampongs, the early, specific phase of nationalism had only a minor effect. But as the movement unified and moved toward eventual triumph, the masses too began to be affected and, as I have pointed out, mainly through the medium of religious symbols. The highly urbanized elite forged their bonds to the peasantry not in terms of complex political and economic theory, which would have had little meaning in a rural context, but in terms of concepts and values already present there. As the major line of demarcation among the elite was between those who took Islamic doctrine as the overall basis of their mass appeal and those who took a generalized philosophical refinement of the indigenous syncretic tradition as such a basis, so in the countryside santri and abangan soon became not simply religious but political categories, denoting the followers of these two diffuse approaches to the organization of the emerging independent society. When the achievement of political freedom strengthened the importance of factional politics in parliamentary government, the santri–abangan distinction became, on the local level at least, one of the primary ideological axes around which the process of party maneuvering took place.

The effect of this development has been to cause political debate and religious propitiation to be carried out in the same vocabulary. A koranic chant becomes an affirmation of political allegiance as well as a paean to God; a burning of incense expresses one's secular ideology as well as one's sacred beliefs. Slametans now tend to be marked by anxious discussions of the various elements in the ritual, of what their "real" significance is; by arguments as to whether a particular practice is essential or optional; by abangan uneasiness when santris lift their eyes to pray and santri uneasiness when abangans recite a protective spell. At death, as we have seen, the traditional symbols tend both to solidify individuals in the face of social loss and to remind them of their differences; to emphasize the broadly human themes of mortality and undeserved suffering and the narrowly social ones of factional opposition and party struggle; to strengthen the values the participants hold in common and to "tune up" their animosities and suspicions. The rituals themselves become matters of political conflict; forms for the sacralization of marriage and death are transformed into important party issues. In such an equivocal cultural setting, the average kampong Javanese finds it increasingly difficult to determine the proper attitude toward a particular event, to choose the meaning of a given symbol appropriate to a given social context.

The corollary of this interference of political meanings with religious meanings also occurs: the interference of religious meanings with political ones. Because the same symbols are used in both political and religious contexts, people often regard party struggle as involving not merely the usual ebb and flow of parliamentary maneuver, the necessary factional give-and-take of democratic government, but involving as well decisions on basic values and ultimates. Kampong people in particular tend to see the open struggle for power explicitly institutionalized in the new republican forms of government as a struggle for the right to establish different brands of essentially religious principles as official: "If the abangans get in, the koranic teachers will be forbidden to hold classes"; "If the santris get in, we shall all have to pray five times a day." The normal conflict involved in electoral striving for office is heightened by the idea that literally everything is at stake: the "If we win, it is our country" idea that the group which gains power has a right, as one man said, "to put his own foundation under the state." Politics thus takes on a kind of sacralized bitterness; and one village election in a suburban Modjokuto village actually had to be held twice because of the intense pressures generated in this way.

The kampong man is, so to speak, caught between his ultimate and his proximate concepts. Because he is forced to formulate his essentially metaphysical ideas, his response to such basic "problems" as fate, suffering, and evil, in the same terms as when he states his claims to secular power, his political rights and aspirations, he experiences difficulty in enacting either a socially and psychologically efficient funeral or a smoothly running election.

But a ritual is not just a pattern of meaning; it is also a form of social interaction. Thus, in addition to creating cultural ambiguity, the attempt to bring a religious pattern from a relatively less differentiated rural background into an urban context also gives rise to social conflict, simply because the kind of social integration demonstrated by the pattern is not congruent with the major patterns of integration in the society generally. The way kampong people go about maintaining solidarity in everyday life is quite different from the way the slametan insists that they should go about maintaining it.

As emphasized earlier, the slametan is essentially a territorially based ritual; it assumes the primary tie between families to be that of residential propinquity. One set of neighbors is considered a significant social unit (politically, religiously, economically) as against another set of neighbors; one village as against another village; one village-cluster as against another village-cluster. In the town, this pattern has in large part changed. Significant social groups are defined by a plurality of factors—class, political commitment, occupation, ethnicity, regional origins, religious preference, age, and sex, as well as residence. The new urban form of organization consists of a careful balance of conflicting forces arising out of diverse contexts: class differences are softened by ideological similarities; ethic conflicts by common economic interests; political opposition, as we have been, by residential intimacy. But in the midst of all this pluralistic checking and balancing, the slametan remains unchanged, blind to the major lines of social and cultural demarcation in urban life. For it, the primary classifying characteristic of an individual is where he lives.

Thus when an occasion arises demanding sacralization—a life-cycle transition, a holiday, a serious illness—the religious form which must be employed acts not with but against the grain of social equilibrium. The slametan ignores those recently devised mechanisms of social insulation which in daily life keep group conflict within fixed bounds, as it also ignores the newly evolved patterns of social integration among opposed groups which balance contradictory tensions in a reasonably effective fashion. People are pressed into an intimacy they would as soon avoid; where the incongruity between the social assumptions of the ritual ("we are all culturally homogeneous peasants together") and what is in fact the case ("we are several different kinds of people who must perforce live together despite our serious value disagreements") leads to a deep uneasiness of which Paidjan's funeral was but an extreme example. In the kampong, the holding of a slametan increasingly serves to remind people that the neighborhood bonds they are strengthening through a dramatic enactment are no longer the bonds which most emphatically hold them together. These latter are ideological, class, occupation, and political bonds, divergent ties which are no longer adequately summed up in territorial relationships.

In sum, the disruption of Paidjan's funeral may be traced to a single source: an incongruity between the cultural framework of meaning and the patterning of social interaction, an incongruity due to the persistence in an urban environment of a religious symbol system adjusted to peasant social structure. Static functionalism, of either the sociological or social psychological sort, is unable to isolate this kind of incongruity because it fails to discriminate between logico-meaningful integration and causal-functional integration; because it fails to realize that cultural structure and social structure are not mere reflexes of one another but independent, yet interdependent, variables. The driving forces in social change can be clearly formulated only by a more dynamic form of functionalist theory, one which takes into account the fact that man's need to live in a world to which he can attribute some significance, whose essential import he feels he can grasp, often diverges from his concurrent need to maintain a functioning social organism. A diffuse concept of culture as "learned behavior," a static view of social structure as an equilibrated pattern of interaction, and a stated or unstated assumption that the two must somehow (save in "disorganized" situations) be simple mirror images of one another, is rather too primitive a conceptual apparatus with which to attack such problems as those raised by Paidjan's unfortunate but instructive funeral.

Chapter 7 /

"Internal Conversion"

in Contemporary Bali

⚜

Every race has its lumber-room of magical beliefs and practices, and many such survivals are gracious and beautiful and maintain the continuity of a civilization. It is to be hoped that modern materialist ideas will not obliterate them entirely and leave Malay culture jejune.
RICHARD WINSTEDT, *The Malay Magician*

We hear much these days about political and economic modernization in the new states of Asia and Africa, but little about religious modernization. When not ignored entirely, religion tends to be viewed either as a rigidly archaic obstacle to needed progress or a beleaguered conservator of precious cultural values threatened by the corrosive powers of rapid change. Little attention is paid to religious development in and of itself, to regularities of transformation which occur in the ritual and belief systems of societies undergoing comprehensive social revolutions. At best, we get studies of the role that established religious commitments and identifications play in political or economic processes. But our view of Asian and African religions as such is oddly static. We expect them to prosper or decline; we do not expect them to change.

With respect to Bali, perhaps the most richly stocked lumber-room of gracious and beautiful magical beliefs and practices in Southeast Asia, such an approach is virtually universal, and the dilemma of choosing between a quixotic cultural antiquarianism and a barren cultural materialism seems, therefore, to be an especially cruel one. In this essay, I want to suggest that this dilemma is, in all likelihood, a false one, that the continuity of Balinese civilization can be maintained though the fundamental nature of its religious life be totally transformed. And further, I want to point to a few faint, uncertain signs that such a transformation is in fact already under way.

The Concept of Religious Rationalization

In his great work on comparative religion, the German sociologist Max Weber set forth a distinction between two idealized polar types of religions in world history, the "traditional" and the "rationalized," which, if it is overgeneralized and incompletely formulated, is yet a useful starting point for a discussion of the process of genuinely religious change.[1]

The axis of this contrast turns upon a difference in the relationship between religious concepts and social forms. Traditional religious concepts (Weber also calls them magical) rigidly stereotype established social practices. Inextricably bound up with secular custom in an almost point-for-point manner, they draw "all branches of human activity . . . into the circle of symbolic magic" and so insure that the stream of everyday existence continues to flow steadily within a fixed and firmly outlined course.[2] Rationalized concepts, however, are not so thoroughly intertwined with the concrete details of ordinary life. They are "apart," "above," or "outside" of them, and the relations of the systems of ritual and belief in which they are embodied to secular society are not intimate and unexamined but distant and problematic. A rationalized religion is, to the degree that it is rationalized, self-conscious and worldly-wise. Its attitude to secular life may be various, from the resigned

---

[1] Weber's main theoretical discussion of religion is contained in a still untranslated section of his *Wirtschaft and Gesellschaft* (Tübingen, 1925), pp. 225–356, but application of his approach can be found in the translations of his *Religionssoziologie* issued as *The Religion of China* (Glencoe, Ill., 1958), *Ancient Judaism* (Glencoe, Ill., 1952), *The Religion of India* (Glencoe, Ill., 1958), and *The Protestant Ethic and the Spirit of Capitalism* (New York, 1958). The best discussions of Weber's work in English are T. Parsons, *The Structure of Social Action* (Glencoe, Ill., 1949), and R. Bendix, *Max Weber: An Intellectual Portrait* (New York, 1960).

[2] Quoted in Parsons, *Social Action,* p. 566.

acceptance of genteel Confucianism to the active mastery of ascetic Protestantism; but it is never naive.[3]

With this difference in relationship between the religious realm and the secular goes a difference also in the structure of the religious realm itself. Traditional religions consist of a multitude of very concretely defined and only loosely ordered sacred entities, an untidy collection of fussy ritual acts and vivid animistic images which are able to involve themselves in an independent, segmental, and immediate manner with almost any sort of actual event. Such systems (for, despite their lack of formal regularity, they are systems) meet the perennial concerns of religion, what Weber called the "problems of meaning"—evil, suffering, frustration, bafflement, and so on—piecemeal. They attack them opportunistically as they arise in each particular instance—each death, each crop failure, each untoward natural or social occurrence—employing one or another weapon chosen, on grounds of symbolic appropriateness, from their cluttered arsenal of myth and magic. (With respect to the less defensive activities of religion—the celebration of human continuity, prosperity, and solidarity—the same strategy is employed.) As the approach to fundamental spiritual issues which traditional religions take is discrete and irregular, so also is their characteristic form.

Rationalized religions, on the other hand, are more abstract, more logically coherent, and more generally phrased. The problems of meaning, which in traditional systems are expressed only implicitly and fragmentarily, here get inclusive formulations and evoke comprehensive attitudes. They become conceptualized as universal and inherent qualities of human existence as such, rather than being seen as inseparable aspects of this or that specific event. The question is no longer put merely in such terms as, to use a classic example from the British anthropologist Evans-Pritchard, "Why has the granary fallen on my brother and not on someone else's brother?" but rather, "Why do the good die young and the evil flourish as the green bay tree?" [4] Or, to escape from the conventions of Christian theodicy, not, "By what means can I discover who practiced witchcraft against my brother, thereby causing the granary to fall on him?" but, "How can one know the truth?" Not, "What specific actions must I perform in order to wreak vengeance upon the witch?" but, "What are the bases upon which punishment of

[3] Weber, *Religion of China*, pp. 226–249.
[4] E. E. Evans-Pritchard, *Witchcraft, Oracles and Magic Among the Azande* (Oxford, 1932).

evildoers can be justified?" The narrower, concrete questions, of course, remain; but they are subsumed under the broader ones, whose more radically disquieting suggestions they therefore bring forward. And with this raising of the broader ones in a stark and general form arises also the need to answer them in an equally sweeping, universal, and conclusive manner.

The so-called world religions developed, Weber argued, as responses to the appearance in an acute form of just this sort of need. Judaism, Confucianism, Philosophical Brahmanism, and, though on the surface it might not seem to be a religion at all, Greek Rationalism, each emerged out of a myriad of parochial cults, folk mythologies, and ad hoc by-beliefs whose power had begun to fail for certain crucial groups in the societies concerned.[5] This sense, on the part, largely, of religious intellectuals, that the traditional conglomerate of rituals and beliefs was no longer adequate, and the rise to consciousness of the problems of meaning in an explicit form, seems to have been part, in each case, of a much wider dislocation in the pattern of traditional life. The details of such dislocations (or of those amidst which later world religions, descended from these first four, appeared) need not detain us. What is important is that the process of religious rationalization seems everywhere to have been provoked by a thorough shaking of the foundations of social order.

Provoked, but not determined. For, aside from the fact that profound social crisis has not always produced profound religious creativity (or any creativity at all), the lines along which such creativity has moved when it has appeared have been most varied. Weber's whole grand comparison of the religions of China, India, Israel, and the West rested on the notion that they represented variant directions of rationalization, contrastive choices among a finite set of possible developments away from magical realism. What these diverse systems had in common was not the specific content of their message, which deepened in its particularity as it expanded in its scope, but the formal pattern, the generic mode, in which it was cast. In all of them, the sense of sacredness was gathered up, like so many scattered rays of light brought to focus in a lens, from the countless tree spirits and garden spells through which it

[5] For a discussion of Weber's analysis of the role of status groups in religious change, see Bendix, *Max Weber,* 103–111. My formulation here and elsewhere in this discussion owes much to an unpublished paper by Robert Bellah, "Religion in the Process of Cultural Differentiation"; see also his *Tokugawa Religion* (Glencoe, Ill., 1957).

was vaguely diffused, and was concentrated in a nucleate (though not necessarily monotheistic) concept of the divine. The world was, in Weber's famous phrase, disenchanted: the locus of sacredness was removed from the rooftrees, graveyards, and road-crossings of everyday life and put, in some sense, into another realm where dwelt Jahweh, Logos, Tao, or Brahman.[6]

With this tremendous increase in "distance," so to speak, between man and the sacred goes the necessity of sustaining the ties between them in a much more deliberate and critical manner. As the divine can no longer be apprehended *en passant* through numberless concrete, almost reflexive ritual gestures strategically interspersed throughout the general round of life, the establishment of a more general and comprehensive relationship to it becomes, unless one is to abandon concern with it altogether, imperative. Weber saw two main ways in which this can be brought about. One is through the construction of a consciously systematized, formal, legal-moral code consisting of ethical commands conceived to have been given to man by the divine, through prophets, holy writings, miraculous indications, and so on. The other is through direct, individual experiential contact with the divine via mysticism, insight, aesthetic intuition, etc., often with the assistance of various sorts of highly organized spiritual and intellectual disciplines, such as yoga. The first approach is, of course, typically, though not exclusively, mid-Eastern; the second typically, though also not exclusively, East Asian. But whether, as seems unlikely, these are the only two possibilities, or not, they both do bridge the enormously widened gap, or attempt to bridge it, between the profane and the sacred in a self-conscious, methodical, explicitly coherent manner. They maintain, for those who are committed to them, a sense of a meaningful tie between man and the removed divine.

As with all Weber's polar contrasts, however, that between traditional and rational (the opposite of which is not irrational, but unrationalized) is as thoroughly blurred in fact as it is sharply drawn in theory. In particular, it must not be assumed that the religions of nonliterate peoples are wholly lacking in rationalized elements and those of literate ones rationalized through and through. Not only do many so-called primitive religions show the results of significant amounts of self-conscious criticism, but a popular religiosity of a traditional sort persists with great strength in societies where religious thought has attained its

[6] Bellah, "Differentiation."

highest reaches of philosophical sophistication.[7] Yet, in relative terms, it is hardly to be doubted that the world religions show greater conceptual generalization, tighter formal integration, and a more explicit sense of doctrine than do the "little" ones of clan, tribe, village, or folk. Religious rationalization is not an all-or-none, an irreversible, or an inevitable process. But, empirically, it is a real one.

Traditional Balinese Religion

As the Balinese are, in a broad sense, Hindus, one might expect that a significant part, at least, of their religious life would be relatively well rationalized, that over and above the usual torrent of popular religiosity there would exist a developed system of either ethical or mystical theology. Yet this is not the case. A number of overintellectualized descriptions of it to the contrary notwithstanding, Balinese religion, even among the priests, is concrete, action-centered, thoroughly interwoven with the details of everyday life, and touched with little, if any, of the philosophical sophistication or generalized concern of classical Brahmanism or its Buddhist offshoot.[8] Its approach to the problems of meaning remains implicit, circumscribed and segmental. The world is still enchanted and (some recent stirrings aside for the moment) the tangled net of magical realism is almost completely intact, broken only here and there by individual qualms and reflections.

How far this absence of a developed body of doctrine is a result of the persistence of the indigenous (that is, pre-Hindu) element, of the relative isolation of Bali from the outside world after the fifteenth century or so and the consequent parochialization of its culture, or of the rather unusual degree to which Balinese social structure has been able to maintain a solidly traditional form, is a moot question. In Java, where the pressure of external influences has been relentless, and where

[7] On rationalized elements in "primitive" religions see P. Radin, *Primitive Man as a Philosopher* (New York, 1957). On popular religion in developed civilizations, Bendix, *Weber*, 112–116.
[8] The very partial nature of the one slight exception to this can be seen from the brief description of a priest's intellectual training in V. E. Korn, "The Consecration of a Priest," in J. L. Swellengrebel et al., *Bali: Studies in Life, Thought and Ritual* (The Hague and Bandung, 1960), pp. 133–153.

traditional social structure has lost much of its resilience, not just one but several relatively well-rationalized systems of belief and worship have developed, giving a conscious sense of religious diversity, conflict, and perplexity still quite foreign to Bali.[9] Thus, if one comes, as I did, to Bali after having worked in Java, it is the near total absence of either doubt or dogmatism, the metaphysical nonchalance, that almost immediately strikes one. That, and the astounding proliferation of ceremonial activity. The Balinese, perpetually weaving intricate palm-leaf offerings, preparing elaborate ritual meals, decorating all sorts of temples, marching in massive processions, and falling into sudden trances, seem much too busy practicing their religion to think (or worry) very much about it.

Yet, again, to say that Balinese religion is not methodically ordered is not to say that it is not ordered at all. Not only is it pervaded with a consistent, highly distinctive tone (a kind of sedulous theatricalism which only extended description could evoke), but the elements which comprise it cluster into a number of relatively well-defined ritual complexes which exhibit, in turn, a definite approach to properly religious issues no less reasonable for being implicit. Of these, three are of perhaps greatest importance: (1) the temple system; (2) the sanctification of social inequality; and (3) the cult of death and witches. As the relevant ethnographic details are readily available in the literature, my description of these complexes can be cursory.[10]

1. *The temple system* is a type example of the wholesale fashion in which the diverse strands of a traditional religion twine themselves through the social structure within which they are set. Though all the temples, of which there are literally thousands, are built on a generally similar open-court plan, each is entirely focused on one or another of a number of quite specifically defined concerns: death, neighborhood patriotism, kin-group solidarity, agricultural fertility, caste pride, political loyalty, and so on. Every Balinese belongs to from two or three to a dozen such temples; and, as the congregation of each is composed of those families who happen to use the same graveyard, live in the same neighborhood, farm the same fields, or have other links, such memberships and the heavy ritual obligations they involve buttress rather directly the sort of social relationships out of which Balinese daily life is built.

[9] On Java, see C. Geertz, *The Religion of Java* (Glencoe, Ill., 1960).
[10] For a general survey, see M. Covarrubias, *Island of Bali* (New York, 1956).

The religious forms associated with the various temples, like the architecture broadly similar from temple to temple, are almost wholly ceremonial in nature. Beyond a minimal level, there is almost no interest in doctrine, or generalized interpretation of what is going on, at all. The stress is on orthopraxy, not orthodoxy—what is crucial is that each ritual detail should be correct and in place. If one is not, a member of the congregation will fall, involuntarily, into a trance, becoming thereby the chosen messenger of the gods, and will refuse to revive until the error, announced in his ravings, has been corrected. But the conceptual side is of much less moment: the worshippers usually don't even know who the gods in the temples are, are uninterested in the meaning of the rich symbolism, and are indifferent to what others may or may not believe. You can believe virtually anything you want to actually, including that the whole thing is rather a bore, and even say so. But if you do not perform the ritual duties for which you are responsible you will be totally ostracized, not just from the temple congregation, but from the community as a whole.

Even the execution of ceremonies has an oddly externalized air about it. The main such ceremony occurs on each temple's "birthday," every 210 days, at which time the gods descend from their homes atop the great volcano in the center of the island, enter iconic figurines placed on an altar in the temple, remain three days, and then return. On the day of their arrival the congregation forms a gay parade, advancing to meet them at the edge of the village, welcoming them with music and dance, and escorting them to the temple where they are further entertained; on the day of their departure they are sent off with a similar, though sadder, more restrained procession. But most of the ritual between the first and the last day is performed by the temple priest alone, the congregation's main obligation being to construct tremendously complex offerings and bring them to the temple. There is, on the first day, an important collective ritual at which holy water is sprinkled on members of the congregation as, palms to forehead, they make the classic Hindu obeisance gesture to the gods. But even in this seemingly sacramental ceremony only one member of the household need participate, and it is usually a woman or an adolescent who is so delegated, the men being generally unconcerned so long as a few drops of the charmed water falls protectively upon some representative of their family.

2. *The sanctification of social inequality* centers on the one hand around the Brahmana priesthood and on the other around the enormous

ceremonies which the dozens of kings, princes, and lordlings of Bali give to express and reinforce their ascendency. In Bali, the symbolization of social inequality, of rank, has always been the linchpin of supravillage political organization. From the very earliest stages, the primary moving forces in the process of state formation have been more stratificatory than political, have been concerned more with status than with statecraft. It was not a drive toward higher levels of administrative, fiscal, or even military efficiency that acted as the fundamental dynamic element in the shaping of the Balinese polity, but rather an intense emphasis on the ceremonial expression of delicately graduated distinctions in social standing. Governmental authority was made to rest, secondarily and quite precariously, on more highly valued prestige differences between social strata; and the actual mechanisms of political control through which an authoritarian oligarchy exercises its power were much less elaborately developed than were those through which a traditional cultural elite demonstrates its spiritual superiority— that is, state ritual, court art, and patrician etiquette.

Thus, where the temples are primarily associated with egalitarian village groups—perhaps the fundamental structural principle around which they are organized is that within the temple context all differences in social rank between members of the congregation are irrelevant —the priesthood and the spectacular ceremonies of the upper caste tie gentry and peasantry together into relationships that are frankly asymmetrical.

While any male member of the Brahmana caste is eligible to become a priest, only a minority undertake the extended period of training and purification that is prerequisite to actual practice in the role.[11] Though it has no organization as such, each priest operating independently, the priesthood as a whole is very closely identified with the nobility. The ruler and the priest are said to stand side by side as "full brothers." Each without the other would fall, the first for lack of charismatic potency, the second for lack of armed protection. Even today, each noble house has a symbiotic tie with a particular priestly house which is considered to be its spiritual counterpart, and in the precolonial period not only were the royal courts largely manned by priests, but no priest could be consecrated without permission of the local ruler and no ruler legitimately installed except by a priest.

[11] A priest usually must have a Brahmana wife in order to be consecrated, and his wife may fill his role after his death as a full-fledged priest.

On the commoner or lower-caste side each priest "owns" a number of followers, allotted to his house at one point or another by this or that noble house and subsequently inherited from generation to generation. These followers are scattered, if not altogether randomly, at least very widely—say three in one village, four in the next, several more in a third, and so on—the reason for this practice evidently being a wish on the part of the nobility to keep the priesthood politically weak. Thus, in any one village a man and his neighbor will ordinarily be dependent upon different priests for their religious needs, the most important of which is the obtaining of holy water, an element essential not just for temple ceremonies but for virtually all important rituals. Only a Brahmana priest can address the gods directly in order to sanctify water, as only he has, as the result of his ascetic regimen and his caste purity, the spiritual strength to traffic safely with the tremendous magical power involved. The priests are thus more professional magicians than true priests: they do not serve the divine nor elucidate it, but, through the agency of ill-understood sanskritic chants and beautifully stylized sacred gestures, they utilize it.

A priest's followers refer to him as their *siwa,* after the god by whom he is possessed during the entranced portions of his rite, and he refers to them as his *sisija,* roughly "clients"; and in such a way the hierarchical social differentiation into upper and lower castes is symbolically assimilated to the spiritual contrast between priests and ordinary men. The other means through which rank is given religious expression and support, the prodigious ceremonies of the nobility, employs an institution of political rather than ritual clientage—*corvée*—to underscore the legitimacy of radical social inequality. Here, it is not the content of the ceremonial activity which is important, but the fact that one is in a position to mobilize the human resources to produce such an extravaganza at all.

Usually focused around life-cycle events (tooth-filing, cremation), these ceremonies involve the collective efforts of great masses of subjects, dependents, etc., over a considerable stretch of time, and form, therefore, not just the symbol but the very substance of political loyalty and integration. In precolonial times the preparation and performance of such grand spectacles seem to have consumed more time and energy than all other state activities, including warfare, put together, and so, in a sense, the political system can be said to have existed to support the ritual system, rather than the other way round. And, despite colonialism, occupation, war, and independence, the pattern in great part persists—the gentry is still, in Cora Du Bois's fine phrase, "the symbolic expression of the peasantry's greatness," and the peasantry, still the lifeblood of the gentry's pretensions.[12]

3. *The cult of death and witches* is the "dark" side of Balinese religion, and, though it penetrates into virtually every corner of daily life, adding an anxious note to the otherwise equable tenor of existence, it finds its most direct and vivid expression in the ecstatic ritual combat of those two strange mythological figures: Rangda and Barong. In Rangda, monstrous queen of the witches, ancient widow, used-up prostitute, child-murdering incarnation of the goddess of death, and, if Margaret Mead is correct, symbolic projection of the rejecting mother, the Balinese have fashioned a powerful image of unqualified evil.[13] In Barong, a vaguely benign and slightly ludicrous deity, who looks and acts like a cross between a clumsy bear, a foolish puppy, and a strutting Chinese dragon, they have constructed an almost parodic representation of human strength and weakness. That in their headlong encounters these two demons, each saturated with that mana-like power the Balinese call *sakti,* arrive inevitably at an exact stand-off is therefore not without a certain ultimate significance for all its magical concreteness.

The actual enactments of the battle between Rangda and Barong usually, though not inevitably, take place during a death temple's "birthday" ceremony. One villager (a man) dances Rangda, donning the fierce mask and repulsive costume; two others, arranged fore and aft as in a vaudeville horse, dance the elegant Barong. Both entranced, the hag and dragon advance warily from opposite sides of the temple yard amid curses, threats, and growing tension. At first Barong fights alone, but soon members of the audience begin falling involuntarily into trance, seizing krisses, and rushing to his aid. Rangda advances toward Barong and his helpers, waving her magical cloth. She is hideous and terrifying, and, although they hate her with a terrible rage and want to destroy her, they fall back. When she, held at bay by Barong's *sakti,* then turns away, she suddenly becomes irresistibly attractive (at least so my informants reported) and they advance on her eagerly from the rear, sometimes even trying to mount her from behind; but, with a turn of

[12] C. Du Bois, *Social Forces in Southeast Asia* (Cambridge, Mass., 1959), p. 31.
[13] G. Bateson and M. Mead, *Balinese Character: A Photographic Analysis* (New York, 1942).

her head and a touch of her cloth, they fall helpless into a coma. Finally she withdraws from the scene, undefeated, but at least checked, and Barong's desperately frustrated assistants burst into wild self-destructive rages, turning their krisses (ineffectively, because they are in trance) against their chests, desperately hurling themselves about, devouring live chicks, and so on. From the long moment of tremulous expectancy which precedes the initial appearance of Rangda to this final dissolution into an orgy of futile violence and degradation, the whole performance has a most uncomfortable air of being about to descend at any moment into sheer panic and wild destruction. Evidently it never does, but the alarming sense of touch-and-go, with the diminishing band of the entranced desperately attempting to keep the situation minimally in hand, is altogether overwhelming, even for a mere observer. The razor-thin dimensions of the line dividing reason from unreason, eros from thanatos, or the divine from the demonic, could hardly be more effectively dramatized.

The Rationalization of Balinese Religion

Except for a few odd sports of limited consequence such as Bahai or Mormonism (and leaving aside, as equivocal cases, the so-called political religions such as Communism and Fascism), no new rationalized world religions have arisen since Mohammed. Consequently, almost all of the tribal and peasant peoples of the world who have shed, to whatever degree, the husk of their traditional faiths since that time, have done so through conversion to one or another of the great missionary religions—Christianity, Islam, or Buddhism. For Bali, however, such a course seems precluded. Christian missionaries have never made much progress on the island and, connected as they are with the discredited colonial regime, their chances would now seem poorer than ever. Nor are the Balinese likely to become Muslims in large numbers, despite the general Islamism of Indonesia. They are, as a people, intensely conscious and painfully proud of being a Hindu island in a Muslim sea, and their attitude toward Islam is that of the duchess to the bug. To become either Christian or Muslim would be tantamount, in their eyes, to ceasing to be Balinese, and, indeed, an occasional individual who is converted is still considered, even by the most tolerant and sophisticated, to have abandoned not just Balinese religion but Bali, and perhaps reason, itself. Both Christianity and Islam may influence further religious developments on the island; but they have virtually no chance of controlling them.[14]

Yet, that a comprehensive shaking of the foundations of the Balinese social order is, if not already begun, in the very immediate offing, is apparent on all sides. The emergence of the unitary Republic and the enclosure of Bali as a component within it has brought modern education, modern governmental forms, and modern political consciousness to the island. Radically improved communications have brought increased awareness of, and contact with, the outside world, and provided novel criteria against which to measure the worth both of their own culture and that of others. And inexorable internal changes—increased urbanization, growing population pressure, and so on—have made maintenance of traditional systems of social organization in unchanged form progressively more difficult. What happened in Greece or China after the fifth century B.C.—the disenchantment of the world—seems about to happen, in an altogether different historical context and with an altogether different historical meaning, in mid-twentieth century Bali.

Unless, as is of course a real possibility, events move too fast for them to maintain their cultural heritage at all, the Balinese seem likely to rationalize their religious system through a process of "internal conversion." Following, generally and not uncritically, the guidelines of the Indian religions to which they have been so long nominally affiliated, but from whose doctrinal spirit they have been almost wholly cut off, they seem on the verge of producing a self-conscious "Bali-ism" which, in its philosophical dimensions, will approach the world religions both in the generality of the questions it asks and in the comprehensiveness of the answers it gives.

The questions, at least, are already being asked; particularly by the youth. Among the educated or semieducated young men of eighteen to thirty who formed the ideological vanguard of the Revolution, there have appeared scattered but distinct signs of a conscious interest in

---

[14] For a similar judgment by a missionary linguist, see J. L. Swellengrebel, Introduction, in Swellengrebel et al., *Bali,* pp. 68–76. As the present paper was drafted in the field before Swellengrebel's appeared, the convergence of some of the material he presents with mine serves as something of an independent support for the reality of the process outlined here.

spiritual issues of a sort which still seem largely meaningless to their elders or their less *engagés* contemporaries.

For example, one night, at a funeral in the village where I was living, a full-scale philosophical discussion of such issues broke out among eight or ten young men squatted around the courtyard "guarding" the corpse. As the other aspects of traditional Balinese religion which I have described, funeral ceremonies consist largely of a host of detailed little busy-work routines, and whatever concern with first and last things death may stimulate is well submerged in a bustling ritualism. But these young men, who involved themselves but minimally in all this, the necessary observances being mostly performed by their elders, fell spontaneously into a searching discussion of the nature of religion as such.

At first they addressed themselves to a problem which has haunted the religious and the students of religion alike: how can you tell where secular custom leaves off and religion, the truly sacred, begins? Are all the items in the detailed funeral rite really necessary homage to the gods, genuinely sacred matters? Or are many simply human customs performed out of blind habit and tradition? And, if so, how can you differentiate the one from the other?

One man offered the notion that practices which were clearly connected with grouping people together, strengthening their bonds with one another—for example, the communal construction of the corpse litter by the village as a whole, or the kin-group's preparation of the body —were custom, and so not sacred, while those connected directly with the gods—the family obeisance to the spirit of the deceased, the purification of the body with holy water, and so on—were properly religious. Another argued that those elements which appeared generally in ritual observances, which you find virtually everywhere, from birth to death, in the temples and at the Rangda plays (again, holy water is a good example), were religious, but those which occurred only here and there, or were limited to one or two rites, were not.

Then the discussion veered, as such discussions will, to the grounds of validity for religion as such. One man, somewhat Marxist-influenced, propounded social relativism: when in Rome do as the Romans do, a phrase he quoted in its Indonesian form. Religion is a human product. Man thought up God and then named him. Religion is useful and valuable, but it has no supernatural validity. One man's faith is another man's superstition. At bottom, everything comes down to mere custom. This was greeted with universal disagreement, disapproval, and dismay. In response, the son of the village head offered a simple, nonrational belief position. Intellectual arguments are totally irrelevant. He knows in his heart that the gods exist. Faith is first, thought secondary. The truly religious person, such as himself, just knows that the gods truly come into the temples—he can feel their presence. Another man, more intellectually inclined, erected, more or less on the spot, a complex allegorical symbology to solve the problem. Tooth-filing symbolizes man becoming more like the gods and less like the animals, who have fangs. This rite means this, that that; this color stands for justice, that for courage, etc. What seems meaningless is full of hidden meaning, if only you have the key. A Balinese cabalist. Yet another man, more agnostic, though not a disbeliever, produced the golden mean for us. You can't really think about these things because they don't lie within human comprehension. We just don't know. The best policy is a conservative one—believe just about half of everything you hear. That way you won't go overboard.

And so it went through a good part of the night. Clearly these young men, all of whom (save the village chief's son who was a government clerk in a nearby town) were peasants and smiths, were better Weberians than they knew. They were concerned on the one hand with segregating religion from social life in general, and on the other with trying to close the gap between this world and the other, between secular and sacred, which was thus opened up, by means of some sort of deliberately systematic attitude, some general commitment. Here is the crisis of faith, the breaking of the myths, the shaking of the foundations in a pretty unvarnished form.

The same sort of new seriousness is beginning to appear, here and there, in liturgical contexts as well. In a number of the temple ceremonies—particularly those at which, as is increasingly the case, a Brahmana priest officiates directly rather than, as has been customary, merely providing holy water for the use of the low-caste temple priest —there is appearing an almost pietistic fervor on the part of some of the young male (and a few of the young female) members of the congregation. Rather than permitting but one member of their family to participate for all in the genuflexion to the gods, they all join in, crowding toward the priest so as to have more holy water sprinkled on them. Rather than the context of screaming children and idly chatting adults within which this sacrament usually takes place, they demand, and get, a hushed and reverent atmosphere. They talk, afterward, about the holy water not in magical but emotionalist terms, saying that their inward unease and uncertainty is "cooled" by the water as it falls upon them, and they too speak of feeling the gods' presence directly and immediately. Of all this, the older and the more traditional can make little; they look on it, as they themselves say, like a cow looking at a gamelan orchestra—with an uncomprehending, bemused (but in no way hostile) astonishment.

Such rationalizing developments on the more personal level demand, however, a comparable sort of rationalization at the level of dogma and creed if they are to be sustained. And this is in fact occurring, to a limited extent, through the agency of several recently established publishing firms which are attempting to put scholarly order into the classical palm-leaf literature upon which the Brahmana priesthoods' claim to learning rests, to translate it into modern Balinese or Indonesian, to interpret it in moral-symbolic terms, and to issue it in cheap editions for the increasingly literate masses. These firms are also publishing translations of Indian works, both Hindu and Buddhist, are importing theosophical books from Java, and have even issued several original works by Balinese writers on the history and significance of their religion.[15]

It is, again, the young educated men who for the most part buy these books, but they often read them aloud at home to their families. The interest in them, especially in the old Balinese manuscripts, is very great, even on the part of quite traditional people. When I bought some books of this sort and left them around our house in the village, our front porch became a literary center where groups of villagers would come and sit for hours on end and read them to one another, commenting now and then on their meaning, and almost invariably remarking that it was only since the Revolution that they had been permitted to see such writings, that in the colonial period the upper castes prevented their dissemination altogether. This whole process represents, thus, a spreading of religious literacy beyond the traditional priestly castes—for whom the writings were in any case more magical esoterica than canonical scriptures—to the masses, a vulgarization, in the root sense, of religious knowledge and theory. For the first time, at least a few ordinary Balinese are coming to feel that they can get some understanding of what their religion is all about; and more important, that they have a need for and a right to such understanding.

[15] See Swellengrebel, *Bali,* Introduction, pp. 70–71, for descriptions of some of this literature.

Against such a background, it might seem paradoxical that the main force behind this religious literacy and philosophical-moral interpretation movement is the nobility, or part of it, that it is certain, again generally younger, members of the aristocracy who are collating and translating the manuscripts and founding the firms to publish and distribute them.

But the paradox is only an apparent one. As I have noted, much of the nobility's traditional status rested on ceremonial grounds; a great part of the traditional ceremonial activity was designed so as to produce an almost reflexive acceptance of their eminence and right to rule. But today this simple assumption of eminence is becoming increasingly difficult. It is being undermined by the economic and political changes of Republican Indonesia and by the radically populist ideology which has accompanied these changes. Though a good deal of large-scale ceremonialism still persists on Bali, and though the ruling class continues to express its claim to superiority, in terms of ritual extravagance, the day of the colossal cremation and the titanic tooth-filing seems to be drawing to a close.

To the more perceptive of the aristocracy the handwriting on the wall is thus quite clear: if they persist in basing their right to rule on wholly traditional grounds they will soon lose it. Authority now demands more than court ceremonialism to justify it; it demands "reasons"—that is, doctrine. And it is doctrine that they are attempting to provide through reinterpreting classical Balinese literature and re-establishing intellectual contact with India. What used to rest on ritual habit is now to rest on rationalized dogmatic belief. The main concerns upon which the content of the "new" literature focuses—the reconciliation of polytheism and monotheism, the weighing of the relative importance of "Hindu" and "Balinese" elements in "Hindu-Balinese" religion, the relation of outward form to inward content in worship, the tracing of the historico-mythological origins of caste rankings, and so on—all serve to set the traditional hierarchical social system in an explicitly intellectual context. The aristocracy (or part of it) have cast themselves in the role of the leaders of the new Bali-ism so as to maintain their more general position of social dominance.

To see in all this a mere Machiavellianism, however, would be to give the young nobles both too much credit and too little. Not only are they at best partially conscious of what they are doing, but, like my village theologians, they too are at least in part religiously rather than politically motivated. The transformations which the "new Indonesia" has brought have hit the old élite as hard as any other group in Balinese society by questioning the foundations of their belief in their own vocation and thus their view of the very nature of reality in which they conceive that vocation to be rooted. Their threatened displacement from power appears to them as not just a social but a spiritual issue. Their sudden concern with dogma is, therefore, in part a concern to justify themselves morally and metaphysically, not only in the eyes of the mass of the population but in their own, and to maintain at least the essentials of the established Balinese world view and value system in a radically changed social setting. Like so many other religious innovators, they are simultaneously reformists and restorationists.

Aside from the intensification of religious concern and the systematization of doctrine, there is a third side to this process of rationalization —the social-organizational. If a new "Bali-ism" is to flourish, it needs not only a popular change of heart and an explicit codification, but a more formally organized institutional structure in which it can be socially embodied. This need, essentially an ecclesiastical one, is coming to revolve around the problem of the relation of Balinese religion to the national state, in particular around its place—or lack thereof—in the Republican Ministry of Religion.

The Ministry, which is headed by a full cabinet member, is centered in Djakarta, but has offices scattered over much of the country. It is entirely dominated by Muslims, and its main activities are building mosques, publishing Indonesian translations of the Koran and commentaries, appointing Muslim marriage-closers, supporting Koranic schools, disseminating information about Islam, and so on. It has an elaborate bureaucracy, in which there are special sections for Protestants and Catholics (who largely boycott it anyway on separatist grounds) as distinct religions. But Balinese religion is thrown into the general residual category perhaps best translated as "wild"—that is, pagan, heathen, primitive, etc.—the members of which have no genuine rights in, or aid from, the Ministry. These "wild" religions are considered, in the classical Muslim distinction between "peoples of the Book" and "religions of ignorance," as threats to true piety and fair game for conversion.[16]

The Balinese naturally take a dim view of this and have constantly petitioned Djakarta for equal recognition with Protestantism, Catholicism, and Islam as a fourth major religion. President Sukarno, himself half-Balinese, and many other national leaders sympathize, but they

[16] See Swellengrebel, *Bali,* Introduction, pp. 72–73, for some parliamentary exchanges on this issue.

cannot, as yet, afford to alienate the politically powerful orthodox Muslims and so have vacillated, giving little effective support. The Muslims say that the adherents of Balinese Hinduism are all in one place, unlike the Christians who are scattered all over Indonesia; the Balinese point out that there are Balinese communities in Djakarta and elsewhere in Java, as well as in south Sumatra (transmigrants), and instance the recent erection of Balinese temples in east Java. The Muslims say, you have no Book, how can you be a world religion? The Balinese reply, we have manuscripts and inscriptions dating from before Mohammed. The Muslims say, you believe in many gods and worship stones; the Balinese say, God is One but has many names and the "stone" is the vehicle of God, not God himself. A few of the more sophisticated Balinese even claim that the real reason why the Muslims are unwilling to admit them to the Ministry is the fear that if "Bali-ism" were to become an officially recognized religion, many Javanese, who are Islamic in name only and still very Hindu-Buddhist in spirit, would convert, and "Bali-ism" would grow rapidly at the expense of Islam.

In any case, there is an impasse. And, as a result, the Balinese have set up their own independent, locally financed "Ministry of Religion," and are attempting through it to reorganize some of their most central religious institutions. The main effort, so far, has been concentrated (with largely indifferent results) upon regularizing the qualifications for Brahmana priests. Instead of resting the priestly role mainly on its hereditary aspect, which in itself they, of course, do not question, or on the ritual virtuosity involved, the "Ministry" wishes to rest it on religious knowledge and wisdom. It wants to insure that the priests know what the scriptures mean and can relate them to contemporary life, are of good moral character, have attained at least some degree of genuine scholarship, and so on. Our young men will no longer follow a man just because he is a Brahmana, the officials say; we must make him a figure of moral and intellectual respect, a true spiritual guide. And to this end they are attempting to exercise some control over ordination, even to the point of setting qualifying examinations, and to make the priesthood a more corporate body by holding meetings of all the priests in an area. The representatives of the "Ministry" also tour the villages giving educational speeches on the moral significance of Balinese religion, on the virtues of monotheism and the dangers of idol worship, and so on. They are even attempting to put some order into the temple system, to establish a systematic classification of temples, and perhaps eventually to elevate one kind, most likely the village origin-temple, to pre-eminence in a universalistic pattern comparable to that of a mosque or a church.

All this is, however, still largely in the paper-planning stage, and it cannot be claimed that very much actual reorganization of the institutional structure of Balinese religion has in fact taken place. But there is an office of the "Ministry" in each Balinese regency now, headed by a salaried Brahmana priest (a regularly paid "official" priesthood being in itself something of a revolution), assisted by three or four clerks, most of them also members of the Brahmana caste. A religious school, independent of the "Ministry" but encouraged by it, has been established, and even a small religious political party centered around a ranking noble and dedicated to forwarding these changes has been founded, so that at least the faint beginnings of religious bureaucratization are manifest.

What will come of all this—the intensified religious questioning, the spread of religious literacy, and the attempt to reorganize religious institutions—remains simply to be seen. In many ways, the whole drift of the modern world would seem to be against the sort of movement toward religious rationalization which these developments portend, and perhaps Balinese culture will, in the end, be swamped and left jejune by just the sort of "modern materialist ideas" which Sir Richard Winstedt fears. But not only do such overall drifts—when they do not turn out to be mirages altogether—often pass over deeply rooted cultural configurations with rather less effect upon them than we would have thought possible, but, for all its present weakness, the regenerative potential of a triangular alliance of troubled youth, threatened aristocrats, and aroused priests should not be underestimated. Today in Bali some of the same social and intellectual processes which gave rise to the fundamental religious transformations of world history seem to be at least well begun, and whatever their vicissitudes or eventual outcome, their career can hardly help but be an instructive one. By looking closely at what happens on this peculiar little island over the next several decades we may gain insights into the dynamics of religious change of a specificity and an immediacy that history, having already happened, can never give us.[17]

[17] In 1962, "Balinese Religion" was finally admitted as an official "Great Religion" in Indonesia. Since that time, and particularly since the 1965 massacres, conversions from Islam to "Bali-ism" have indeed markedly increased in Java. And on Bali itself, the Hindu reform movement has grown into a major force. On all this, see C. Geertz, "Religious Change and Social Order in Soeharto's Indonesia," *Asia* 27 (Autumn 1972):62–84.

PART IV

Chapter 8 / Ideology

As a Cultural System

I

It is one of the minor ironies of modern intellectual history that the term "ideology" has itself become thoroughly ideologized. A concept that once meant but a collection of political proposals, perhaps somewhat intellectualistic and impractical but at any rate idealistic—"social romances" as someone, perhaps Napoleon, called them—has now become, to quote *Webster's*, "the integrated assertions, theories, and aims constituting a politico-social program, often with an implication of factitious propagandizing; as, Fascism was altered in Germany to fit the Nazi *ideology*"—a much more formidable proposition. Even in works that, in the name of science, profess to be using a neutral sense of the term, the effect of its employment tends nonetheless to be distinctly polemical: in Sutton, Harris, Kaysen, and Tobin's in many ways excellent *The American Business Creed,* for example, an assurance that "one has no more cause to feel dismayed or aggrieved by having his own views described as 'ideology' than had Molière's famous character by the discovery that all his life he had been talking prose," is followed immediately by the listing of the main characteristics of ideology as bias, oversimplification, emotive language, and adaption to public prejudice.[1] No

[1] F. X. Sutton, S. E. Harris, C. Kaysen, and J. Tobin, *The American Business Creed* (Cambridge, Mass., 1956), pp. 3–6.

one, at least outside the Communist bloc, where a somewhat distinctive conception of the role of thought in society is institutionalized, would call himself an ideologue or consent unprotestingly to be called one by others. Almost universally now the familiar parodic paradigm applies: "I have a social philosophy; you have political opinions; he has an ideology."

The historical process by which the concept of ideology came to be itself a part of the very subject matter to which it referred has been traced by Mannheim; the realization (or perhaps it was only an admission) that sociopolitical thought does not grow out of disembodied reflection but "is always bound up with the existing life situation of the thinker" seemed to taint such thought with the vulgar struggle for advantage it had professed to rise above.[2] But what is of even more immediate importance is the question of whether or not this absorption into its own referent has destroyed its scientific utility altogether, whether or not having become an accusation, it can remain an analytic concept. In Mannheim's case, this problem was the animus of his entire work—the construction, as he put it, of a "nonevaluative conception of ideology." But the more he grappled with it the more deeply he became engulfed in its ambiguities until, driven by the logic of his initial assumptions to submit even his own point of view to sociological analysis, he ended, as is well known, in an ethical and epistemological relativism that he himself found uncomfortable. And so far as later work in this area has been more than tendentious or mindlessly empirical, it has involved the employment of a series of more or less ingenious methodological devices to escape from what may be called (because, like the puzzle of Achilles and the tortoise, it struck at the very foundations of rational knowledge) Mannheim's Paradox.

As Zeno's Paradox raised (or, at least, articulated) unsettling questions about the validity of mathematical reasoning, so Mannheim's Paradox raised them with respect to the objectivity of sociological analysis. Where, if anywhere, ideology leaves off and science begins has been the Sphinx's Riddle of much of modern sociological thought and the rustless weapon of its enemies. Claims to impartiality have been advanced in the name of disciplined adherence to impersonal research procedures, of the academic man's institutional insulation from the immediate con-

---

[2] K. Mannheim, *Ideology and Utopia,* Harvest ed. (New York, n.d.), pp. 59–83; see also R. Merton, *Social Theory and Social Structure* (New York, 1949), pp. 217–220.

cerns of the day and his vocational commitment to neutrality, and of deliberately cultivated awareness of and correction for one's own biases and interests. They have been met with denial of the impersonality (and the effectiveness) of the procedures, of the solidity of the insulation, and of the depth and genuineness of the self-awareness. "I am aware," a recent analyst of ideological preoccupations among American intellectuals concludes, somewhat nervously, "that many readers will claim that my position is itself ideological." [3] Whatever the fate of his other predictions, the validity of this one is certain. Although the arrival of a scientific sociology has been repeatedly proclaimed, the acknowledgment of its existence is far from universal, even among social scientists themselves; and nowhere is resistance to claims to objectivity greater than in the study of ideology.

A number of sources for this resistance have been cited repeatedly in the apologetic literature of the social sciences. The value-laden nature of the subject matter is perhaps most frequently invoked: men do not care to have beliefs to which they attach great moral significance examined dispassionately, no matter for how pure a purpose; and if they are themselves highly ideologized, they may find it simply impossible to believe that a disinterested approach to critical matters of social and political conviction can be other than a scholastic sham. The inherent elusiveness of ideological thought, expressed as it is in intricate symbolic webs as vaguely defined as they are emotionally charged; the admitted fact that ideological special pleading has, from Marx forward, so often been clothed in the guise of "scientific sociology"; and the defensiveness of established intellectual classes who see scientific probing into the social roots of ideas as threatening to their status, are also often mentioned. And, when all else fails, it is always possible to point out once more that sociology is a young science, that it has been so recently founded that it has not had time to reach the levels of institutional solidity necessary to sustain its claims to investigatory freedom in sensitive areas. All these arguments have, doubtless, a certain validity. But what—by a curious selective omission the unkind might well indict as ideological—is not so often considered is the possibility that a great part of the problem lies in the lack of conceptual sophistication within social science itself, that the resistance of ideology to sociological analysis is so great because such analyses are in fact fundamentally inade-

[3] W. White, *Beyond Conformity* (New York, 1961), p. 211.

quate; the theoretical framework they employ is conspicuously incomplete.

I shall try in this essay to show that such is indeed the case: that the social sciences have not yet developed a genuinely nonevaluative conception of ideology; that this failure stems less from methodological indiscipline than from theoretical clumsiness; that this clumsiness manifests itself mainly in the handling of ideology as an entity in itself—as an ordered system of cultural symbols rather than in the discrimination of its social and psychological contexts (with respect to which our analytical machinery is very much more refined); and that the escape from Mannheim's Paradox lies, therefore, in the perfection of a conceptual apparatus capable of dealing more adroitly with meaning. Bluntly, we need a more exact apprehension of our object of study, lest we find ourselves in the position of the Javanese folk-tale figure, "Stupid Boy," who, having been counseled by his mother to seek a quiet wife, returned with a corpse.

II

That the conception of ideology now regnant in the social sciences is a thoroughly evaluative (that is, pejorative) one is readily enough demonstrated. " [The study of ideology] deals with a mode of thinking which is thrown off its proper course," Werner Stark informs us; "ideological thought is . . . something shady, something that ought to be overcome and banished from our mind." It is not (quite) the same as lying, for, where the liar at least attains to cynicism, the ideologue remains merely a fool: "Both are concerned with untruth, but whereas the liar tries to falsify the thought of others while his own private thought is correct, while he himself knows well what the truth is, a person who falls for an ideology is himself deluded in his private thought, and if he misleads others, does so unwillingly and unwittingly." [4] A follower of Mannheim, Stark holds that all forms of thought are socially conditioned in the very nature of things, but that ideology has in addition the unfortunate quality of being psychologically "deformed" ("warped," "contaminated," "falsified," "distorted," "clouded") by the pressure of personal

[4] W. Stark, The Sociology of Knowledge (London, 1958), p. 48.

emotions like hate, desire, anxiety, or fear. The sociology of knowledge deals with the social element in the pursuit and perception of truth, its inevitable confinement to one or another existential perspective. But the study of ideology—an entirely different enterprise—deals with the causes of intellectual error:

Ideas and beliefs, we have tried to explain, can be related to reality in a double way: either to the *facts* of reality, or to the *strivings* to which this reality, or rather the reaction to this reality, gives rise. Where the former connection exists, we find thought which is, in principle, truthful; where the latter relation obtains, we are faced with ideas which can be true only by accident, and which are likely to be vitiated by bias, the word taken in the widest possible sense. The former type of thought deserves to be called theoretical; the latter must be characterized as paratheoretical. Perhaps one might also describe the former as rational, the latter as emotionally tinged —the former as purely cognitive, the latter as evaluative. To borrow Theodor Geiger's simile . . . thought determined by social fact is like a pure stream, crystal-clear, transparent; ideological ideas like a dirty river, muddied and polluted by the impurities that have flooded into it. From the one it is healthy to drink; the other is poison to be avoided.[5]

This is primitive, but the same confinement of the referent of the term "ideology" to a form of radical intellectual depravity also appears in contexts where the political and scientific arguments are both far more sophisticated and infinitely more penetrating. In his seminal essay on "Ideology and Civility," for example, Edward Shils sketches a portrait of "the ideological outlook," which is, if anything, even grimmer than Stark's.[6] Appearing "in a variety of forms, each alleging itself to be unique"—Italian Fascism, German National Socialism, Russian Bolshevism, French and Italian Communism, the Action Française, the British Union of Fascists, "and their fledgling American kinsman, 'McCarthyism,' which died in infancy"—this outlook "encircled and invaded public life in the Western countries during the 19th century and in the 20th century . . . threatened to achieve universal domination." It consists, most centrally, of "the assumption that politics should be conducted from the standpoint of a coherent, comprehensive set of beliefs which must override every other consideration." Like the politics it supports, it is dualistic, opposing the pure "we" to the evil "they," pro-

[5] Ibid., pp. 90–91. Italics in the original. For approximation of the same argument in Mannheim, formulated as a distinction between "total" and "particular" ideology, see *Ideology and Utopia*, pp. 55–59.

[6] E. Shils, "Ideology and Civility: On the Politics of the Intellectual," *The Sewanee Review* 66 (1958): 450–480.

claiming that he who is not with me is against me. It is alienative in that it distrusts, attacks, and works to undermine established political institutions. It is doctrinaire in that it claims complete and exclusive possession of political truth and abhors compromise. It is totalistic in that it aims to order the whole of social and cultural life in the image of its ideals, futuristic in that it works toward a utopian culmination of history in which such an ordering will be realized. It is, in short, not the sort of prose any good bourgeois gentleman (or even any good demo- crat) is likely to admit to speaking.

Even on more abstract and theoretical levels, where the concern is more purely conceptual, the notion that the term "ideology" properly applies to the views of those "stiff in opinions, and always in the wrong" does not disappear. In Talcott Parsons's most recent contempla- tion of Mannheim's Paradox, for example, "deviations from [social] scientific objectivity" emerge as the "essential criteria of an ideology": "The problem of ideology arises where there is a *discrepancy* between what is believed and what can be [established as] scientifically correct." [7] The "deviations" and "discrepancies" involved are of two general sorts. First, where social science, shaped as is all thought by the overall values of the society within which it is contained, is selective in the sort of questions it asks, the particular problems it chooses to tackle, and so forth, ideologies are subject to a further, cognitively more pernicious "secondary" selectivity, in that they emphasize some aspects of social reality—that reality, for example, as revealed by current social scientific knowledge—and neglect or even suppress other aspects. "Thus the business ideology, for instance, substantially exaggerates the contribution of businessmen to the national welfare and underplays the contribution of scientists and professional men. And in the current ide- ology of the 'intellectual,' the importance of social 'pressures to con- formity' is exaggerated and institutional factors in the freedom of the individual are ignored or played down." Second, ideological thought, not content with mere overselectivity, positively distorts even those as- pects of social reality it recognizes, distortion that becomes apparent only when the assertions involved are placed against the background of the authoritative findings of social science. "The criterion of distortion is that statements are made about society which by social-scientific

[7] T. Parsons, "An Approach to the Sociology of Knowledge," *Transactions of the Fourth World Congress of Sociology* (Milan and Stressa, 1959), pp. 25–49. Ital- ics in original.

methods can be shown to be positively in error, whereas selectivity is involved where the statements are, at the proper level, 'true,' but do not constitute a balanced account of the available truth." That in the eyes of the world there is much to choose between being positively in error and rendering an unbalanced account of the available truth seems, however, rather unlikely. Here, too, ideology is a pretty dirty river.

Examples need not be multiplied, although they easily could be. More important is the question of what such an egregiously loaded concept is doing among the analytic tools of a social science that, on the basis of a claim to cold-blooded objectivity, advances its theoretical interpretations as "undistorted" and therefore normative visions of social reality. If the critical power of the social sciences stems from their disinterestedness, is not this power compromised when the analysis of political thought is governed by such a concept, much as the analysis of religious thought would be (and, on occasion, has been) compromised when cast in terms of the study of "superstition"?

The analogy is not farfetched. In Raymond Aron's *The Opium of the Intellectuals,* for example, not only the title—ironically echoic of Marx's bitter iconoclasm—but the entire rhetoric of the argument ("political myths," "the idolatry of history," "churchmen and faithful," "secular clericalism," and so forth) reminds one of nothing so much as the literature of militant atheism.[8] Shils's tack of invoking the extreme pathologies of ideological thought—Nazism, Bolshevism, or whatever—as its paradigmatic forms is reminiscent of the tradition in which the Inquisition, the personal depravity of Renaissance popes, the savagery of Reformation wars, or the primitiveness of Bible-belt fundamentalism is offered as an archetype of religious belief and behavior. And Parsons's view that ideology is defined by its cognitive insufficiencies vis-à-vis science is perhaps not so distant as it might appear from the Comtean view that religion is characterized by an uncritically figurative conception of reality, which a sober sociology, purged of metaphor, will soon render obsolete: We may wait as long for the "end of ideology" as the positivists have waited for the end of religion. Perhaps it is even not too much to suggest that, as the militant atheism of the Enlightenment and after was a response to the quite genuine horrors of a spectacular outburst of religious bigotry, persecution, and strife (and to a broadened knowledge of the natural world), so the militantly hostile approach to

[8] R. Aron, *The Opium of the Intellectuals* (New York, 1962).

ideology is a similar response to the political holocausts of the past half-century (and to a broadened knowledge of the social world). And, if this suggestion is valid, the fate of ideology may also turn out to be similar—isolation from the mainstream of social thought.[9]

Nor can the issue be dismissed as merely a semantic one. One is, naturally, free to confine the referent of the term "ideology" to "something shady" if one wishes; and some sort of historical case for doing so can perhaps be made. But if one does so limit it, one cannot then write works on the ideologies of American businessmen, New York "literary" intellectuals, members of the British Medical Association, industrial labor-union leaders, or famous economists and expect either the subjects or interested bystanders to credit them as neutral.[10] Discussions of sociopolitical ideas that indict them *ab initio,* in terms of the very words used to name them, as deformed or worse, merely beg the questions they pretend to raise. It is also possible, of course, that the term "ideology" should simply be dropped from scientific discourse altogether and left to its polemical fate—as "superstition" in fact has been. But, as there seems to be nothing at the moment with which to replace it and as it is at least partially established in the technical lexicon of the social sciences, it seems more advisable to proceed with the effort to defuse it.[11]

[9] As the danger of being misinterpreted here is serious, may I hope that my criticism will be credited as technical and not political if I note that my own general ideological (as I would frankly call it) position is largely the same as that of Aron, Shils, Parsons, and so forth; that I am in agreement with their plea for a civil, temperate, unheroic politics? Also it should be remarked that the demand for a nonevaluative concept of ideology is not a demand for the nonevaluation of ideologies, any more than a nonevaluative concept of religion implies religious relativism.

[10] Sutton, et al., *American Business Creed;* White, *Beyond Conformity;* H. Eckstein, *Pressure Group Politics: The Case of the British Medical Association* (Stanford, 1960); C. Wright Mills, *The New Men of Power* (New York, 1948); J. Schumpeter, "Science and Ideology," *American Economic Review* 39 (1949): 345–359.

[11] There have been, in fact, a number of other terms used in the literature for the general range of phenomena that "ideology" denotes, from Plato's "noble lies" through Sorel's "myths" to Pareto's "derivations"; but none of them has managed to reach any greater level of technical neutrality than has "ideology." See H. D. Lasswell, "The Language of Power," in Lasswell, N. Leites, and Associates, *Language of Politics* (New York, 1949), pp. 3–19.

III

As the flaws hidden in a tool show up when it is used, so the intrinsic weaknesses of the evaluative concept of ideology reveal themselves when it is used. In particular, they are exposed in the studies of the social sources and consequences of ideology, for in such studies this concept is coupled to a highly developed engine of social- and personality-system analysis whose very power only serves to emphasize the lack of a similar power on the cultural (that is, the symbol-system) side. In investigations of the social and psychological contexts of ideological thought (or at least the "good" ones), the subtlety with which the contexts are handled points up the awkwardness with which the thought is handled, and a shadow of imprecision is cast over the whole discussion, a shadow that even the most rigorous methodological austerity cannot dispel.

There are currently two main approaches to the study of the social determinants of ideology: the interest theory and the strain theory.[12] For the first, ideology is a mask and a weapon; for the second, a symptom and a remedy. In the interest theory, ideological pronouncements are seen against the background of a universal struggle for advantage; in the strain theory, against the background of a chronic effort to correct sociopsychological disequilibrium. In the one, men pursue power; in the other, they flee anxiety. As they may, of course, do both at the same time—and even one by means of the other—the two theories are not necessarily contradictory; but the strain theory (which arose in response to the empirical difficulties encountered by the interest theory), being less simplistic, is more penetrating, less concrete, more comprehensive.

The fundamentals of the interest theory are too well known to need review; developed to perfection of a sort by the Marxist tradition, they are now standard intellectual equipment of the man-in-the-street, who is only too aware that in political argumentation it all comes down to whose ox is gored. The great advantage of the interest theory was and is its rooting of cultural idea-systems in the solid ground of social structure, through emphasis on the motivations of those who profess such systems and on the dependence of those motivations in turn upon social

[12] Sutton, et al., *American Business Creed*, pp. 11–12, 303–310.

position, most especially social class. Further, the interest theory welded political speculation to political combat by pointing out that ideas are weapons and that an excellent way to institutionalize a particular view of reality—that of one's group, class, or party—is to capture political power and enforce it. These contributions are permanent; and if interest theory has not now the hegemony it once had, it is not so much because it has been proved wrong as because its theoretical apparatus turned out to be too rudimentary to cope with the complexity of the interaction among social, psychological, and cultural factors it itself uncovered. Rather like Newtonian mechanics, it has not been so much displaced by subsequent developments as absorbed into them.

The main defects of the interest theory are that its psychology is too anemic and its sociology too muscular. Lacking a developed analysis of motivation, it has been constantly forced to oscillate between a narrow and superficial utilitarianism that sees men as impelled by rational calculation of their consciously recognized personal advantage and a broader, but no less superficial, historicism that speaks with a studied vagueness of men's ideas as somehow "reflecting," "expressing," "corresponding to," "emerging from," or "conditioned by" their social commitments. Within such a framework, the analyst is faced with the choice of either revealing the thinness of his psychology by being so specific as to be thoroughly implausible or concealing the fact that he does not have any psychological theory at all by being so general as to be truistic. An argument that for professional soldiers "domestic [governmental] policies are important mainly as ways of retaining and enlarging the military establishment [because] that is their business; that is what they are trained for" seems to do scant justice to even so uncomplicated a mind as the military mind is reputed to be; while an argument that American oil men "cannot very well be pure-and-simple oil men" because "their interests are such" that "they are also political men" is as enlightening as the theory (also from the fertile mind of M. Jourdain) that the reason opium puts you to sleep is that it has dormitive powers.[13]

On the other hand, the view that social action is fundamentally an unending struggle for power leads to an unduly Machiavellian view of ideology as a form of higher cunning and, consequently, to a neglect of its broader, less dramatic social functions. The battlefield image of so-

<hr>

[13] The quotations are from the most eminent recent interest theorist, C. Wright Mills, *The Causes of World War Three* (New York, 1958), pp. 54, 65.

ciety as a clash of interests thinly disguised as a clash of principles turns attention away from the role that ideologies play in defining (or obscuring) social categories, stabilizing (or upsetting) social expectations, maintaining (or undermining) social norms, strengthening (or weakening) social consensus, relieving (or exacerbating) social tensions. Reducing ideology to a weapon in a *guerre de plume* gives to its analysis a warming air of militancy, but it also means reducing the intellectual compass within which such analysis may be conducted to the constricted realism of tactics and strategy. The intensity of interest theory is—to adapt a figure from Whitehead—but the reward of its narrowness.

As "interest," whatever its ambiguities, is at one and the same time a psychological and sociological concept—referring both to a felt advantage of an individual or group of individuals and to the objective structure of opportunity within which an individual or group moves—so also is "strain," for it refers both to a state of personal tension and to a condition of societal dislocation. The difference is that with "strain" both the motivational background and the social structural context are more systematically portrayed, as are their relations with one another. It is, in fact, the addition of a developed conception of personality systems (basically Freudian), on the one hand, and of social systems (basically Durkheimian) on the other, and of their modes of interpenetration—the Parsonian addition—that transforms interest theory into strain theory.[14]

The clear and distinct idea from which strain theory departs is the chronic malintegration of society. No social arrangement is or can be completely successful in coping with the functional problems it inevitably faces. All are riddled with insoluble antinomies: between liberty and political order, stability and change, efficiency and humanity, precision and flexibility, and so forth. There are discontinuities between norms in different sectors of the society—the economy, the polity, the family, and so on. There are discrepancies between goals within the different sectors—between the emphases on profit and productivity in business firms or between extending knowledge and disseminating it in universities, for example. And there are the contradictory role expectations of which so much has been made in recent American sociological litera-

[14] For the general schema, see Parsons, *The Social System* (New York, 1951), especially Chaps. 1 and 7. The fullest development of the strain theory is in Sutton et al., *American Business Creed*, especially Chap. 15.

ture on the foreman, the working wife, the artist, and the politician. Social friction is as pervasive as is mechanical friction—and as irremovable.

Further, this friction or social strain appears on the level of the
individual personality—itself an inevitably malintegrated system of conflicting desires, archaic sentiments, and improvised defenses—as psychological strain. What is viewed collectively as structural inconsistency
is felt individually as personal insecurity, for it is in the experience of
the social actor that the imperfections of society and contradictions of
character meet and exacerbate one another. But at the same time, the
fact that both society and personality are, whatever their shortcomings,
organized systems, rather than mere congeries of institutions or clusters of motives, means that the sociopsychological tensions they induce
are also systematic, that the anxieties derived from social interaction
have a form and order of their own. In the modern world at least, most
men live lives of patterned desperation.

Ideological thought is, then, regarded as (one sort of) response to this
desperation: "Ideology is a patterned reaction to the patterned strains of
a social role." [15] It provides a "symbolic outlet" for emotional disturbances generated by social disequilibrium. And as one can assume that
such disturbances are, at least in a general way, common to all or most
occupants of a given role or social position, so ideological reactions to
the disturbances will tend to be similar, a similarity only reinforced by
the presumed commonalities in "basic personality structure" among
members of a particular culture, class, or occupational category. The
model here is not military but medical: An ideology is a malady (Sutton, et al., mention nail-chewing, alcoholism, psychosomatic disorders,
and "crotchets" among the alternatives to it) and demands a diagnosis.
"The concept of strain is not in itself an explanation of ideological patterns but a generalized label for the kinds of factors to look for in
working out an explanation." [16]

But there is more to diagnosis, either medical or sociological, than
the identification of pertinent strains; one understands symptoms not
merely etiologically but teleologically—in terms of the ways in which
they act as mechanisms, however unavailing, for dealing with the disturbances that have generated them. Four main classes of explanation have
been most frequently employed: the cathartic, the morale, the solidarity,

[15] Sutton, et al., *American Business Creed*, pp. 307–308.
[16] Parsons, "An Approach."

and the advocatory. By the "cathartic explanation" is meant the venerable safety-valve or scapegoat theory. Emotional tension is drained off by being displaced onto symbolic enemies ("The Jews," "Big Business," "The Reds," and so forth). The explanation is as simple-minded as the device; but that, by providing legitimate objects of hostility (or, for that matter, of love), ideology may ease somewhat the pain of being a petty bureaucrat, a day laborer, or a small-town storekeeper is undeniable. By the "morale explanation" is meant the ability of an ideology to sustain individuals (or groups) in the face of chronic strain, either by denying it outright or by legitimizing it in terms of higher values. Both the struggling small businessman rehearsing his boundless confidence in the inevitable justness of the American system and the neglected artist attributing his failure to his maintenance of decent standards in a Philistine world are able, by such means, to get on with their work. Ideology bridges the emotional gap between things as they are and as one would have them be, thus insuring the performance of roles that might otherwise be abandoned in despair or apathy. By the "solidarity explanation" is meant the power of ideology to knit a social group or class together. To the extent that it exists, the unity of the labor movement, the business community, or the medical profession obviously rests to a significant degree on common ideological orientation; and the South would not be The South without the existence of popular symbols charged with the emotions of a pervasive social predicament. Finally, by the "advocatory explanation" is meant the action of ideologies (and ideologists) in articulating, however partially and indistinctly, the strains that impel them, thus forcing them into the public notice. "Ideologists state the problems for the larger society, take sides on the issues involved and 'present them in the court' of the ideological market place." [17] Although ideological advocates (not altogether unlike their legal counterparts) tend as much to obscure as to clarify the true nature of the problems involved, they at least call attention to their existence and, by polarizing issues, make continued neglect more difficult. Without Marxist attack, there would have been no labor reform; without Black Nationalists, no deliberate speed.

It is here, however, in the investigation of the social and psychological roles of ideology, as distinct from its determinants, that strain theory itself begins to creak and its superior incisiveness, in comparison with interest theory, to evaporate. The increased precision in the

[17] White, *Beyond Conformity*, p. 204.

location of the springs of ideological concern does not, somehow, carry over into the discrimination of its consequences, where the analysis becomes, on the contrary, slack and ambiguous. The consequences envisaged, no doubt genuine enough in themselves, seem almost adventitious, the accidental by-products of an essentially nonrational, nearly automatic expressive process initially pointed in another direction—as when a man stubbing his toe cries an involuntary "ouch!" and incidentally vents his anger, signals his distress, and consoles himself with the sound of his own voice; or as when, caught in a subway crush, he issues a spontaneous "damn!" of frustration and, hearing similar oaths from others, gains a certain perverse sense of kinship with fellow sufferers.

This defect, of course, can be found in much of the functional analysis in the social sciences: a pattern of behavior shaped by a certain set of forces turns out, by a plausible but nevertheless mysterious coincidence, to serve ends but tenuously related to those forces. A group of primitives sets out, in all honesty, to pray for rain and ends by strengthening its social solidarity; a ward politician sets out to get or remain near the trough and ends by mediating between unassimilated immigrant groups and an impersonal governmental bureaucracy; an ideologist sets out to air his grievances and finds himself contributing, through the diversionary power of his illusions, to the continued viability of the very system that grieves him.

The concept of latent function is usually invoked to paper over this anomalous state of affairs, but it rather names the phenomenon (whose reality is not in question) than explains it; and the net result is that functional analyses—and not only those of ideology—remain hopelessly equivocal. The petty bureaucrat's anti-Semitism may indeed give him something to do with the bottled anger generated in him by constant toadying to those he considers his intellectual inferiors and so drain some of it away; but it may also simply increase his anger by providing him with something else about which to be impotently bitter. The neglected artist may better bear his popular failure by invoking the classical canons of his art; but such an invocation may so dramatize for him the gap between the possibilities of his environment and the demands of his vision as to make the game seem unworth the candle. Commonality of ideological perception may link men together, but it may also provide them, as the history of Marxian sectarianism demonstrates, with a vocabulary by means of which to explore more exquisitely the differences among them. The clash of ideologists may bring a social problem to public attention, but it may also charge it with such passion that any possibility of dealing with it rationally is precluded. Of all these possibilities, strain theorists are, of course, very well aware. Indeed they tend to stress negative outcomes and possibilities rather more than the positive, and they but rarely think of ideology as more than a *faute de mieux* stopgap—like nail-chewing. But the main point is that, for all its subtlety in ferreting out the motives of ideological concern, strain theory's analysis of the consequences of such concern remains crude, vacillatory, and evasive. Diagnostically it is convincing; functionally it is not.

The reason for this weakness is the virtual absence in strain theory (or in interest theory either) of anything more than the most rudimentary conception of the processes of symbolic formulation. There is a good deal of talk about emotions "finding a symbolic outlet" or "becoming attached to appropriate symbols"—but very little idea of how the trick is really done. The link between the causes of ideology and its effects seems adventitious because the connecting element—the autonomous process of symbolic formulation—is passed over in virtual silence. Both interest theory and strain theory go directly from source analysis to consequence analysis without ever seriously examining ideologies as systems of interacting symbols, as patterns of interworking meanings. Themes are outlined, of course; among the content analysts, they are even counted. But they are referred for elucidation, not to other themes nor to any sort of semantic theory, but either backward to the effect they presumably mirror or forward to the social reality they presumably distort. The problem of how, after all, ideologies transform sentiment into significance and so make it socially available is short-circuited by the crude device of placing particular symbols and particular strains (or interests) side by side in such a way that the fact that the first are derivatives of the second seems mere common sense—or at least post-Freudian, post-Marxian common sense. And so, if the analyst be deft enough, it does.[18] The connection is not thereby explained but merely educed. The nature of the relationship between the sociopsychological stresses that incite ideological attitudes and the elaborate symbolic structures through which those attitudes are given a public existence is much too complicated to be comprehended in terms of a vague and unexamined notion of emotive resonance.

[18] Perhaps the most impressive tour de force in this paratactic genre is Nathan Leites's *A Study of Bolshevism* (New York, 1953).

IV

It is of singular interest in this connection that, although the general stream of social scientific theory has been deeply influenced by almost every major intellectual movement of the last century and a half— Marxism, Darwinism, Utilitarianism, Idealism, Freudianism, Behaviorism, Positivism, Operationalism—and has attempted to capitalize on virtually every important field of methodological innovation from ecology, ethology, and comparative psychology to game theory, cybernetics, and statistics, it has, with very few exceptions, been virtually untouched by one of the most important trends in recent thought: the effort to construct an independent science of what Kenneth Burke has called "symbolic action." [19] Neither the work of such philosophers as Peirce, Wittgenstein, Cassirer, Langer, Ryle, or Morris nor of such literary critics as Coleridge, Eliot, Burke, Empson, Blackmur, Brooks, or Auerbach seems to have had any appreciable impact on the general pattern of social scientific analysis.[20] Aside from a few more venturesome (and largely programmatic) linguists—a Whorf or a Sapir—the question of how symbols symbolize, how they function to mediate meanings has simply been bypassed. "The embarrassing fact," the physician *cum* novelist Walker Percy has written, "is that there does not exist today— a natural empirical science of symbolic behavior *as such*. . . . Sapir's gentle chiding about the lack of a science of symbolic behavior and the need of such a science is more conspicuously true today than it was thirty-five years ago." [21]

---

[19] K. Burke, *The Philosophy of Literary Form, Studies in Symbolic Action* (Baton Rouge, 1941). In the following discussion, I use "symbol" broadly in the sense of any physical, social, or cultural act or object that serves as the vehicle for a conception. For an explication of this view, under which "five" and "the Cross" are equally symbols, see S. Langer, *Philosophy in a New Key,* 4th ed. (Cambridge, Mass., 1960), pp. 60–66.

[20] Useful general summaries of the tradition of literary criticism can be found in S. E. Hyman, *The Armed Vision* (New York, 1948) and in R. Welleck and A. Warren, *Theory of Literature,* 2nd ed. (New York, 1958). A similar summary of the somewhat more diverse philosophical development is apparently not available, but the seminal works are C. S. Peirce, *Collected Papers,* ed. C. Hartshorne and P. Weiss, 8 vols. (Cambridge, Mass., 1931–1958); E. Cassirer, *Die Philosophie der symbolischen Foremen,* 3 vols. (Berlin, 1923–1929); C. W. Morris, *Signs, Language and Behavior* (Englewood Cliffs, N.J., 1944); and L. Wittgenstein, *Philosophical Investigations* (Oxford, 1953).

[21] W. Percy, "The Symbolic Structure of Interpersonal Process," *Psychiatry* 24 (1961):39–52. Italics in original. The reference is to Sapir's "The Status of Lin-

It is the absence of such a theory and in particular the absence of any analytical framework within which to deal with figurative language that have reduced sociologists to viewing ideologies as elaborate cries of pain. With no notion of how metaphor, analogy, irony, ambiguity, pun, paradox, hyperbole, rhythm, and all the other elements of what we lamely call "style" operate—even, in a majority of cases, with no recognition that these devices are of any importance in casting personal attitudes into public form, sociologists lack the symbolic resources out of which to construct a more incisive formulation. At the same time that the arts have been establishing the cognitive power of "distortion" and philosophy has been undermining the adequacy of an emotivist theory of meaning, social scientists have been rejecting the first and embracing the second. It is not therefore surprising that they evade the problem of construing the import of ideological assertions by simply failing to recognize it as a problem.[22]

In order to make explicit what I mean, let me take an example that is, I hope, so thoroughly trivial in itself as both to still any suspicions that I have a hidden concern with the substance of the political issue involved and, more important, to bring home the point that concepts developed for the analysis of the more elevated aspects of culture— poetry, for example—are applicable to the more lowly ones without in any way blurring the enormous qualitative distinctions between the two. In discussing the cognitive inadequacies by which ideology is defined for them, Sutton et al. use as an example of the ideologist's tendency to "oversimplify" the denomination by organized labor of the Taft-Hartley Act as a "slave labor law":

Ideology tends to be simple and clear-cut, even where its simplicity and clarity do less than justice to the subject under discussion. The ideological picture uses sharp lines and contrasting blacks and whites. The ideologist exaggerates and caricatures in the fashion of the cartoonist. In contrast, a scientific description of social phenomena is likely to be fuzzy and indistinct. In recent labor ideology the Taft-Hartley Act has been a "slave labor act." By no dispassionate examination does the Act merit this label. Any detached

guistics as a Science," originally published in 1929 and reprinted in D. Mandlebaum, ed., *Selected Writings of Edward Sapir* (Berkeley and Los Angeles, 1949), pp. 160–166.

[22] A partial exception to this stricture, although marred by his obsession with power as the sum and substance of politics, is Lasswell's "Style in the Language of Politics," in Lasswell et al., *Language of Politics,* pp. 20–39. It also should be remarked that the emphasis on verbal symbolism in the following discussion is merely for the sake of simplicity and is not intended to deny the importance of plastic, theatrical, or other nonlinguistic devices—the rhetoric of uniforms, floodlit stages, and marching bands—in ideological thought.

assessment of the Act would have to consider its many provisions individually. On any set of values, even those of trade unions themselves, such an assessment would yield a mixed verdict. But mixed verdicts are not the stuff of ideology. They are too complicated, too fuzzy. Ideology must categorize the Act as a whole with a symbol to rally workers, voters and legislators to action.[23]

Leaving aside the merely empirical question of whether or not it is in fact true that ideological formulations of a given set of social phenomena are inevitably "simpler" than scientific formulations of the same phenomena, there is in this argument a curiously depreciatory—one might even say "oversimple"—view of the thought processes of labor-union leaders on the one hand and "workers, voters and legislators" on the other. It is rather hard to believe that either those who coined and disseminated the slogan themselves believed or expected anyone else to believe that the law would actually reduce (or was intended to reduce) the American worker to the status of a slave or that the segment of the public for whom the slogan had meaning perceived it in any such terms. Yet it is precisely this flattened view of other people's mentalities that leaves the sociologist with only two interpretations, both inadequate, of whatever effectiveness the symbol has: either it deceives the uninformed (according to interest theory), or it excites the unreflective (according to strain theory). That it might in fact draw its power from its capacity to grasp, formulate, and communicate social realities that elude the tempered language of science, that it may mediate more complex meanings than its literal reading suggests, is not even considered. "Slave labor act" may be, after all, not a label but a trope.

More exactly, it appears to be a metaphor or at least an attempted metaphor. Although very few social scientists seem to have read much of it, the literature on metaphor—"the power whereby language, even with a small vocabulary, manages to embrace a multi-million things"— is vast and by now in reasonable agreement.[24] In metaphor one has, of course, a stratification of meaning, in which an incongruity of sense on one level produces an influx of significance on another. As Percy has pointed out, the feature of metaphor that has most troubled philosophers (and, he might have added, scientists) is that it is "wrong": "It asserts of one thing that it is something else." And, worse yet, it tends to

[23] Sutton, et al., *American Business Creed*, pp. 4–5.
[24] An excellent recent review is to be found in P. Henle, ed., *Language, Thought and Culture* (Ann Arbor, 1958), pp. 173–195. The quotation is from Langer, *Philosophy*, p. 117.

be most effective when most "wrong." [25] The power of a metaphor derives precisely from the interplay between the discordant meanings it symbolically coerces into a unitary conceptual framework and from the degree to which that coercion is successful in overcoming the psychic resistance such semantic tension inevitably generates in anyone in a position to perceive it. When it works, a metaphor transforms a false identification (for example, of the labor policies of the Republican Party and of those of the Bolsheviks) into an apt analogy; when it misfires, it is a mere extravagance.

That for most people the "slave labor law" figure was, in fact, pretty much a misfire (and therefore never served with any effectiveness as "a symbol to rally workers, voters and legislators to action") seems evident enough, and it is this failure, rather than its supposed clear-cut simplicity, that makes it seem no more than a cartoon. The semantic tension between the image of a conservative Congress outlawing the closed shop and of the prison camps of Siberia was—apparently—too great to be resolved into a single conception, at least by means of so rudimentary a stylistic device as the slogan. Except (perhaps) for a few enthusiasts, the analogy did not appear; the false identification remained false. But failure is not inevitable, even on such an elementary level. Although, a most unmixed verdict, Sherman's "War is hell" is no social-science proposition, even Sutton and his associates would probably not regard it as either an exaggeration or a caricature.

More important, however, than any assessment of the adequacy of the two tropes as such is the fact that, as the meanings they attempt to spark against one another are after all socially rooted, the success or failure of the attempt is relative not only to the power of the stylistic mechanisms employed but also to precisely those sorts of factors upon which strain theory concentrates its attention. The tensions of the Cold War, the fears of a labor movement only recently emerged from a bitter struggle for existence, and the threatened eclipse of New Deal liberalism after two decades of dominance set the sociopsychological stage both for the appearance of the "slave labor" figure and—when it proved unable to work them into a cogent analogy—for its miscarriage. The militarists of 1934 Japan who opened their pamphlet on *Basic Theory of National Defense and Suggestions for Its Strengthening* with the resounding familial metaphor, "War is the father of creation and the mother of culture," would no doubt have found Sherman's maxim as

[25] W. Percy, "Metaphor as Mistake," *The Sewanee Review* 66 (1958): 79–99.

unconvincing as he would have found theirs.[26] They were energetically preparing for an imperialist war in an ancient nation seeking its footing in the modern world; he was wearily pursuing a civil war in an unrealized nation torn by domestic hatreds. It is thus not truth that varies with social, psychological, and cultural contexts but the symbols we construct in our unequally effective attempts to grasp it. War *is* hell and *not* the mother of culture, as the Japanese eventually discovered—although no doubt they express the fact in a grander idiom.

The sociology of knowledge ought to be called the sociology of meaning, for what is socially determined is not the nature of conception but the vehicles of conception. In a community that drinks its coffee black, Henle remarks, to praise a girl with "You're the cream in my coffee" would give entirely the wrong impression; and, if omnivorousness were regarded as a more significant characteristic of bears than their clumsy roughness, to call a man "an old bear" might mean not that he was crude, but that he had catholic tastes.[27] Or, to take an example from Burke, since in Japan people smile on mentioning the death of a close friend, the semantic equivalent (behaviorally as well as verbally) in American English is not "He smiled," but "His face fell"; for, with such a rendering, we are "translating the accepted social usage of Japan into the corresponding accepted social usage of the West." [28] And, closer to the ideological realm, Sapir has pointed out that the chairmanship of a committee has the figurative force we give it only because we hold that "administrative functions somehow stamp a person as superior to those who are being directed"; "should people come to feel that administrative functions are little more than symbolic automatisms, the chairmanship of a committee would be recognized as little more than a petrified symbol and the particular value that is now felt to inhere in it would tend to disappear." [29] The case is no different for "slave labor law." If forced labor camps come, for whatever reasons, to play a less prominent role in the American image of the Soviet Union, it will not be the symbol's veracity that has dissolved but its very meaning, its capacity to be *either* true or false. One must simply frame the argument —that the Taft-Hartley Act is a mortal threat to organized labor—in some other way.

[26] Quoted in J. Crowley, "Japanese Army Factionalism in the Early 1930's," *The Journal of Asian Studies* 21 (1958): 309–326.

[27] Henle, *Language, Thought and Culture*, pp. 4–5.

[28] K. Burke, *Counterstatement* (Chicago, 1957), p. 149.

[29] Sapir, "Status of Linguistics," p. 568.

In short, between an ideological figure like "slave labor act" and the social realities of American life in the midst of which it appears, there exists a subtlety of interplay, which concepts like "distortion," "selectivity," or "oversimplification" are simply incompetent to formulate.[30] Not only is the semantic structure of the figure a good deal more complex than it appears on the surface, but an analysis of that structure forces one into tracing a multiplicity of referential connections between it and social reality, so that the final picture is one of a configuration of dissimilar meanings out of whose interworking both the expressive power and the rhetorical force of the final symbol derive. This interworking is itself a social process, an occurrence not "in the head" but in that public world where "people talk together, name things, make assertions, and to a degree understand each other." [31] The study of symbolic action is no less a sociological discipline than the study of small groups, bureaucracies, or the changing role of the American woman; it is only a good deal less developed.

V

Asking the question that most students of ideology fail to ask—what, precisely, do we mean when we assert that sociopsychological strains are "expressed" in symbolic forms?—gets one, therefore, very quickly

[30] Metaphor is, of course, not the only stylistic resource upon which ideology draws. Metonymy ("All I have to offer is blood, sweat and tears"), hyperbole ("The thousand-year Reich"), meiosis ("I shall return"), synechdoche ("Wall Street"), oxymoron ("Iron Curtain"), personification ("The hand that held the dagger has plunged it into the back of its neighbor"), and all the other figures the classical rhetoricians so painstakingly collected and so carefully classified are utilized over and over again, as are such syntactical devices as antithesis, inversion, and repetition; such prosodic ones as rhyme, rhythm, and alliteration; such literary ones as irony, eulogy, and sarcasm. Nor is all ideological expression figurative. The bulk of it consists of quite literal, not to say flat-footed, assertions, which, a certain tendency toward *prima facie* implausibility aside, are difficult to distinguish from properly scientific statements: "The history of all hitherto existing society is the history of class struggles"; "The whole of the morality of Europe is based upon the values which are useful to the herd"; and so forth. As a cultural system, an ideology that has developed beyond the stage of mere sloganeering consists of an intricate structure of interrelated meanings—interrelated in terms of the semantic mechanisms that formulate them—of which the two-level organization of an isolated metaphor is but a feeble representation.

[31] Percy, "Symbolic Structure."

into quite deep water indeed; into, in fact, a somewhat untraditional and apparently paradoxical theory of the nature of human thought as a public and not, or at least not fundamentally, a private activity.[32] The details of such a theory cannot be pursued any distance here, nor can any significant amount of evidence be marshaled to support it. But at least its general outlines must be sketched if we are to find our way back from the elusive world of symbols and semantic process to the (apparently) more solid one of sentiments and institutions, if we are to trace with some circumstantiality the modes of interpenetration of culture, personality, and social system.

The defining proposition of this sort of approach to thought *en plein air*—what, following Galanter and Gerstenhaber, we may call "the extrinsic theory"—is that thought consists of the construction and manipulation of symbol systems, which are employed as models of other systems, physical, organic, social, psychological, and so forth, in such a way that the structure of these other systems—and, in the favorable case, how they may therefore be expected to behave—is, as we say, "understood." [33] Thinking, conceptualization, formulation, comprehension, understanding, or what-have-you, consists not of ghostly happenings in the head but of a matching of the states and processes of symbolic models against the states and processes of the wider world:

Imaginal thinking is neither more nor less than constructing an image of the environment, running the model faster than the environment, and predicting that the environment will behave as the model does. . . . The first step in the solution of a problem consists in the construction of a model or image of the "relevant features" of the [environment]. These models can be constructed from many things, including parts of the organic tissue of the body and, by man, paper and pencil or actual artifacts. Once a model has been constructed it can be manipulated under various hypothetical conditions and constraints. The organism is then able to "observe" the outcome of these manipulations, and to project them onto the environment so that prediction is possible. According to this view, an aeronautical engineer is thinking when he manipulates a model of a new airplane in a wind tunnel. The motorist is thinking when he runs his finger over a line on a map, the finger serving as a model of the relevant aspects of the automobile, the map as a model of the road. External models of this kind are often used in thinking about complex [environments]. Images used in covert thinking depend

[32] G. Ryle, *The Concept of Mind* (New York, 1949).
[33] E. Galanter and M. Gerstenhaber, "On Thought: The Extrinsic Theory," *Psychol. Rev.* 63 (1956):218–227.

upon the availability of the physico-chemical events of the organism which must be used to form models.[34]

This view does not, of course, deny consciousness: it defines it. Every conscious perception is, as Percy has argued, an act of recognition, a pairing in which an object (or an event, an act, an emotion) is identified by placing it against the background of an appropriate symbol:

It is not enough to say that one is conscious *of* something; one is also conscious of something being something. There is a difference between the apprehension of a gestalt (a chicken perceived the Jastrow effect as well as a human) and the grasping of it under its symbolic vehicle. As I gaze about the room, I am aware of a series of almost effortless acts of *matching:* seeing an object and knowing what it is. If my eye falls upon an unfamiliar something, I am immediately aware that one term of the match is missing, I ask what [the object] is—an exceedingly mysterious question.[35]

What is missing and what is being asked for are an applicable symbolic model under which to subsume the "unfamiliar something" and so render it familiar:

If I see an object at some distance and do not quite recognize it, I may see it, actually see it, as a succession of different things, each rejected by the criterion of fit as I come closer, until one is positively certified. A patch of sunlight in a field I may actually see as a rabbit—a seeing which goes much further than the guess that it may be a rabbit; no, the perceptual gestalt is so construed, actually stamped by the essence of rabbitness: I could have sworn it was a rabbit. On coming closer, the sunlight pattern changes enough so that the rabbit-cast is disallowed. The rabbit vanishes and I make another cast: it is a paper bag, and so on. But most significant of all, even the last, the "correct" recognition is quite as mediate an apprehension as the incorrect ones; it is also a cast, a pairing, an approximation. And let us note in passing that even though it is correct, even though it is borne out by all indices, it may operate quite as effectively to conceal as to discover. When I recognize a strange bird as a sparrow, I tend to dispose of the bird under its appropriate formulation: it is only a sparrow.[36]

Despite the somewhat intellectualist tone of these various examples, the extrinsic theory of thought is extendable to the affective side of human

---

[34] Ibid. I have quoted this incisive passage above (pp. 77–78), in attempting to set the extrinsic theory of thought in the context of recent evolutionary, neurological, and cultural anthropological findings.

[35] W. Percy, "Symbol, Consciousness and Intersubjectivity," *Journal of Philosophy* 55 (1958): 631–641. Italics in original. Quoted by permission.

[36] Ibid. Quoted by permission.

mentality as well.[37] As a road map transforms mere physical locations into "places," connected by numbered routes and separated by measured distances, and so enables us to find our way from where we are to where we want to go, so a poem like, for example, Hopkins's "Felix Randal" provides, through the evocative power of its charged language, a symbolic model of the emotional impact of premature death, which, if we are as impressed with its penetration as with the road map's, transforms physical sensations into sentiments and attitudes and enables us to react to such a tragedy not "blindly" but "intelligently." The central rituals of religion—a mass, a pilgrimage, a corroboree—are symbolic models (here more in the form of activities than of words) of a particular sense of the divine, a certain sort of devotional mood, which their continual re-enactment tends to produce in their participants. Of course, as most acts of what is usually called "cognition" are more on the level of identifying a rabbit than operating a wind tunnel, so most of what is usually called "expression" (the dichotomy is often overdrawn and almost universally misconstrued) is mediated more by models drawn from popular culture than from high art and formal religious ritual. But the point is that the development, maintenance, and dissolution of "moods," "attitudes," "sentiments," and so forth are no more "a ghostly process occurring in streams of consciousness we are debarred from visiting" than is the discrimination of objects, events, structures, processes, and so forth in our environment. Here, too, "we are describing the ways in which . . . people conduct parts of their predominantly public behavior." [38]

Whatever their other differences, both so-called cognitive and so-called expressive symbols or symbol-systems have, then, at least one thing in common: they are extrinsic sources of information in terms of which human life can be patterned—extrapersonal mechanisms for the perception, understanding, judgment, and manipulation of the world. Culture patterns—religious, philosophical, aesthetic, scientific, ideological—are "programs"; they provide a template or blueprint for the organization of social and psychological processes, much as genetic systems provide such a template for the organization of organic processes:

These considerations define the terms in which we approach the problem of "reductionism" in psychology and social science. The levels we have tenta-

[37] S. Langer, *Feeling and Form* (New York, 1953).
[38] The quotations are from Ryle, *Concept of Mind*, p. 51.

tively discriminated [organism, personality, social system, culture] . . . are
. . . levels of organization and control. The lower levels "condition," and
thus in a sense "determine" the structures into which they enter, in the same
sense that the stability of a building depends on the properties of the materials out of which it is constructed. But the physical properties of the materials do not determine the *plan* of the building; this is a factor of another
order, one of *organization*. And the organization controls the *relations* of
the materials to each other, the *ways* in which they are utilized in the building by virtue of which it constitutes an ordered system of a particular type
—looking "downward" in the series, we can always investigate and discover
sets of "conditions" in which the function of a higher order of organization
is dependent. There is, thus, an immensely complicated set of physiological
conditions on which psychological functioning is dependent, etc. Properly
understood and evaluated, these conditions are always authentic determinants of process in the organized systems at the next higher levels. We may,
however, also look "upward" in the series. In this direction we see "structures," organization patterns, patterns of meaning, "programs," etc., which
are the focus of the organization of the system at the level on which we
have concentrated our attention.[39]

The reason such symbolic templates are necessary is that, as has been
often remarked, human behavior is inherently extremely plastic. Not
strictly but only very broadly controlled by genetic programs or models
—intrinsic sources of information—such behavior must, if it is to have
any effective form at all, be controlled to a significant extent by extrinsic ones. Birds learn how to fly without wind tunnels, and whatever reactions lower animals have to death are in great part innate, physiologically preformed.[40] The extreme generality, diffuseness, and variability

[39] T. Parsons, "An Approach to Psychological Theory in Terms of the Theory
of Action," in *Psychology: A Study of a Science,* ed. S. Koch (New York, 1959),
vol. 3. Italics in original. Compare: "In order to account for this selectivity, it is
necessary to assume that the structure of the enzyme is related in some way to
the structure of the gene. By a logical extension of this idea we arrive at the concept that the gene is a representation—blueprint so to speak—of the enzyme
molecule, and that the function of the gene is to serve as a source of information
regarding the structure of the enzyme. It seems evident that the synthesis of an
enzyme—a giant protein molecule consisting of hundreds of amino acid units arranged end-to-end in a specific and unique order—requires a model or set of instructions of some kind. These instructions must be characteristic of the species;
they must be automatically transmitted from generation to generation, and they
must be constant yet capable of evolutionary change. The only known entity that
could perform such a function is the gene. There are many reasons for believing
that it transmits information, by acting as a model or template." N. H. Horowitz,
"The Gene," *Scientific American,* February 1956, p. 85.
[40] This point is perhaps somewhat too baldly put in light of recent analyses of
animal learning; but the essential thesis—that there is a general trend toward a
more diffuse, less determinate control of behavior by intrinsic (innate) parameters

of man's innate response capacities mean that the particular pattern his behavior takes is guided predominantly by cultural rather than genetic templates, the latter setting the overall psychophysical context within which precise activity sequences are organized by the former. The tool-making, laughing, or lying animal, man, is also the incomplete—or, more accurately, self-completing—animal. The agent of his own realization, he creates out of his general capacity for the construction of symbolic models the specific capabilities that define him. Or—to return at last to our subject—it is through the construction of ideologies, schematic images of social order, that man makes himself for better or worse a political animal.

Further, as the various sorts of cultural symbol-systems are extrinsic sources of information, templates for the organization of social and psychological processes, they come most crucially into play in situations where the particular kind of information they contain is lacking, where institutionalized guides for behavior, thought, or feeling are weak or absent. It is in country unfamiliar emotionally or topographically that one needs poems and road maps.

So too with ideology. In polities firmly embedded in Edmund Burke's golden assemblage of "ancient opinions and rules of life," the role of ideology, in any explicit sense, is marginal. In such truly traditional political systems the participants act as (to use another Burkean phrase) men of untaught feelings; they are guided both emotionally and intellectually in their judgments and activities by unexamined prejudices, which do not leave them "hesitating in the moment of decision, sceptical, puzzled and unresolved." But when, as in the revolutionary France Burke was indicting and in fact in the shaken England from which, as perhaps his nation's greatest ideologue, he was indicting it, those hallowed opinions and rules of life come into question, the search for systematic ideological formulations, either to reinforce them or to replace them, flourishes. The function of ideology is to make an autonomous politics possible by providing the authoritative concepts that render it meaningful, the suasive images by means of which it can be sensibly grasped.[41]

---

as one moves from lower to higher animals—seems well established. See above, Chapter 3, pp. 70–76.

[41] Of course, there are moral, economic, and even aesthetic ideologies, as well as specifically political ones, but as very few ideologies of any social prominence lack political implications, it is perhaps permissible to view the problem here in this somewhat narrowed focus. In any case, the arguments developed for political ideologies apply with equal force to nonpolitical ones. For an analysis of a moral

It is, in fact, precisely at the point at which a political system begins to free itself from the immediate governance of received tradition, from the direct and detailed guidance of religious or philosophical canons on the one hand and from the unreflective precepts of conventional moralism on the other, that formal ideologies tend first to emerge and take hold.[42] The differentiation of an autonomous polity implies the differentiation, too, of a separate and distinct cultural model of political action, for the older, unspecialized models are either too comprehensive or too concrete to provide the sort of guidance such a political system demands. Either they trammel political behavior by encumbering it with transcendental significance, or they stifle political imagination by binding it to the blank realism of habitual judgment. It is when neither a society's most general cultural orientations nor its most down-to-earth, "pragmatic" ones suffice any longer to provide an adequate image of political process that ideologies begin to become crucial as sources of sociopolitical meanings and attitudes.

In one sense, this statement is but another way of saying that ideology is a response to strain. But now we are including *cultural* as well as social and psychological strain. It is a loss of orientation that most directly gives rise to ideological activity, an inability, for lack of usable models, to comprehend the universe of civic rights and responsibilities in which one finds oneself located. The development of a differentiated polity (or of greater internal differentiation within such a polity) may and commonly does bring with it severe social dislocation and psychological tension. But it also brings with it conceptual confusion, as the established images of political order fade into irrelevance or are driven into disrepute. The reason why the French Revolution was, at least up to its time, the greatest incubator of extremist ideologies, "progressive" and "reactionary" alike, in human history was not that either personal insecurity or social disequilibrium were deeper and more pervasive than at many earlier periods—though they were deep and pervasive enough

---

ideology cast in terms very similar to those developed in this paper, see A. L. Green, "The Ideology of Anti-Fluoridation Leaders," *The Journal of Social Issues* 17 (1961):13–25.

[42] That such ideologies may call, as did Burke's or De Maistre's, for the reinvigoration of custom or the reimposition of religious hegemony is, of course, no contradiction. One constructs arguments for tradition only when its credentials have been questioned. To the degree that such appeals are successful they bring, not a return to naive traditionalism, but ideological retraditionalization—an altogether different matter. See Mannheim, "Conservative Thought," in his *Essays on Sociology and Social Psychology* (New York, 1953), especially pp. 94–98.

—but because the central organizing principle of political life, the divine right of kings, was destroyed.[43] It is a confluence of sociopsychological strain and an absence of cultural resources by means of which to make sense of the strain, each exacerbating the other, that sets the stage for the rise of systematic (political, moral, or economic) ideologies.

And it is, in turn, the attempt of ideologies to render otherwise incomprehensible social situations meaningful, to so construe them as to make it possible to act purposefully within them, that accounts both for the ideologies' highly figurative nature and for the intensity with which, once accepted, they are held. As metaphor extends language by broadening its semantic range, enabling it to express meanings it cannot or at least cannot yet express literally, so the head-on clash of literal meanings in ideology—the irony, the hyperbole, the overdrawn antithesis—provides novel symbolic frames against which to match the myriad "unfamiliar somethings" that, like a journey to a strange country, are produced by a transformation in political life. Whatever else ideologies may be—projections of unacknowledged fears, disguises for ulterior motives, phatic expressions of group solidarity—they are, most distinctively, maps of problematic social reality and matrices for the creation of collective conscience. Whether, in any particular case, the map is accurate or the conscience creditable is a separate question to which one can hardly give the same answer for Nazism and Zionism, for the nationalisms of McCarthy and of Churchill, for the defenders of segregation and its opponents.

VI

Though ideological ferment is, of course, widespread in modern society, perhaps its most prominent locus at the moment lies in the new (or renewed) states of Asia, Africa, and some parts of Latin America; for it is in these states, Communist or not, that the initial steps away from a

[43] It is important to remember, too, that the principle was destroyed long before the king; it was to the successor principle that he was, in fact, a ritual sacrifice: "When [Saint-Just] exclaims: 'To determine the principle in virtue of which the accused [Louis XVI] is perhaps to die, is to determine the principle by which the society that judges him lives,' he demonstrates that it is the philosophers who are going to kill the King: the King must die in the name of the social contract." A. Camus, *The Rebel* (New York, 1958), p. 114.

traditional politics of piety and proverb are just now being taken. The attainment of independence, the overthrow of established ruling classes, the popularization of legitimacy, the rationalization of public administration, the rise of modern elites, the spread of literacy and mass communications, and the propulsion willy-nilly of inexperienced governments into the midst of a precarious international order that even its older participants do not very well understand all make for a pervasive sense of disorientation, a disorientation in whose face received images of authority, responsibility, and civic purpose seem radically inadequate. The search for a new symbolic framework in terms of which to formulate, think about, and react to political problems, whether in the form of nationalism, Marxism, liberalism, populism, racism, Caesarism, ecclesiasticism, or some variety of reconstructed traditionalism (or, most commonly, a confused melange of several of these) is therefore tremendously intense.

Intense—but indeterminate. For the most part, the new states are still groping for usable political concepts, not yet grasping them; and the outcome in almost every case, at least in every non-Communist case, is uncertain not merely in the sense that the outcome of any historical process is uncertain but in the sense that even a broad and general assessment of overall direction is extremely difficult to make. Intellectually, everything is in motion, and the words of that extravagant poet in politics, Lamartine, written of nineteenth century France, apply to the new states with perhaps even greater appropriateness than they did to the dying July Monarchy:

These times are times of chaos; opinions are a scramble; parties are a jumble; the language of new ideas has not been created; nothing is more difficult than to give a good definition of oneself in religion, in philosophy, in politics. One feels, one knows, one lives, and at need, one dies for one's cause, but one cannot name it. It is the problem of this time to classify things and men. . . . The world has jumbled its catalog.[44]

This observation is no truer anywhere in the world right now [1964] than it is in Indonesia, where the whole political process is mired in a slough of ideological symbols, each attempting and so far each failing to unjumble the Republic's catalogue, to name its cause, and to give point and purpose to its polity. It is a country of false starts and frantic revi-

---

[44] Alphonse de Lamartine, "Declaration of Principles," in *Introduction to Contemporary Civilization in the West, A Source Book* (New York, 1946), 2: 328–333.

sions, of a desperate search for a political order whose image, like a mirage, recedes more rapidly the more eagerly it is approached. The salving slogan amid all this frustration is, "The Revolution Is Unfinished!" And so, indeed, it is. But only because no one knows, not even those who cry most loudly that they do, precisely how to go about the job of finishing it.[45]

The most highly developed concepts of government in traditional Indonesia were those upon which the classic Hinduized states of the fourth to fifteenth centuries were built, concepts that persisted in somewhat revised and weakened form even after these states were first Islamicized and then largely replaced or overlaid by the Dutch colonial regime. And of these concepts the most important was what might be called the theory of the exemplary center, the notion that the capital city (or more accurately the king's palace) was at once a microcosm of the supernatural order—"an image of . . . the universe on a smaller scale"—and the material embodiment of political order.[46] The capital was not merely the nucleus, the engine, or the pivot of the state; it *was* the state.

In the Hindu period, the king's castle comprehended virtually the entire town. A squared-off "heavenly city" constructed according to the ideas of Indic metaphysics, it was more than a locus of power; it was a synoptic paradigm of the ontological shape of existence. At its center was the divine king (an incarnation of an Indian deity), his throne symbolizing Mount Meru, seat of the gods; the buildings, roads, city walls, and even, ceremonially, his wives and personal staff were deployed quadrangularly around him according to the directions of the four sacred winds. Not only the king himself but his ritual, his regalia, his court, and his castle were shot through with charismatic significance. The castle and the life of the castle were the quiddity of the kingdom, and he who (often after meditating in the wilderness to attain the appropriate spiritual status) captured the castle captured the whole empire,

[45] The following very schematic and necessarily *ex cathedra* discussion is based mainly on my own research and represents only my own views, but I have also drawn heavily on the work of Herbert Feith for factual material. See especially, *The Decline of Constitutional Democracy in Indonesia* (New York, 1962) and "Dynamics of Guided Democracy," in *Indonesia,* ed. R. McVey (New Haven, 1963), pp. 309–409. For the general cultural analysis within which my interpretations are set, see C. Geertz, *The Religion of Java* (New York, 1960).

[46] R. Heine-Geldern, "Conceptions of State and Kinship in Southeast Asia," *Far Eastern Quarterly* 2 (1942): 15–30.

grasped the charisma of office, and displaced the no-longer-sacred king.[47]

The early polities were thus not so much solidary territorial units as loose congeries of villages oriented toward a common urban center, each such center competing with others for ascendency. Whatever degree of regional or, at moments, interregional hegemony prevailed depended, not on the systematic administrative organization of extensive territory under a single king, but on the varying abilities of kings to mobilize and apply effective striking forces with which to sack rival capitals, abilities that were believed to rest on essentially religious—that is, mystical—grounds. So far as the pattern was territorial at all, it consisted of a series of concentric circles of religio-military power spreading out around the various city-state capitals, as radio waves spread from a transmitter. The closer a village to a town, the greater the impact, economically and culturally, of the court on that village. And, conversely, the greater the development of the court—priests, artisans, nobles, and king—the greater its authenticity as an epitome of cosmic order, its military strength, and the effective range of its circles of outward-spreading power. Spiritual excellence and political eminence were fused. Magical power and executive influence flowed in a single stream outward and downward from the king through the descending ranks of his staff and whatever lesser courts were subordinate to him, draining out finally into the spiritually and politically residual peasant mass. Theirs was a facsimile concept of political organization, one in which the reflection of the supernatural order microscopically mirrored in the life of the capital was in turn further and more faintly reflected in the countryside as a whole, producing a hierarchy of less and less faithful copies of an eternal, transcendent realm. In such a system, the administrative, military, and ceremonial organization of the court orders the world around it iconically by providing it with a tangible paragon.[48]

---

[47] Ibid.

[48] The whole expanse of Yawa-land [Java] is to be compared with one town in the Prince's reign.

By thousands are [counted] the people's dwelling places, to be compared with the manors of Royal servants, surrounding the body of the Royal compound.

All kinds of foreign islands; to be compared with them are the cultivated land's areas, made happy and quiet.

Of the aspect of parks, then, are the forests and mountains, all of them set foot on by Him, without feeling anxiety.

Canto 17, stanza 3 of the "Nagara-Kertagama," a fourteenth century royal

When Islam came, the Hindu political tradition was to some extent weakened, especially in the coastal trade kingdoms surrounding the Java Sea. The court culture nevertheless persisted, although it was overlaid and interfused with Islamic symbols and ideas and set among an ethnically more differentiated urban mass, which looked with less awe on the classical order. The steady growth—especially on Java—of Dutch administrative control in the mid-nineteenth and early twentieth centuries constricted the tradition still further. But, since the lower levels of the bureaucracy continued to be manned almost entirely by Indonesians of the old upper classes, the tradition remained, even then, the matrix of supravillage political order. The Regency or the District Office remained not merely the axis of the polity but the embodiment of it, a polity with respect to which most villagers were not so much actors as audience.

It was this tradition with which the new elite of republican Indonesia was left after the revolution. That is not to say that the theory of the exemplary center persisted unchanged, drifting like some Platonic archetype through the eternity of Indonesian history, for (like the society as a whole) it evolved and developed, becoming ultimately perhaps more conventional and less religious in general temper. Nor does it mean that foreign ideas, from European parliamentarianism, from Marxism, from Islamic moralism, and so forth did not come to play an essential role in Indonesian political thought, for modern Indonesian nationalism is very far from being merely old wine in a new bottle. It is simply that, as yet, the conceptual transition from the classic image of a polity as a concentrated center of pomp and power, alternately providing a cynosure for popular awe and lashing out militarily at competing centers, to one of a polity as a systematically organized national community has, for all these changes and influences, still not been completed. Indeed, it has been arrested and to some extent reversed.

This cultural failure is apparent from the growing, seemingly unquenchable ideological din that has engulfed Indonesian politics since the revolution. The most prominent attempt to construct, by means of a figurative extension of the classic tradition, an essentially metaphoric reworking of it, a new symbolic framework within which to give form and meaning to the emerging republican polity, was President Sukarno's fa-

epic. Translated in Th. Piegeaud, *Java in the 14th Century* (The Hague, 1960), 3:21. The term *nagara* still means, indifferently, "palace," "capital city," "state," "country," or "government"—sometimes even "civilization"—in Java.

mous Pantjasila concept, first set forth in a public speech toward the end of the Japanese occupation.[49] Drawing on the Indic tradition of fixed sets of numbered precepts—the three jewels, the four sublime moods, the eightfold path, the twenty conditions of successful rule, and so forth—it consisted of five (*pantja*) principles (*sila*) that were intended to form the "sacred" ideological foundations of an independent Indonesia. Like all good constitutions, the Pantjasila was short, ambiguous, and impeccably high-minded, the five points being "nationalism," "humanitarianism," "democracy," "social welfare," and (pluralistic) "monotheism." Finally, these modern concepts, set so nonchalantly in a medieval frame, were explicitly identified with an indigenous peasant concept, *gotong rojong* (literally, "the collective bearing of burdens"; figuratively, "the piety of all for the interests of all"), thus drawing together the "great tradition" of the exemplary state, the doctrines of contemporary nationalism, and the "little traditions" of the villages into one luminous image.[50]

The reasons why this ingenious device failed are many and complex, and only a few of them—like the strength in certain sectors of the population of Islamic concepts of political order, which are difficult to reconcile with Sukarno's secularism—are themselves cultural. The Pantjasila, playing upon the microcosm-macrocosm conceit and upon the traditional syncretism of Indonesian thought, was intended to contain within it the political interests of the Islamic and Christian, gentry and peasantry, nationalist and communist, commercial and agrarian, Javanese and "Outer Island" groups in Indonesia—to rework the old facsimile pattern into a modern constitutional structure in which these various tendencies would, each emphasizing one or another aspect of the doctrine, find a *modus vivendi* at each level of administration and party struggle. The attempt was not so totally ineffective or so intellectually fatuous as it has sometimes been painted. The cult of the Pantjasila (for that is what it literally became, complete with rites and commentaries) did provide for a while a flexible ideological context within which parliamentary institutions and democratic sentiments were being soundly, if gradually, forged at both local and national levels. But the combination of a deteriorating economic situation, a hopelessly pathological relationship with the former metropole, the rapid growth of a subversive (in

[49] For a description of the Pantjasila speech, see G. Kahin, *Nationalism and Revolution in Indonesia* (Ithaca, 1952), pp. 122–127.
[50] The quotations are from the Pantjasila speech, as quoted in ibid., p. 126.

principle) totalitarian party, a renascence of Islamic fundamentalism, the inability (or unwillingness) of leaders with developed intellectual and technical skills to court mass support, and the economic illiteracy, administrative incapacity, and personal failings of those who were able (and only too willing) to court such support soon brought the clash of factions to such a pitch that the whole pattern dissolved. By the time of the Constitutional Convention of 1957, the Pantjasila had changed from a language of consensus to a vocabulary of abuse, as each faction used it more to express its irreconcilable opposition to other factions than its underlying rules-of-the-game agreement with them, and the Convention, ideological pluralism, and constitutional democracy collapsed in a single heap.[51]

What has replaced them is something very much like the old exemplary center pattern, only now on a self-consciously doctrinaire rather than an instinctive religion-and-convention basis and cast more in the idiom of egalitarianism and social progress than in that of hierarchy and patrician grandeur. On the one hand, there has been, under President Sukarno's famous theory of "guided democracy" and his call for the reintroduction of the revolutionary (that is, authoritarian) constitution of 1945, both an ideological homogenization (in which discordant streams of thought—notably those of Moslem modernism and democratic socialism—have simply been suppressed as illegitimate) and an accelerated pace of flamboyant symbol-mongering, as though, the effort to make an unfamiliar form of government work having misfired, a desperate attempt to breathe new life into a familiar one was being launched. On the other hand, the growth of the political role of the army, not so much as an executive or administrative body as a backstop enforcement agency with veto power over the whole range of politically relevant institutions, from the presidency and the civil service to the parties and the press, has provided the other—the minatory—half of the traditional picture.

Like the Pantjasila before it, the revised (or revivified) approach was introduced by Sukarno in a major speech—"The Rediscovery of Our Revolution"—given on Independence Day (August 17) in 1959, a speech that he later decreed, along with the expository notes on it pre-

---

[51] The proceedings of the Convention, unfortunately still untranslated, form one of the fullest and most instructive records of ideological combat in the new states available. See *Tentang Negara Republik Indonesia Dalam Konstituante*, 3 vols. (n.p. [Djakarta?], n.d. [1958?]).

pared by a body of personal attendants known as The Supreme Advisory Council, to be the "Political Manifesto of the Republic":

There thus came into existence a catechism on the basis, aims and duties of the Indonesian revolution; the social forces of the Indonesian revolution, its nature, future and enemies; and its general program, covering the political, economic, social, mental, cultural, and security fields. Early in 1960 the central message of the celebrated speech was stated as consisting of five ideas —the 1945 constitution, Socialism a la Indonesia, Guided Democracy, Guided Economy, and Indonesian Personality—and the first letters of these five phrases were put together to make the acronym USDEK. With "Political Manifesto" becoming "Manipol," the new creed became known as "Manipol-USDEK." [52]

And, as the Pantjasila before it, the Manipol-USDEK image of political order found a ready response in a population for whom opinions have indeed become a scramble, parties a jumble, the times a chaos:

Many were attracted by the idea that what Indonesia needed above all was men with the right state of mind, the right spirit, the true patriotic dedication. "Returning to our own national personality" was attractive to many who wanted to withdraw from the challenges of modernity, and also to those who wanted to believe in the current political leadership but were aware of its failures to modernize as fast as such countries as India and Malaya. And for members of some Indonesian communities, notably for many [Indic-minded] Javanese, there was real meaning in the various complex schemes which the President presented in elaboration of Manipol-USDEK, explaining the peculiar significance and tasks of the current stage of history. [But] perhaps the most important appeal of Manipol-USDEK, however, lay in the simple fact that it promised to give men a *pegangan*—something to which to hold fast. They were attracted not so much by the content of this *pegangan* as by the fact that the President had offered one at a time when the lack of a sense of purpose was sorely felt. Values and cognitive patterns being in flux and in conflict, men looked eagerly for dogmatic and schematic formulations of the political good. [53]

While the President and his entourage concern themselves almost entirely with the "creation and recreation of mystique," the army concerns itself mainly with combating the numerous protests, plots, mutinies, and rebellions that occur when that mystique fails to achieve its hoped-for

[52] Feith, "Dynamics of Guided Democracy," p. 367. A vivid, if somewhat shrill, description of "Manipol-USDEKism" in action can be found in W. Hanna, *Bung Karno's Indonesia* (New York, 1961).
[53] Feith, "Dynamics of Guided Democracy," 367–368. *Pegang* literally means "to grasp"; thus *pegangan*, "something graspable."

effect and when rival claims to leadership arise.[54] Although involved in some aspects of the civil service, in the managing of the confiscated Dutch enterprises, and even in the (nonparliamentary) cabinet, the army has not been able to take up, for lack of training, internal unity, or sense of direction, the administrative, planning, and organizational tasks of the government in any detail or with any effectiveness. The result is that these tasks are either not performed or very inadequately performed, and the supralocal polity, the national state, shrinks more and more to the limits of its traditional domain, the capital city—Djakarta —plus a number of semi-independent tributary cities and towns held to a minimal loyalty by the threat of centrally applied force.

That this attempt to revive the politics of the exemplary court will long survive is rather doubtful. It is already being severely strained by its incapacity to cope with the technical and administrative problems involved in the government of a modern state. Far from arresting Indonesia's decline into what Sukarno has called "the abyss of annihilation," the retreat from the hesitant, admittedly hectic and awkwardly functioning parliamentarianism of the Pantjasila period to the Manipol-USDEK alliance between a charismatic president and a watchdog army has probably accelerated it. But what will succeed this ideological framework when, as seems certain, it too dissolves, or from where a conception of political order more adequate to Indonesia's contemporary needs and ambitions will come, if it does come, is impossible to say.

Not that Indonesia's problems are purely or even primarily ideological and that they will—as all too many Indonesians already think—melt away before a political change of heart. The disorder is more general, and the failure to create a conceptual framework in terms of which to shape a modern polity is in great part itself a reflection of the tremendous social and psychological strains that the country and its population are undergoing. Things do not merely *seem* jumbled—they *are* jumbled, and it will take more than theory to unjumble them. It will take administrative skill, technical knowledge, personal courage and resolution, endless patience and tolerance, enormous self-sacrifice, a virtually incorruptible public conscience, and a very great deal of sheer (and unlikely) good luck in the most material sense of the word. Ideological formulation, no matter how elegant, can substitute for none of these elements; and, in fact, in their absence, it degenerates, as it has in Indonesia, into a smokescreen for failure, a diversion to stave off de-

[54] Ibid.

spair, a mask to conceal reality rather than a portrait to reveal it. With a tremendous population problem; extraordinary ethnic, geographical, and regional diversity; a moribund economy; a severe lack of trained personnel; popular poverty of the bitterest sort; and pervasive, implacable social discontent, Indonesia's social problems seem virtually insoluble even without the ideological pandemonium. The abyss into which Ir. Sukarno claims to have looked is a real one.

Yet, at the same time, that Indonesia (or, I should imagine, any new nation) can find her way through this forest of problems without any ideological guidance at all seems impossible.[55] The motivation to seek (and, even more important, to *use*) technical skill and knowledge, the emotional resilience to support the necessary patience and resolution, and the moral strength to sustain self-sacrifice and incorruptibility must come from somewhere, from some vision of public purpose anchored in a compelling image of social reality. That all these qualities may not be present; that the present drift to revivalistic irrationalism and unbridled fantasy may continue; that the next ideological phase may be even further from the ideals for which the revolution was ostensibly fought than is the present one; that Indonesia may continue to be, as Bagehot called France, the scene of political experiments from which others profit much but she herself very little; or that the ultimate outcome may be viciously totalitarian and wildly zealotic is all very true. But whichever way events move, the determining forces will not be wholly sociological or psychological but partly cultural—that is, conceptual. To forge a theoretical framework adequate to the analysis of such three-dimensional processes is the task of the scientific study of ideology—a task but barely begun.

[55] For an analysis of the role of ideology in an emerging African nation, conducted along lines similar to our own, see L. A. Fallers, "Ideology and Culture in Uganda Nationalism," *American Anthropologist* 63 (1961): 677–686. For a superb case study of an "adolescent" nation in which the process of thorough-going ideological reconstruction seems to have been conducted with reasonable success, see B. Lewis, *The Emergence of Modern Turkey* (London, 1961), especially Chap. 10.

VII

Critical and imaginative works are answers to questions posed by the situation in which they arose. They are not merely answers, they are *strategic* answers, *stylized* answers. For there is a difference in style or strategy, if one says "yes" in tonalities that imply "thank God!" or in tonalities that imply "alas!" So I should propose an initial working distinction between "strategies" and "situations" whereby we think of . . . any work of critical or imaginative cast . . . as the adopting of various strategies for the encompassing of situations. These strategies size up the situations, name their structure and outstanding ingredients, and name them in a way that contains an attitude toward them.

This point of view does not, by any means, vow us to personal or historical subjectivism. The situations are real; the strategies for handling them have public content; in so far as situations overlap from individual to individual, or from one historical period to another, the strategies possess universal relevance.

KENNETH BURKE, *The Philosophy of Literary Form*

As both science and ideology are critical and imaginative "works" (that is symbolic structures), an objective formulation both of the marked differences between them and of the nature of their relationship to one another seems more likely to be achieved by proceeding from such a concept of stylistic strategies than from a nervous concern with comparative epistemological or axiological status of the two forms of thought. No more than scientific studies of religion ought to begin with unnecessary questions about the legitimacy of the substantive claims of their subject matter ought scientific studies of ideology to begin with such questions. The best way to deal with Mannheim's, as with any true paradox, is to circumvent it by reformulating one's theoretical approach so as to avoid setting off yet once more down the well-worn path of argument that led to it in the first place.

The differentiae of science and ideology as cultural systems are to be sought in the sorts of symbolic strategy for encompassing situations that they respectively represent. Science names the structure of situations in

such a way that the attitude contained toward them is one of disinterestedness. Its style is restrained, spare, resolutely analytic: by shunning
the semantic devices that most effectively formulate moral sentiment, it
seeks to maximize intellectual clarity. But ideology names the structure
of situations in such a way that the attitude contained toward them is
one of commitment. Its style is ornate, vivid, deliberately suggestive: by
objectifying moral sentiment through the same devices that science
shuns, it seeks to motivate action. Both are concerned with the definition of a problematic situation and are responses to a felt lack of
needed information. But the information needed is quite different, even
in cases where the situation is the same. An ideologist is no more a
poor social scientist than a social scientist is a poor ideologist. The two
are—or at least they ought to be—in quite different lines of work, lines
so different that little is gained and much obscured by measuring the activities of the one against the aims of the other.[56]

Where science is the diagnostic, the critical, dimension of culture,
ideology is the justificatory, the apologetic one—it refers "to that part
of culture which is actively concerned with the establishment and defense of patterns of belief and value." [57] That there is natural tendency
for the two to clash, particularly when they are directed to the interpretation of the same range of situations, is thus clear; but that the clash is
inevitable and that the findings of (social) science necessarily will undermine the validity of the beliefs and values that ideology has chosen
to defend and propagate seem most dubious assumptions. An attitude at
once critical and apologetic toward the same situation is no intrinsic
contradiction in terms (however often it may in fact turn out to be an
empirical one) but a sign of a certain level of intellectual sophistication.
One remembers the story, probably *ben trovato,* to the effect that when
Churchill had finished his famous rally of isolated England, "We shall
fight on the beaches, we shall fight on the landing grounds, we shall fight
in the fields and in the streets, we shall fight in the hills . . . ," he

[56] This point is, however, not quite the same as saying that the two sorts of
activity may not in practice be carried on together, any more than a man cannot,
for example, paint a portrait of a bird that is both ornithologically accurate and
aesthetically effective. Marx is, of course, the outstanding case, but for a more recent successful synchronization of scientific analysis and ideological argument, see
E. Shils, *The Torment of Secrecy* (New York, 1956). Most such attempts to mix
genres are, however, distinctly less happy.

[57] Fallers, "Ideology and Culture." The patterns of belief and value defended
may be, of course, those of a socially subordinate group, as well as those of a socially dominant one, and the "apology" therefore for reform or revolution.

turned to an aide and whispered, "and we shall hit them over the head with soda-water bottles, because we haven't any guns."

The quality of social rhetoric in ideology is thus not proof that the vision of sociopsychological reality upon which it is based is false and that it draws its persuasive power from any discrepancy between what is believed and what can, now or someday, be established as scientifically correct. That it may indeed lose touch with reality in an orgy of autistic fantasy—even that, in situations where it is left uncriticized by either a free science or competing ideologies well-rooted in the general social structure, it has a very strong tendency to do so—is all too apparent. But however interesting pathologies are for clarifying normal functioning (and however common they may be empirically), they are misleading as prototypes of it. Although fortunately it never had to be tested, it seems most likely that the British would have indeed fought on the beaches, landing grounds, streets, and hills—with soda-water bottles too, if it came to that—for Churchill formulated accurately the mood of his countrymen and, formulating it, mobilized it by making it a public possession, a social fact, rather than a set of disconnected, un-realized private emotions. Even morally loathsome ideological expressions may still catch most acutely the mood of a people or a group. Hitler was not distorting the German conscience when he rendered his countrymen's demonic self-hatred in the tropological figure of the magically corrupting Jew; he was merely objectifying it—transforming a prevalent personal neurosis into a powerful social force.

But though science and ideology are different enterprises, they are not unrelated ones. Ideologies do make empirical claims about the condition and direction of society, which it is the business of science (and, where scientific knowledge is lacking, common sense) to assess. The social function of science vis-à-vis ideologies is first to understand them —what they are, how they work, what gives rise to them—and second to criticize them, to force them to come to terms with (but not necessarily to surrender to) reality. The existence of a vital tradition of scientific analysis of social issues is one of the most effective guarantees against ideological extremism, for it provides an incomparably reliable source of positive knowledge for the political imagination to work with and to honor. It is not the only such check. The existence, as mentioned, of competing ideologies carried by other powerful groups in the society is at least as important; as is a liberal political system in which dreams of total power are obvious fantasies; as are stable social conditions in which conventional expectations are not continually frustrated and conventional ideas not radically incompetent. But, committed with a quiet intransigence to a vision of its own, it is perhaps the most indomitable.

Chapter 9/

After the Revolution:

The Fate of Nationalism

in the New States

✣

Between 1945 and 1968 sixty-six "countries"—the actualities demand the quotation marks—attained political independence from colonial rule. Unless one counts the American engagement in Vietnam, an ambiguous case, the last great struggle for national liberation was that which triumphed in Algeria in the summer of 1962. Though a few other collisions are apparently still to come—in the Portuguese territories of Africa, for example—the great revolution against Western governance of Third World peoples is essentially over. Politically, morally, and sociologically, the results are mixed. But from the Congo to Guyana the wards of imperialism are, formally anyway, free.[1]

Considering all that independence seemed to promise—popular rule,

---

[1] The term "new states," indeterminate to begin with, becomes even more so as time passes and the states age. Though my main referent is the countries that have gained independence since World War II, I do not hesitate, where it suits my purposes and seems realistic, to extend the term to cover states like those of the Middle East, whose formal independence came earlier, or even those, like Ethiopia, Iran, or Thailand, which in the strict sense were never colonies at all.

rapid economic growth, social equality, cultural regeneration, national greatness and, above all, an end to the ascendancy of the West—it is not surprising that its actual advent has been anticlimactic. It is not that nothing has happened, that a new era has not been entered. Rather, that era having been entered, it is necessary now to live in it rather than merely imagine it, and that is inevitably a deflating experience.

The signs of this darkened mood are everywhere: in nostalgia for the emphatic personalities and well-made dramas of the revolutionary struggle; in disenchantment with party politics, parliamentarianism, bureaucracy, and the new class of soldiers, clerks, and local powers; in uncertainty of direction, ideological weariness, and the steady spread of random violence; and, not the least, in a dawning realization that things are more complicated than they look, that social, economic, and political problems, once thought to be mere reflexes of colonial rule, to disappear when it disappeared, have less superficial roots. Philosophically, the lines between realism and cynicism, between prudence and apathy, and between maturity and despair may be very broad; but sociologically, they are always very narrow. And in most of the new states right now they have thinned almost to the vanishing point.

Behind the mood, which is of course not unmixed, lie the realities of postcolonial social life. The sacred leaders of the national struggle are either gone (Gandhi, Nehru, Sukarno, Nkrumah, Muhammed V, U Nu, Jinnah, Ben Bella, Keita, Azikiwe, Nasser, Bandaranaike), replaced by less confident heirs or less theatrical generals, or have been diminished to mere heads of state (Kenyatta, Nyerere, Bourguiba, Lee, Sekou Touré, Castro). The near-millennial hopes of political deliverance once invested in a handful of extraordinary men are not only now diffused among a larger number of distinctly less extraordinary ones but are themselves attenuated. The enormous concentration of social energies that charismatic leadership can, whatever its other defects, clearly accomplish, dissolves when such leadership disappears. The passing of the generation of prophet-liberators in the last decade has been nearly as momentous, if not quite as dramatic, an event in the history of the new states as was their appearance in the thirties, forties, and fifties. Here and there, new ones will doubtless from time to time emerge, and some may make a considerable impact upon the world. But, unless a wave of Communist uprisings, of which there is now little indication, sweeps through the Third World throwing up a cloud of Che Guevaras, there will not soon again be such a galaxy of successful revolutionary heroes as there were in the Olympian days of the Bandung Conference. Most new states are in for a period of commonplace rulers.

In addition to the reduction in the grandeur of leadership, there has been a solidification of the white collar patriciate—what American sociologists like to call "the new middle class" and the French, less euphemistic, call *la classe dirigeante*—which surrounds and in many places engulfs that leadership. Just as colonial rule tended almost everywhere to transform those who happened to be socially ascendant (and submissive to its demands) at the time of its advent into a privileged corps of officials and overseers, so independence tended almost everywhere to create a similar, though larger, corps out of those who happened to be ascendant (and responsive to its spirit) at its advent. In some cases, the class continuity between the new elite and the old is great, in some less great; determining its composition has been the major internal political struggle of the revolutionary and immediate postrevolutionary periods. But accommodative, parvenu, or something in between, it is now rather definitely in place, and the avenues of mobility that for a moment seemed so wide open seem now, to most people, distinctly less so. As political leadership has slipped back toward the "normal," or anyway appearing such, so too has the stratification system.

So too, indeed, has society as a whole. The consciousness of massive, univocal, irresistible movement, the stirring to action of an entire people, that the attack upon colonialism almost everywhere induced has not wholly disappeared, but it has powerfully lessened. There is much less talk, both inside the new states and in the scholarly literature concerning them, about "social mobilization" than there was five, not to say ten, years ago (and what there is seems increasingly hollow). And this is because there is in fact much less social mobilization. Change continues, and indeed may even be accelerating under a general illusion that nothing much is happening, an illusion in good part generated by the great expectations that accompanied liberation in the first place.[2] But the general forward motion of "the nation as a whole" has been replaced by

[2] For an incisive, if anecdotal, discussion of the way in which contemporary social conditions in the Third World hamper the recognition of change on the part of "the natives" and foreign observers alike, see A. Hirschman, "Underdevelopment, Obstacles to the Perception of Change, and Leadership," *Daedalus* 97 (1968): 925–937. For some comments of my own relative to the tendency of Western scholars—and, inferentially, Third World intellectuals—to underestimate the present rate (and to misconceive the direction) of change in the new states, see "Myrdal's Mythology," *Encounter,* June 1969, pp. 26–34.

a complex, uneven, and many-directioned movement by its various parts, which conduces to a sense less of progress than of agitated stagnation.

Yet, despite the sense of diluted leadership, renascent privilege, and arrested movement, the force of the great political emotion upon which the independence movement was everywhere built remains but slightly dimmed. Nationalism—amorphous, uncertainly focused, half-articulated, but for all that highly inflammable—is still the major collective passion in most new states, and in some it is virtually the only one. That, like the Trojan War, the world revolution may not take place as scheduled, that poverty, inequality, exploitation, superstition, and great power politics are going to be around for a while, is an idea, however galling, that most people at least can somehow contrive to live with. But, once aroused, the desire to become a people rather than a population, a recognized and respected somebody in the world who counts and is attended to, is, short of its satisfaction, apparently unappeasable. At least it has nowhere yet been appeased.

Actually, the novelties of the postrevolutionary period have, in many ways, exacerbated it. The realization that the power imbalance between the new states and the West has not only not been corrected by the destruction of colonialism, but has in some respects increased, while at the same time the buffer colonial rule provided against the direct impact of that imbalance has been removed, leaving fledgling states to fend for themselves against stronger, more practiced, established states, renders nationalist sensitivity to "outside interference" just that much more intense and that much more general. In the same way, emerging into the world as an independent state has led to a similar sensitivization to the acts and intentions of neighboring states—most of them likewise just emerged—that was not present when such states were not free agents but, as oneself, "belonged" to a distant power. And internally, removing European rule has liberated the nationalisms within nationalisms that virtually all the new states contain and produced as provincialism or separatism, a direct and in some cases—Nigeria, India, Malaysia, Indonesia, Pakistan—immediate threat to the new-wrought national identity in whose name the revolution was made.

The effects of this persistent nationalistic sentiment amid national disappointment have been naturally varied: a withdrawal into don't-touch-me isolationism, as in Burma; a surge of neotraditionalism, as in Algeria; a turn toward regional imperialism, as in precoup Indonesia;

an obsession with a neighboring enemy, as in Pakistan; a collapse into ethnic civil war, as in Nigeria; or, in the majority of the cases where the conflict is for the moment less severe, an underdeveloped version of muddling-through, which contains a little of all these plus a certain amount of whistling in the dark. The postrevolutionary period was envisioned to be one of organizing rapid, large-scale, broadly coordinated social, economic, and political advance. But it has turned out to be rather more a continuation, under changed, and in some ways even less propitious, circumstances, of the main theme of the revolutionary and immediate prerevolutionary periods: the definition, creation, and solidification of a viable collective identity.

In this process, the formal liberation from colonial rule turns out not to have been the climax but a stage; a critical and necessary stage, but a stage nonetheless, and quite possibly far from the most consequential one. As in medicine the severity of surface symptoms and the severity of underlying pathology are not always in close correlation, so in sociology the drama of public events and the magnitude of structural change are not always in precise accord. Some of the greatest revolutions occur in the dark.

Four Phases of Nationalism

The tendency for the velocities of outward change and inward transformation to be out of phase with one another is clearly enough demonstrated in the general history of decolonization.

If, keeping all the limitations of periodization in mind, one divides that history into four major phases—that in which the nationalist movements formed and crystallized; that in which they triumphed; that in which they organized themselves into states; and that (the present one) in which, organized into states, they find themselves obliged to define and stabilize their relationships both to other states and to the irregular societies out of which they arose—this incongruence comes plainly into view. The most obvious changes, those which caught and held the attention of the entire world, occurred in the second and third of these phases. But the bulk of the more far-reaching changes, those altering the general shape and direction of social evolution, occurred or are occurring in the less spectacular first and fourth.

The first, formative stage of nationalism consisted essentially of confronting the dense assemblage of cultural, racial, local, and linguistic categories of self-identification and social loyalty that centuries of uninstructed history had produced with a simple, abstract, deliberately constructed, and almost painfully self-conscious concept of political ethnicity—a proper "nationality" in the modern manner. The granular images into which individuals' views of who they are and who they aren't are so intensely bound in traditional society, were challenged by the more general, vaguer, but no less charged conceptions of collective identity, based on a diffuse sense of common destiny, that tend to characterize industrialized states. The men who raised this challenge, the nationalist intellectuals, were thus launching a revolution as much cultural, even epistemological, as it was political. They were attempting to transform the symbolic framework through which people experienced social reality, and thus, to the extent that life is what we make of it all, that reality itself.

That this effort to revise the frames of self-perception was an uphill battle, that in most places it was hardly more than just begun, and that in all it remained confused and incomplete goes without saying—or would, had not the contrary so often been asserted. Indeed, the very success of the independence movements in rousing the enthusiasm of the masses and directing it against foreign domination tended to obscure the frailty and narrowness of the cultural foundations upon which those movements rested, because it led to the notion that anticolonialism and collective redefinition are the same thing. But for all the intimacy (and complexity) of their interconnections, they are not. Most Tamils, Karens, Brahmins, Malays, Sikhs, Ibos, Muslims, Chinese, Nilotes, Bengalis, or Ashantis found it a good deal easier to grasp the idea that they were not Englishmen than that they were Indians, Burmese, Malayans, Ghanaians, Pakistanis, Nigerians, or Sudanese.

As the mass attack (more massive, and more violent, in some places than others) upon colonialism developed, it seemed to create, in and of itself, the basis of a new national identity that independence would merely ratify. The popular rallying behind a common, extremely specific political aim—an occurrence that surprised the nationalists nearly as much as it did the colonialists—was taken for a sign of a deeper solidarity, which produced by it would yet outlive it. Nationalism came to mean, purely and simply, the desire—and the demand—for freedom. Transforming a people's view of themselves, their society, and their culture—the sort of thing that absorbed Gandhi, Jinnah, Fanon, Su-

karno, Senghor, and indeed all the bitter theorists of national
awakening—was identified, to a large extent by some of these same
men, with the access of such peoples to self-government. "Seek ye first
the political kingdom"—the nationalists would make the state, and the
state would make the nation.

The task of making the state turned out to be exacting enough to permit this illusion, indeed the whole moral atmosphere of the revolution,
to be sustained for some time beyond the transfer of sovereignty. The
degree to which this proved possible, necessary, or even advisable, varied widely from Indonesia or Ghana at one extreme to Malaysia or
Tunisia at the other. But, with a few exceptions, by now all the new
states have organized governments that maintain general dominion
within their borders, and well or badly, function. And as government
shakes down into some reasonably recognizable institutional form—
party oligarchy, presidential autocracy, military dictatorship, reconditioned monarchism, or, very partially in the best of cases, representative democracy—it becomes less and less easy to avoid confronting the
fact that to make Italy is not to make Italians. Once the political revolution is accomplished, and a state, if hardly consolidated, is at least established, the question: Who are we, who have done all this? re-emerges
from the easy populism of the last years of decolonization and the first
of independence.

Now that there is a local state rather than a mere dream of one, the
task of nationalist ideologizing radically changes. It no longer consists
in stimulating popular alienation from a foreign-dominated political
order, nor with orchestrating a mass celebration of that order's demise.
It consists in defining, or trying to define, a collective subject to whom
the actions of the state can be internally connected, in creating, or
trying to create, an experiential "we" from whose will the activities of
government seem spontaneously to flow. And as such, it tends to revolve around the question of the content, relative weight, and proper relationship of two rather towering abstractions: "The Indigenous Way of
Life" and "The Spirit of the Age."

To stress the first of these is to look to local mores, established institutions, and the unities of common experience—to "tradition," "culture," "national character," or even "race"—for the roots of a new
identity. To stress the second is to look to the general outlines of the
history of our time, and in particular to what one takes to be the overall
direction and significance of that history. There is no new state in which

both these themes (which, merely to have names for them, I shall call "essentialism" and "epochalism") are not present; few in which they are not thoroughly entangled with one another; and only a small, incompletely decolonized minority in which the tension between them is not invading every aspect of national life from language choice to foreign policy.

Language choice is, in fact, a good, even a paradigmatic, example. I cannot think of a new state in which this question has not in some form or other risen to the level of national policy.[3] The intensity of the disturbance it has thereby generated, as well as the effectiveness with which it has been handled, varies quite widely; but for all the diversity of its expressions, the "language issue" turns precisely on the essentialism-epochalism dilemma.

For any speaker of it, a given language is at once either more or less his own or more or less someone else's, and either more or less cosmopolitan or more or less parochial—a borrowing or a heritage; a passport or a citadel. The question of whether, when, and for what purposes to use it is thus also the question of how far a people should form itself by the bent of its genius and how far by the demands of its times.

The tendency to approach the "language issue" from the linguistic standpoint, homemade or scientific, has somewhat obscured this fact. Most discussion, inside the new states and out, concerning the "suitability" of a given language for national use has suffered from the notion that this suitability turns on the inherent nature of the language—on the adequacy of its grammatical, lexical, or "cultural" resources to the expression of complex philosophical, scientific, political, or moral ideas. But what it really turns on is the relative importance of being able to give one's thoughts, however crude or subtle, the kind of force that speaking one's mother tongue permits as against being able to participate in movements of thought to which only "foreign," or in some cases "literary," languages can give access.

It doesn't matter therefore whether, in concrete form, the problem is the status of classical as against colloquial Arabic in Middle Eastern countries; the place of an "elite" Western language amid a collection of "tribal" languages in sub-Saharan Africa; the complex stratification of local, regional, national, and international languages in India or the Philippines; or the replacement of a European language of limited

[3] For a general review, see J. A. Fishman et al., eds., *Language Problems of Developing Nations* (New York, 1968).

world significance by others of greater significance in Indonesia. The underlying issue is the same. It is not whether this or that language is "developed" or "capable of development"; it is whether this or that language is psychologically immediate and whether it is an avenue to the wider community of modern culture.

It is not because Swahili lacks a stable syntax or Arabic cannot build combining forms—dubious propositions in any case[4]—that language problems are so prominent in the Third World: it is because, for the overwhelming majority of speakers of the overwhelming majority of languages in the new states, the two sides of this double question tend to work out inversely. What, from the ordinary speaker's view, is the natural vehicle of thought and feeling (and particularly in cases like Arabic, Hindi, Amharic, Khmer, or Javanese—the repository of an advanced religious, literary, and artistic tradition to boot) is, from the view of the main current of twentieth century civilization, virtually a patois. And what for that current are the established vehicles of its expression, are for that ordinary speaker at best but half-familiar languages of even less familiar peoples.[5]

Formulated this way, the "language problem" is only the "nationality problem" writ small, though in some places the conflicts arising from it are intense enough to make the relationship seem reversed. Generalized, the "who are we" question asks what cultural forms—what systems of meaningful symbols—to employ to give value and significance to the activities of the state, and by extension to the civil life of its citizens. Nationalist ideologies built out of symbolic forms drawn from local

[4] For the first (not accepted, but attacked), see L. Harries, "Swahili in Modern East Africa," in Fishman et al., *Language Problems,* p. 426. For the second (accepted during an incisive discussion along the general lines here being developed), see C. Gallagher, "North African Problems and Prospects: Language and Identity," in *Language Problems,* p. 140. My point, of course, is not that technical linguistic matters have no relevance to language problems in the new states, but merely that the roots of those problems are much deeper and that expanding lexicons, standardizing usages, improving writing systems, and rationalizing instruction, though valuable in themselves, do not touch the central difficulty.

[5] The main exception so far as the Third World generally is concerned is Latin America, but there—proving the rule—language issues are very much less prominent than in the new states proper and tend to reduce to education and minority group problems. (For an example, see D. H. Burns, "Bilingual Education in the Andes of Peru," in Fishman et al., *Language Problems,* pp. 403–413.) To what degree the fact that Spanish (or, more, Portuguese) is just enough of a carrier of modern thought to be felt to be an avenue to it and just marginal enough a carrier of it not actually to be a very good one has played a part in the intellectual provincialization of Latin America—so that it has in fact had a language problem without quite realizing it—is an interesting and separate question.

traditions—which are, that is, essentialist—tend, like vernaculars, to be psychologically immediate but socially isolating; built out of forms implicated in the general movement of contemporary history—that is, epochalist—they tend, like lingua francas, to be socially deprovincializing but psychologically forced.

However, rarely is such an ideology anywhere purely essentialist or purely epochalist. All are mixed and one can speak at best only of a bias in one direction or another, and often not even of that. Nehru's image of "India" was doubtless heavily epochalist, Gandhi's doubtless heavily essentialist; but the fact that the first was the disciple of the second and the second the patron of the first (and neither managed to convince all Indians that he was not, in the one case, a brown Englishman, or, in the other, a medieval reactionary) demonstrates that the relation between these two routes to self-discovery is a subtle and even paradoxical one. Indeed, the more ideologized new states—Indonesia, Ghana, Algeria, Egypt, Ceylon, and the like—have tended to be both intensely epochalist and intensely essentialist at the same time, whereas countries more purely essentialist like Somalia or Cambodia, or epochalist like Tunisia or the Philippines, have been rather the exceptions.

The tension between these two impulses—to move with the tide of the present and to hold to an inherited course—gives new state nationalism its peculiar air of being at once hell-bent toward modernity and morally outraged by its manifestations. There is a certain irrationality in this. But it is more than a collective derangement; it is a social cataclysm in the process of happening.

Essentialism and Epochalism

The interplay of essentialism and epochalism is not, therefore, a kind of cultural dialectic, a logistic of abstract ideas, but a historical process as concrete as industrialization and as tangible as war. The issues are being fought out not simply at the doctrine and argument level—though there is a great deal of both—but much more importantly in the material transformations that the social structures of all the new states are undergoing. Ideological change is not an independent stream of thought running alongside social process and reflecting (or determining) it, it is a dimension of that process itself.

The impact within any new state society of the desire for coherence and continuity on the one hand and for dynamism and contemporaneity on the other is both extremely uneven and highly nuanced. The pull of indigenous tradition is felt most heavily by its appointed, and these days rather besieged, guardians—monks, mandarins, pandits, chiefs, ulema, and so on; that of what is usually referred to (not altogether accurately) as "the West," by the urban youth, the troubled schoolboys of Cairo, Djakarta, or Kinshasa who have surrounded words like *shabb, pemuda,* and *jeunesse* with an aura of energy, idealism, impatience, and menace. But stretching out between these all-too-visible extremes is the great bulk of the population, among whom essentialist and epochalist sentiments are scrambled into a vast confusion of outlooks, which, because the current of social change produced it, only the current of social change can sort out.

As illustrative cases, compressed to the dimensions of historical anecdotes, of the generation of this confusion and of the efforts now being made to dissolve it, Indonesia and Morocco can serve as well as any. My reason for choosing them is that they are the cases I happen to know firsthand and, in dealing with the interplay between institutional change and cultural reconstruction, the degree to which one can substitute a synoptic vision for an intimate one is limited. Their experiences are, as all social experiences, unique. But they are not so different either from one another or from those of new states as a whole as to be unable to reveal, in their very particularity, some generic outlines of the problems faced by societies struggling to bring what they like to call their "personality" into a workable alignment with what they like to call their "destiny."

In Indonesia, the essentialist element is, and long has been, extremely unhomogeneous. To an extent, this is true for virtually all the new states, which tend to be bundles of competing traditions gathered accidentally into concocted political frameworks rather than organically evolving civilizations. But in Indonesia, the outlands at once of India, China, Oceania, Europe, and the Middle East, cultural diversity has been for centuries both especially great and especially complex. The edge of everything classical, it has been itself shamelessly eclectic.

Up until about the third decade of this century, the several ingredient traditions—Indic, Sinitic, Islamic, Christian, Polynesian—were suspended in a kind of half-solution in which contrasting, even opposed styles of life and world outlooks managed to coexist, if not wholly without tension, or even without violence, at least in some sort of usually workable, to-each-his-own sort of arrangement. This *modus vivendi* began to show signs of strain as early as the mid-nineteenth century, but its dissolution got genuinely under way only with the rise, from 1912 on, of nationalism; its collapse, which is still not complete, only in the revolutionary and postrevolutionary periods. For then what had been parallel traditionalisms, encapsulated in localities and classes, became competing definitions of the essence of the New Indonesia. What was once, to employ a term I have used elsewhere, a kind of "cultural balance of power" became an ideological war of a peculiarly implacable sort.

Thus, in apparent paradox (though, in fact, it has been a nearly universal occurrence in the new states) the move toward national unity intensified group tensions within the society by raising settled cultural forms out of their particular contexts, expanding them into general allegiances, and politicizing them. As the nationalist movement developed, it separated into strands. In the Revolution these strands became parties, each promoting a different aspect of the eclectic tradition as the only true basis of Indonesian identity. Marxists looked mainly to the folk melange of peasant life for the essence of the national heritage; the technicians, clerks, and administrators of the *classe dirigeante* to the Indic aestheticism of the Javanese aristocracy; and the more substantial merchants and landholders to Islam. Village populism, cultural elitism, religious puritanism: some differences of ideological opinion can perhaps be adjusted, but not these.

Rather than adjusted they were accentuated, as each strand attempted to graft a modernist appeal onto its traditionalist base. For the populist element, this was Communism; and the Indonesian Communist party, professing to discern an indigenous radical tradition in the collectivism, social egalitarianism, and anticlericalism of rural life, became the chief spokesman both for peasant essentialism, especially Javanese peasant essentialism, and for a revolutionary epochalism of the usual "rise of the masses" sort. For the salaried element, the modernist appeal was industrial society as found (or imagined) in Europe and the United States, and it proposed a marriage of convenience between oriental spirituality and occidental drive, between "wisdom" and "technique," that would somehow preserve cherished values while transforming the material basis of the society out of which those values had arisen. And for the pious, it was naturally enough religious reform, a celebration of the effort to renovate Islamic civilization in such a way as to regain its lost, rightful leadership of the moral, material, and intellectual progress of mankind. But, in the event, none of these things—Peasant Revolution, The Meeting of East and West, or The Cultural Resurgence of Islam—happened. What happened was the mass slaughter of 1965, in which somewhere between a quarter and three-quarters of a million people lost their lives. The blood bath in which the Sukarno regime with painful slowness drowned was the result of a vast complex of causes, and it would be absurd to reduce it to an ideological explosion. Yet, whatever the role of economic, political, psychological, or—for that matter—accidental factors in bringing it on (and, what is even harder to explain, sustaining it), it marked the end of a distinct phase in the progress of Indonesian nationalism. Not only were the slogans of unity ("one people, one language, one nation"; "from many, one"; "collective harmony"; and so on), which had not been easy to credit in the first place, now rendered implausible altogether, but the theory that the native eclecticism of Indonesian culture would yield easily to a generalized modernism clamped onto one or another element of it was definitively disproved. Multiform in the past, it would seem also to have to be multiform in the present.

In Morocco, the main obstacle to defining an integral national self has not been cultural heterogeneity, which in comparative terms has not been so very great, but social particularism, which in comparative terms has been extreme. Traditional Morocco consisted of an enormous, ill-organized field of rapidly forming and rapidly dissolving political constellations on every level from the court to the camp, every basis from the mystical to the occupational, and every scale from the grand to the microscopic. The continuity of the social order lay less in any durability of the arrangements composing it or the groups embodying it, for the sturdiest of them were fugitive, than in the constancy of the processes by which, incessantly reworking those arrangements and redefining those groups, it formed, reformed, and re-reformed itself.

Insofar as this unsettled society had a center, it was the Alawite monarchy. But even in the best times the monarchy was hardly more than the largest bear in the garden. Embedded in a patrimonial bureaucracy of the most classic sort, a haphazard assortment of courtiers, chieftains, scribes, and judges, it struggled continuously to bring competing centers of power—of which there were literally hundreds, each resting on slightly different ground from the next—within its control. Although between its founding in the seventeenth century and its submission in 1912 it never altogether failed in this, it also never more than very partially succeeded. Not quite an anarchy and not quite a polity, the Moroccan state had, with its endemic particularism, just enough reality to persist.

Initially the effect of colonial domination, which only formally lasted about forty years, was to eviscerate the monarchy and turn it into a kind of Moorish *tableau vivant;* but intentions are one thing and events are another, and the ultimate result of European rule was to establish the king as the axis of the Moroccan political system rather more emphatically than had originally been the case. Though the earliest movements toward independence were undertaken by an uneasy, and as it turned out unstable, coalition of Western-educated intellectuals and neo-traditional Muslim reformers, it was the arrest, exile, and triumphant restoration of Muhammed V in 1953–1955 that finally secured the independence movement, and, in securing it, turned the throne into the focus of Morocco's growing but still intermittent sense of nationhood. The country got, revived, ideologized, and better organized, its center back. But, it soon turned out, it also got, similarly improved, its particularism back.

Much postrevolutionary political history has demonstrated this fact: that however transformed, the crucial struggle still consists in an attempt by the king and his staff to sustain the monarchy as a viable institution in a society in which everything from landscape and kinship structure to religion and national character conspires to partition political life into disparate and disconnected exhibitions of parochial power. The first such exhibitions came with a series of so-called tribal uprisings—in part foreign-stimulated, in part the result of domestic political maneuvering, in part a return of the culturally repressed—that harried the new state during the first few years of independence. These were eventually put down with a combination of royal force and royal intrigue. But they were merely the first, rather elemental indications of what life was going to be like for a classical monarchy that, returning from the limbo of colonial subservience, had to establish itself as at once the authentic expression of the nation's soul and the appropriate vehicle of its modernization.

As Samuel Huntington has pointed out, the peculiar fate of traditional monarchies almost everywhere in the new states is to have also to be modernizing monarchies, or at least to look like such.[6] A king content merely to reign can remain a political icon, a piece of cultural bric-a-brac. But if he wants also to rule, as Moroccan kings have always very much wanted to do, he must make himself the expression of a powerful force in contemporary social life. For Muhammed V, and, since 1961, his son Hassan II, this force has been the emergence for the first time in the country's history of a Western-educated class large enough to permeate the entire society and discrete enough to represent a distinctive interest. Though their styles have been somewhat different—Hassan is remote where Muhammed was paternal—they have each struggled at once to organize and to place themselves at the head of The New Middle Class, The Intermediate Sectors, *La Classe Dirigeante,* The National Elite, or whatever this forming crowd of officials, officers, managers, educators, technicians, and publicists ought properly to be called.

Suppressing the tribal rebellions was thus less the end of the old order than the end of an ineffective strategy for dominating it. After 1958, the essentials of what has become the palace's established approach to securing a firmer grip on the Moroccan half-polity emerged —the construction of a constitutional monarchy, constitutional enough to attract the support of the educated elite and monarchical enough to maintain the substance of royal power. Desiring the fate of neither the English monarchy nor the Iraqi, Muhammed V, and even more Hassan II, have sought to create an institution which, invoking Islam, Arabism, and three centuries of Alawite rule, could draw its legitimacy from the past and, calling for rationalism, *dirigisme,* and technocracy, its authority from the present.

The stages in the recent history of this effort to turn Morocco, by a kind of political miscegenation, into what can only be called a royalist republic—the separation of the secularist, religious, and traditionalist wings of the nationalist movement and the consequent formation of a

[6] S. P. Huntington, "The Political Modernization of Traditional Monarchies," *Daedalus* 95 (1966):763–768; see also his *Political Order in Changing Societies* (New Haven, 1968). With Huntington's general analysis, too much influenced, in my opinion, by the analogy of the king vs. aristocracy struggle in premodern Europe, I am, however, in some disagreement. For Morocco, anyway, the image of a populist monarchy "out of style in middle-class circles," appealing over the heads of "local privilege, corporate autonomy [and] feudal power" to the masses in the interests of progressive reform, seems to me very nearly the reverse of the truth. For more realistic views of postindependence Moroccan politics, see J. Waterbury, *The Commander of the Faithful* (London, 1970).

multiparty system in 1958–1959; the failure of the king's own coalition party, the Front for the Defense of Constitutional Institutions, to gain a parliamentary majority in the 1963 general elections; the royal suspension, ostensibly temporary, of parliament in 1965; the dime-novel murder (in France) of the major opponent of the whole project, Mehdi Ben Barka, in 1968—need not be traced out here. The point is that the tension between essentialism and epochalism is as observable in the vicissitudes of the postrevolutionary Moroccan political system as in those of the Indonesian; and if it has not as yet attained so flamboyant a denouement, and one may hope never will, it has been moving in the same direction of increasing unmanageability, as the relationship between what Edward Shils has called the "will to be modern" and what Mazzini called the "need to exist and have a name" grows steadily more involved.[7] And though the form it takes and the speed at which it moves naturally vary, the same process is occurring in, if perhaps not all, at least the overwhelming majority of the new states as, the revolution accomplished, the point of it is sought.

Concepts of Culture

Until Talcott Parsons, carrying forward Weber's double rejection (and double acceptance) of German idealism and Marxist materialism, provided a viable alternative, the dominant concept of culture in American social science identified culture with learned behavior. This concept can hardly be called "wrong"—isolated concepts are neither "wrong" nor "right"—and for many, rather routine purposes it was, and remains, serviceable. But it is now clear to virtually everyone whose interests extend any distance beyond the descriptive that it is very difficult to generate analyses of much theoretical power from such a diffuse, empiricist notion. The day when social phenomena were explained by redescribing them as culture patterns and noting that such patterns are handed down from generation to generation is very nearly past. And Parsons, insisting in his grave and toneless voice that to interpret the way a group of human beings behave as an expression of their culture while defining

[7] E. Shils, "Political Development in the New States," *Comparative Studies in Society and History* 2 (1960): 265–292, 379–411.

their culture as the sum of the ways in which they have learned to behave is not terribly informative, is as responsible for its passing as any
single figure in contemporary social science.

In place of this near-idea, Parsons, following not only Weber but a
line of thought stretching back at least to Vico, has elaborated a concept
of culture as a system of symbols by which man confers significance
upon his own experience. Symbol systems, man-created, shared, conventional, ordered, and indeed learned, provide human beings with a meaningful framework for orienting themselves to one another, to the world
around them, and to themselves. At once a product and a determinant
of social interaction, they are to the process of social life as a computer's program is to its operations, the genic helix to the development
of the organism, the blueprint to the construction of the bridge, the
score to the performance of the symphony, or, to choose a humbler
analogy, the recipe to the baking of the cake—so the symbol system is
the information source that, to some measurable extent, gives shape,
direction, particularity, and point to an ongoing flow of activity.

Yet these analogies, which suggest a pre-existing template stamping
form onto a process external to it, pass rather facilely over what has
emerged as the central theoretical problem for this more sophisticated
approach: namely, how to conceptualize the dialectic between the crystallization of such directive "patterns of meaning" and the concrete
course of social life.

There is a sense in which a computer's program is an outcome of
prior developments in the technology of computing, a particular helix of
phylogenetic history, a blueprint of earlier experiments in bridge building, a score of the evolution of musical performance, and a recipe of a
long series of successful and unsucccessful cakes. But the simple fact
that the information elements in these cases are materially separable
from the processual—one can, in principle anyhow, write out the program, isolate the helix, draw the blueprint, publish the score, note down
the recipe—makes them less useful as models for the interaction of cultural patterns and social processes where, a few more intellectualized
realms like music and cake-baking in part aside, the very question at
issue is precisely how such a separation is, even in thought, actually to
be effected. The workability of the Parsonian concept of culture rests
almost entirely on the degree to which such a model can be constructed
—on the degree to which the relationship between the development of
symbol systems and the dynamics of social process can be circumstan-

tially exposed, thereby rendering the depiction of technologies, rituals, myths, and kinship terminologies as man-made information sources for the directive ordering of human conduct more than a metaphor.

This problem has haunted Parsons' writings on culture from the earliest days when he regarded it as a set of Whiteheadian "external objects" psychologically incorporated into personalities and thus, by extension, institutionalized in social systems, to the most recent where he sees it more in the control-mechanism terms of cybernetics. But nowhere has it come home more to roost than in discussing ideology; for, of all the realms of culture, ideology is the one in which the relationship between symbolic structures and collective behavior is at once the most conspicuous and the least clear.

For Parsons, an ideology is but a special sort of symbol system:

A system of beliefs held in common by members of a collectivity . . . which is oriented to the evaluative integration of the collectivity, by *interpretation of the empirical nature of the collectivity* and *of the situation in which it is placed,* the processes by which it developed to its given state, the goals to which its members are collectively oriented, and their relation to the future course of events.[8]

Yet, left at that, this formulation fuses together modes of self-interpretation that do not entirely go together, and, glossing over the moral tension inherent in ideological activity, obscures the interior sources of its enormous sociological dynamism. In particular, the two clauses I have underscored, the "interpretation of the empirical nature of the collectivity," and " [the interpretation] of the situation in which [that collectivity] is placed," are not, as I hope I have by now demonstrated, as coordinate as practical enterprises in social self-definition as the mere "and" conjoining them might suggest. So far as new state nationalism is concerned, they are in fact very deeply, in some places irreconcilably, at odds. To deduce what the nation is from a conception of the world-historical situation in which it is thought to be enclosed— "epochalism"—produces one sort of moral-political universe; to diagnose the situation with which the nation is faced from a prior conception of what it is intrinsically—"essentialism"—produces quite another; and to combine the two (the most common approach) produces a confused assortment of mixed cases. For this reason, among others, nationalism is not a mere by-product but the very stuff of social change in

[8] T. Parsons, *The Social System* (Glencoe, Ill., 1951), p. 349. Italics added.

so many new states; not its reflection, its cause, its expression, or its engine, but the thing itself.

To see one's country as the product of "the processes by which it developed to its given state," or, alternatively, to see it as the ground of
"the future course of events," is, in short, to see it rather differently.
But, more than that, it is to look in rather different places to see it: to
parents, to traditional authority figures, to custom and legend; or, to
secular intellectuals, to the oncoming generation, to "current events,"
and the mass media. Fundamentally, the tension between essentialist
and epochalist strains in new state nationalism is not a tension between
intellectual passions but between social institutions charged with discordant cultural meanings. An increase in newspaper circulation, an up-
surge of religious activity, a decline in family cohesion, an expansion of
universities, a reassertion of hereditary privilege, a proliferation of folklore societies are—like their contraries—themselves elements in the
process by which the character and content of that nationalism as an
"information source" for collective behavior are determined. The organized "systems of belief" propagated by professional ideologists represent attempts to raise aspects of this process to the level of conscious
thought and so deliberately control it.

But, no more than consciousness exhausts mentality does nationalist
ideology exhaust nationalism; what it does, selectively and incompletely,
is articulate it. The images, metaphors, and rhetorical turns from which
nationalist ideologies are built are essentially devices, cultural devices
designed to render one or another aspect of the broad process of collective self-redefinition explicit, to cast essentialist pride or epochalist hope
into specific symbolic forms, where more than dimly felt, they can be
described, developed, celebrated, and used. To formulate an ideological
doctrine is to make (or try to make—there are more failures than suc-
cesses) what was a generalized mood into a practical force.

The scuffle of political sects in Indonesia and the shifting foundations
of monarchy in Morocco, the first so far an apparent failure, the second
so far an ambiguous success, represent such attempts to draw the intan-
gibilities of conceptual change into articulate cultural forms. They represent, also, of course, and even more immediately, a struggle for
power, place, privilege, wealth, fame, and all the other so-called "real"
rewards of life. Indeed, it is because of the fact that they also represent
this that their ability to focus and transform men's views of who they
are and how they should act is so great.

The "patterns of meaning" by which social change is formed grow from the processes of that change itself and, crystallized into proper ideologies or embedded in popular attitudes, serve in turn, to some inevitably limited degree, to guide it. The progress from cultural diversity to ideological combat to mass violence in Indonesia, or the attempt to dominate a field of social particularisms by fusing the values of a republic with the facts of an autocracy in Morocco, are without doubt the hardest of hard political, economic, and stratificatory realities; real blood has flowed, real dungeons have been built—and, to be fair, real pain has been relieved. But they are also without doubt the record of those would-be countries' efforts to breathe intelligibility into an idea of "nationhood," in terms of which these realities, and worse to come, can be confronted, shaped, and understood.

And this is true for the new states generally. As the heroic excitements of the political revolution against colonial domination recede into an inspirational past to be replaced by the shabbier, but no less convulsive movements of the dispiriting present, the secular analogues of Weber's famous "problems of meaning" grow more and more desperate. It is not only in religion that things are not "merely there and happen" but "have a 'meaning' and are there because of this meaning," but in politics as well, and in new-state politics in particular. The questions "What is it all for?" "What's the use?" and "Why go on?" arise in the context of mass poverty, official corruption, or tribal violence as much as in those of wasting illness, defeated hope, or premature death. They get no better answers, but insofar as they get any at all it is from images of a heritage worth preserving or a promise worth pursuing, and though these need not necessarily be nationalist images, almost all of them—Marxist ones included—are.[9]

Rather like religion, nationalism has a bad name in the modern world, and, rather like religion, it more or less deserves it. Between them (and sometimes in combination) religious bigotry and nationalist hatred have probably brought more havoc upon humanity than any two forces in history, and doubtless will bring a great deal more. Yet also

[9] The question of the relationship between Marxism and nationalism is a vexed one which it would take another essay even to outline. Suffice it here to say that, as far as the new states are concerned, Marxist movements, Communist or non-Communist, have almost everywhere been heavily nationalistic in both aim and idiom, and there is very little sign that they are becoming any less so. Actually, the same point could be made about religio-political movements—Muslim, Buddhist, Hindu, or whatever; they too tend to be as localized in fact as they are placeless in principle.

rather like religion, nationalism has been a driving force in some of the most creative changes in history, and doubtless will be so again in many yet to come. It would seem, then, well to spend less time decrying it—which is a little like cursing the winds—and more in trying to figure out why it takes the forms it does and how it might be prevented from tearing apart even as it creates the societies in which it arises, and beyond that the whole fabric of modern civilization. For in the new states the age of ideology is not only not over, but, as the inchoate changes of self-conception wrought by the dramatic events of the past forty years emerge into the public light of explicit doctrine, only just beginning. In preparing ourselves to understand and deal with it, or perhaps only to survive it, the Parsonian theory of culture, suitably emended, is one of our most powerful intellectual tools.

Chapter 10 /

The Integrative Revolution:
Primordial Sentiments
and Civil Politics
in the New States

I

In 1948, scarcely a year after Independence, Pandit Nehru found himself in the always unsettling position for an opposition politician finally come to power of being obliged to place in practice a policy he had long espoused but never liked. With Patel and Sitaramayya, he was appointed to the Linguistic Provinces Committee.

The Congress had supported the principle of linguistic determination of state boundaries within India almost since its founding, arguing, ironically enough, that British maintenance of "arbitrary"—that is, nonlinguistic—administrative units was part of a divide-and-rule policy. In 1920 it had actually reorganized its own regional chapters along linguistic lines so as better to secure its popular appeal. But with the echoes of partition perhaps still ringing in his ears, Nehru was deeply shaken by his experience on the Linguistic Committee, and with the candor that made him virtually unique among the leaders of the new states, he admitted it:

[This inquiry] has been in some ways an eye-opener for us. The work of 60 years of the Indian National Congress was standing before us, face to face with centuries-old India of narrow loyalties, petty jealousies and ignorant prejudices engaged in mortal conflict and we were simply horrified to see how thin was the ice upon which we were skating. Some of the ablest men in the country came before us and confidently and emphatically stated that language in this country stood for and represented culture, race, history, individuality, and finally a sub-nation.[1]

But, horrified or not, Nehru, Patel, and Sitaramayya in the end were forced to endorse the claims of Andhra as a Telugu-speaking state, and the thin ice was broken. Within the decade India had been almost entirely reorganized along linguistic lines, and a wide range of observers, both domestic and foreign, were wondering aloud whether the country's political unity would survive this wholesale concession to "narrow loyalties, petty jealousies, and ignorant prejudices."[2]

The problem that opened Nehru's eyes in such wide astonishment is phrased in linguistic terms, but the same problem phrased in a wide variety of terms is, of course, literally pandemic to the new states, as the countless references to "dual" or "plural" or "multiple" societies, to "mosaic" or "composite" social structures, to "states" that are not "nations" and "nations" that are not "states," to "tribalism," "parochialism," and "communalism," as well as to pan-national movements of various sorts demonstrate.

When we speak of communalism in India, we refer to religious contrasts; when we speak of it in Malaya, we are mainly concerned with racial ones, and in the Congo with tribal ones. But the grouping under a common rubric is not simply adventitious; the phenomena referred to are in some way similar. Regionalism has been the main theme in Indonesian disaffection, differences in custom in Moroccan. The Tamil mi-

[1] Quoted in S. Harrison, "The Challenge to Indian Nationalism," *Foreign Affairs* 34 (April 1956): 3.
[2] For a very dim view, see S. Harrison, *India: The Most Dangerous Decades* (Princeton, N.J., 1960). For a lively Indian view that sees the "scheme of dividing India in the name of Linguistic States" as "full of poison" but yet necessary "to make easy the way to democracy and to remove racial and cultural tension," see B. R. Ambedkar, *Thoughts on Linguistic States* (Delhi, ca. 1955).

nority in Ceylon is set off from the Sinhalese majority by religion, language, race, region, and social custom; the Shiite minority in Iraq is set off from the dominant Sunnis virtually by an intra-Islamic sectarian difference alone. Pan-national movements in Africa are largely based on race, in Kurdistan, on tribalism; in Laos, the Shan States, and Thailand, on language. Yet all these phenomena, too, are in some sense of a piece. They form a definable field of investigation.

That is, they would, could we but define it. The stultifying aura of conceptual ambiguity that surrounds the terms "nation," "nationality," and "nationalism" has been extensively discussed and thoroughly deplored in almost every work that has been concerned to attack the relationship between communal and political loyalties.[3] But as the preferred remedy has been to adopt a theoretical eclecticism that, in its attempt to do justice to the multifaceted nature of the problems involved, tends to confuse political, psychological, cultural, and demographic factors, actual reduction of that ambiguity has not proceeded very far. Thus a recent symposium on the Middle East refers indiscriminately to the efforts of the Arab League to destroy existing nation-state boundaries, those of the Sudan Government to unify a somewhat arbitrary and accidentally demarcated sovereign state, and those of the Azerin Turks to separate from Iran and join the Soviet Republic of Azerbaijan as "nationalism." [4] Operating with a similarly omnibus concept, Coleman sees Nigerians (or some of them) as displaying five different sorts of nationalism at once—"African," "Nigerian," "Regional," "Group," and "Cultural." [5] And Emerson defines a nation as a "terminal community —the largest community that, when the chips are down, effectively commands men's loyalty, overriding the claims both of the lesser communities within it and those that cut across it or potentially enfold it within a still greater society . . . ," which simply shifts the ambiguity from the term "nation" to the term "loyalty," as well as seeming to leave such questions as whether India, Indonesia, or Nigeria are nations to the determination of some future, unspecified historical crisis.[6]

---

[3] See, for example, K. Deutsch, *Nationalism and Social Communication* (New York, 1953), pp. 1–14; R. Emerson, *From Empire to Nation* (Cambridge, Mass., 1960); J. Coleman, *Nigeria: Background to Nationalism* (Berkeley, 1958), p. 419 ff; F. Hertz, *Nationalism in History and Politics* (New York, 1944), pp. 11–15.

[4] W. Z. Laqueur, ed., *The Middle East in Transition: Studies in Contemporary History* (New York, 1958).

[5] Coleman, *Nigeria,* pp. 425–426.

[6] Emerson, *Empire to Nation,* pp. 95–96.

Some of this conceptual haze is burned away, however, if it is realized that the peoples of the new states are simultaneously animated by two powerful, thoroughly interdependent, yet distinct and often actually opposed motives—the desire to be recognized as responsible agents whose wishes, acts, hopes, and opinions "matter," and the desire to build an efficient, dynamic modern state. The one aim is to be noticed: it is a search for an identity, and a demand that the identity be publicly acknowledged as having import, a social assertion of the self as "being somebody in the world." [7] The other aim is practical: it is a demand for progress, for a rising standard of living, more effective political order, greater social justice, and beyond that of "playing a part in the larger arena of world politics," of "exercising influence among the nations." [8] The two motives are, again, most intimately related, because citizenship in a truly modern state has more and more become the most broadly negotiable claim to personal significance, and because what Mazzini called the demand to exist and have a name is to such a great extent fired by a humiliating sense of exclusion from the important centers of power in world society. But they are not the same thing. They stem from different sources and respond to different pressures. It is, in fact, the tension between them that is one of the central driving forces in the national evolution of the new states; as it is, at the same time, one of the greatest obstacles to such evolution.

This tension takes a peculiarly severe and chronic form in the new states, both because of the great extent to which their peoples' sense of self remains bound up in the gross actualities of blood, race, language, locality, religion, or tradition, and because of the steadily accelerating importance in this century of the sovereign state as a positive instrument for the realization of collective aims. Multiethnic, usually multilinguistic, and sometimes multiracial, the populations of the new states tend to regard the immediate, concrete, and to them inherently meaningful sorting implicit in such "natural" diversity as the substantial content of their individuality. To subordinate these specific and familiar identifications in favor of a generalized commitment to an overarching and somewhat alien civil order is to risk a loss of definition as an autonomous person, either through absorption into a culturally undifferentiated mass or, what is even worse, through a domination by some other

[7] I. Berlin, *Two Concepts of Liberty* (New York, 1958), p. 42.
[8] E. Shils, "Political Development in the New States," *Comparative Studies in Society and History* 2 (1960): 265–292, 379–411.

rival ethnic, racial, or linguistic community that is able to imbue that order with the temper of its own personality. But at the same time, all but the most unenlightened members of such societies are at least dimly aware—and their leaders are acutely aware—that the possibilities for social reform and material progress they so intensely desire and are so determined to achieve rest with increasing weight on their being enclosed in a reasonably large, independent, powerful, well-ordered polity. The insistence on recognition as someone who is visible and matters and the will to be modern and dynamic thus tend to diverge, and much of the political process in the new states pivots around an heroic effort to keep them aligned.

II

A more exact phrasing of the nature of the problem involved here is that, considered as societies, the new states are abnormally susceptible to serious disaffection based on primordial attachments.[9] By a primordial attachment is meant one that stems from the "givens"—or, more precisely, as culture is inevitably involved in such matters, the assumed "givens"—of social existence: immediate contiguity and kin connection mainly, but beyond them the givenness that stems from being born into a particular religious community, speaking a particular language, or even a dialect of a language, and following particular social practices. These congruities of blood, speech, custom, and so on, are seen to have an ineffable, and at times overpowering, coerciveness in and of themselves. One is bound to one's kinsman, one's neighbor, one's fellow believer, ipso facto; as the result not merely of personal affection, practical necessity, common interest, or incurred obligation, but at least in great part by virtue of some unaccountable absolute import attributed to the very tie itself. The general strength of such primordial bonds, and the types of them that are important, differ from person to person, from society to society, and from time to time. But for virtually every person, in every society, at almost all times, some at-

---

[9] E. Shils, "Primordial, Personal, Sacred and Civil Ties," *British Journal of Sociology* 8 (1957): 130–145.

tachments seem to flow more from a sense of natural—some would say spiritual—affinity than from social interaction.

In modern societies the lifting of such ties to the level of political supremacy—though it has, of course, occurred and continues to occur —has more and more come to be deplored as pathological. To an increasing degree national unity is maintained not by calls to blood and land but by a vague, intermittent, and routine allegiance to a civil state, supplemented to a greater or lesser extent by governmental use of police powers and ideological exhortation. The havoc wreaked, both upon themselves and others, by those modern (or semimodern) states that did passionately seek to become primordial rather than civil political communities, as well as a growing realization of the practical advantages of a wider-ranging pattern of social integration than primordial ties can usually produce or even permit, have only strengthened the reluctance publicly to advance race, language, religion, and the like as bases for the definition of a terminal community. But in modernizing societies, where the tradition of civil politics is weak and where the technical requirements for an effective welfare government are poorly understood, primordial attachments tend, as Nehru discovered, to be repeatedly, in some cases almost continually, proposed and widely acclaimed as preferred bases for the demarcation of autonomous political units. And the thesis that truly legitimate authority flows only from the inherent coerciveness such attachments are conceived somehow to possess is frankly, energetically, and artlessly defended:

The reasons why a unilingual state is stable and a multilingual state unstable are quite obvious. A state is built on fellow feeling. What is this fellow feeling? To state briefly it is a feeling of a corporate sentiment of oneness which makes those who are charged with it feel that they are kith and kin. This feeling is a double-edged feeling. It is at once a feeling of "consciousness of kind" which, on the one hand, binds together those who have it so strongly that it overrides all differences arising out of economic conflicts or social gradations and, on the other, severs them from those who are not of their kind. It is a longing not to belong to any other group. The existence of this fellow feeling is the foundation of a stable and democratic state.[10]

    [10] Ambedkar, *Thoughts on Linguistic States,* p. 11. Noting that the modern bilingual states of Canada, Switzerland, and (white) South Africa might be quoted against him, Ambedkar adds: "It must not be forgotten that the genius of India is quite different than the genius of Canada, Switzerland, and South Africa. The genius of India is to divide—the genius of Switzerland, South Africa and Canada to unite." [In 1972, both this note and my passage about the declining role of primordial divisions in "modern" countries seem, to put it mildly, rather less con-

It is this crystallization of a direct conflict between primordial and civil sentiments—this "longing not to belong to any other group"—that gives to the problem variously called tribalism, parochialism, communalism, and so on, a more ominous and deeply threatening quality than most of the other, also very serious and intractable, problems the new states face. Here we have not just competing loyalties, but competing loyalties of the same general order, on the same level of integration. There are many other competing loyalties in the new states, as in any state—ties to class, party, business, union, profession, or whatever. But groups formed of such ties are virtually never considered as possible self-standing, maximal social units, as candidates for nationhood. Conflicts among them occur only within a more or less fully accepted terminal community whose political integrity they do not, as a rule, put into question. No matter how severe they become, they do not threaten, at least not intentionally, its existence as such. They threaten governments, or even forms of government, but they rarely at best—and then usually when they have become infused with primordial sentiments— threaten to undermine the nation itself, because they do not involve alternative definitions of what the nation is, of what its scope of reference is. Economic or class or intellectual disaffection threatens revolution, but disaffection based on race, language, or culture threatens partition, irredentism, or merger, a redrawing of the very limits of the state, a new definition of its domain. Civil discontent finds its natural outlet in the seizing, legally or illegally, of the state apparatus. Primordial discontent strives more deeply and is satisfied less easily. If severe enough, it wants not just Sukarno's or Nehru's or Moulay Hasan's head, it wants Indonesia's or India's or Morocco's.

The actual foci around which such discontent tends to crystallize are various, and in any given case several are usually involved concurrently, sometimes at cross-purposes with one another. On a merely descriptive level they are, nevertheless, fairly readily enumerable: [11]

Assumed Blood Ties. Here the defining element is quasi-kinship. "Quasi" because kin units formed around known biological relationship

---

vincing than they did in 1962, when this essay was originally written. But if events in Canada, Belgium, Ulster, and so on have made primordial definition seem less predominantly a "new state" phenomenon, they have made the general argument developed here seem even more germane.]

[11] For a similar but rather differently conceived and organized listing, see Emerson, *Empire to Nation,* Chaps. 6, 7, and 8.

(extended families, lineages, and so on) are too small for even the most tradition-bound to regard them as having more than limited significance, and the referent is, consequently, to a notion of untraceable but yet sociologically real kinship, as in a tribe. Nigeria, the Congo, and the greater part of sub-Saharan Africa are characterized by a prominence of this sort of primordialism. But so also are the nomads or seminomads of the Middle East—the Kurds, Baluchis, Pathans, and so on; the Nagas, Mundas, Santals, and so on, of India; and most of the so-called hill tribes of Southeast Asia.

Race. Clearly, race is similar to assumed kinship, in that it involves an ethnobiological theory. But it is not quite the same thing. Here, the reference is to phenotypical physical features—especially, of course, skin color, but also facial form, stature, hair type, and so on—rather than any very definite sense of common descent as such. The communal problems of Malaya in large part focus around these sorts of differences, between, in fact, two phenotypically very similar Mongoloid peoples. "Negritude" clearly draws much, though perhaps not all, of its force from the notion of race as a significant primordial property, and the pariah commercial minorities—like the Chinese in Southeast Asia or the Indians and Lebanese in Africa—are similarly demarcated.

Language. Linguism—for some yet to be adequately explained reasons—is particularly intense in the Indian subcontinent, has been something of an issue in Malaya, and has appeared sporadically elsewhere. But as language has sometimes been held to be the altogether essential axis of nationality conflicts, it is worth stressing that linguism is not an inevitable outcome of linguistic diversity. As indeed kinship, race, and the other factors to be listed below, language differences need not in themselves be particularly divisive; they have not been so for the most part in Tanganyika, Iran (not a new state in the strict sense, perhaps), the Philippines, or even in Indonesia, where despite a great confusion of tongues linguistic conflict seems to be the one social problem the country has somehow omitted to demonstrate in extreme form. Furthermore, primordial conflicts can occur where no marked linguistic differences are involved, as in Lebanon, among the various sorts of Batak-speakers in Indonesia, and to a lesser extent perhaps between the Fulani and Hausa in northern Nigeria.

Region. Although a factor nearly everywhere, regionalism naturally tends to be especially troublesome in geographically heterogeneous areas. Tonkin, Annam, and Cochin in prepartitioned Vietnam, the two baskets on the long pole, were opposed almost purely in regional terms, sharing language, culture, race, and so on. The tension between East and West Pakistan [now separated into Bangladesh and Pakistan] involved differences in language and culture too, but the geographic element was of great prominence owing to the territorial discontinuity of the country. Java versus the Outer Islands in archipelagic Indonesia, and the Northeast versus the West Coast in mountain-bisected Malaya, are other examples in which regionalism has been an important primordial factor in national politics.

Religion. Indian partition is the outstanding case of the operation of this type of attachment. But Lebanon, the Christian Karens and the Moslem Arakenese in Burma, the Toba Bataks, Ambonese, and Minahassans in Indonesia, the Moros in the Philippines, the Sikhs in Indian Punjab and the Ahmadiyas in Pakistan, and the Hausa in Nigeria are other well-known examples of its force in undermining or inhibiting a comprehensive civil sense.

Custom. Again, differences in custom form a basis for a certain amount of national disunity almost everywhere, and are of especial prominence in those cases in which an intellectually and / or artistically rather sophisticated group sees itself as the bearer of a "civilization" amid a largely barbarian population that would be well advised to model itself upon it: the Bengalis in India, the Javanese in Indonesia, the Arabs (as against the Berbers) in Morocco, the Amhara in— another "old" new state—Ethiopia, and so forth. But it is important also to point out that even vitally opposed groups may differ rather little in their general style of life: Hindu Gujeratis and Maharashtrians in India; Baganda and Bunyoro in Uganda; Javanese and Sundanese in Indonesia. And the reverse holds also: the Balinese have far and away the most divergent pattern of customs in Indonesia, but they have been, so far, notable for the absence of any sense of primordial discontent at all.

But beyond such a mere listing of the sorts of primordial ties that tend, in one place or another, to become politicized, it is necessary to go further and attempt also to classify, or somehow order, the concrete patterns of primordial diversity and conflict that in fact exist in the various new states and of which these ties are the components.

This seemingly routine exercise in political ethnography is a rather more delicate task than at first appears, however, not only because those communalistic challenges to the integrity of the civil state that are at the moment being openly pressed must be discerned, but also because those that are latent, lying concealed in the enduring structure of primordial identifications, ready to take explicit political form given only the proper sorts of social conditions, must be revealed. The fact that the Indian minority in Malaya has not so far posed a very serious threat to the viability of the state does not mean that it might not do so if something odd happened to the world price of rubber or if Mrs. Gandhi's hands-off policy toward overseas Indians should be replaced by one more like that of Mao toward the overseas Chinese. The Moro problem, which provided postgraduate field training for select members of several generations of West Pointers, now merely simmers in the Philippines, but it may not do so forever. The Free Thai movement seems dead at the moment, but it could revive with a change in Thailand's foreign policy or even with Pathet success in Laos. Iraq's Kurds, several times ostensibly mollified, continue to show signs of restlessness. And so on. Primordially based political solidarities have a deeply abiding strength in most of the new states, but it is not always an active and immediately apparent one.

    Initially, a useful analytic distinction can be made with respect to this matter of classification between those allegiances that operate more or less wholly within the confines of a single civil state and those that do not but which run across them. Or, put somewhat differently, one can contrast those cases in which the racial, tribal, linguistic, and so on, reference group that is charged with a "corporate sentiment of oneness" is smaller than the existing civil state, and those where it is larger, or at least transcends its borders in some fashion. In the first instance primordial discontent arises from a sense of political suffocation; in the second, from a sense of political dismemberment. Karen separatism in Burma, Ashanti in Ghana, or Baganda in Uganda are examples of the former; pan-Arabism, greater Somaliism, pan-Africanism, of the latter.

    Many of the new states are plagued by both these sorts of problems at once. In the first place, most interstate primordial movements do not involve entire separate countries, as the pan-movements at least tend to do, but rather minorities scattered through several, for example: the Kurdistan movement to unite Kurds in Iran, Syria, Turkey, and the Soviet Union, perhaps the most unlikely-to-succeed political movement of all time; the Abako movement of the late Mr. Kasuvubu and his Republic of The Congo and Angola allies; the Dravidistan movement, insofar as it comes to see itself as extending across Palk Strait from

South India into Ceylon; the movement, or perhaps it is so far only a formless sentiment, for a unified and sovereign Bengal—greater Bangladesh—independent of both India and Pakistan. And there are even a few classical irredentist-type problems scattered among the new states—the Malays in South Thailand, the Pushtu speakers along the Afghan border of Pakistan, and so on; and when political boundaries become more firmly established in sub-Saharan Africa there will be a great many more of them. In all these cases, there is—or there may develop—both a desire to escape the established civil state and a longing to reunite a politically divided primordial community.[12]

In the second place, interstate and intrastate primordial attachments often cross-cut one another in a complex network of balanced—if most precariously balanced—commitments. In Malaya one of the more effective binding forces that has, so far at least, held Chinese and Malays together in a single state despite the tremendous centrifugal tendencies the racial and cultural difference generates is the fear on the part of either group that should the Federation dissolve they may become a clearly submerged minority in some other political framework: the Malays through the turn of the Chinese to Singapore or China; the Chinese through the turn of the Malays to Indonesia. In a similar way, in Ceylon both the Tamils and Sinhalese manage to see themselves as minorities: the Tamils because 70 percent of the Ceylonese are Sinhalese; the Sinhalese because the eight million of them in Ceylon are all there are, while in addition to the two million Tamils on the island there are 28 million more in South India. In Morocco, there has tended to be both a within-state split between Arab and Berber, and an extrastate split between partisans of Nasser's pan-Arabism and of Bourguiba's *regroupement maghrebin*. And Nasser himself, until his death perhaps the new states' most accomplished virtuoso in the primordial arts, was absorbed in juggling pan-Arabist, pan-Islamic, and pan-African sentiments in the interests of Egyptian hegemony among the Bandung powers.

But whether the relevant attachments outrun state boundaries or not, most of the major primordial battles are for the moment being fought within them. A certain amount of international conflict focusing around, or at least animated by, primordial issues does exist among the new

[12] The intensity, prevalence, or even the reality of such desires in each case is another matter, about which nothing is being asserted here. How much, if any, feeling in favor of assimilation to Malaya exists among the South Thailand Malays, the actual strength of the Abako idea, or the attitudes of Tamils in Ceylon toward the Dravidian separatists of Madras are matters for empirical research.

states. The hostility between Israel and her Arab neighbors and the quarrel of India and Pakistan over Kashmir are the most prominent cases, of course. But the embroilment of two older states, Greece and Turkey, over Cyprus is another case; the tension between Somalia and Ethiopia concerning an essentially irredentist problem a third; the Indonesian difficulties vis-à-vis Peking with respect to the issue of "dual citizenship" for Chinese residents of Indonesia a fourth, and so on. As the new states solidify politically, such disputes may well grow both more frequent and more intense. But as of now they have not yet become—with the exception of the Israeli-Arab conflict and, sporadically, the Kashmir problem—paramount political issues, and the immediate significance of primordial differences is almost everywhere primarily domestic, though this is not to say that they are therefore without important international implications.[13]

The construction of a typology of the concrete patterns of primordial diversity that are found within the various new states is severely hampered, however, by the simple lack of detailed and reliable information in the overwhelming majority of the cases. But, again, a gross and merely empirical classification can nonetheless fairly easily be devised, and should prove useful as a rough-and-ready guide to a wilderness otherwise uncharted, and facilitate a more incisive analysis of the role of primordial sentiments in civil politics than is possible in terms of "pluralism," "tribalism," "parochialism," "communalism," and the other cliches of common-sense sociology:

1. One common and, relatively speaking, simple pattern seems to be that of a single dominant and usually, though not inevitably, larger group set over against a single strong and chronically troublesome minority: Cyprus with Greeks and Turks; Ceylon with Sinhalese and Tamils; Jordan with Jordanians and Palestinians, though in this last case the dominant group is the smaller.

2. Similar in some ways to this first pattern, but more complex, is

---

[13] Nor does the interstate significance of primordial sentiments lie wholly in their divisive power. Pan-African attitudes, weak and ill-defined as they may be, have provided a useful context of mild solidarity for the confrontation of leaders of major African countries. Burma's strenuous (and expensive) efforts to strengthen and revitalize international Buddhism, as in the Sixth Great Council at Yegu in 1954, served, at least temporarily, to link her more effectively with the other Theravada countries—Ceylon, Thailand, Laos, and Cambodia. And a vague, mainly racial, feeling of common "Malayness" has played a positive role in the relations between Malaya and Indonesia and Malaya and the Philippines, and even, more recently, between Indonesia and the Philippines.

that of one central—often enough in a geographic sense as well as a
political—group and several mediumly large and at least somewhat opposed peripheral groups: the Javanese versus the Outer Island peoples
in Indonesia; the Irrawaddy Valley Burmese versus the various hill
tribes and upland valley peoples in Burma; the central plateau Persians
and the various tribes in Iran (though, again, this is not strictly a new
state); the Atlantic Plain Arabs encircled by the diverse Berber tribes
of the Rif, the Atlas, and the Sous; the Mekong Lao and the tribal peoples in Laos; and so on. How far such a pattern is to be found in black
Africa is unclear. In the one case where it might have crystallized, with
the Ashanti in Ghana, the power of the central group seems to have, at
least temporarily, been broken. And whether in a new state the Baganda will be able to maintain [or, perhaps now, regain] their dominant position vis-à-vis the other Uganda groups through their greater
education, political sophistication, and so on, and despite their compris-
ing but about a fifth of the population, remains to be seen.

3. Another pattern that forms an internally even less homogeneous
type is a bipolar one of two nearly evenly balanced major groups: Malays and Chinese in Malaya (though there is also a smaller Indian
group); or Christians and Moslems in Lebanon (though here both
groups are actually aggregates of smaller sects); or Sunnis and Shiis in
Iraq. The two regions of Pakistan, although the Western region is far
from wholly homogeneous within itself, gave that state a sharply bipolar
primordial pattern, which has now torn it in half. Vietnam before partition tended to take this form—Tonkin versus Cochin—this problem
now having been "solved" with the assistance of the great powers,
though reunification of the country might revive it. Even Libya, which
has scarcely enough people to develop decent group conflicts, has something of this pattern with the Cyrenecia-Tripolitania contrast.

4. Next, there is the pattern of a relatively even gradation of groups
in importance, from several large ones through several medium-sized
ones to a number of small ones, with no clearly dominant ones and no
sharp cut-off points. India, the Philippines, Nigeria, and Kenya are perhaps examples.

5. Finally, there is simple ethnic fragmentation, as Wallerstein has
called it, with multiple small groups, into which somewhat residual category it is necessary to toss much of Africa, at least until more is
known about it.[14] One proposal, issuing from the nothing-if-not-exper-

[14] I. Wallerstein, "The Emergence of Two West African Nations: Ghana and
the Ivory Coast" (Ph.D. thesis, Columbia University, 1959).

imental Leopoldville Government, suggesting a grouping of the Congo Republic's estimated two hundred and fifty or so separate tribal-linguistic groups into eighty autonomous tribal regions, which would then be organized into twelve federated states, gives something of an indication of the extent to which such fragmentation can go, and the complexity of primordial allegiances it may involve.

The world of personal identity collectively ratified and publicly expressed is thus an ordered world. The patterns of primordial identification and cleavage within the existing new states are not fluid, shapeless, and infinitely various, but are definitely demarcated and vary in systematic ways. And as they vary, the nature of the individual's problem of social self-assertion varies with them, as it does also according to his position within any one type of pattern. The task of securing recognition as someone who is somebody to whom attention must be paid appears in a different form and light to a Sinhalese in Ceylon than it does to a Javanese in Indonesia or a Malay in Malaya, because to be a member of a major group set over against one minor one is a quite different matter from being a member of such a group over against a plurality of minor ones or another major one. But it appears also in a different form and light to a Turk in Cyprus than to a Greek, to a Karen in Burma than to a Burmese, to a Tiv in Nigeria than to a Hausa, because membership in a minor group places one in a different position from that in which membership in a major group places one, even within a single system.[15] The so-called pariah communities of "foreign" traders that are found in so many of the new states—the Lebanese in West Africa, the Indians in East Africa, the Chinese in Southeast Asia and, in a somewhat different way, the Marwaris in South India—live in an altogether different social universe, so far as the problem of the maintenance of a recognized identity is concerned, than do the settled agricultural groups, no matter how small and insignificant, in the same societies. The network of primordial alliance and opposition is a dense, intricate, but yet precisely articulated one, the product, in most cases, of centuries of gradual crystallization. The unfamiliar civil state, born yesterday from the meager remains of an exhausted colonial regime, is su-

[15] For a brief discussion of this problem with respect to Indonesia, see C. Geertz, "The Javanese Village," in Local, Ethnic and National Loyalties in Village Indonesia, ed. G. W. Skinner, Yale University, Southeast Asia Studies, Cultural Report Series, No. 8 (New Haven, 1959), pp. 34–41.

perimposed upon this fine-spun and lovingly conserved texture of pride and suspicion, and must somehow contrive to weave it into the fabric of modern politics.

III

The reduction of primordial sentiments to civil order is rendered more difficult, however, by the fact that political modernization tends initially not to quiet such sentiments but to quicken them. The transfer of sovereignty from a colonial regime to an independent one is more than a mere shift of power from foreign hands to native ones; it is a transformation of the whole pattern of political life, a metamorphosis of subjects into citizens. Colonial governments, like the aristocratic governments of premodern Europe in whose image they were fashioned, are aloof and unresponsive; they stand outside the societies they rule, and act upon them arbitrarily, unevenly, and unsystematically. But the governments of the new states, though oligarchic, are popular and attentive; they are located in the midst of the societies they rule, and as they develop act upon them in progressively more continuous, comprehensive, and purposeful manner. For the Ashanti cocoa farmer, the Gujerati shopkeeper, or the Malayan Chinese tin miner, his country's attainment of political independence is also his own attainment, willy-nilly, of modern political status, no matter how culturally traditional he may remain nor how ineffectively and anachronistically the new state may in practice function. He now becomes an integral part of an autonomous and differentiated polity that begins to touch his life at every point except the most strictly private. "The same people which has hitherto been kept as far as possible from government affairs must now be drawn into them," the Indonesian nationalist Sjahrir wrote on the eve of World War II, defining exactly the character of the "revolution" that was in fact to follow in the Indies over the next decade—"That people must be made politically conscious. Its political interest must be stimulated and maintained." [16]

This thrusting of a modern political consciousness upon the mass of a still largely unmodernized population does indeed tend to lead to the

[16] S. Sjahrir, *Out of Exile* (New York, 1949), p. 215.

stimulation and maintenance of a very intense popular interest in the affairs of government. But, as a primordially based "corporate feeling of oneness," remains for many the *fons et origo* of legitimate authority—the meaning of the term "self" in "self-rule"—much of this interest takes the form of an obsessive concern with the relation of one's tribe, region, sect, or whatever to a center of power that, while growing rapidly more active, is not easily either insulated from the web of primordial attachments, as was the remote colonial regime, or assimilated to them as are the workaday authority systems of the "little community." Thus, it is the very process of the formation of a sovereign civil state that, among other things, stimulates sentiments of parochialism, communalism, racialism, and so on, because it introduced into society a valuable new prize over which to fight and a frightening new force with which to contend.[17] The doctrines of the nationalist propagandists to the contrary notwithstanding, Indonesian regionalism, Malayan racialism, Indian linguism, or Nigerian tribalism are, in their political dimensions, not so much the heritage of colonial divide-and-rule policies as they are products of the replacement of a colonial regime by an independent, domestically anchored, purposeful unitary state. Though they rest on historically developed distinctions, some of which colonial rule helped to accentuate (and others of which it helped to moderate), they are part and parcel of the very process of the creation of a new polity and a new citizenship.

For a telling example in this connection one may look to Ceylon, which, having made one of the quietest of entries into the family of new states is now [1962] the scene of one of its noisiest communal uproars. Ceylonese independence was won largely without struggle; in fact, without even very much effort. There was no embittered nationalist mass movement, as in most of the other new states, no loudly passionate hero-leader, no diehard colonial opposition, no violence, no arrests—no

17 As Talcott Parsons has pointed out, defined as the capacity to mobilize social resources for social goals, is not a "zero-sum" quantity within a social system, but, like wealth, is generated by the working of particular, in this case political rather than economic, institutions. "The Distribution of Power in American Society," *World Politics* 10 (1957): 123–143. The growth of a modern state within a traditional social context represents, therefore, not merely the shifting or transfer of a fixed quantity of power between groups in such a manner that aggregatively the gains of certain groups or individuals match the losses of others, but rather the creation of a new and more efficient machine for the production of power itself, and thus an increase in the general political capacity of the society. This is a much more genuinely "revolutionary" phenomenon than a mere redistribution, however radical, of power within a given system.

revolution really, for the 1947 transfer of sovereignty consisted of the replacement of conservative, moderate, aloof British civil servants by conservative, moderate, aloof British-educated Ceylonese notables who, to more nativistic eyes at least, "resembled the former colonial rulers in everything but the color of their skin." [18] The revolution was to come later, nearly a decade after formal independence and the British governor's valedictory expression of "profound satisfaction that Ceylon has reached its goal of freedom without strife or bloodshed along the path of peaceful negotiation" [19] proved to be somewhat premature: in 1956 wild Tamil-Sinhalese riots claimed more than a hundred lives, in 1958, perhaps as many as two thousand.

The country, 70 percent Sinhalese, 23 percent Tamil, has been marked by a certain amount of group tension for centuries.[20] But such tension has taken the distinctively modern form of an implacable, comprehensive, and ideologically instigated mass hatred mainly since the late S. W. R. D. Bandaranaike was swept into the premiership on a sudden wave of Sinhalese cultural, religious, and linguistic revivalism in 1956. Himself Oxford-educated, vaguely Marxist, and essentially secularist in civil matters, Bandaranaike undermined the authority of the English-speaking (and biethnic Colombo) patriciate by appealing openly, and one suspects somewhat cynically, to the primordial sentiments of the Sinhalese, promising a "Sinhala-only" linguistic policy, a place of pride for Buddhism and the Buddhist clergy, and a radical reversal of the supposed policy of "pampering" the Tamils, as well as rejecting Western dress for the traditional "cloth and banian" of the Sinhalese countryman.[21] And if, as one of his more uncritical apologists claims, his "supreme ambition" was not "to set up an outmoded, paro-

[18] D. K. Rangenekar, "The Nationalist Revolution in Ceylon," *Pacific Affairs* 33 (1960): 361–374.

[19] Quoted in M. Weiner, "The Politics of South Asia," in G. Almond and J. Coleman, *The Politics of the Developing Areas* (Princeton, N.J., 1960), pp. 153–246.

[20] About half the Tamils are stateless "Indian Tamils"—that is, individuals transported to Ceylon in the nineteenth century to work on British tea estates, and now rejected as citizens by India on the ground that they live in Ceylon, and by Ceylon on the ground that they are but sojourners from India.

[21] Commenting on the spectacular failure of Sir Ivor Jennings' 1954 prediction that Bandaranaike was unlikely to win the leadership of the nationalist movement because he was a "political Buddhist," having been educated as a Christian, Rangenekar shrewdly remarks, "In an Asian setting a Western-educated politician who renounces his Westernization and upholds indigenous culture and civilization wields a much greater influence than the most dynamic local thoroughbred can ever hope to do." Rangenekar, "Nationalist Revolution in Ceylon."

chial, racialist government," but to "stabilize democracy and convert his country into a modern welfare state based on Nehru-style socialism," [22] he soon found himself the helpless victim of a rising tide of primordial fervor, and his death, after thirty hectic and frustrating months in power, at the hands of an obscurely motivated Buddhist monk, was merely that much more ironic.

The first definite move toward a resolute, popularly based, social reform government led, therefore, not to heightened national unity, but to the reverse—increased linguistic, racial, regional, and religious parochialism, a strange dialectic whose actual workings have been well-described by Wriggins.[23] The institution of universal suffrage made the temptation to court the masses by appealing to traditional loyalties virtually irresistible, and led Bandaranaike and his followers to gamble, unsuccessfully as it turned out, on being able to tune primordial sentiments up before elections and down after them. The modernizing efforts of his government in the fields of health, education, administration, and so on, threatened the status of consequential rural personages—monks, ayurvedic doctors, village schoolteachers, local officials—who were thereby rendered that much more nativistic and insistent upon communal tokens of reassurance in exchange for their political support. The search for a common cultural tradition to serve as the content of the country's identity as a nation now that it had become, somehow, a state, led only to the revivification of ancient, and better forgotten, Tamil-Sinhalese treacheries, atrocities, insults, and wars. The eclipse of the Western-educated urban elite, within which class loyalties and old-school ties tended to override primordial differences, removed one of the few important points of amicable contact between the two communities. The first stirrings of fundamental economic change aroused fears that the position of the industrious, frugal, aggressive Tamils would be strengthened at the expense of the less methodical Sinhalese. The intensified competition for government jobs, the increasing importance of the vernacular press, and even government-instituted land-reclamation programs—because they threatened to alter population distribution and so communal representation in the parliament—all acted in a similarly provocative manner. Ceylon's aggravated primordial problem is not a mere legacy, an inherited impediment to her political, social, and eco-

[22] Ibid.
[23] H. Wriggins, "Impediments to Unity in New Nations—The Case of Ceylon" (unpublished).

nomic modernization; it is a direct and immediate reflex of her first serious—if still rather ineffective—attempt to achieve such modernization.

And this dialectic, variously expressed, is a generic characteristic of new-state politics. In Indonesia, the establishment of an indigenous unitary state made the fact that the thinly populated but mineral-rich Outer Islands produced the bulk of the country's foreign-exchange earnings, while densely populated, resource-poor Java consumed the bulk of its income, painfully apparent in a way it could never become in the colonial era, and a pattern of regional jealousy developed and hardened to the point of armed revolt.[24] In Ghana, hurt Ashanti pride burst into open separatism when, in order to accumulate development funds, Nkrumah's new national government fixed the cocoa price lower than what Ashanti cocoa growers wished it to be.[25] In Morocco, Riffian Berbers, offended when their substantial military contribution to the struggle for independence was not followed by greater governmental assistance in the form of schools, jobs, improved communications facilities, and so on, revived a classic pattern of tribal insolence—refusal to pay taxes, boycott of marketplaces, retreat to a predatory mountain life—in order to gain Rabat's regard.[26] In Jordan, Abdullah's desperate attempt to strengthen his newly sovereign civil state through the annexation of Cis-Jordan, negotiation with Israel, and modernization of the army provoked his assassination by an ethnically humiliated pan-Arab Palestinian.[27] Even in those new states where such discontent has not progressed to the point of open dissidence, there has almost universally arisen around the developing struggle for governmental power as such a broad penumbra of primordial strife. Alongside of, and interacting with, the usual politics of party and parliament, cabinet and bureau-

[24] H. Fieth, "Indonesia," in G. McT. Kahin, ed., *Government and Politics of Southeast Asia* (Ithaca, N.Y., 1959), pp. 155–238; and Kahin, G. McT., ed., *Major Governments of Asia* (Ithaca, N.Y., 1958), pp. 471–592. This is not to say that the crystallization of regional enmities was the sole motivating force in the Padang rebellion, nor that the Java-Outer Islands contrast was the only axis of opposition. In all the quoted examples in this essay, the desire to be recognized as a responsible agent whose wishes, acts, hopes, and opinions matter is intertwined with the more familiar desires for wealth, power, prestige, and so on. Simple primordial determinism is no more defensible a position than economic determinism.

[25] D. Apter, *The Gold Coast in Transition* (Princeton, N.J., 1955), p. 68.

[26] W. Lewis, "Feuding and Social Change in Morocco," *Journal of Conflict Resolution* 5 (1961): 43–54.

[27] R. Nolte, "The Arab Solidarity Agreement," American University Field Staff Letter, Southwest Asia Series, 1957.

cracy, or monarch and army, there exists, nearly everywhere, a sort of parapolitics of clashing public identities and quickening ethnocratic aspirations.

What is more, this parapolitical warfare seems to have its own characteristic battlegrounds; there are certain specific institutional contexts outside the customary arenas of political combat into which it has a strong inclination to settle. Though primordial issues do, of course, turn up from time to time in parliamentary debates, cabinet deliberations, judicial decisions, and, more often, in electoral campaigns, they show a persistent tendency to emerge in purer, more explicit, and more virulent form in some places where other sorts of social issues do not ordinarily, or at least so often or so acutely, appear.

One of the most obvious of these is the school system. Linguistic conflicts, in particular, tend to emerge in the form of school crises—witness the fierce dispute between Malay and Chinese teachers' unions over the degree to which Malay should replace Chinese in Chinese schools in Malaya, the three-way guerrilla war between partisans of English, Hindi, and various local vernaculars as instruction media in India, or the bloody riots staged by Bengali-speaking university students to block the imposition of Urdu by West on East Pakistan. But religious issues, too, tend to penetrate educational contexts quite readily. In Moslem countries there is the enduring question of the reform of traditional Koranic schools toward Western forms; in the Philippines there is the clash between the American-introduced tradition of the secular public school and the intensified clerical effort to increase the teaching of religion in such schools; and in Madras there are the Dravidian separatists announcing sanctimoniously that "education must be free from political, religious or communal bias," by which they in fact mean that it "must not stress Hindu writings such as the epic Ramayana." [28] Even largely regional struggles tend to engulf the school system: in Indonesia the rise of provincial discontent was accompanied by a competitive multiplication of local institutions of higher learning to the point where, despite the extreme shortage of qualified instructors, there is now a faculty in nearly every major region of the country, monuments to past resentments and perhaps cradles for future ones; and a similar pattern may now be developing in Nigeria. If the general strike is the classical political expression of class warfare, and the coup d'état of the struggle be-

[28] P. Talbot, "Raising a Cry for Secession," American University Field Staff Letter, South Asia Series, 1957.

tween militarism and parliamentarianism, then the school crisis is perhaps becoming the classical political—or parapolitical—expression of the clash of primordial loyalties.

There are a number of other poles around which parapolitical vortices tend to form, but so far as the literature is concerned they have been more noted in passing than analyzed in detail. Social statistics is an example. In Lebanon there has not been a census since 1932, for fear that taking one would reveal such changes in the religious composition of the population as to make the marvelously intricate political arrangements designed to balance sectarian interests unviable. In India, with its national language problem, just what constitutes a Hindi speaker has been a matter of some rather acrimonious dispute, because it depends upon the rules of counting: Hindi enthusiasts use census figures to prove that as many as half of India's people speak "Hindi" (including Urdu and Punjabi), while anti-Hindiists force the figure down as low as 30 percent by considering such matters as script differences, and evidently even religious affiliation of the speaker, as linguistically significant. Then, too, there is the closely related problem of what, in connection with the strange fact that according to the 1941 census of India there were 25 million tribal peoples but in the 1951 census only 1.7 million, Weiner has aptly called "genocide by census redefinition." [29] In Morocco, published figures for the percentage of the population that is Berber run all the way from 35 to 60 percent, and some nationalist leaders would like to believe, or have others believe, that the Berbers are a French invention altogether.[30] Statistics, real or fancied, concerning the ethnic composition of the civil service are a favorite weapon of primordial demagogues virtually everywhere, being particularly effective where a number of local officials are members of a group other than the one they administrate. And in Indonesia a leading newspaper was banned, at the height of the regionalist crisis, for print-

[29] M. Weiner, "Community Associations in Indian Politics" (unpublished). The reverse process, "ethnogenesis by census redefinition," also occurs, as when in Libreville, the Gabon capital, Togolese and Dahomeans are lumped statistically into a new category, "the Popo," or in Northern Rhodesia copperbelt towns Henga, Tonga, Tambuka, and so on, are "by common consent" grouped together as Nyasalanders, these manufactured groupings then taking on a real "ethnic" existence. I. Wallerstein, "Ethnicity and National Integration in West Africa," Cahiers d'études africaines 3 (1960): 129–139.

[30] The 35 percent figure can be found in N. Barbour, ed., A Survey of North West Africa (New York, 1959), p. 79; the 60 percent figure in D. Rustow, "The Politics of the Near East," in Almond and Coleman, Politics of Developing Areas, pp. 369–453.

ing, in mock innocence, a simple bar graph depicting export earnings and government expenditure by province.

Dress (in Burma hundreds of frontier tribesmen brought to Rangoon for Union day to improve their patriotism are cannily sent home with gifts of Burmese clothing), historiography (in Nigeria a sudden proliferation of tendentious tribal histories strengthens the already very powerful centrifugal tendencies plaguing the country), and the official insignia of public authority (in Ceylon, Tamils have refused to use automobile license plates marked with Sinhala characters, and in South India they have painted over Hindi railroad signs) are other as yet but impressionistically observed spheres of parapolitical controversy.[31] So, also, is the rapidly expanding complex of tribal unions, caste organizations, ethnic fraternities, regional associations, and religious sodalities that seems to be accompanying urbanization in virtually all the new states, and has made the major cities in some of them—Lagos, Beirut, Bombay, Medan—caldrons of communal tension.[32] But, details aside, the point is that there swirl around the emerging governmental institutions of the new states, and the specialized politics they tend to support, a whole host of self-reinforcing whirlpools of primordial discontent, and that this parapolitical maelstrom is in great part an outcome—to continue the metaphor, a backwash—of that process of political development itself. The growing capacity of the state to mobilize social resources for public ends, its expanding power, roils primordial sentiments because, given the doctrine that legitimate authority is but an extension of the inherent moral coerciveness such sentiments possess, to permit oneself to be ruled by men of other tribes, other races, or other religions is to submit not merely to oppression but to degradation—to exclusion from the moral community as a lesser order of being whose opinions, attitudes, wishes, and so on, simply do not fully count, as those of children, the simple-minded, and the insane do not fully count in the eyes of those who regard themselves as mature, intelligent, and sane.

Though it can be moderated, this tension between primordial sentiments and civil politics probably cannot be entirely dissolved. The

[31] On Burmese dress, see H. Tinker, *The Union of Burma* (New York, 1957), p. 184. On Nigerian tribal histories, see Coleman, *Nigeria*, pp. 327–328. On Ceylonese license plates, see Wriggins, "Ceylon's Time of Troubles, 1956–8," *Far Eastern Survey* 28 (1959): 33–38. On Hindi railroad signs, see Weiner, "Community Associations."

[32] For a general discussion of the role of voluntary associations in the urbanization process in modernizing societies, see Wallerstein, "The Emergence of Two West African Nations," pp. 144–230.

power of the "givens" of place, tongue, blood, looks, and way-of-life to shape an individual's notion of who, at bottom, he is and with whom, indissolubly, he belongs is rooted in the nonrational foundations of personality. And, once established, some degree of involvement of this unreflective sense of collective selfhood in the steadily broadening political process of the national state is certain, because that process seems to touch on such an extraordinarily wide range of matters. Thus, what the new states—or their leaders—must somehow contrive to do as far as primordial attachments are concerned is not, as they have so often tried to do, wish them out of existence by belittling them or even denying their reality, but domesticate them. They must reconcile them with the unfolding civil order by divesting them of their legitimizing force with respect to governmental authority, by neutralizing the apparatus of the state in relationship to them, and by channeling discontent arising out of their dislocation into properly political rather than parapolitical forms of expression.

This goal, too, is not fully achievable or at least has never yet been achieved—even in Mr. Ambedkar's Canada and Switzerland (the less said of South Africa in this connection, the better) with their supposed "genius to unite." But it is relatively so, and it is upon the possibility of such relative achievement that the hope of the new states to turn the attack upon their integrity and their legitimacy by unfettered primordial enthusiasms rests. As with industrialization, urbanization, restratification, and the various other social and cultural "revolutions" these states seem fated to undergo, the containment of diverse primordial communities under a single sovereignty promises to tax the political capacity of their peoples to its utmost limits—in some cases, no doubt, beyond them.

IV

This "integrative revolution" has, of course, already begun, and a desperate search for ways and means to create a more perfect union is everywhere under way. But it has merely begun and just got under way, so that if one surveys the new states on a broadly comparative basis, one is confronted with a bewildering picture of diverse institutional and ideological responses to what, for all its variation in outward form, is

essentially a common problem—the political normalization of primordial discontent.

The new states are, today, rather like naive or apprentice painters or
poets or composers, seeking their own proper style, their own distinctive mode of solution for the difficulties posed by their medium. Imitative, poorly organized, eclectic, opportunistic, subject to fads, ill-defined, uncertain, they are exceedingly difficult to order typologically,
either in classical categories or invented ones, in the same paradoxical
way that it is usually so much more difficult to classify immature artists
firmly into schools or traditions than it is mature ones who have found
their own unique style and identity. Indonesia, India, Nigeria, and the
rest share, in the matter at hand, only a predicament; but a predicament
that is one of the main stimuli to political creativity for them, pressing
them on to a restless experimentation in order to find ways to extricate
themselves from it and triumph over it. Again, this is not to say that all
this creativity will ultimately be successful; there are *manqué* states as
there are *manqué* artists, as France perhaps demonstrates. But it is the
recalcitrance of primordial issues that, among other things, keeps the
process of incessant political, and even constitutional, innovation going,
and gives to any attempt at systematic classification of new state polities
a radically provisional, if not simply premature, quality.

An attempt to order the various governmental arrangements now
emerging in the new states as means for coping with problems arising
from linguistic, racial, and so on, heterogeneity must begin, therefore,
with a simple empirical review of a number of such arrangements, a
mere setting out in model form of existing experiments. From such a review it should be possible to derive a sense of at least the ranges of variation involved, a notion of the general dimensions of the social field
within which these arrangements are taking shape. Typologizing becomes, in this approach, a matter, not of devising constructed types,
ideal or otherwise, which will isolate fundamental constancies of structure amid the confusion of phenomenal variation, but of determining
the limits with which such variation takes place, the domain over which
it plays. Here, a sense of such ranges, dimensions, limits, and domains
can perhaps best be conveyed, in a kaleidoscopic sort of way, by the
rapid presentation of a series of snapshot pictures of the "integrative
revolution" as it seems to be proceeding in several selected new states
showing different concrete patterns of primordial diversity and different
modes of political response to those patterns. Indonesia, Malaya,

Burma, India, Lebanon, Morocco, and Nigeria, culturally distinct and geographically scattered, are as appropriate subjects as any for this type of flying survey of divided nations en route—*ex hypothesi*—to unity.[33]

[33] As, with the partial exception of Indonesia [and now—1972—Morocco], all the following summaries are based on the literature rather than on field research, a full bibliography of sources would obviously be too lengthy for inclusion in an essay. I therefore list below only those works upon which I have relied rather heavily. The best general survey including the countries discussed is Almond and Coleman, *Politics of Developing Areas,* and for Asia I have found the two previously cited symposia edited by Kahin, *Governments and Politics of Southeast Asia* and *Major Governments of Asia,* most useful. Emerson, *Empire to Nation,* also offers some valuable comparative materials.

INDONESIA: H. Feith, *The Wilopo Cabinet, 1952–1953* (Ithaca, N.Y., 1958); H. Feith, *The Indonesian Elections of 1955* (Ithaca, N.Y., 1952); G. Pauker, "The Role of Political Organization in Indonesia," *Far Eastern Survey* 27 (1958): 129–142; G. W. Skinner, *Local, Ethnic, and National Loyalties in Village Indonesia.*

MALAYA: M. Freedman, "The Growth of a Plural Society in Malaya," *Pacific Affairs* 33 (1960): 158–167; N. Ginsburg and C. F. Roberts, Jr., *Malaya* (Seattle, 1958); J. N. Parmer, "Malaya's First Year of Independence," *Far Eastern Survey* 27 (1958): 161–168; T. E. Smith, "The Malayan Elections of 1959," *Pacific Affairs* 33 (1960): 38–47.

BURMA: L. Bigelow, "The 1960 Elections in Burma," *Far Eastern Survey* 29 (1960): 70–74; G. Fairbairn, "Some Minority Problems in Burma," *Pacific Affairs* 30 (1957): 299–311; J. Silverstein, "Politics in the Shan State: The Question of the Secession from the Union of Burma," *The Journal of Asian Studies* 18 (1958): 43–58; H. Tinker, *The Union of Burma.*

INDIA: Ambedkar, *Thoughts on Linguistic States;* S. Harrison, *India;* R. L. Park and I. Tinker, eds., *Leadership and Political Institutions in India* (Princeton, N.J., 1959); *Report of the States Reorganization Commission* (New Delhi, 1955); M. Weiner, *Party Politics in India* (Princeton, N.J., 1957).

LEBANON: V. Ayoub, "Political Structure of a Middle East Community: A Druze Village in Mount Lebanon" (Ph.D. thesis, Harvard University, 1955); P. Rondot, *Les Institutions politiques du Liban* (Paris, 1957); N. A. Ziadeh, *Syria and Lebanon* (London, 1957); N. A. Ziadeh, "The Lebanese Elections, 1960," *Middle East Journal* 14 (1960): 367–381.

MOROCCO: D. Ashford, *Political Change in Morocco* (Princeton, N.J., 1961); N. Barbour, ed., *A Survey of North West Africa* (New York, 1959); H. Favre, "Le Maroc A L'Epreuve de la Démocratisation" (unpublished, 1958); J. and S. Lacouture, *Le Maroc A L'Epreuve* (Paris, 1958); W. Lewis, "Rural Administration in Morocco," *Middle East Journal* 14 (1960): 45–54; W. Lewis, "Feuding and Social Change in Morocco," *The Journal of Conflict Resolution* 5 (1961): 43–54.

NIGERIA: J. Coleman, *Nigeria; Report of the Commission Appointed to Enquire into the Fears of Minorities and the Means of Allaying Them* (London, 1958); H. and M. Smythe, *The New Nigerian Elite* (Stanford, Calif., 1960).

For current events I have found the American University Field Staff Letters, particularly those on Indonesia (W. Hanna), Malaya (W. Hanna), India (P. Talbot), Morocco (C. Gallagher), and Nigeria (R. Frodin), very useful.

[Since the above list was compiled, a decade ago, an enormous number of new works bearing on our subject have appeared. So far as I know, however, a comprehensive bibliography in this field does not yet exist.]

INDONESIA

Until about the beginning of 1957, the regional tension between Java and the Outer Islands was kept in bounds by a combination of the continuing momentum of revolutionary solidarity, a broadly representative multiparty system, and a characteristically Indonesian bisection of paramount executive power in an institution called the Dwi-Tunggal— loosely, "dual leadership"—in which the two veteran nationalist leaders, Sukarno, a Javanese, and Mohammed Hatta, a Sumatran, shared primacy as President and Vice-President of the Republic. Since then, the solidarity has faded, the party system collapsed, and the Dwi-Tunggal split. Despite the effective military suppression of the regional rebellion of 1958, and despite Sukarno's feverish attempts to focus the government on his person as the incarnation of "the spirit of '45," the political equilibrium thus lost has not been restored, and the new nation has become an almost classic case of integrative failure. With every step toward modernity has come increased regional discontent; with each increase in regional discontent has come a new revelation of political incapacity; and with each new revelation of political incapacity has come a loss of political nerve and a more desperate resort to an unstable amalgam of military coercion and ideological revivalism.

It was the first general elections of 1955 that, by completing the general outlines of a parliamentary system, made it inescapably apparent to reflective Indonesians that they had either to find some way of solving their problems within the framework of the modern civil order that they had almost reluctantly created or face a rising crescendo of primordial discontent and parapolitical conflict. Having been expected to clear the air, the elections only stirred it. They shifted the political center of gravity away from the Dwi-Tunggal toward the parties. They crystallized the popular strength of the Communist Party, which not only gained some 16 percent of the total vote, but drew nearly 90 percent of its support from Java, thus fusing regional and ideological tensions. They dramatized the fact that the interest of some of the more important centers of power in the society—the army, the Chinese, certain Outer Island export traders, and so on—were not adequately represented in the formal political system. And they shifted the basis of qualification for political leadership away from revolutionary distinction toward mass appeal. At once the elections demanded that, if the existing

civil order were to be maintained and developed, a whole new set of relationships among the president, vice-president, parliament, and cabinet
be worked out; that an aggressive, well-organized totalitarian party hostile to the very conception of democratic, multiparty politics be contained; that important groups outside the parliamentary framework be
brought into effective relation to it; and that a new basis for elite solidarity other than the shared experiences of 1945–1949 be found. Given
extremely intractable economic problems, a cold-war international environment, and a large number of long-standing personal vendettas among
the highly placed, it would perhaps have been surprising had this multiple demand been met. But there is no reason to believe that given the
requisite political talents, it could not have been.

In any case, it was not. By the end of 1956 the always delicate relationship between Sukarno and Hatta became so strained that the latter
resigned, an action that in essence withdrew the stamp of legitimacy
from the central government so far as many of the leading military, financial, political, and religious groups in the Outer Islands were concerned. The duumvirate had been the symbolic, and to a great extent
the real, guarantee of the recognition of the various Outer Island peoples as full and equal partners with the so much more numerous Javanese in the Republic, a quasi-constitutional warranty that the Javanese tail would not be permitted to wag the Indonesian dog. Sukarno,
part Javanese mystic and part inveterate eclectic, and Hatta, part
Sumatran puritan and part shirtsleeve administrator, supplemented one
another not only politically but primordially. Sukarno summed up the
syncretic high culture of the elusive Javanese; Hatta, the Islamic mer-
cantilism of the less subtle Outer Islanders. The major political parties
—particularly the Communists, fusing Marxist ideology with traditional
Javanese "folk religion," and the Moslem Masjumi, which having
gained nearly half of its popular vote in the more orthodox regions outside Java became their major spokesman—aligned themselves accordingly. Thus, when the Vice-President resigned and the President moved
to become, under his conception of a back-to-1945 (that is, pre-elec-
tions) "guided democracy," the sole axis of Indonesian national life, the
Republic's political balance was upset and the advance toward regional
disaffection entered its radical phase.

Since then, spasmodic violence has alternated with a frantic search
for political panaceas. Abortive coups, misfired assassination attempts,
and unsuccessful insurrections have followed one after the other, punc-

tuated by an astounding wealth of ideological and institutional experiments. New Life movements have given way to Guided Democracy movements, and Guided Democracy movements to "Back to the 1945 Constitution" movements, while governmental structures—national councils, state planning commissions, constitutional conventions, and so on—have multiplied like weeds in a neglected garden. But from all this nervous tinkering and breathless sloganeering no form competent to contain the country's diversity has appeared, because such random improvisation represents not a realistic search for a solution to the nation's integrative problems but a desperately laid smoke screen behind which to hide a growing conviction of impending political catastrophe. For the moment, a new, de facto duumvirate divides leadership—Sukarno, calling ever more shrilly for a renewal of the "revolutionary spirit of unity," and Lieutenant General A. H. Nasution, Defense Minister and former Army Chief of Staff (and another colorless Sumatran professional), directing the military in its expanded role as a quasi-civil service. But their relationship to each other, as well as the extent of their effective power, remains, like just about everything else in Indonesian political life, undetermined.

The "growing conviction of an impending political catastrophe" turned out to be all too accurate. President Sukarno's frenzied ideologism continued to rise until the night of September 30, 1965, when the Commander of the Presidential Guard mounted an attempted coup d'état. Six ranking Army generals were murdered (General Nasution narrowly escaped), but the coup failed when another General, Suharto, rallied the army and crushed the rebels. There followed several months of extraordinary popular savagery—mainly in Java and Bali, but also sporadically in Sumatra—directed against individuals considered to be followers of the Indonesian Communist Party, which was generally regarded to have been behind the coup. Several hundred thousand people were massacred, largely villagers by other villagers (though there were some army executions as well), and, in Java at least, mainly along the primordial lines—pious Moslems killing Indic syncretists—described above. (There were some anti-Chinese actions, too, especially in Sumatra, but the bulk of the killings were of Javanese by Javanese, Balinese by Balinese, and so on.) Sukarno was gradually replaced as leader of the country by Suharto and died in June 1970, Suharto having officially succeeded to the presidency two years earlier. Since then the country

has been run by the army with the assistance of various civilian techni-
cal experts and administrators. A second general election, held in the
summer of 1971, resulted in the victory of a government-sponsored and
-controlled party and the severe weakening of the older political parties.
At the moment, though tension between primordially defined groups,
religious, regional, and ethnic, remains intense, and in fact may have
been deepened by the events of 1965, open expression of it is largely
absent. That it will long remain so seems—to me at least—unlikely.

MALAYA

In Malaya, the striking thing is the degree to which the overall integration of the diverse groups in a rigidly multiracial society is taking
place not so much in terms of state structure as such, but of that much
more recent political invention, party organization. It is the Alliance, a
confederation of the United Malays National Organization, the Malayan
Chinese Association, and the less important Malayan Indian Congress,
within which primordial conflicts are being informally and realistically
adjusted and where the strong centrifugal tendencies, as intense as perhaps any state—new, old, or middle-aged—has ever faced, are, so far,
being effectively absorbed, deflected, and contained. Formed in 1952, at
the height of the terrorist "emergency," by conservative, English-edu-
cated, upper-class elements in the Malay and Chinese communities (the
Indians, never quite certain which way to jump, joined a year or two
later), the Alliance is one of the most remarkable examples of the successful practice of the art of the impossible in the whole sphere of new-
state politics—a federated, noncommunal party of subparties, themselves frankly, explicitly, and on occasion enthusiastically communal in
appeal, set in a context of primordial suspicion and hostility that would
make the Habsburg Empire seem like Denmark or Australia. On the
mere surface of things, it ought not to work.

The important question is, anyway, whether it will continue to work.
Malaya has been independent only since mid-1957, has benefited from
relatively favorable economic conditions, from—the Communist in-
surrection aside—a fairly smooth transfer of sovereignty and the continuing *présence anglaise* this has made possible, and the ability of a
conservative, somewhat rationalistic oligarchy to convince the mass of
the population that it is a more suitable vehicle for their aspirations

than the left-wing, emotionally populist sort of leadership that characterizes most of the other new states. Is Alliance rule merely the lull before the storm as was United National Party rule, which it rather resembles, in Ceylon? Is it destined to weaken and disintegrate when the social and economic seas roughen as did the Indonesian Dwi-Tunggal-multiparty system? Is it, in a word, too good to last?

The omens are mixed. In the first general election, held prior to revolution, the Alliance captured 80 percent of the popular vote and 51 of the 52 elected seats in the federal legislative council, to become virtually the sole legitimate heir to the colonial regime; but in the 1959 elections, the first held subsequent to independence, it lost a good deal of ground to more simply communal parties, its popular vote falling to 51 percent and its seats to 73 of 103. The Malay sector, the UMNO, was weakened by the unexpected sweep of the pious, rural, heavily Malay northeast by an intensely communal party calling for an Islamic theocratic state, "the restoration of Malay sovereignty," and "Greater Indonesia." The Chinese and Indian wings were undercut by Marxist parties in the large towns along the tin- and rubber-rich central west coast, where large numbers of new, lower-class Chinese and Indian voters had entered the rolls under the liberalized postindependence citizenship laws, the Marxism adapting itself, here as elsewhere, to primordial loyalties with little difficulty. Buffeted by these loses—which first became apparent in the state elections held a couple of months prior to the federal ones—the Alliance in fact came very close to splitting altogether. The losses of the UMNO tempted younger, less conservative elements in the MCA to press for a greater number of Chinese candidacies, for an explicit condemnation by the Alliance of Malay racialism, and for a review of state educational policy with respect to the language problem in Chinese schools. Hothead elements in the UMNO responded in kind, and though the rift was patched, or patched over, in time for the elections, several of the younger leaders of the MCA resigned, and the UMNO girded itself to expel primordial "agitators" in its own midst.

Thus, although as in Indonesia, the holding of general elections brought latent primordial issues into such a focus that they had to be faced directly rather than concealed behind a facade of nationalist rhetoric, in Malaya political talents seem, so far, to have been rather more competent to this task. Though the Alliance is less absolutely dominant and perhaps somewhat less integrated than it was in the immediate postindependence period, it is still quite comfortably in power and still an effective civil framework within which very intense primordial issues can be adjusted and contained rather than allowed to run free in parapolitical confusion. The pattern that seems to be developing, and perhaps crystallizing, is one in which a comprehensive national party, with its three subparts or subparties, comes almost to comprise the state and is multiply assailed by a field of small parties—by class parties for being too communal, and communal parties for not being communal enough (and by both for being "undemocratic" and "reactionary")— each of which is trying to knock chips off one or another part of it by attacking the points of strain that develop within it as it functions and by appealing more openly to primordial sentiments. The intricate inner working of the Alliance as it endeavors to hold the vital center against efforts from all directions to undermine its basic source of strength—a matter-of-fact, quid-pro-quo, all-in-the-same-boat political understanding among Malay, Chinese, and Indian leaders—is thus the quintessence of the integrative revolution as it is proceeding in Malaya.

In 1963 Malaya became Malaysia, a federation of Malaya proper (i.e., the peninsula), Singapore, and the north Bornean territories of Sarawak and Sabah. The Alliance remained the majority party, but the major Singapore party, the People's Action Party, sought to make inroads among the peninsula Chinese, undercutting the MCA and thus threatening the Alliance and the Chinese-Malay political balance. In August 1965 the strains became such that Singapore left the Federation and became independent. Intense opposition to the new Federation from Indonesia and to Sabah's inclusion in it from the Philippines only added to the stresses involved in the forming of the new political entity. In the general elections of May 1969 the narrow Alliance majority was lost, mainly because of the failure of the MCA to hold Chinese support (much of which went to the essentially Chinese Democratic Action Party), but also to further gains by the Islamist Malay communalist party mentioned in the text, which got nearly a quarter of the vote. The MCA, feeling it had lost the confidence of the Chinese community, then quit the Alliance, bringing on a full-fledged crisis. Later in the same month savage communal riots broke out in the capital, Kuala Lumpur, in which about 150 persons were killed, most of them in an extremely brutal fashion, and communications between the Chinese and Malay communities broke down almost totally. Emergency rule was imposed, and the situation calmed. In September 1970, Teunku Abdul Rahman, who had headed the UMNO and the Alliance since their founding, retired and was replaced by his long-time deputy and the strong man of the regime, Tun Abdul Razak. The state of emergency was finally ended and parliamentary government restored after twenty-one months, in February of 1971. For the moment the situation seems to have stabilized, and the Alliance still holds against the communalist attempts to chip away at it (a continuing Chinese Communist guerrilla revolt persists, however, in Sarawak), though the country as a whole may be in fact further away from communal accord than it was in the first years of its existence.

BURMA

In Burma, the case is almost diametrically opposite to the Malayan. Although again, and unlike Indonesia, a comprehensive national party (U Nu's "clean faction" of the Anti-Fascist People's Freedom League) governs [1962] a formally federal state with only weak, if bitter, opposition, its power is mainly based on a direct appeal to the cultural pride of the Burmans (that is, speakers of Burmese), while the minorities, some of whom helped keep the country in a multisided civil war for the first few years after independence, are catered to by a rather intricate and highly peculiar constitutional system that protects them in theory against the Burman dominance that the party system tends to produce in fact. Here the government itself is to a very great extent the obvious agency of a single, central primordial group, and it is faced, therefore, with a very serious problem of maintaining legitimacy in the eyes of members of peripheral groups—more than one-third of the population —who are naturally inclined to see it as alien, a problem it has attempted to solve largely by a combination of elaborate legal gestures of reassurance and a good deal of aggressive assimilationism.

Briefly, the constitutional system designed to allay minority fears consists of—to date [1962]—six juridically nonuniform "states," demarcated largely along regional-linguistic-cultural lines and possessing dissimilar formal powers. Some states have a—surely nominal—right of secession; others not. Each state has somewhat different electoral arrangements, and controls its own elementary schools. The elaboration of state governmental structure varies from the Chin, which has hardly any local autonomy whatever, to the Shan, where traditional "feudal" chiefs have been able to maintain a goodly number of their traditional rights; while Burma proper is not viewed as a constituent state within the Union at all, but as virtually indistinguishable from it. The degree to which territorial boundaries match primordial realities varies—with the Karen the most chronically discontented, and the small Kayah State evidently resting on the politically convenient invention of a "Red Karen" race. From each of these states a delegation is elected to the upper house of the bicameral Union legislature, the Chamber of Nationalities, which is heavily weighted in favor of the minority peoples. In the Union government this chamber is overshadowed by the popularly chosen lower house, the Chamber of Deputies; but as each state delegation to it sits, along with the lower-house representatives from its state, to form the State Council that governs the state, it has significant local importance. Further, the head of the state (that is, of the State Council) is appointed at the same time to be minister for the state in the Union government, and constitutional amendments demand two-thirds approval of both houses, so that the minorities are given at least a formal check on the powers of the government and the lower chamber to which it is responsible. And finally, the presidency of the Union, a largely ceremonial office, is rotated, by informal agreement rather than explicit constitutional provision, among ethnic groups.

It is within this finely wrought constitutional structure, which so artfully blurs the distinction between the Union and its constituent members at precisely the time it seems to be formalizing it most exactly, that the vigorously assimilationist policies of the AFPFL are pursued. This tradition of "Burmanization," or of what some minority groups more bluntly call "AFPFL imperialism," traces back to the very beginnings of the nationalist movement in the Buddhist student clubs at the turn of the century; and by the thirties the Thakins were calling for an independent nation in which Burmese would be the national language, Burman dress would be the national costume, and the classical role of the (predominantly Burman) Buddhist monkhood as teacher, guide, and counselor to the secular government would be restored. Since independence and the accession of the pietistic Thakin Nu to the premiership, the government has moved strenuously to bring about these ends, the noticeable relaxation of the assimilative pressure during the year and a half of military rule being followed by an even more intense assertion of such pressure following U Nu's landslide re-election on a

Buddhism-as-a-state-religion platform in 1960. (In Burma proper his "clean" AFPFL captured outright about 80 percent of the lower-house seats; in the states and the disaffected Arakan area, about a third.)

As a result, most of the political adjustments of primordial interests in Burma have tended to be cast, in form at least, in juristic terms, to be carried out in a rather odd and artificial vocabulary of constitutional legalism. The Karens' conviction that the official boundaries of their state were too circumscribed to compensate for the loss of the special privileges they enjoyed under the colonial regime helped send them into revolt; their submission following military defeat by Union forces was in turn sealed and symbolized by their acceptance of those boundaries, plus a number of additional legal penalties imposed as object lessons: an explicit denial of the right of secession, the reduction of their representation in both houses of parliament, and the revocation of an earlier decision to unite the Kayah State with the Karen. Similarly, the primordial discontent of the Arakanese and the Mons—which has also periodically flared into open violence—has been expressed in demands for Arakanese and Mon states, which U Nu has at length been forced to support despite his oft-reiterated opposition to the formation of any more states. In Shan State the traditional chiefs have brandished their constitutional right to secession and a states' rights doctrine that they claim is written into the constitution, as bargaining weapons in their higgle with the Union over the amount and kind of compensation to be paid them for the surrender of various of their traditional powers. And so on. This irregular and unorthodox constitutional framework, which is so nicely exact in language and so usefully vague in meaning that "not even [Burmese] lawyers seem able to tell whether the Union is in fact a federal or a unitary state," [34] allows the single-party, Burman-centered AFPFL regime to pursue its strongly assimilationist policies in almost all aspects of actual government, while maintaining at least minimal loyalty from the non-Burman Burmese, something it did not have a decade ago—though if its ethnic enthusiasm is not contained, it may not have it a decade hence either.

In March of 1962 General Ne Win took over the Burmese government via a military coup d'état from U Nu, who was imprisoned. Ne Win instituted a policy of extreme isolationism for Burma, which,

[34] Fairbairn, "Some Minority Problems in Burma."

among other things, has made it difficult to find out much in detail concerning what is going on in the country. What does seem clear is that armed opposition by ethnic minority groups has continued at about the previous level and has indeed become almost institutionalized as a regular aspect of the national scene. In January 1971, U Nu (who had by then been released from prison) set up headquarters for a "National Liberation Front" in Western Thailand, adjoining the rebellious Burmese Shan States. Little seems yet to have come of that, but the Karen, Shan, and Kachin revolts seem to be continuing apace. (The Karens were awarded a "state" in South Burma in 1969 by Ne Win, but, regarding the grant of "autonomy" as too limited, launched an offensive in early 1971 aimed at toppling Ne Win.) In February of 1971 a United National Liberation Front was formed including (the rebel elements of) the Karens, Mons, Chins, and Shans. (The Kachins, who have their own Independence Army, agreed to cooperate but not to join.) Thus, although it is very difficult to tell, given the near-closure of Burma to outside observation, how much all of this comes to on the ground, it seems apparent that not only has the characteristic pattern of Burmese primordial dissidence not changed under Ne Win but it has hardened into an enduring feature of the political landscape.

INDIA

India, that vast and various labyrinth of religious, linguistic, regional, racial, tribal, and caste allegiances, is developing a many-sided political form to match for baffling irregularity her daedalian social and cultural structure. Waddling in (in E. M. Forster's gently mocking image) at this late hour to take her seat among the nations, she is beset by virtually the entire range of primordial conflicts complexly superimposed one upon the other. One peels off Punjabi linguism and finds Sikh religious communalism, scratches Tamil regionalism and finds anti-Brahman racialism, views Bengali cultural arrogance from a slightly different angle and sees Greater Bengal patriotism. No general and uniform political solution to the problem of primordial discontent seems possible in such a situation, only a loose assemblage of diverse, locally adapted, ad hoc solutions, related to one another only incidentally and pragmatically. The policies suitable for the tribal dissidence of the Assam Naga are not generalizable to the caste-based disaffection of peasant landlords in Andhra. The central government stance taken toward Orissa princes cannot be taken toward Gujerati industrialists. The problem of Hindu fundamentalism in Uttar Pradesh, the heartland of Indic culture, takes a rather different form in Dravidian Mysore. So far as primordial issues are concerned, Indian civil politics amounts to a disconnected series of attempts to make the temporary endure.

The major institutional vehicle through which these attempts are being made is, of course, the Indian National Congress. Though, like the Malayan Alliance and the Burmese AFPFL, the Congress is a comprehensive national party that has largely pre-empted the governmental apparatus of the new state and become its most important centralizing force, it has done so neither as a confederation of frankly primordial subparties nor as an agency of majority-group assimilationism. The first of these courses is precluded by the multifarious nature of the primordial pattern—the sheer number of different groups involved—and the second by the absence of any one clearly central group within this pattern. As a result, the Congress, its slightly North Indian complexion aside, has tended to become an ethnically neutral, resolutely modernist, somewhat cosmopolitan force on the national level at the same time that it has built up a multiplicity of separate, and to a large extent independent, parochial party machines to secure its power on the local level. The image the Congress presents is thus a double one: in one focus, lecturing Hindi zealot and Tamil xenophobe alike, stands Nehru, "a reflective, cultivated, modern intellectual, full of wistfulness, skepticism, dogmatism, and self-doubt in the presence of his own country"; [35] in the other, deliberately manipulating (among other things) the local realities of language, caste, culture, and religion to keep the party dominant, stand a whole set of less pensive regional bosses—Kamaraj Nadar in Madras, Chavan in Bombay, Atulya Ghosh in Maharashtra, Patnaik in Orissa, Kairon in Punjab, and Sukhadia in Rajahstan.

The States Reorganization Act of 1956—itself, as has been mentioned, the culmination of a process begun within the Congress several decades before independence—gave this pattern of civil hub and primordial rim its official institutionalization. The division of the country into linguistically demarcated subunits is, in fact, part and parcel of the

[35] E. Shils, *The Intellectual Between Tradition and Modernity: The Indian Situation,* Comparative Studies in Society and History, Supplement 1 (The Hague, 1961), p. 95. [Now, of course, it is his daughter, Mrs. Gandhi, who stands there, and rather less wistfully, but the pattern remains.]

general approach of attempting to insulate parapolitical forces from national concerns by sequestering them in local contexts. Unlike those of Burma, the states of India have real and explicitly—perhaps too explicitly—spelled out constitutional powers in every field from education and agriculture to taxation and public health, so that the political process centering around the state assemblies and the formation of state governments is far from being an inconsequential matter. It is on the state level that perhaps the bulk of the bitter hand-to-hand clashes that form the everyday substance of Indian domestic politics are coming to take place, and where the adjustments of parochial interests are coming to be effected, insofar as they are effected at all.

Thus, in the 1957 elections, even more than in those of 1952, the Congress found itself engaged in a multifront war, fighting different election battles in the various states, against different sorts of opponents capitalizing on different sorts of discontents—against the Communists in Kerala, Bengal, and Andhra; against communal religious parties in Punjab, Uttar and Madhya Pradesh, and Rajahstan; against tribal unions in Assam and Bihar; against ethno-linguistic fronts in Madras, Maharashtra, and Gujerat; against feudal-prince restorationist parties in Orissa, Bihar, and Rajahstan; against the Praja Socialists in Bombay. Not all these struggles pivoted around primordial issues, but virtually all—even those involving leftist "class" parties—seem to have been significantly influenced by them.[36] In any case, as none of these opposition parties was able to spread beyond the few strongholds where the particular veins they tapped proved comparatively rich, the Congress as the only genuinely national party was able to maintain overwhelming control of both the central and—with a few exceptions—the state governments, even though it captured less than half the popular vote.

How, out of this conglomerate hodgepodge of courthouse machinations arises the rather cerebral, dispassionate, moralistic central Congress government to serve as a kind of extraordinary committee for the conduct of foreign policy, as a comprehensive social and economic planning commission, and as a symbolic expression of all-India national

[36] "The success of the Kerala Communist Party as the first regional Communist Party in India to capture control of a state government can be explained, above all, by its ability to manipulate the regional patriotism of all Kerala at the same time that it manipulated politically strategic class lobbies within linguistic boundaries."—Harrison, *India*, p. 193. In Bombay, both the Communists and the Praja Socialists joined in the Maharashtra linguistic front; in opposed Gujerat, the Gujerati one.

identity, is something of an Eastern mystery. Most observers put it
down, rather without analysis, to Nehru's charismatic force as a nationalist hero. His position as apostolic heir to Gandhi and avatar of independence bridges the gulf between his own cosmopolitan intellectualism
and the provincial horizons of the mass of his people. And it is perhaps
for this reason, as well as for his matchless ability to keep local bosses
loyal, in line, and reasonably unambitious, that the problem of
succession—"after Nehru, who?"—has in India even more of a fundamentally disquieting quality than in most of the other new states where
succession is also nearly always a prominent anxiety. The fact that
India has been held together up to now, Ambedkar says flatly, is due to
the force of Congress Party discipline—"but how long is the Congress
to last? The Congress is Pandit Nehru and Pandit Nehru is Congress.
But is Pandit Nehru immortal? Anyone who applies his mind to these
questions will realize that the Congress will not last until the sun and
the moon." [37] If the Burmese integrative problem is to restrain primordial enthusiasm at the center, the Indian seems to be to restrain it at the
periphery.

*The fears surrounding the succession problem, real enough when the
above was written, proved to be baseless. After Nehru's death in May
1964, and a brief period of rule by Lal Bahadur Shastri, the "apostolic"
succession pattern was re-established with the accession to the Prime
Ministership of Nehru's daughter and Gandhi's namesake, Mrs. Indira
Gandhi. In the early phases of her regime, the Congress lost ground,
and a series of upheavals on the state level led to the imposition of direct central government rule in several states. In May 1969, President
Zakir Husein, a Muslim, died, threatening the Hindu-Muslim understanding within India and precipitating a showdown between Mrs. Gandhi and the traditional Congress bosses, which Mrs. Gandhi decisively
won. Though faced with continued upheaval on the state level, Mrs.
Gandhi won a decisive victory in the general elections of March 1971,
capturing undisputed control of the government. The Bangladesh revolt,
perhaps the most dramatic, and certainly the most successful, primordial separatism in the new states so far, broke out later in the year,
followed by Indian intervention and the short, successful war with Pakistan. With all this, the Congress' ability to keep India's multiple pri-*

[37] Ambedkar, *Thoughts on Linguistic States*, p. 12. The Chinese attack may, of
course, provide an even more powerful cement than Nehru—a common enemy.

mordial groups under control has surely at least temporarily increased.
But that the problem persists is clear from a wide range of "events,"
stretching from the continuing Naga revolt in Assam to continuing Sikh
riots in Punjab. Indeed, the Bangladesh example may prove a two-sided
one for India in the long run, not only in Bengal itself, but elsewhere:
in February of this year (1972), the Dravidian Advancement Party
launched a campaign for Tamil Nadu, an autonomous Tamil state in
South India, drawing an open parallel with Bangladesh and accusing
Mrs. Gandhi of behaving like General Yahya Khan. Thus, though the
increased strength of the Congress central government has for one mo-
ment somewhat cooled down India's multifront war against primordial-
ism, it has very far from ended it.

LEBANON

Lebanon may be—as Phillip Hitti has pointed out—not much larger
than Yellowstone Park, but it is a good deal more astonishing. Although its population is almost entirely Arabic-speaking and shares a
generally "Levantine" ethos, it is rigidly partitioned into seven major
Moslem (Sunni, Shi'a, and Druze) and Christian (Maronites, Greek Orthodox, Greek Catholic, and Armenian Orthodox) sects and about that
many minor ones (Protestants, Jews, Armenian Catholics, and so on), a
confessional heterogeneity that not only forms the principal public
framework of individual self-identification, but is woven directly into
the whole structure of the state. Seats in the parliament are allotted on a
strictly sectarian basis according to demographic proportions that are
fixed by law and that have remained essentially unchanged in the five
elections held since independence. Paramount executive authority is not
merely bisected, but trisected, with the president of the country conventionally a Maronite, the prime minister a Sunni, and the chairman of
parliament a Shi'i. Cabinet posts are carefully doled out on a confessional basis, and a similar balance is maintained in the civil service
from ministry secretaries, district administrators, and diplomatic posts
all the way down to rank-and-file clerical jobs. The judicial system is
equally a maze of religious pluralism, with both the laws themselves
and the courts applying them varying as to sect, final authority in personal law cases sometimes lying outside the boundaries of the country
altogether. Arab province and Christian outpost, modern commercial

entrepôt and last relic of the Ottoman millet system, Lebanon is almost as much an entente as a state.

The sort of politics this entente supports are equally wondrous. Political parties, though formally present, play as yet but a marginal role. The struggle for pelf and power pivots instead around strong local leaders, who tend to be either important absentee landlords or, in the freehold sections of the country, heads of large and prominent extended families. Each of these faction chiefs, whose following is bound to him in essentially traditional rather than ideological terms, then forms alliances with similar faction chiefs from other locally represented sects, yielding in the election campaign a Tammany Hall sort of "one Irishman, one Jew, one Italian" ticket-balancing.

This process is encouraged by the device of having the entire electorate in any one district vote in all the local races regardless of sect. Thus a Maronite voting in a district where there are also Sunni, Greek Orthodox, and Druze seats at stake chooses among the Sunni, Greek Orthodox, and Druze candidates as well as among his own—the Maronite ones—and vice versa. This, in turn, leads to the forming of composite lists through which the candidates in each sect attempt to link themselves with popular candidates in other sects so as to attract the necessary external votes. As lists are rarely split, because the possibility of a candidate making effective alliances rests on his ability to bring loyal voters with him (and because the average voter has little knowledge of candidates of other sects on which to base rational judgments of their worth, anyway), this means that although, for any given seat, Maronite competes against Maronite, or Sunni against Sunni, and so on, it is actually lists that are elected. The electoral process thus acts to align certain leaders from the various sects over against certain other such leaders in such a way that political ties tend to cross-cut sectarian ones. Members of different sects are driven into each other's arms in interconfessional coalitions; members of the same sect are driven apart into intraconfessional factions.

Such calculated forging (and breaking) of alliances between significant political personalities is not confined merely to campaign tactics, but extends over the whole of political life. Among the strongest leaders the same principles come into play with respect to the higher national offices; so that, in example, a leading Maronite who considers himself as a possible president will attempt to align himself in public life with a leading Sunni who is aiming for the premiership, and so on, both in

order to gain Sunni support and to prevent his immediate Maronite rivals for the presidency from making so effective an alliance themselves.
Similar patterns operate throughout the system, at every level and in
every aspect of government.

As such coalitions are so opportunistically rather than ideologically
put together, they frequently dissolve overnight, as seeming bosom companions suddenly fall out and mortal enemies unite amid a storm of accusations and counteraccusations of betrayal, corruption, incompetence,
and ingratitude. The pattern is thus fundamentally an individualistic,
even egoistic, one, despite its grounding in traditional religious, economic, and kinship groupings, with each would-be political power
scheming to advance his career by a skillful manipulation of the system.
Both places on tickets led by strong figures and votes themselves are
bought (during the 1960 elections the amount of money in circulation
rose three million Leb.); rivals are slandered and, on occasion, physically attacked; favoritism, nepotic or otherwise, is accepted procedure;
and spoils are considered the normal reward of office. "There is no
right in Lebanon," Ayoub's Mount Lebanon Druzes say, "there is only
silver and the 'fix.' " [38]

Yet out of all this low cunning has come not only the most democratic state in the Arab world, but the most prosperous; and one that
has in addition been able—with one spectacular exception—to maintain its equilibrium under intense centrifugal pressures from two of the
most radically opposed extrastate primordial yearnings extant: that of
the Christians, especially the Maronites, to be part of Europe, and that
of the Moslems, especially the Sunnis, to be part of pan-Arabia. The
first of these motives finds expression mainly in a so-called isolationist
view of Lebanon as a special and unique phenomenon among the Arab
states, a "nice piece of mosaic," whose distinctiveness must be jealously
conserved; the second takes the form of a call for reunion with Syria.
And insofar as Lebanese politics escapes the merely personal and traditional and becomes involved with general ideas and issues, it is in these
terms that it tends to polarize.

The one spectacular exception to the maintenance of equilibrium, the
1958 civil war and American intervention, was in great part precipi-
tated by just this sort of atypical ideological polarization. On the one
hand President Sham'un's unconstitutional attempt to succeed himself
and, presumably, to align Lebanon more closely with the West in order

[38] Ayoub, "Political Structure," p. 82.

to enhance Christian power against the rising tide of Nasserism, excited the ever-present Moslem fears of Christian domination; on the other, the sudden outburst of pan-Arab enthusiasm stimulated by the Iraqi revolution and Syria's turn toward Cairo led to the equally ever-present Christian fear of drowning in a Moslem sea. But the crisis—and the Americans—passed. Sham'un was, at least temporarily, discredited for "dividing the country." The pan-Arabist fever was, also at least temporarily, checked by a renewed conviction, even within Sunni circles, that the integrity of the Lebanese state must at all costs be preserved. Civil rule was quickly restored, and by 1960 a new election could be held peacefully enough, bringing back most of the old familiar faces to the old familiar stands.

It seems, therefore, that Lebanese politics, as they are now constituted, must remain personalistic, factional, opportunistic, and unprogrammatic if they are to work at all. Given the extreme confessional heterogeneity and the penetration of this heterogeneity throughout the entire organization of the state, any increase in ideologized party politics tends very quickly to lead to an unstable Christian-Moslem polarization over the pan-Arab issue and to the breakdown of the cross-sect links that in the course of normal political maneuvering divide the sects and unite, if somewhat precariously, the government. Machiavellian calculation and religious toleration are opposite sides of the same coin in Lebanon; in the short run, anyway, the alternative to "silver and 'the fix' " may very well be national dissolution.

Though sorely tried by the continuation of the Arab-Israeli confrontation, and especially by the appearance of the Palestinian commandos as an important political force in the area, the Lebanese "nice piece of mosaic" remains intact. Indeed, of all the countries reviewed here, Lebanon has continued to be the most effective in containing its deep primordial cleavages, and though harassed by economic difficulties, by the presence of small radical groups of Left and Right (no major multisectarian parties have yet been able to form), and by frequent outbursts of popular violence, the Lebanese political system continues to function about as it has since the end of World War II. Differences in view as to the appropriate attitude to take toward the Palestine commandos (and toward Israeli incursions into the country) have led to the fall of cabinets, extended government crises, and some realignments among the major sectarian groupings. In 1970, the Christian-supported president

*won by only one vote over his Muslim-backed opponent, despite the un-
written rule that the post is reserved for a Maronite. But as the cabinet
continues to be headed by a Muslim, the established arrangements persist, and the government's authority vis-à-vis the Palestinian commandos and their Lebanese supporters has increased, especially since the
defeat of the commandos by the Jordanian army in September 1970.
Nothing lasts forever, especially in the Eastern Mediterranean, but to
date Lebanon continues to be a proof that although extreme primordial
diversity may make political equilibrium permanently precarious, it
does not necessarily, in and of itself, make it impossible.*

MOROCCO

Across the whole of the Middle East—except for Nile-bound Egypt
—runs an ancient social contrast between, as Coon puts it, "the tame
and the insolent, the domestic and the independent"—between those
living within the political, economic, and cultural orbit of the great generative cities and those living, if not precisely outside that orbit, along
its fringes and providing "the supply of rebels who, since the beginning
of the Bronze Age, have kept the urban civilizations refreshed and in
motion." [39] Between the central power of the shahs and sultans and the
stubborn libertarianism of the outlying tribes there existed (and to a
great extent still exists) a delicate balance. When the state was strong,
the tribes were obliged to give it at least grudging recognition and to
check their anarchic impulses; when it was weak, they ignored it, plun-
dered it, or—one or another of them—even overthrew it to become in
turn the carriers and defenders of the urban great tradition. For the better part of the time, however, neither fully effective despotism nor mere
tribal rampage prevailed. Rather, an uneasy truce between center and
perimeter was maintained, tying them together in "a loose system of
give and take" under which "mountaineers and nomads come to town
freely, their fastnesses are left alone, and they let the caravans of travel-
ers, traders, and pilgrims cross [their territories] without hindrance or
inconvenience over and above the normal rigors of travel." [40]

In Morocco, this contrast has always been particularly strong, in part
because so much of the terrain is mountainous, in part because of the

---

[39] C. Coon, *Caravan* (London, 1952), p. 295.
[40] Ibid., pp. 264–265.

gradual superimposition, after the seventh century, of an Arabic culture migrant from the East upon a relatively large indigenous Berber population, and in part because of the country's relatively great distance from the primary foci of Middle Eastern civilization in Egypt and Mesopotamia.

The complex early history of the region aside, the establishment of the Arabized, Islamic reformist Sherifian dynasty toward the end of the seventeenth century and the subsequent royal efforts to reduce the field of Berber customary law in favor of Koranic law, to repress saint worship and cultic practices, and to purify Islamic belief of local pagan accretions, reinforced the distinction between *bled al makhzen*—"the land of government"—and *bled as siba*—"the land of insolence." Claiming direct descent from the Prophet (the meaning of the term "sherif"), the dynasty, which rules until today, attempted to assert both spiritual and temporal power over the more Arabized population of the Atlantic Plain as well as over the more Berberized ones of the encircling Rif and Atlas mountains; but though the spiritual claim—that of imamship— has been commonly accepted, the temporal has been more of a sometime thing, particularly in the peripheral upland regions. Thus arose perhaps the most striking and distinctive feature of the Moroccan political system: the attachment of the urban and peasant populations of the plain to the sultan as autocratic head of a rather developed patrimonial bureaucracy (the Makhzen) of ministers, notables, soldiers, magistrates, clerks, policemen, and tax collectors; and the attachment of the tribal peoples to his person as "Lord of the Believers," but not to his secular government or its representatives.

By the time of the establishment of the French and Spanish protectorates in 1912, the sultanate had become so seriously weakened by a combination of internal corruption and external subversion that it was unable to exert effective control not merely over the mountains but in the plain as well. Though for a decade or so the seignoral proconsulship of Marshal Lyautey held the tribes in check and, in a somewhat paternalistic way, reinvigorated the Makhzen bureaucracy, after his departure his successors initiated the so-called Berber Policy, dedicated to drawing a sharp distinction between Arab and Berber and isolating the latter from the influence of the Makhzen entirely. Special Berber schools, designed to produce a "Berber elite," were set up; missionization increased; and—most important—the symbolic supremacy of Koranic law (and thus of the sultan as imam) was undermined by the placing of the mountain tribes under the French criminal code and officially recognizing the judicial competence of customary law tribal councils in civil disputes. Coinciding with the rise of the intense Islamic puritanism of the Egyptian and Afghan-Parisian reformers Abduh and Al-Afghani among the notables of the Arabized towns, and particularly those around the ancient Qarawiyin University at Fez, the Berber Policy and its implied threat to Islam stimulated the growth of nationalism under the banner of defending the faith against European-sponsored secularization and Christianization. Thus—even if under rather seriously altered conditions—the national movement in Morocco has also taken the classic form of attempting to strengthen the integrative power of a generally mid-Eastern urban civilization against the centrifugal tendencies of tribal particularism.

The exile of Sultan Mohammed V by the French in 1953 and his wildly triumphant return as a national hero in 1955 put the cap on this political and cultural revival of the Makhzen, and inaugurated, after independence was achieved, a new-state regime perhaps most aptly described as a "modernizing autocracy." [41] With the French and the Spanish gone, the Rabat Sultanate has become again the double-pronged pivot of the system. The major nationalist party, the Istiqlal, its independent power undercut by the lack, thus far, of national elections of a genuine parliament, has become the incumbent of a somewhat modernized but still essentially patrimonial Makhzen. Led by conservative Arabized notables of the lowland cities and towns (and again most especially of Fez—"la ville sainte de l'Islame . . . la métropole de l'arabisme . . . [et] la vraie capitale du Maroc"),[42] it has acted as the administrative arm of the throne, a "college of viziers" dominating the royal-appointed Councils of Government, the party-rationalized civil bureaucracy, and the reinstated (and reformed) Islamic judicial system. But as the attitude toward Istiqlal among the tribesmen has been, like their attitude to earlier palace officialdoms, at best lukewarm and at worst actively hostile, the relationship between the sultan and at least the more intact, peripheral tribes has remained essentially personal. Loyal to the king and resistant to his government, the tribes have been,

[41] For this concept and its analytic implications, see D. Apter, *The Political Kingdom in Uganda* (Princeton, N.J., 1961), pp. 20–28.

[42] Favre, "Le Maroc." [Since working in Morocco, I would now formulate some of these matters a bit differently: see C. Geertz, *Islam Observed: Religious Development in Morocco and Indonesia* (New Haven, 1968), esp. Chap. 3.]

since the transfer of sovereignty as they were before it, the main source of primordial threats to national integration.

Since 1956, heartland–hinterland crises have come thick and fast. The absorption into the Royal Army of the irregular military force formed from among the tribes during the sultan's exile—the so-called Liberation Army—has proved to be a most ticklish task leading to open clashes; only after the king firmly removed the Royal Army from Istiqlal influence and attached it directly to the palace under his son, Prince Moulay Hasan, as chief of staff, was the tension in part eased. In the fall of 1956, a Berber chieftain from the Middle Atlas, an intimate of the king, and a bitter opponent of the Istiqlal, resigned his post as interior minister in the royal cabinet, and returned to the mountains to preach primordialism to the tribes ("It is the tribes who have made the glory of Morocco"), calling for the dissolution of all political parties ("It is contrary to the interests of the country to confer responsibility on men who totally ignore the tribes") and a national rally around the figure of Mohammed V. ("We have in this nation both weak and strong. United on the same mountain and under the same skies, they are equal before the king.") [43] His effort soon ceased—at least openly—evidently upon the advice of the king; but a few months later an even more traditionalistic Berber, the governor of the southeastern province of Tafilelt, went into semirevolt, simultaneously refusing to obey "a party which hinders us from living as we wish," and declaring his undying loyalty to the sultan. The king soon secured his peaceful submission and placed him in forced residence near the imperial palace; but in late 1958 and early 1959 sporadic uprisings also occurred in the north and northeast, they too being contained within narrow limits largely through the agency of the king's personal popularity, diplomatic skill, military strength, and religious charisma.

Yet the modernizing aspect of the new Moroccan state is as real as the autocratic, and probably more enduring. The restlessness of the tribes does not represent merely "the past and the province against the future and the nation," but the concern of the traditional, "land of insolence" groups to find a secure and accepted place in that future and nation.[44] The development, first clandestinely and then—as the various parapolitical expressions of tribal dissatisfaction collapsed—openly, of

[43] Quotations in this sentence from Lahcen al-Youssi and in the following from Addi ou Bihi taken from Lacouture, *Le Maroc*, p. 90.
[44] Ibid., p. 93.

a new national political party, the Popular Movement, as the vehicle of rural aspirations, is but one of the more obvious signs that mere hostility to urban culture and unbending resistance to central authority is coming to be replaced among the outlying peoples by a fear of being relegated to second-class citizenship within a modern civil order. Under the leadership of the former head of the Liberation Army, Ahardane, and with the vaguest of programs—"Moslem Socialism" and a new union around the king as imam, not just for Morocco, but for the whole Maghrib—the new party has at best but one foot in that order. But as a rapid sequence of very serious political mutations—the holding of local elections; the breakaway of the left wing of Istiqlal to form a proletarian party; the sudden, premature death of Mohammed V, and the succession of his less popular son—have cast a cloud of uncertainty over the future of monarchical government in the last couple of years, the new state may well find itself increasingly hard pressed to satisfy and contain the subtle fusion of traditional *siba* sentiments and modern political ambitions neatly summed up in Ahardane's stiff-necked slogan, "We have not acquired independence in order to lose liberty.".[45]

Though it is perhaps true that in the long run the modernizing aspect of the new Moroccan state is more enduring than the autocratic, over the last decade it is the autocratic which has flourished. The king, Hassan II, suspended the constitution and dissolved parliament in 1965 after riots in Casablanca led to the death, largely at the hands of government forces, of anywhere from thirty (the official count) to several hundred people. The king took direct control of the government, ruling by executive fiat and systematically reducing the influence of the two major parties—the Islamist Istiqlal *and the socialist* Union Nationale des Forces Populaires—*and the urban Arab masses which, for the most part, formed their constituencies. The period was one of accelerating neotraditionalism, as Hassan attempted to draw various sorts of local notables, many of them Berber, and army officers, the great majority of them Berber, into direct, personal loyalty to the throne. In 1970, the so-called state of exception was at least nominally ended when the king promulgated a new constitution and announced general elections. The parties (except for the Berber-dominated* Mouvement Populaire) *found the constitution insufficiently democratic and the elections insufficiently free, however, and regarded the whole maneuver as an effort by the*

45 Quoted in Ashford, *Political Change*, p. 322.

king to institutionalize and legitimize the throne-centered system of neo-traditional government he had evolved during his first decade of rule. Thus, though the elections were held and the constitution approved—under conditions generally held to be less than honest—the pattern of court-and-notables politics persisted. This pattern came to something of a dramatic dissolution with the attempted army coup at the king's for-ty-second birthday picnic in July of 1970, in which about a hundred of the approximately five hundred guests (many of them foreign) were killed. A major, five colonels, and four generals were executed almost immediately (others, including its leader, died in the coup attempt it-self), and a number of other officers were imprisoned. The degree to which primordial loyalties played a role in the attack is unclear (almost all the leaders were Berbers, most of them from the Rif; and most were outstanding beneficiaries of the king's favors under the throne-centered policy); but since the attack (which was followed in August 1972 by an-other, which also failed) the king has moved to de-emphasize the Berber role in the army as well as to find a basis of support among the Arab-speaking populations of the large cities that the two major parties, now united into a "National Action Bloc" claim to represent. Thus, what-ever the reality of the bled al makhzen/bled as siba *contrast might, or might not, ever have been (and I would now be inclined to regard it as having never been as clear-cut or simple as European scholarship de-scribed it), the distinction—partly cultural, partly linguistic, partly so-cial, partly a kind of ethnopolitical myth, a traditional, almost instinc-tive way of perceiving group differences—between "Arab" and "Berber" remains an important, if elusive, factor in Moroccan national life.*

NIGERIA

The distinctive feature of Nigerian political life as it has evolved since World War II has been what Coleman has called "the regionaliza-tion of nationalism." [46] Whereas in most of the other new states the final phases of the pursuit of independence saw a progressive unification of diverse elements into an intensely solidary opposition to colonial rule, open dissidence emerging only after devolution and the inevitable waning of revolutionary comradeship, in Nigeria tension between var-

[46] Coleman, *Nigeria*, pp. 319–331.

ious primordial groups increased in the last decade of dependency. After 1946 the Nigerian struggle for freedom was less a matter of defying foreign authority and more a matter of drawing boundaries, founding capitals, and distributing powers in such a way as to dampen and contain sharpening ethnoregional hostilities prior to the disappearance of that authority. It was marked not so much by growing insurgency in order to force the British to leave as by feverish negotiation, in both Lagos and London, in order to create a *modus vivendi* among the Yoruba, Ibo, and Hausa-Fulani so that they could leave.

The arrangement ultimately devised (in a 240-page, fine-print constitution) was a radically federal one, composed of three powerful constituent regions—the Northern, the (south-) Eastern, and the (south-) Western—each with its own capital, its own parliament, cabinet, and high court, and its own budget. Each region was dominated by a particular ethnic group—respectively, the Hausa, Ibo, and Yoruba; a particular political party—the Northern People's Congress (NPC), the National Council of Nigeria and the Cameroons (NCNC), and the Action Group (AG); and a particular political personality—Alhaji Sir Ahmadu Bello, the Sardauna ("Sultan") of Sokoto, Dr. Nnamdi Azikiwe, and Chief Obafemi Awolowo. Perched, somewhat insecurely, on top of these regional strongholds was the federal government at Lagos as the arena in which the sort of two-against-one coalition politics one would naturally expect from this type of three-person game took place and out of whose changeful processes the authoritative leadership to fill the vacuum at the center of the system was supposed at length to emerge.

The sort of form that leadership was to take, who was to provide it, and how, in the working of this Swiss-clock governmental mechanism, it was to actually be produced remained, however, entirely obscure. In the meantime, the triangular pattern of primordial identification crystallized in the country at large, as the tribal societies of traditional Nigeria gradually regrouped themselves into the regional-linguistic (and in the Moslem North, religious) folk societies of modern Nigeria. But though increasingly important as the country's ethnic skeleton, this pattern did not exhaust the full variety of ingrained "consciousness of kind," because in each region there remained a large number of smaller groups outside the core Hausa, Yoruba, and Ibo areas at least somewhat resistant to assimilation to these broader subnational entities. And it was in these marginal areas—the southern half of the North, the eastern edge of the West, and the southern and eastern borders of the East—that the most vital electoral competition between major ethnic groups tended to take place, as each party attempted, with some success, to capitalize on minority resentments within their opponents' strongholds. What appeared at the center as a three-way subnational competition, and at the regional capitals as (more and more) a one-party ethnocracy, represented in the countryside a much more complex and diversified network of tribal alliances and oppositions.[47] It was a tiered system in which local loyalties remained mostly organized in traditional terms, provincial ones became organized in party-political terms, and national ones were only barely organized at all.

Thus, although the regionalization of nationalism process led to the establishment of a party system and constitutional structure in which Nigeria's several hundred primordial groups, ranging from the nearly six million Hausa to tribal fragments of only a few hundred were able, for a while, to live in at least reasonable amity, it also created a void at the very heart of national political life and left the country more or less acephalous.

After independence (in October, 1960), political attention consequently turned toward the federal capital at Lagos as parties and their leaders jockeyed for starting positions from which to launch their campaigns to correct this condition. After an initial attempt to form a governing alliance between the economically and politically more advanced Eastern and Western regions against the more traditional North stumbled over the entrenched hostility between the mobile, aggressive Ibo intelligentsia and the stolid, wealthy Yoruba business class—and between the mercurial Dr. Azikiwe and the lofty Chief Awolowo—the North and East formed such an alliance, isolating the West. Azikiwe resigned the Eastern premiership to become governor general, in theory a

[47] The whole picture was further complicated, not only by the fact that tribal identifications within the three major groups had not altogether given way before the wider ethnolinguistic loyalty, but also that not all members of such larger units were located in their home regions, having migrated or spilled over into the others where they sometimes formed, particularly in the towns, an important oppositional minority. The whole problem of the allegiance of an individual living outside his "home region" is an extremely ticklish one for all new states in which integrative problems have been coped with by creating territorial substates tinged with primordial significance, as Nehru's continual insistence that, for example, a Bengali living in Madras is a citizen of the state level, of Madras, not of Bengal, and that all notions of a "national homeland" for ethnic groups living elsewhere in India must be stamped out demonstrates. The additional fact that some such groups are more mobile than others (in Nigeria, the Ibo; in India, the Marwari and so on) only intensifies this problem.

merely symbolic office, but which he hoped to make into something more; the Sardauna of Sokoto, choosing to remain lion of the North in his regional premiership, sent his lieutenant, Alhaji Sir Abubakar Tafawa Balewa, to serve in his stead as federal prime minister; and Awolowo, odd man out in this first of what was a series of two-against-one coalitions, resigned his post as Western premier to become leader of the opposition in the federal parliament.

Posts taken, the maneuvering began. The federal parliament decided to form a fourth state, the Midwest, out of the minority area of the Western Region; Awolowo shifted from a markedly right- to a markedly left-wing ideological position in an attempt to shake the somewhat tory government and ride the antineocolonialism horse to power, splitting the Action Group in the process; tensions within the NCNC between the increasingly accommodative old guard and the still radical Young Turks increased, and so on.

But all this more confused issues than clarified them; complicated matters rather than simplified them. Independent (as this is written) for less than a year, Nigeria, the newest of the new states considered here, offers but the most unformed materials upon which to base an assessment of its essential character and probable future. Possessed of what would appear to be an extraordinarily unwieldy set of political institutions hurriedly put together in the last hectic years of constitution-making before independence, lacking a comprehensive national party, a supereminent political leader, an overarching religious tradition or a common cultural background, and—seemingly—of several minds about what to do with freedom now that it has, almost as a matter of course, received it, it has an unusually tentative, up-in-the-air quality, even for a new state.

Nigeria was the least well-defined of the generally ill-defined states reviewed as examples in my original essay. At the time, its situation seemed at once the most hopeful and the most ominous. Hopeful, because it seemed to have escaped the usual upheavals of decolonization, to be large enough to be economically viable, and to have inherited a moderate, well-trained, and experienced elite; ominous, because its primordial group tensions were both extremely great and unbelievably complex. The sense of ominousness proved to be the prophetic one. In January 1966 a military coup led to the death of a number of Northern political leaders, including Sir Abubakar Tafawa Balewa, and the estab-

lishment of an Ibo-led military regime. A second coup, led by a North-erner from a minor, that is, non-Hausa, tribe, Colonel Yakubu Gowon, eventuated in the massacre of somewhere between ten and thirty thou-sand Ibos living in the Hausa areas of the North, while anywhere from two hundred thousand to a million and a half Ibos fled from the North to their Eastern region homeland. In May of 1967, Colonel Gowon as-sumed emergency powers and sought to divide the Eastern region into three states as a device to increase the power of the non-Ibo Easterners and decrease that of the Ibos. The Ibos, forming themselves into the Republic of Biafra, rebelled, and, after nearly three years of some of the most bitter warfare of modern times (perhaps more than two million people were killed and countless others died of starvation), were sup-pressed by the federal government under Gowon, now a general and head of the country. After all this, surely one of the most dramatic ex-amples of the power of primordial loyalties and antipathies (though, again, the causes of the coups and the war were not "merely" pri-mordial, as the involvement of the great powers demonstrates), the "ten-tative," "up-in-the-air" quality of the country remains, as does its com-plex, intense, and but narrowly balanced pattern of group distrust.

V

Center-and-arc regionalism and dual leadership in Indonesia, single-party interracial alliance in Malaya, aggressive assimilationism wrapped in constitutional legalism in Burma, a cosmopolitan central party with provincial machines fighting a multifront war against every sort of parochialism known to man (and a few known only to Hindus) in India, sectarian slate-making and log-rolling in Lebanon, Janus-faced autocratic rule in Morocco, and unfocused check-and-balance scrim-maging in Nigeria—are these systems as merely unique as they appear? From this array of efforts after political order, does any evidence emerge for the claim that the integrative revolution is a general process?

Over the cases reviewed here, at least, one common developmental tendency does stand out: the aggregation of independently defined, spe-cifically outlined traditional primordial groups into larger, more diffuse units whose implicit frame of reference is not the local scene but the "nation"—in the sense of the whole society encompassed by the new civil state. The leading principle in terms of which this lumping is mainly carried out varies—region in Indonesia, race in Malaya, language in India, religion in Lebanon, custom in Morocco, and quasi kinship in Nigeria. Whether it involves becoming an Outer Islander in addition to a Minangkabau, a Kachin over and above a Duleng, a Christian as well as a Maronite, or a Yoruba rather than only an Egba, the process, though variously advanced, both as between countries and within them, is general. It is a progressive extension of the sense of primordial similarity and difference generated from the direct and protracted encounter of culturally diverse groups in local contexts to more broadly defined groups of a similar sort interacting within the framework of the entire national society, an extension Freedman has described particularly well for Malaya:

Malaya was and remains a culturally plural society. Paradoxically, from a purely structural point of view, its plural nature is more marked today than ever before. Nationalism and political independence in their early phases have tended to define, on a pan-Malayan basis, ethnic blocs which in former times were merely categories. Then the social map of Malaya was, so to speak, made up of a kaleidoscope of small culturally defined units rearranging themselves in accordance with local conditions. "The Malays" did not interact with "the Chinese" and "the Indians." Some Malays interacted with some Chinese and some Indians. But as "Malays," "Chinese" and "Indians" come to be realized as structural entities on a nationwide scale, they can begin to have total relations with one another.[48]

The emergence of a nationwide system of "ethnic blocs" engaged in "total relations with one another" sets the stage for a direct clash between personal identity and political integrity in the new states. By generalizing and extending tribal, racial, linguistic, or other principles of primordial solidarity, such a system permits the maintenance of a profoundly rooted "consciousness of kind," and relates that consciousness to the developing civil order. It allows one to continue to claim public acknowledgement of one's existence and import in terms of the familiar symbols of group uniqueness, while at the same time becoming more and more drawn into a political society cast in a mold wholly different from the "natural" community those symbols define. But, on the other hand, it also simplifies and concentrates group antagonisms, raises the specter of separatism by superimposing a comprehensive political sig-

[48] Freedman, "Plural Society in Malaya."

nificance upon those antagonisms, and, particularly when the crystallizing ethnic blocs outrun state boundaries, stirs international controversies. The integrative revolution does not do away with ethnocentrism; it merely modernizes it.

Yet modernizing ethnocentrism does render it more easily reconciled to the presence of developed national political institutions. The effective operation of such institutions does not require the simple replacement of primordial ties and identifications by civil ones. In all probability, such a replacement is a sheer impossibility. What it does demand is an adjustment between them, an adjustment such that the processes of government can proceed freely without seriously threatening the cultural framework of personal identity, and such that whatever discontinuities in "consciousness of kind" happen to exist in the general society do not radically distort political functioning. At least as they have been conceived here, primordial and civil sentiments are not ranged in direct and implicitly evolutionary opposition to one another in the manner of so many of the theoretical dichotomies of classical sociology—
Gemeinschaft and *Gesellschaft*, mechanical and organic solidarity, folk and urban society; the history of their development does not consist simply of the expansion of the one at the expense of the other. Their marked tendency to interfere with one another in the new states stems not from any natural and irremovable antipathy between them but rather from dislocations arising from the differing patterns of change intrinsic to each of them as they respond to the disequilibrating forces of the mid-twentieth century. Their clash is an outcome of the contrasting sorts of transformation that traditional political institutions and traditional modes of self-perception undergo as they move along their separate paths toward modernity.

On the self-perception side, the nature of the modernizing process is virtually uninvestigated; it is not usually even recognized that such a process exists. The already mentioned aggregation of narrowly circumscribed tribal, linguistic, religious, and so on, groups into larger more generalized ethnic blocs set within the context of a common social frame is certainly a crucial part of it. A simple, coherent, broadly defined ethnic structure, such as is found in most industrial societies, is not an undissolved residue of traditionalism but an earmark of modernity. But how this reconstruction of the system of primordial affiliation takes place, the stages through which it passes, the forces that advance or retard it, the transformations in personality structure it involves, all are largely unknown. The comparative sociology (or social psychology) of ethnic change remains to be written.

With respect to the political side, it can hardly be said that the problem is unrecognized, for the notion of a civil society, of the nature of citizenship and the diffuse social sentiments on which it rests, has been a central concern of political science since Aristotle. But it remains nonetheless vague; much easier to point to than describe; much easier to sense than to analyze. What the civic sense more than anything else seems to involve is a definite concept of the public as a separate and distinct body and an attendant notion of a genuine public interest, which though not necessarily superior to, is independent of and at times even in conflict with, both private and other sorts of collective interest. When we talk about the changing forms of civil politics in the new states or elsewhere, it is the vicissitudes of just this sense of the public and the public interest, its waxings and wanings, its alterations in mode of expression, to which we refer. Again, however, though we have at least a general idea of the nature of civility and the range of forms through which it is materialized in industrial states, very little is known about the processes by which the present patterns have come to be what they are. A genuine civil sense is often even denied—incorrectly in my opinion—to traditional states at all. In any case, the stages through which a modern sense of political community arises out of a traditional one have been at best but impressionistically traced, and thus both the roots and the character of civility remain obscure.

A satisfactory understanding of the reasons for the chronic tension in the new states between the need to maintain a socially ratified personal identity and the desire to construct a powerful national community demands, therefore, a more circumstantial tracing of the stages through which their relationship to one another passes as each proceeds along the special lines of its own development. And it is in the histories of those states as they unfold before our eyes that such a tracing is most readily to be accomplished. The diverse constitutional, quasi-constitutional, or simply ad hoc experiments in government that characterize at least those new states described here represent, among other things, an attempt to establish a pattern of politics in which the looming headlong clash of primordial and civil loyalties can be averted. Whether ethnic differentiation is given its political expression in terms of territorial subunits, political parties, government posts, executive leadership, or, as is most common, one or another combination of these, the effort is everywhere to find a formula that will keep the pace of modernization of the nation's sense of selfhood in step with the parallel modernization not only of its political, but of its economic, stratificatory, domestic, and so on, institutions as well. It is by watching the integrative revolution happen that we shall understand it. This may seem like a mere wait-and-see policy, inappropriate to the predictive ambitions of science. But such a policy is at least preferable, and more scientific, to waiting and not seeing, which has been largely the case to date.

At any rate, the success of the efforts to find a formula for balance in the midst of change now taking place in the new states is nowhere assured. A high degree of governmental immobilism resulting from the attempt to reconcile divergent primordial groups is everywhere apparent. The mere prejudices that must be tolerated in order to effect such reconciliations are often repugnant. But as the alternatives to such attempts as these to construct a civil politics of primordial compromise would seem to be either Balkanization, *Herrenvolk* fanaticism, or the forcible suppression of ethnic assertion by a leviathan state, can they be viewed, especially by members of a society that has notably failed to resolve its own most troublesome primordial problem, with either indifference or contempt?

Chapter 11 /

The Politics of Meaning

I

One of the things that everyone knows but no one can quite think how to demonstrate is that a country's politics reflect the design of its culture. At one level, the proposition is indubitable—where else could French politics exist but France? Yet, merely to state it is to raise doubts. Since 1945, Indonesia has seen revolution, parliamentary democracy, civil war, presidential autocracy, mass murder, and military rule. Where is the design in that?

Between the stream of events that make up political life and the web of beliefs that comprises a culture it is difficult to find a middle term. On the one hand, everything looks like a clutter of schemes and surprises; on the other, like a vast geometry of settled judgments. What joins such a chaos of incident to such a cosmos of sentiment is extremely obscure, and how to formulate it is even more so. Above all, what the attempt to link politics and culture needs is a less breathless view of the former and a less aesthetic view of the latter.

In the several essays which make up *Culture and Politics in Indonesia,* the sort of theoretical reconstruction necessary to produce such a change of perspective is undertaken, mainly from the cultural side by Benedict Anderson and Taufik Abdullah, mainly from the political by

Daniel Lev and G. William Liddle, more or less evenly from both by Sartono Kartodirdjo.[1] Whether the subject be law or party organization, the Javanese idea of power or the Minangkabau idea of change, ethnic conflict or rural radicalism, the effort is the same: to render Indonesian political life intelligible by seeing it, even at its most erratic, as informed by a set of conceptions—ideals, hypotheses, obsessions, judgments—derived from concerns which far transcend it, and to give reality to those conceptions by seeing them as having their existence not in some gauzy world of mental forms but in the concrete immediacy of partisan struggle. Culture, here, is not cults and customs, but the structures of meaning through which men give shape to their experience; and politics is not coups and constitutions, but one of the principal arenas in which such structures publicly unfold. The two being thus reframed, determining the connection between them becomes a practicable enterprise, though hardly a modest one.

The reason the enterprise is immodest, or anyway especially venturesome, is that there is almost no theoretical apparatus with which to conduct it; the whole field—what shall we call it? thematic analysis? —is wedded to an ethic of imprecision. Most attempts to find general cultural conceptions displayed in particular social contexts are content to be merely evocative, to place a series of concrete observations in immediate juxtaposition and to pull out (or read in) the pervading element by rhetorical suggestion. Explicit argument is rare because there are, as much by design as neglect, hardly any terms in which to cast it, and one is left with a collection of anecdotes connected by insinuation, and with a feeling that though much has been touched little has been grasped.[2]

The scholar who wishes to avoid this sort of perfected impressionism has thus to build his theoretical scaffold at the same time that he conducts his analysis. That is why the authors in the [Holt] book have such diverse approaches—why Liddle moves out from group conflicts and Anderson from art and literature; why Lev's puzzle is the politicization of legal institutions, Sartono's the durability of popular millenarianism, Abdullah's the fusion of social conservatism and ideological dynamism. The unity here is neither of topic nor argument, but of

---

[1] See C. Holt, ed., *Culture and Politics in Indonesia* (Ithaca, 1972), in which the present essay first appeared as an "Afterword," pp. 319–336.

[2] Perhaps the foremost, as well as the most uncompromising, practitioner of this paratactic approach to relating politics to culture is Nathan Leites. See especially his *A Study of Bolshevism* (Glencoe, Ill., 1953), and *The Rules of the Game in Paris* (Chicago, 1969).

analytical style—of aim and of the methodological issues the pursuit of such an aim entails.

These issues are multiple, involving questions of definition, verification, causality, representativeness, objectivity, measurement, communication. But at base they all boil down to one question: how to frame an analysis of meaning—the conceptual structures individuals use to construe experience—which will be at once circumstantial enough to carry conviction and abstract enough to forward theory. These are equal necessities; choosing one at the expense of the other yields blank descriptivism or vacant generality. But they also, superficially at least, pull in opposite directions, for the more one invokes details the more he is bound to the peculiarities of the immediate case, the more one omits them the more he loses touch with the ground on which his arguments rest. Discovering how to escape this paradox—or more exactly, for one never really escapes it, how to keep it at bay—is what, methodologically, thematic analysis is all about.

And it is, consequently, what, beyond the particular findings concerning particular subjects, the [Holt] book is about. Each study struggles to draw broad generalizations out of special instances, to penetrate deeply enough into detail to discover something more than detail. The strategies adopted to accomplish this are again various, but the effort to make parochial bodies of material speak for more than themselves is uniform. The scene is Indonesia; but the goal, still far enough away to sustain ambition, is an understanding of how it is that every people gets the politics it imagines.

II

Indonesia is an excellent place to take up such a quest. As heir to Polynesian, Indic, Islamic, Chinese, and European traditions, it probably has more hieratic symbols per square foot than any other large land expanse in the world, and moreover it had in Sukarno (who it is a mistake to think was untypical in anything but his genius) a man both wildly anxious and supremely equipped to assemble those symbols into a pan-doctrinal *Staatsreligion* for the new-formed Republic. "Socialism, Communism, incarnations of Vishnu Murti," a newspaper call to arms cried in 1921: "Abolish capitalism, propped up by the imperialism that is its slave! God grant Islam the strength that it may succeed." [3] "I am a follower of Karl Marx. . . . I am also a religious man," Sukarno announced some decades later; "I have made myself the meeting place of all trends and ideologies. I have blended, blended, and blended them until finally they became the present Sukarno."[4]

Yet, on the other hand, the very density and variety of symbolic reference has made of Indonesian culture a swirl of tropes and images into which more than one incautious observer has merely disappeared.[5] With so much meaning lying scattered openly around it is nearly impossible to frame an argument relating political events to one or another strain of it which is totally lacking in plausibility. In one sense, seeing cultural reflections in political activities is extremely easy in Indonesia; but this only makes the isolation of precise connections that much more difficult. Because in this garden of metaphors almost any hypothesis discerning a form of thought in a piece of action has a certain logic, developing hypotheses that have truth as well is more a matter of resisting temptations than of seizing opportunities.

The main temptation to be resisted is jumping to conclusions and the main defense against it is explicitly to trace out the sociological links between cultural themes and political developments, rather than to move deductively from one to the other. Ideas—religious, moral, practical, aesthetic—must, as Max Weber, among others, never tired of insisting, be carried by powerful social groups to have powerful social effects; someone must revere them, celebrate them, defend them, impose them. They have to be institutionalized in order to find not just an intellectual existence in society, but, so to speak, a material one as well. The ideological wars which have wracked Indonesia for the past twenty-five years must be seen not, as they so often have, as clashes of opposed mentalities—Javanese "mysticism" versus Sumatran "pragmatism," Indic "syncretism" versus Islamic "dogmatism"—but as the substance of a struggle to create an institutional structure for the country that

[3] Quoted (from *Utusan Hindia*) in B. Dahm, *Sukarno and the Struggle for Indonesian Independence* (Ithaca, 1969), p. 39.

[4] Quoted in L. Fischer, *The Story of Indonesia* (New York, 1959), p. 154. For a similar statement from a public speech of Sukarno, see Dahm, *Sukarno and the Struggle*, p. 200.

[5] For an example, see H. Luethy, "Indonesia Confronted," *Encounter* 25 (1965): 80–89; 26 (1966): 75–83, along with my comment "Are the Javanese Mad?" and Luethy's "Reply," ibid., August 1966, pp. 86–90.

enough of its citizens would find sufficiently congenial to allow it to function.

Hundreds of thousands of political dead testify to the fact that nowhere nearly enough citizens did so, and it is questionable how far they do so now. Organizing a cultural hodgepodge into a workable polity is more than a matter of inventing a promiscuous civil religion to blunt its variety. It requires either the establishment of political institutions within which opposing groups can safely contend, or the elimination of all groups but one from the political stage. Neither of these has, so far, been more than marginally effected in Indonesia; the country has been as incapable of totalitarianism as of constitutionalism. Rather, almost every institution in the society—army, bureaucracy, court, university, press, party, religion, village—has been swept by great tremors of ideological passion which seem to have neither end nor direction. If Indonesia gives any overall impression, it is of a state manqué, a country which, unable to find a political form appropriate to the temper of its people, stumbles on apprehensively from one institutional contrivance to the next.

A great part of the problem, of course, is that the country is archipelagic in more than geography. Insofar as it displays a pervasive temper, it is one riven with internal contrasts and contradictions. There are the regional differences (the rhetorical combativeness of the Minangkabau and the reflective elusiveness of the Javanese, for example); there are the faith-and-custom "ethnic" divergences among even closely related groups, as in the East Sumatran "boiling pot"; there are the class conflicts reflected in the nativistic movement material and the vocational ones reflected in that of the struggle for a workable legal system. There are racial minorities (Chinese and Papuans); religious minorities (Christians and Hindus); local minorities (Djakarta Batak, Surabaja Madurese). The nationalist slogan, "One People, One Country, One Language," is a hope, not a description.

The hope that the slogan represents, however, is not necessarily unreasonable. Most of the larger nations of Europe grew out of a cultural heterogeneity hardly less marked; if Tuscans and Sicilians can live together in the same state and conceive of themselves as natural compatriots, so can Javanese and Minangkabau. Rather than the mere fact of internal diversity, it has been the refusal, at all levels of the society, to come to terms with it that has impeded Indonesia's search for effective political form. The diversity has been denied as a colonial slander, de-

plored as a feudal remnant, clouded over with ersatz syncretisms, tendentious history, and utopian fantasies, while all the time the bitter
combat of groups who see in one another rivals not merely for political
and economic power, but for the right to define truth, justice, beauty,
and morality, the very nature of reality, rages on virtually unguided by
formal political institutions. By acting as though it were culturally homogeneous like Japan or Egypt instead of heterogeneous like India or Nigeria, Indonesia (or more exactly, I suppose, the Indonesian elite) has
managed to create anarchic politics of meaning outside the established
structures of civil government.

This politics of meaning is anarchic in the literal sense of unruled,
not the popular one of unordered. As each of the essays in the [Holt]
volume shows in its own way, what I have elsewhere called "the struggle
for the real," the attempt to impose upon the world a particular conception of how things at bottom are and how men are therefore obliged to
act, is, for all the inability thus far to bring it to workable institutional
expression, not a mere chaos of zeal and prejudice. It has a shape,
trajectory, and force of its own.

The political processes of all nations are wider and deeper than the
formal institutions designed to regulate them; some of the most critical
decisions concerning the direction of public life are not made in parlia-
ments and presidiums; they are made in the unformalized realms of
what Durkheim called "the collective conscience" (or "consciousness";
the useful ambiguity of *conscience* is unavailable in English). But in Indonesia the pattern of official life and the framework of popular sentiment within which it sits have become so disjoined that the activities of
government, though centrally important, seem nevertheless almost be-
side the point, mere routinisms convulsed again and again by sudden ir-
ruptions from the screened-off (one almost wants to say, repressed) political course along which the country is in fact moving.

The more accessible events of public life, political facts in the
narrower sense, do about as much to obscure this course as to reveal it.
Insofar as they reflect it, as of course they do, they do so obliquely and
indirectly, as dreams reflect desires or ideologies interests; discerning it
is more like interpreting a constellation of symptoms than tracing a
chain of causes. The studies in the [Holt] book therefore diagnose and
assess, rather than measure and predict. Fragmentation in the party system bespeaks an intensification of ethnic self-consciousness; enfeeble-
ment of formal law, renewed commitment to conciliatory methods of
dispute settlement. Behind the moral quandaries of provincial modern-

izers lie complexities in traditional accounts of tribal history; behind the explosiveness of rural protest, enthrallment with cataclysmic images of change; behind the theatrics of Guided Democracy, archaic conceptions of the sources of authority. Taken together, these exercises in political exegesis begin to expose the faint outlines of what the Indonesian Revolution in fact amounts to: an effort to construct a modern state in contact with its citizens' conscience; a state with which they can, in both senses of the word, come to an understanding. One of the things Sukarno was right about, though in fact he had something rather different in mind, was that it is, this Revolution, not over.

III

The classical problem of legitimacy—how do some men come to be credited with the right to rule over others—is peculiarly acute in a country in which long-term colonial domination created a political system that was national in scope but not in complexion. For a state to do more than administer privilege and defend itself against its own population, its acts must seem continuous with the selves of those whose state it pretends it is, its citizens—to be, in some stepped-up, amplified sense, *their* acts. This is not a mere question of consensus. A man does not have to agree with his government's acts to see himself as embodied in them any more than he has to approve of his own acts to acknowledge that he has, alas, himself performed them. It is a question of immediacy, of experiencing what the state "does" as proceeding naturally from a familiar and intelligible "we." A certain amount of psychological sleight of hand is always required on the part of government and citizenry in this in the best of cases. But when a country has been governed for two hundred years or so by foreigners, it is, even after they have been displaced, a yet more difficult trick.

The political tasks that loomed so formidable as independence was reached for—ending the domination of outside powers, creating leadership cadres, stimulating economic growth, and sustaining a sense of national unity—have indeed turned out to be that and more since independence has been gained. But they have been joined by another task, less clearly envisaged then and less consciously recognized now, that of dispelling the aura of alienness from the institutions of modern government. Much of the symbol-mongering that went on under the Sukarno regime, and which has been moderated rather than ended under its successor, was a half-deliberate attempt to close the cultural gulf between the state and society that, if not altogether created by colonial rule, had been enormously widened by it. The great crescendo of slogans, movements, monuments, and demonstrations which reached a pitch of almost hysterical intensity in the early sixties was, in part anyway, designed to make the nation-state seem indigenous. As it was not indigenous, disbelief and disorder spiraled upward together, and Sukarno was destroyed, along with his regime, in the collapse which ensued.

Even without the complicating factor of colonial rule, however, the modern state would seem alien to local tradition in a country like Indonesia, if only because such a state's conception of itself as a specialized instrument for the coordination of all aspects of public life has no real counterpart in such a tradition. Traditional rulers, and not only in Indonesia, may have been, when they could manage it and were so inclined, despotic, arbitrary, selfish, unresponsive, exploitative, or merely cruel (though, under the influence of the Cecil B. DeMille view of history, the degree to which they were has commonly been exaggerated); but they never imagined themselves, nor did their subjects imagine them, to be executives of an omnicompetent state. Mostly they governed to proclaim their status, protect (or, where possible, enlarge) their privileges, and exercise their style of life; and insofar as they regulated matters beyond their immediate reach—which was commonly very little—they did so only derivatively, as a reflex of concerns more stratificatory than properly political. The notion that the state is a machine whose function is to organize the general interest comes into such a context as something of a strange idea.

So far as popular reaction is concerned, the results of that strangeness have been the usual ones: a degree of curiosity, a degree more of fear, heightened expectancy, and a great deal of puzzlement. It was to such a confusion of sentiment that Sukarno's symbol-wielding was a failed response; but the various matters discussed in the [Holt] book are others, less concocted so less ephemeral. In them, one can see in concrete detail what being abruptly confronted with the prospect of an activist, comprehensive central government—what de Jouvenel has called "the power-house state"—means to a people used to masters but not to managers.[6]

[6] B. de Jouvenel, *On Power* (Boston, 1962).

Such a confrontation means that the received concepts of justice, power, protest, authenticity, identity (as well, of course, as a host of others these essays do not explicitly treat) are all thrown into jeopardy by the requirements, or seeming such, of effective national existence in the contemporary world. This conceptual dislocation—the putting into question of the most familiar frames of moral and intellectual perception and the vast shift of sensibility thereby set in motion—forms the proper subject of cultural studies of new state politics. "What this country needs," Sukarno once said, in a characteristic burst of linguistic syncretism, "is *ke-up-to-date-an.*" He didn't quite give it that, merely gestures toward it, but they were gestures graphic enough to convince all but the most provincial of Indonesians that not just the form but the nature of government had changed and that they had, in result, some mental adjustments to make.[7]

IV

This sort of social changing of the mind is a great deal easier to sense than to document, not only because its manifestations are so various and indirect, but because it is so hesitant, shot through with uncertainty and contradiction. For every belief, practice, ideal, or institution that is condemned as backward, one, often the same one and by the same people, is celebrated as the very essence of contemporaneity; for every one attacked as alien, one, again often the same one, is hailed as a sacred expression of the national soul.

There is, in such matters, no simple progression from "traditional" to "modern," but a twisting, spasmodic, unmethodical movement which turns as often toward repossessing the emotions of the past as disowning them. Some of Sartono's peasants read their future in medieval myths, some in Marxist visions, some in both. Lev's lawyers waver between the formal dispassion of Justice's scales and the sheltering paternalism of the banyan tree. The publicist whose career Abdullah traces as an example of his society's reaction to the challenge of modernism, editorial-

[7] The quotation is from Sukarno's letters attacking traditionalist Islam, written while he was in prison exile in Flores, *Surat-surat Dari Endeh,* eleventh letter, August 18, 1936, in K. Goenadi and H. M. Nasution, eds., *Dibawah Bendera Revolusi* 1 (Djakarta, 1959): 340.

izes simultaneously for the restoration of "the genuine Minangkabau
adat [custom]," and for headlong entry "unto the path of *kemadjuan*
[progress]." In Java, Anderson finds "archaic-magical" and "devel-
oped-rational" theories of power existing side by side; in Sumatra, Liddle finds localism and nationalism advancing *pari passu*.

This undeniable, commonly denied, fact—that whatever the curve of
progress may be, it fits no graceful formula—disables any analysis of
modernization which starts from the assumption that it consists of the
replacement of the indigenous and obsolescent with the imported and
up-to-date. Not just in Indonesia, but throughout the Third World—
throughout the world—men are increasingly drawn to a double goal: to
remain themselves and to keep pace, or more, with the twentieth century. A tense conjunction of cultural conservatism and political radicalism is at the nerve of new state nationalism, and nowhere more
conspicuously so than in Indonesia. What Abdullah says of the
Minangkabau—that accommodating to the contemporary world has required "continuing revision of the meaning of modernization," involved
"new attitudes toward tradition itself and [an unending] search for a
suitable basis of modernization"—is said, in one manner or another,
throughout each of the essays. What they reveal is not a linear advance
from darkness to light, but a continuous redefinition of where "we"
(peasants, lawyers, Christians, Javanese, Indonesians . . .) have been,
now are, and have yet to go—images of group history, character, evolution, and destiny that have only to emerge to be fought over.

In Indonesia, such bending backward and forward at the same time
has been apparent from the beginning of the nationalist movement and
merely grown more marked since.[8] Sarekat Islam, the first really siz-
able organization (its membership increased from approximately four
thousand in 1912 to approximately four hundred thousand in 1914),
appealed at once to visionary mystics, Islamic purists, Marxist radicals,
trading-class reformers, paternal aristocrats, and messianic peasants.
When this commotion disguised as a party came to pieces, as it did in

[8] For the history of Indonesian nationalism, on which my remarks here are
but passing commentary, see J. M. Pluvier, *Overzicht van de Ontwikkeling der
Nationalistische Beweging in Indonesie in de Jaren 1930 tot 1942* (The Hague,
1953); A. K. Pringgodigdo, *Sedjarah Pergerakan Rakjat Indonesia* (Djakarta,
1950); D. M. G. Koch, *Om de Vrijheid* (Djakarta, 1950); Dahm, *Sukarno and the
Struggle;* G. McT. Kahin, *Nationalism and Revolution in Indonesia* (Ithaca,
1952); H. Benda, *The Crescent and the Rising Sun: Indonesian Islam under the
Japanese Occupation, 1942–1945* (The Hague, 1958); W. F. Wertheim, *Indonesian Society in Transition* (The Hague, 1956).

the twenties, it separated not into the "reactionary" and "progressive" wings of revolutionary mythology, but into a whole series of factions, movements, ideologies, clubs, conspiracies—what Indonesians call *aliran* (streams)—seeking to fasten one or another form of modernism on to one or another strand of tradition.

"Enlightened" gentry—physicians, lawyers, schoolteachers, sons of civil servants—attempted to marry "spiritual" East and "dynamic" West by fusing a sort of cultic aestheticism with an evolutionary, *noblesse oblige* program of mass uplift. Rural Koranic religious teachers sought to transform anti-Christian sentiments into anticolonial ones, and themselves into links between urban activism and village piety. Muslim modernists tried at once to purify popular faith of heterodox accretions and work out a properly Islamic program of social and economic reform. Left-wing revolutionaries sought to identify rural collectivism and political, peasant discontent and class struggle; Eurasian half-castes to reconcile their Dutch and Indonesian identities and provide a rationale for multiracial independence; Western-educated intellectuals to reconnect themselves to Indonesian reality by tapping indigenous, antifeudal (and to some extent anti-Javanese) attitudes in the interests of democratic socialism. Everywhere one looks, in the fevered days of the nationalist awakening (ca. 1912–1950), someone is matching advanced ideas and familiar sentiments in order to make some variety of progress look less disruptive and some pattern of custom less dispensable.

The heterogeneity of Indonesian culture and that of modern political thought thus played into one another to produce an ideological situation in which a highly generalized consensus at one level—that the country must collectively storm the heights of modernity while clinging, also collectively, to the essentials of its heritage—was countered on another by an accelerating dissensus as to what direction the heights should be stormed from and what the essentials were. After Independence, the fragmentation of the elite and the active sectors of the population along such lines was completed as the society regrouped into competing *familles d'esprit,* some huge, some minute, some in between, which were concerned not just with governing Indonesia but with defining it.

Thus, a paralyzing incongruity grew up between the ideological framework within which the formal institutions of the would-be powerhouse state were constructed and operated and that within which the overall political formation of the, also would-be, nation took shape; between the "blended, blended, blended" integralism of Guided Democracy, the Pantjasila, Nasakom, and the like, and the "boiling pot" com-partmentalization of popular sentiment.[9] The contrast was not a simple center and periphery one—integralism in Djakarta, compartmentalism in the provinces; but it appeared, and in not very different form, on all levels of the political system. From the village coffee shops where Sartono's peasants laid their small plans to the bureaus of Merdeka Square where Anderson's "ministeriales" laid their larger ones, political life proceeded in a curious kind of double-level way, in which a rivalry, again not just for power but for the power above power—the right to specify the terms under which direction of the state, or even mere official existence, is granted—went on, wrapped in the generous phrases of common struggle, historic identity, and national brotherhood.

That is, political life proceeded in this way until October 1, 1965. The bungled coup and its savage aftermath—perhaps a quarter of a million dead in three or four months—brought to open view the cultural disarray fifty years of political change had created, advanced, dramatized, and fed upon.[10] The wash of nationalist cliches soon

---

[9] For the state ideology of the Republic until the mid-sixties, see H. Feith, "Dynamics of Guided Democracy," in R. T. McVey, ed., *Indonesia* (New Haven, 1963), pp. 309–409; for popular divisions, R. R. Jay, *Religion and Politics in Rural Central Java*, Southeast Asia Studies, Cultural Reports Series no. 12 (New Haven, 1963); G. W. Skinner, ed., *Local, Ethnic and National Loyalties in Village Indonesia*, Southeast Asia Studies, Cultural Report Series no. 8 (New Haven, 1959); and R. W. Liddle, *Ethnicity, Party, and National Integration* (New Haven, 1970). The rather schizoid political atmosphere thus created can be sensed in the debates of the constitutional convention of 1957–1958; see *Tentang Dasar Negara Republik Indonesia Dalam Konstituante*, 3 vols. [Djakarta (?), 1958(?)].

[10] The death estimate is that of John Hughes, *The End of Sukarno* (London, 1968), p. 189. Estimates range from 50,000 to a million; no one really knows, and the killing was on so grand a scale that to debate numbers seems obtuse. Hughes' account of the coup, the massacres, and the ascendency of Suharto, though not very analytic, is probably as reliable and evenhanded as any. For other discussions, from varying points of view, see R. Shaplen, *Time Out of Hand* (New York, 1969); D. S. Lev, "Indonesia 1965: The Year of the Coup," *Asian Survey* 6, no. 2 (1966): 103–110; W. F. Wertheim, "Indonesia Before and After the Untung Coup," *Pacific Affairs* 39 (1966): 115–127; B. Gunawan, *Kudeta: Staatsgreep in Djakarta* (Meppel, 1968); J. M. van der Kroef, "Interpretations of the 1965 Indonesian Coup: A Review of the Literature," *Pacific Affairs* 43, no. 4 (1970–1971): 557–577; E. Utrecht, *Indonesie's Nieuwe Orde: Ontbinding en Herkolonisatie* (Amsterdam, 1970); H. P. Jones, *Indonesia: The Possible Dream* (New York, 1971); L. Rey, "Dossier on the Indonesian Drama," *New Left Review* (1966): 26–40; A. C. Brackman, *The Communist Collapse in Indonesia* (New York, 1969). To my mind, the literature on the coup, right, left, and center, has been marred by obsessive concern with the exact roles of Sukarno and of the Indonesian Communist Party in the immediate events of the plot (not unimportant issues, but more important for understanding the moment than for understanding the country), at the expense of its meaning for the development of Indonesian political consciousness.

clouded the scene again, for one can no more stare at the abyss than at the sun. But there can be very few Indonesians now who do not know that, however clouded, the abyss is there, and they are scrambling along the edge of it, a change of awareness which may prove to be the largest step in the direction of a modern mentality they have yet made.

V

Whatever social scientists might desire, there are some social phenomena whose impact is immediate and profound, even decisive, but whose significance cannot effectively be assessed until well after their occurrence; and one of these is surely the eruption of great domestic violence. The Third World has seen a number of these eruptions over the twenty-five years it has been coming into being—the partition of India, the Congo mutiny, Biafra, Jordan. But none can have been more shattering than the Indonesian, nor more difficult to evaluate. Since the terrible last months of 1965, all scholars of Indonesia, and especially those trying to penetrate the country's character, are in the uncomfortable situation of knowing that a vast internal trauma has shaken their subject but not knowing, more than vaguely, what its effects have been. The sense that something has happened for which no one was prepared, and about which no one yet quite knows what to say, haunts the essays [in the Holt volume], making them read, sometimes, like the *agon* of a play with the crisis left out. But there is no help for this: the crisis is still happening.[11]

Of course, some of the outward effects are clear. The Indonesian Communist Party, on its claims the third largest in the world, has been, at least for the present, essentially destroyed. There is military rule. Sukarno was first immobilized, then, with that controlled, relentless grace the Javanese call *halus,* deposed, and has since died. The "confronta-

[11] The fact that no one predicted the massacres has sometimes been instanced as an example of the futility of social science. Many studies did stress the enormous tensions and the potential for violence in Indonesian society. Moreover, anyone who announced before the fact that a quarter of a million or so people were about to be slaughtered in three months of rice-field carnage would have been regarded, and rightly, as having a rather warped mind. What this says about reason faced with unreason is a complicated matter; but what it does not say is that reason is powerless because not clairvoyant.

tion" with Malaysia has ended. The economic situation has markedly improved. Domestic security, at the cost of large-scale political detentions, has come to virtually the entire country for almost the first time since Independence. The flamboyant desperation of what now is called the "Old Order" has been replaced by the muted desperation of the "New Order." But the question "What has changed?" is still, when it refers to the culture, a baffling one. Surely, so great a catastrophe, especially as it mostly occurred in villages among villagers, can hardly have left the country unmoved, yet how far and how permanently it has been moved is impossible to say. Emotions surface extremely gradually, if extremely powerfully, in Indonesia: "The crocodile is quick to sink," they say, "but slow to come up." Both writings on Indonesian politics and those politics themselves are permeated right now with the inconfidence derived from waiting for that crocodile to come up.

In the history of comparable political seizures, however (and when one looks at the history of the modern world, they are easy enough to find), some outcomes seem more common than others. Perhaps the most common is a failure of nerve, a constriction of the sense of possibility. Massive internal bloodlettings like the American or the Spanish civil wars have often subjected political life to the sort of muffled panic we associate with psychic trauma more generally: obsession with signs, most of them illusory, that "it is about to happen again"; perfection of elaborate precautions, most of them symbolic, to see that it doesn't; and irremovable conviction, most of it visceral, that it is going to anyway— all resting, perhaps, on the half-recognized desire that it do so and to get it over with. For a society, as for an individual, an inner catastrophe, especially when it occurs in the process of a serious attempt to change, can be both a subtly addictive and a profoundly rigidifying force.

This is particularly so (and here the analogy—which, as public disasters refract through private lives, is not entirely an analogy—with individual response continues) when the truth of what has happened is obscured by convenient stories, and passions are left to flourish in the dark. Accepted for what they were, as terrible as they were, the events of 1965 could free the country from many of the illusions which permitted them to happen, and most especially the illusion that the Indonesian population is embarked as a body on a straight-line march to modernity, or that, even guided by the Koran, the Dialectic, the Voice in the Quiet, or Practical Reason, such a march is possible. Denied, by means of another cooked-up ideological synthesis, the half-suppressed memory of the events will perpetuate and infinitely widen the gulf between the processes of government and the struggle for the real. At an enormous cost, and one which need not have been paid, the Indonesians would seem to an outsider to have now demonstrated to themselves with convincing force the depth of their dissensus, ambivalence, and disorientation. Whether the demonstration has in fact been convincing to the insiders, for whom such revelations about themselves must inevitably be terrifying, is another question; indeed, it is the central question of Indonesian politics at this juncture of history. For all their before-the-storm quality, the studies in the [Holt] volume contribute, if not an answer, at least a sense of what the probabilities are.

However great a disruptive force the massacres may (or may not) have been, the conceptual matrix within which the country has been moving cannot have changed radically, if only because it is deeply embedded in the realities of Indonesian social and economic structure, and they have not. Java is still spectacularly overcrowded, the export of primary products is still the main source of foreign exchange, there are still as many islands, languages, religions, and ethnic groups as there ever were (even, now that West New Guinea has been added, a few more), and the cities are still full of intellectuals without places, the towns of merchants without capital, and the villages of peasants without land.[12]

Lev's lawyers, Abdullah's reformers, Liddle's politicians, Sartono's peasants, and Anderson's functionaries, as well as the soldiers who now police them, face the same range of problems with about the same range of alternatives and the same stock of prejudices as they did before the holocaust. Their frame of mind may be different—after such horrors it is hard to believe that it is not—but the society within which they are enclosed and the structures of meaning which inform it are largely the same. Cultural interpretations of politics are powerful to the degree that they can survive, in an intellectual sense, the events of politics; and their ability to do that depends on the degree to which they are well

[12] It should perhaps be remarked that the external parameters have also not changed very much—China, Japan, the United States, and the Soviet Union are still more or less where and what they were, and so, for that matter, are the terms of trade. If so-called outside factors seem to have been slighted in favor of so-called inside ones [in the Holt volume], it is not because they are considered unimportant, but because in order to have local effects they must first have local expressions, and any attempt to trace them beyond such expressions to their sources would, in studies of this scale, soon get out of hand.

326 THE INTERPRETATION OF CULTURES

grounded sociologically, not on their inner coherence, their rhetorical plausibility, or their aesthetic appeal. When they are properly anchored, whatever happens reinforces them; when they are not, whatever happens explodes them.

So what is written [in the Holt volume] is, if not predictive, still testable. The worth of these essays—the authors of which may or may not agree with my interpretation of their findings—will, in the long run, be determined less by their fit to the facts from which they are derived, though it is that which recommends them to our attention in the first place, than by whether they illumine the future course of Indonesian politics. As the consequences of the last decade appear in the next, we shall begin to see whether what has been said here about Indonesian culture is penetrating or wrongheaded, whether it enables us to construe what happens in terms of it or leaves us straining for understanding against the grain of what we thought was so. Meanwhile, we can only wait for the crocodile along with everyone else, recalling, as a bar to the sort of moral presumptuousness that neither Americans nor Indonesians are at this time very well positioned to affect, what Jakob Burckhardt, who perhaps deserves to be called the founder of thematic analysis, said in 1860 about the dubious business of judging peoples:

It may be possible to indicate many contrasts and shades of difference among different nations, but to strike the balance of the whole is not given to human insight. The ultimate truth with respect to the character, the conscience, and the guilt of a people remains for ever a secret; if only for the reason that its defects have another side, where they reappear as peculiarities or even as virtues. We must leave those who find pleasure in passing sweeping censures on whole nations, to do so as they like. The people of Europe can maltreat, but happily not judge one another. A great nation, interwoven by its civilization, its achievements, and its fortunes with the whole life of the modern world, can afford to ignore both its advocates and its accusers. It lives on with or without the approval of theorists.[13]

13 J. Burckhardt, *The Civilization of the Renaissance in Italy* (New York, 1954); orig. (1860), p. 318.

Chapter 12 / Politics Past, Politics Present: Some Notes on the Uses of Anthropology in Understanding the New States

I

In recent years, the main meeting ground of the various branches of learning which in some uncertain way make up the social sciences has been the study of the so-called Third World: the forming nations and tottering states of Asia, Africa, and Latin America. In this enigmatical setting, anthropology, sociology, political science, history, economics, psychology, as well as that oldest of our disciplines, soothsaying, have found themselves in the unfamiliar position of dealing severally with essentially the same body of data.

The experience has not always been a comfortable one. The meeting ground has often turned into a battleground, and the lines of professional demarcation have hardened: as Englishmen abroad are often more British than in London, so economists abroad are often more econometrical than at M.I.T. Then, too, a few of the more enthusiastic have abandoned their professions almost altogether for a kind of Alexandrian eclecticism which has produced some very strange hippogriffs indeed: Freud, Marx, and Margaret Mead in one ungainly package.

But the general effect has certainly been salutary. The sense of intellectual self-sufficiency, that peculiar conceptual and methodological arrogance which comes from dealing too long and too insistently with a pocket universe all one's own (the American business cycle; French party politics; class mobility in Sweden; the kinship system of some up-country African tribe), and which is perhaps the most formidable enemy of a general science of society, has been seriously, and I think permanently, shaken. The closed society has been as thoroughly exploded for most of those who have studied the new nations as it has for most of those who live in them. It is coming at last to dawn upon even the most isolationist-minded of such scholars that theirs is not only a special science, but a special science which cannot even function without a great deal of help from other special sciences previously despised. Here, anyway, the notion that we are all members of one another has made a certain measure of progress.

Among the more striking examples of this convergence from several directions upon the same body of material is the revival of interest in the structure and functioning of traditional states. In the past several years the need to develop a general political science of preindustrial societies in order to have, as the sociologist Frank Sutton has put it, "a base point from which to understand the transitional societies which crowd the present scene" has been felt with increasing intensity on a wide variety of quarters.[1] As the quarters have been various, so too have the responses. But Max Weber's half-century-old essay on patrimonialism in *Wirtschaft und Gesellschaft* is no longer the "isolated monument" that Sutton, writing only a decade or so ago, then rightly called it. It is now but one among a whole set of discourses, some more monumental than others and a few too monumental altogether, on the nature of government in, to have a word for them, peasant societies:

[1] F. X. Sutton, "Representation and the Nature of Political Systems," *Comparative Studies in Society and History* 2 (1959): 1–10.

societies with too many resemblances to our own for us to stigmatize them as primitive and too few for us to celebrate them as modern.

To simplify, there have been four major lines of attack developing over the last decade or so on this question of the nature of traditional politics.

First, there has been the revival, largely in the hands of Karl Wittfogel, of Marx's old notion of an Asiatic mode of production, now interpreted to be hydraulic agriculture, and of a radically despotic state—"total terror, total submission, total loneliness," in Wittfogel's broadsheet rhetoric—regarded as causally reflective of it.[2]

Second, there has been the work by social anthropologists, most of them British and virtually all of them Africanists, on the so-called segmentary states—states in which kinship groups and kinship loyalties play a central role—and which, quite contrary to the monolithic view of traditional states that emerges from the Wittfogel approach, sees such states as delicate balances among scattered centers of semi-independent power, now building up under the guidance of tribal myth and civic ritual toward some apical point, now sliding away into clan jealousy, local rivalry, and fraternal intrigue.[3]

Third, there has been a renewed emphasis on what might be called comparative feudalism, on the question of whether feudalism is an historical category with one, itself rather unhomogeneous, instance, the European, or a scientific category with many at least roughly similar instances. Here, the motive figure is beyond doubt Marc Bloch, the depth of whose impact upon the social sciences is still not fully appreciated, even by many of those upon whom the impact has been exercised.[4] But this interest is also, of course, the main continuation of the Weberian tradition, and in the hands of a sociologist like Eisenstadt with his interest in the role of bureaucracy in early empires, or of an economic historian like Karl Polanyi with his interest in the political management of commercial activity in such empires, it widens out beyond feudalism proper to concern itself with the range of authority structures found in societies in which feudalization is only one of a number, but a limited number, of institutional possibilities.[5]

[2] K. Wittfogel, *Oriental Despotism* (New Haven, 1957).
[3] For a representative example of this line of thought, see A. Southall, *Alur Society* (Cambridge, England, 1954).
[4] R. Coulburn, ed., *Feudalism in History* (Princeton, 1956), presents a useful review of such studies. For M. Bloch, see his *Feudal Society* (Chicago, 1961).
[5] S. M. Eisenstadt, *The Political Systems of Empires* (New York, 1963); K. Polanyi, C. Arensberg, and H. Pearson, eds., *Trade and Markets in Early Empires* (Glencoe, Ill., 1957).

And fourth, there has been the reconsideration among prehistorians —archeologists mostly, but some orientalists and ethnologists as well— of the size and scope of ancient states and of the developmental stages through which those states seem to have passed. Maya, Teotihuacan, Indus, Angkor, Madjapahit, Inca, Mesopotamia, Egypt—all the magical names—stand less these days for glittering bronze-age barbarisms born adult out of Gordon Childe's "Urban Revolution" and more for extended, gradualistic developmental cycles, some of them similar, some of them different. Or, rather, they stand for phases, momentary ones often, in such cycles; phases which may have been both less grandiose than their legends proclaim or their architectural remains seem at first glance to indicate, and more complexly related to the material conditions upon which they rested than Marxist theorists, even revisionist Marxist theorists, usually imagine.[6]

Anthropologists have been deeply involved in all four of these lines of attack upon the nature of government in peasant societies. Two of them—the study of segmentary states and of the developmental cycles of prehistorical states—have been almost exclusively anthropological. But Wittfogel's theories have had an enormous impact as well. We have had applications of them by anthropologists to Tibet, the Valley of Mexico, the Pueblos of the Southwestern United States, and certain parts of Africa. The comparative-institutions approach has been less frequently pursued, partly because Weber tends to frighten anthropologists, but his fine Germanic hand can be seen quite clearly in a number of recent studies of some of the more developed of black African states —Buganda, Busoga, Fulani, Ethiopia, Ashanti.

In becoming thus involved, anthropologists have, as I have suggested, been drawn willy-nilly into an enterprise far wider than the confines of their own discipline and so find themselves faced with the unforeseen question of what, *qua* anthropologists rather than as self-made sociologists, historians, political scientists or whatever, they have to offer to this wider enterprise. The easy answer to this, still preferred in certain circles, is data, preferably anomalous data which will demolish some sociologist's high-wrought theory. But to accept that answer is to reduce anthropology to a kind of spiteful ethnography, capable, like some literary censor, of disapproving of intellectual constructions but not of creating, or perhaps even of understanding, any.

[6] For a survey and examination of such work, see R. Braidwood and G. Willey, *Courses toward Urban Life* (New York, 1962). See also R. M. Adams, *The Evolution of Urban Society* (New York/Chicago, 1966).

With respect to Professor Sutton's large vision of "a general comparative political science of pre-industrial societies," I, for one, think it can contribute more than that. And in order to indicate (certainly not, in the space available to me here, to establish) what sort of thing that "more" might be, I want to do two things which are quintessentially anthropological: to discuss a curious case from a distant land; and to draw from that case some conclusions of fact and method more far-reaching than any such isolated example can possibly sustain.

II

The distant land is Bali; the curious case the state as it existed there during the nineteenth century. Though in formal terms part of the Netherlands East Indies from, I suppose you would have to say, about 1750 on, Bali was in any realistic sense a part of the Dutch empire only after the invasion of the Southern part of the island in 1906. For all intents and purposes, the Balinese state in the nineteenth century was an indigenous structure; and although, like any social institution, it had changed over the course of the centuries—not the least as a result of the Dutch presence in Java, it had done so but slowly and marginally.

To simplify my description of what, in fact, totally resists simplification, I shall first discuss the cultural foundations of the state—the beliefs and values, for the most part religious ones, which animated it, gave it direction, meaning, and form; and second, I shall discuss the social structural arrangements, the political instruments, in terms of which it attempted, with but intermittent success, to sustain such direction and achieve such form. This separation between ideas and institutions will later turn out not to have been so merely pragmatic as it looks, however, but to have been the very axis of my argument.

In connection with the cultural foundations of the state, let me present briefly three Balinese notions of what, speaking now in the ethnographic present, supralocal politics are all about. The first of these I shall call the doctrine of the exemplary center; the second, the concept of sinking status; and the third, the expressive conception of politics—the conviction that the principal instrumentalities of rule lie less in the techniques of administration than in the arts of the theatre.

The doctrine of the exemplary center is in essence a theory of the nature and basis of sovereignty. This theory holds that the court-and-capital is at once a microcosm of supernatural order—"an image," as Robert Heine-Geldern has put it, "of the universe on a smaller scale"—and the material embodiment of political order.[7] It is not just the nucleus, the engine, or the pivot of the state: it *is* the state.

And this curious equation of the seat of rule with the dominion of rule is more than a passing metaphor, it is a statement of a ruling political idea: namely, that by the mere act of providing a model, a paragon, a faultless image of civilized existence, the court shapes the world around it into at least a rough facsimile of its own excellence. The ritual life of the court, and in fact the life of the court generally, is thus paradigmatic, not merely reflective of social order. What it is reflective of, as the priests declare, is the supernatural order, "the timeless Indian world of the gods" upon which men should, in strict proportion to their status, seek to pattern their lives.[8]

The crucial task of legitimation, the reconciliation of this political metaphysic with the actual distribution of power in classical Bali, was effected by means of a myth; characteristically enough a colonizing myth. In 1343, the armies of the great East Javanese kingdom of Madjapahit were supposed to have defeated, near a place called Gelgel, those of "the king of Bali," a supernatural monster with the head of a pig—a surpassing event in which the Balinese see the source of virtually their entire civilization, even (as, with but a handful of exceptions, they regard themselves as descendents of the Javanese invaders, not the ur-Balinese defenders) of themselves. Like the myth of "The Founding Fathers" in the United States, the myth of "The Madjapahit Conquest" became the origin tale by means of which actual relations of command and obedience were explained and justified.

Whatever scattered elements of genuine historicity this legend may have aside (and I have in any case given only the most schematized summary of what is a very involved and multiversioned tale indeed), it expresses in the concrete images of a just-so story the Balinese view of their political development. In Balinese eyes, the foundation of a Javanese court at Gelgel (where, it is held, the palace was designed to

---

[7] R. Heine-Geldern, "Conceptions of State and Kingship in Southeast Asia," *Far Eastern Quarterly* 2 (1942): 15–30.

[8] J. L. Swellengrebel, Introduction in J. L. Swellengrebel et al., *Bali: Life, Thought and Ritual* (The Hague/Bandung, 1960).

mirror in exact detail the palace of that most exemplary of exemplary centers, Madjapahit itself) created not just a center of power—that had existed before—but a standard of civilization. The Madjapahit Conquest was considered the great watershed of Balinese history because it cut off the ancient Bali of animal barbarism from the renascent Bali of aesthetic elegance and liturgical splendor. The transfer of the capital (and the dispatch of a Javanese noble, draped with magical paraphernalia, to inhabit it) was the transfer of a civilization, the establishment of a court which in the very act of reflecting divine order generated human order.

This reflection and this ordering were not, however, conceived to have maintained their purity and their force until the nineteenth century, but rather to have clouded and weakened as time passed. Despite the fact that they are both in a sense "colonial" myths, beginning with settlement from more cultured foreign shores, the Balinese conception of their political history does not, like the American, present a picture of the forging of unity out of an original diversity, but the dissolution of an original unity into a growing diversity; not a relentless progress toward the good society, but a gradual fading from view of a classic model of perfection.

This fading is conceived to have taken place both over space and through time. The notion, certainly incorrect, is that during the Gelgel period (from about 1300 to about 1700) Bali was ruled from a single capital, but that after that period a series of revolts and fissions took place leading to the establishment of capitals in each of the major regions as lesser members of the royal house fled to them to set up shop as exemplary rulers on their own. In turn, splinters from these splinters led to tertiary capitals in the regions of the various secondary capitals, and so on, if not quite *ad infinitum,* very nearly so.

Details aside, the final (that is, nineteenth century) result was an acrobat's pyramid of "kingdoms" of varying degrees of substantial autonomy and effective power, the main lords of Bali holding the paramount lord upon their shoulders and standing in turn upon the shoulders of the lords whose status was derivative for their own as theirs was from him, and so on down the line. The exemplary center among exemplary centers was still Gelgel, or rather its direct heir, Klungkung, its radiance dimming, naturally, as it diffused through this progressively coarser medium.

More than that, however, its own luster weakened as its pristine concentration of charisma, brought over as a package from Java, diffused out into these lesser centers. The general picture is one of an overall decline in status and spiritual power, not only of peripheral lines as they move away from the core of the ruling class, but of the core itself as the peripheral lines move away from it. Through the course of its development the exemplary force of the once unitary Balinese state weakened at its heart as it thinned at its edges. Or so the Balinese think; and it is this dying-fire view of history, which permeates actually into the very corners of Balinese society, that I refer to as the concept of sinking status.

Yet this was not felt to be an inevitable deterioration, a predestined decline from a golden age. For the Balinese, the decline was the way history had happened to happen, not the way it had had to happen. And the efforts of men, and especially of their spiritual and political leaders, ought consequently to be directed neither toward reversing it (which as events are incorrigible is impossible) nor celebrating it (which as it amounted to a series of retreats from an ideal would be pointless) but rather toward nullifying it, toward re-expressing directly, immediately, and with the greatest possible force and vividness the cultural paradigm by which the men of Gelgel and Madjapahit had in their time guided their lives. As Gregory Bateson has pointed out, the Balinese view of the past is not, in the proper sense of the term, really historical at all. For all their explanatory myth-making, the Balinese search the past not so much for the causes of the present as for the standard by which to judge it, for the unchanging pattern upon which the present ought properly to be modeled but, which through accident, ignorance, indiscipline, or neglect, it so often fails to follow.

This almost aesthetic correction of the present on the basis of what the past had at one point been, the lords sought to effect through the holding of great ceremonial *tableaux*. From the most petty to the most high they were continuously trying to establish, each at his own level, a more truly exemplary center, which if it could not match or even approach Gelgel in brilliance (and a few of the more ambitious hoped even for that) could at least seek to imitate it ritually and so re-create, to some degree, the radiant image of civilization the classic state had embodied and postclassic history had obscured.

The expressive nature of the Balinese state, and of the political life it supported, was apparent through the whole of its known history, for it was always pointed, not toward tyranny, whose systematic concentration of power it was hopelessly incompetent to effect, not even very method-

ically toward government, which it pursued indifferently and even hesi-
tantly, but rather toward spectacle, toward ceremony, toward the public
dramatization of the ruling obsessions of Balinese culture: social inequality and status pride. It was a theatre-state in which the kings and
princes were the impresarios, the priests the directors, the peasantry the
supporting cast, stage crew, and audience. The stupendous cremations,
teeth-filings, temple dedications, the pilgrimages and blood sacrifices,
mobilizing hundreds, even thousands of people and great quantities of
wealth, were not means to political ends, they were the ends themselves,
they were what the state was for. Court ceremonialism was the driving
force of court politics. Mass ritual was not a device to shore up the
state; the state was a device for the enactment of mass ritual. To govern
was not so much to choose as to perform. Ceremony was not form but
substance. Power served pomp, not pomp power.

Turning to the social framework which was designed to support this
effort but in fact acted more to undercut it, I shall have to be even more
ruthless in reducing facts to their shadows, for classical Balinese political institutions were about as complicated as such institutions can get
and still function. But the main point to grasp about the Balinese state
as a concrete structure of authority is that, far from conducing toward
the centralization of power, it conduced, and mightily, toward its dis-
persion. Very few political elites can have as intensely sought loyalty by
means so ingeniously designed to produce treachery as did the Balinese.

In the first place, the elite itself was, as I have indicated, not an organized ruling class, but a crowd of intensely competitive sovereigns, or
rather would-be sovereigns. Even noble lineages, the various royal
houses which formed the various courts, were not solidary units but
were faction-ridden factions, collections of sublineages and sub-sublin-
eages each intent on weakening the others to its own profit.

In the second place, most effective government in the proper sense of
the term was local. Hamlets not only had written constitutions, popular
councils, and executive arms, but they resisted, quite effectively, court
participation in local affairs. Irrigation was in the hands of a separate,
also local, corporate body, of which there were hundreds over the countryside; and rather than leading to the development of a centralized bureaucracy to manage waterworks this system effectively precluded the
emergence of such a bureaucracy. Local lineages, temple congregations,
voluntary groups were equally autonomous, equally jealous of their
rights vis-à-vis both one another and the state.

In the third place, the structural ties between the state (that is, any particular court) and this complex of local institutions (the "village," if you will) were themselves multiple and noncoordinate. The three main obligations laid by the gentry on the peasantry—military-ritual support, land rent, and taxation—were not fused but distributed among three different sorts of ties. A man might well owe ritual and military support to one lord, render rent to a second, and pay taxes to yet a third. Even worse, such ties were not, for the most part, territorially concentrated, so a man and his neighbor, who might well be his brother, could, and often did, owe political allegiance to different lords.

But to break this off before we disappear into the enchanted woods altogether, the point is that supralocal political organization in Bali did not consist in a neat set of hierarchically organized sovereign states, sharply demarcated from one another and engaged in "foreign relations" across well-drawn frontiers. Still less did it consist in any overall domination by a "single-centered apparatus state" under an absolute despot, "hydraulic" or otherwise. What it consisted in was an extended field of highly dissimilar political ties, thickening into nodes of varying size and solidity at strategic points on the landscape and then thinning out again to connect, in a marvelously convolute way, virtually everything with everything else.

The struggle at each point in this diverse and mobile field was more for men, for their deference, their support and their personal loyalty, than it was for land. Political power was embodied less in property than in people, was more a matter of the accumulation of prestige than of territory. The disagreements among the various princedoms were virtually never concerned with border problems but with delicate questions of mutual status and most especially with right to mobilize particular bodies of men, even particular men, for state ritual and (what was really the same thing) warfare.

Korn relates an anecdote concerning South Celebes, where political arrangements approximated those of Bali, which makes this point with the grave irony of traditional wit.[9] The Dutch, who wanted, for the usual administrative reasons, to get the boundary between two petty princedoms straight once and for all, called in the princes concerned and asked them where indeed the borders lay. Both agreed that the border of princedom *A* lay at the furthest point from which a man could still see the swamps, while the border of princedom *B* lay at the furthest point from which a man could still see the sea. Had they, then, never

[9] V. E. Korn, *Het Adatrecht van Bali* (The Hague, 1932), p. 440.

fought over the land in between, from which one could see neither
swamp nor sea? "Mijnheer," one of the old princes replied, "we had
much better reasons to fight with one another than these shabby hills."

In sum, nineteenth century Balinese politics can be seen as stretched
taut between two opposing forces; the centripetal one of state ritual and
the centrifugal one of state structure. On the one hand, there was the
unifying effect of mass ceremonial under the leadership of this or that
lord; on the other there was the intrinsically dispersive, segmental character of the polity considered as a concrete social institution, a power
system, composed as it was of dozens of independent, semi-independent,
and quarter-independent rulers.

The first, the cultural element, came from the top down, the center
outward; the second, the power element, came from the bottom up and
from the periphery inward. As a result, the broader the scope to which
exemplary leadership aspired, the more fragile the political structure
supporting it, for the more it was forced to rest on alliance, intrigue, ca-
jolery and bluff. The lords, pulled on by the cultural ideal of the consummately expressive state, strove constantly to extend their ability to
mobilize men and material so as to hold larger and more splendid ceremonies and larger and more splendid temples and palaces in which to
hold them.

In so doing they were working directly against a form of political organization whose natural tendency, especially under intensified pressures for unification, was toward progressive fragmentation. But, against
the grain or not, they struggled with this paradox of cultural megalo-
mania and organizational pluralism to the very end, and not always
without some degree of temporary success. Had not the modern world,
in the form of Dutch battalions, at length caught up with them, they
would, no doubt, be struggling with it still.

III

To redeem, now, my promise to generalize beyond the data, let me
make two points in conclusion about the contribution of anthropology
to a general comparative political science of peasant societies.

The first is that distinguishing the cultural ambitions of traditional states on the one hand and the social institutions in terms of which these cultural ambitions were, usually quite incompletely, realized on the other, makes for what we may call sociological realism. Professor Sutton's "base point" for understanding more recent developments becomes less a kind of retrospective ideal type, a model constructed to account for what its designer takes to be the more interesting features of the present, and more a historical reality rooted in its own time and place; the sort of thing out of which presents in the world, rather than merely in books, grow.

And second, this increase in sociological realism makes it possible to approach the central question in this area—what in fact *are* the relationships between the way in which New State polities behave and the way in which traditional ones behaved—without succumbing to either of two equally misleading (and, at the moment, equally popular) propositions: that contemporary states are the mere captives of their pasts, re-enactments in thinly modern dress of archaic dramas; or that such states have completely escaped their pasts, are absolute products of an age which owes nothing to anything but itself.

On the first point, it is apparent that the Balinese data, if they are as I say they are, support much better the segmentary state concept of traditional polities as consisting of unstable pyramids of power wreathed in symbols of a grandeur more wished for than achieved, than they do the "Despotic Power—Total and not Benevolent" vision of Wittfogel. But the question is not whether Wittfogel (who has been uncautious enough to quote Bali in support of his arguments) has given us a viable theory or not. I myself think not; but I don't want to try to counter assertions about China with facts about Bali. My argument is merely that in separating, as any close ethnographic study of actual traditional polities inevitably must separate, the ambitions of rulers, the ideas and ideals which pull them on toward some consummating end, from the social instrumentalities by means of which those ends are sought, anthropology contributes to the realization that, in traditional states as in modern ones, the reach of a politician is not quite the same thing as his grasp.

Thus stated, my message may seem the usual negative one for which anthropology is justly famous: "Not on Easter Island." In fact, I think the work on segmentary states, as well as that of the developmental archeologists, promises to make, has already made, an important contribution to a more just image of traditional polities, and along precisely the lines I have indicated. What Evans-Pritchard did for the Shilluk di-

vine king (disentangled his ritual role from his political and thus dissolved at least one African despotism into its true fragility) and a host
of scholars have done for the Maya (distinguished the splendid religious
edifice of the society from the rather more ordinary sort of shifting cul-
tivation community which underlay it, and thus resolved the paradox of
Byzantium in a jungle) is going to be done, I am sure, for more and
more traditional states with results which not only will not be negative
but will transform our whole conception of the sources of power, the
nature of authority, and the techniques of administration in such
states.[10]

But, so far as the politics past, politics present question is concerned,
my second point is the more significant. The conceptual separation of the
ideas of order by which the actors in any polity are guided and the institutional context within which they act makes it possible to approach
the issue of the relations between what once was and what now is with
more than reversible truisms—"There is nothing in the present but the
past"; "The past is a bucket of ashes"—to assist one. More specifically,
it makes it possible to distinguish the ideological contribution to a contemporary state of the cultural traditions to which it is heir from the organizational contribution to such a state of the systems of government
which preceded it, and to see that the former, the ideological contribution, is, with some exceptions, of much greater significance than the latter. As concrete governmental structures, today's Ghana, today's Indonesia, or even today's Morocco, have but the most distant of relations
with the institutions of the Ashanti Confederation, the Javano-Balinese
theatre-state, or that motley collection of bodyguards and tax farmers,
the Magrebine Makhzen. But as embodiments of one or another view of
what government and politics are all about, the relation between traditional states and transitional ones may be a great deal less distant
than the borrowed vocabularies within which Third World ideologies
are usually stated might lead one to believe.

As the cultural apparatus of a traditional state—the detailed myths,
the elaborate rituals, the high-wrought politesse—dissolves, as it has in
the majority of Third World states and doubtless will shortly in most of
the rest, it comes to be replaced by a rather more abstract, rather more

---

[10] On the Shilluk, E. E. Evans-Pritchard, *The Divine Kingship of the Shilluk
of the Nilotic Sudan* (Oxford, 1948). The Maya discussion is more scattered and
still developing, but for a useful summary, see G. Willey, "Mesoamerica," in
Braidwood and Willey, *Courses toward Urban Life,* pp. 84–101.

willed, and, in the formal sense of the term anyway, rather more reasoned set of notions concerning the nature and purpose of politics.
Whether written down in a formal constitution, built into a new set of
governmental institutions, or puffed up into a universal creed (or, as is
not uncommon, all three), these notions, which I would call ideology in
the proper sense of the term, play a similar role to the less-tutored,
preideological ones they have succeeded. That is to say, they provide a
guide for political activity; an image by which to grasp it, a theory by
which to explain it, and a standard by which to judge it. This carrying
forward into a more self-conscious, or anyway more explicit dimension,
of what were once but established attitudes and received conventions is
one of the central features of what we have come to call, half wistfully,
half worriedly, "nation building."

All this is not to say that the ideological frameworks within which
the Third World states operate are merely updated versions of the ideas
and ideals of the past. Their elites have clearly learned much from
other, quite nontraditional sources. Sukarno's close-up observation of
the Japanese in action was probably the most revelatory experience of
his career; we can assume that Nkrumah read at least some of those
tracts his successors so demonstratively burned; and one has only to
glance at the political publics of either India or Algeria to see that neither Harold Laski nor Jean-Paul Sartre have labored entirely in vain.

It is in fact just this confusion of the more recognizable voices of the
present with the stranger, but no less insistent voices of the past which
makes it so difficult to determine just what the politicians, civilian or
military, of any particular Third World state think they are up to. At one
moment they seem Jacobin beyond compare; at the next haunted by
ghosts as ancient and unshakable as the furies. At one moment they
seem to be so many self-taught Madisons and Jeffersons building ingenious political contrivances such as have never before been seen on land
or sea; at the next, so many preening Mussolinis erecting inferior imitations of the more comic-opera examples of European Fascism. At one
moment they seem confident possessors of a settled sense of direction,
full of hope and high purpose; at the next frantic opportunists, swept by
confusion, fear, and boundless self-hatred.

It will not do, however, either to plump for one or another side of
these several antinomies or merely to announce sagely that they are antinomies, that both sides are indeed present and the situation is complex. The mingled voices must be distinguished so that we can hear

what each of them is saying and assess the ideological climate, if not with very great assurance at least with some definiteness and circumstantiality.

In such an effort, the precise determination of the ideological contribution of politics past to politics present—in the case at hand, of exemplary leadership, waning charisma, and dramaturgical statecraft—is an essential element. And for the providing of this element, anthropology, to give one last rap on my drum, is ideally placed. At least it is if it can now remember what, on a Pacific island, it was so easy to forget: that it is not alone in the world.

PART V

Chapter 13/

The Cerebral Savage:

On the Work

of Claude Lévi-Strauss

> Today I sometimes wonder if I was not attracted to an-
> thropology, however unwittingly, by a structural affinity
> between the civilisations which are its subject matter
> and my own thought processes. My intelligence is neo-
> lithic.
>
> Claude Lévi-Strauss, *Tristes Tropiques*

I

What, after all, is one to make of savages? Even now, after three centuries of debate on the matter—whether they are noble, bestial, or even
as you and I; whether they reason as we do, are sunk in a demented
mysticism, or possessors of higher forms of truth we have in our avarice
lost; whether their customs, from cannibalism to matriliny, are mere alternatives, no better and no worse, to our own, or crude precursors of
our own now outmoded, or simply passing strange, impenetrable ex-
otica amusing to collect; whether they are bound and we are free, or we
are bound and they are free—after all this we still don't know. For the
anthropologist, whose profession it is to study other cultures, the puzzle
is always with him. His personal relationship to his object of study is,

perhaps more than for any other scientist, inevitably problematic. Know what he thinks a savage is and you have the key to his work. You know what he thinks he himself is and, knowing what he thinks he himself is, you know in general what sort of thing he is going to say about whatever tribe he happens to be studying. All ethnography is part philosophy, and a good deal of the rest is confession.

In the case of Claude Lévi-Strauss, Professor of Social Anthropology in the *Collège de France* and the center right now of a degree of general attention which men who spend their lives studying far-off peoples do not usually get, sorting out the spiritual elements from the descriptive is particularly difficult. On the other hand, no anthropologist has been more insistent on the fact that the practice of his profession has consisted of a personal quest, driven by a personal vision, and directed toward a personal salvation:

I owe myself to mankind just as much as to knowledge. History, politics, the social and economic universe, the physical world, even the sky, all surround me in concentric circles and I can only escape from those circles in thought if I concede to each of them some part of my being. Like the pebble which marks the surface of the wave with circles as it passes through it, I must throw myself into the water if I am to plumb the depths.

On the other hand, no anthropologist has made greater claims for ethnology as a positive science:

The ultimate goal of the human sciences is not to constitute man but to dissolve him. The critical importance of ethnology is that it represents the first step in a process which includes others. Ethnographic analysis tries to arrive at invariants beyond the empirical diversity of societies. . . . This initial enterprise opens the way for others . . . which are incumbent on the natural sciences: the reintegration of culture into nature and generally of life into the whole of its physico-chemical conditions. . . . One can understand, therefore, why I find in ethnology the principle of all research.

In Lévi-Strauss' work the two faces of anthropology—as a way of going at the world and as a method for uncovering lawful relations among empirical facts—are turned in toward one another so as to force a direct confrontation between them rather than (as is more common among ethnologists) out away from one another so as to avoid such a confrontation and the inward stresses which go with it. This accounts both for the power of his work and for its general appeal. It rings with boldness and a kind of reckless candor. But it also accounts for the more intraprofessional suspicion that what is presented as High Science may really be an ingenious and somewhat roundabout attempt to defend a metaphysical position, advance an ideological argument, and serve a moral cause.

There is, perhaps, nothing so terribly wrong about this, but, as with Marx, it is well to keep it in mind, lest an attitude toward life be taken for a simple description of it. Every man has a right to create his own savage for his own purposes. Perhaps every man does. But to demonstrate that such a constructed savage corresponds to Australian Aborigines, African Tribesmen, or Brazilian Indians is another matter altogether.

The spiritual dimensions of Lévi-Strauss' encounter with his object of study, what trafficking with savages has meant to him personally, are particularly easy to discover, for he has recorded them with figured eloquence in a work which, though it is very far from being a great anthropology book, or even an especially good one, is surely one of the finest books ever written by an anthropologist: *Tristes Tropiques*.[1] Its design is in the form of the standard legend of the Heroic Quest—the precipitate departure from ancestral shores grown familiar, stultifying, and in some uncertain way menacing (a philosophy post at a provincial *lycée* in Le Brun's France); the journey into another, darker world, a magical realm full of surprises, tests, and revelations (the Brazilian jungles of the Cuduveo, Bororo, Nambikwara, and Tupi-Kawahib); and the return, resigned and exhausted, to ordinary existence ("farewell to savages, then, farewell to journeying") with a deepened knowledge of reality and the obligation to communicate what one has learned to those who, less adventurous, have stayed behind. The book is a combination autobiography, traveler's tale, philosophical treatise, ethnographic report, colonial history, and prophetic myth.

For what, after all, have I learnt from the masters I have listened to, the philosophers I have read, the societies I have investigated and that very Science in which the West takes a pride? Simply a fragmentary lesson or two which, if laid end to end would reconstitute the meditations of [Buddha] at the foot of his tree.

The sea journey was uneventful, a prelude. Reflecting upon it twenty years later he compares his position to that of the classical navigators. They were sailing toward an unknown world, one hardly touched by mankind, a Garden of Eden "spared the agitations of 'history' for some

[1] *Tristes Tropiques* (Paris, 1955), translated minus several chapters into English by John Russell (New York, 1964).

ten or twenty millennia." He was sailing toward a spoiled world, one which these navigators (and the colonists who followed them) had destroyed in their greed, their cultural arrogance, and their rage for progress. Nothing was left of the terrestrial Garden but remnants. Its very nature had been transformed and had become "historical where it once was eternal, and social where it once was metaphysical." Once the traveler found civilizations radically different from his own awaiting him at the end of his journey. Now he finds impoverished imitations of his own, set off here and there by the relics of a discarded past. It is not surprising that he finds Rio disappointing. The proportions are all wrong. Sugar Loaf Mountain is too small, the bay is placed the wrong way round, the tropical moon seems overblown with only shanties and bungalows to set it off. He arrived as a delayed Columbus to make a flattening discovery: "The tropics are not so much exotic as out of date."

Ashore, the descent into the depths begins. The plot thickens, grows phantasmagorial, and arrives at a dénouement wholly unforeseen. There are no Indians in the outskirts of São Paulo as he had been promised in Paris by, of all people, the head of the *Ecole Normale*. Where in 1918 two-thirds of the state was marked on the map as "unexplored territory, inhabited only by Indians," not a single native Indian was left by 1935, when, in search of "a human society reduced to its basic expression," he took up his post as Professor of Sociology in the new university there. The nearest were several hundred miles away on a reservation; but they were not very satisfying. Neither true Indians nor true savages, "they were a perfect example of that social predicament which is becoming ever more widespread in the second half of the 20th century: they were 'former savages,' that is to say [ones] on whom civilisation had been abruptly forced; and, as soon as they were no longer 'a danger to society,' civilisation took no further interest in them." Nonetheless, the encounter was instructive, as all initiations are, for they disabused him of "the ingenuous and poetical notion of what is in store for us that is common to all novices in anthropology," and so prepared him to confront with more objectivity the less "contaminated" Indians with whom he was to have to do later.

There were four groups of these, each a little farther into the jungle, a little more untouched, a little more promising of final illumination. The Caduveo in the middle Paraguay intrigued him for their body tattoos in whose elaborate designs he thought he could see a formal repre-

sentation of their aboriginal social organization, by then largely de-
cayed. The Bororo, deeper into the forest, were rather more intact.
Their numbers had been radically reduced by disease and exploitation,
but they still lived in the old village pattern and struggled to maintain
both their clan system and their religion. Deeper yet, the childlike Nambikwara were so simple that he could find in their political organization
—a matter of small, constantly re-forming nomadic bands led by temporary chiefs—support for Rousseau's theory of the social contract.
And finally, near the Bolivian border, in "Crusoe country," gnosis appeared at last at hand in the form of the Tupi-Kawahib, who were not
only uncontaminated, but, the savant's dream, *unstudied:*

Nothing is more exciting for an anthropologist than the prospect of being
the first white man to penetrate a native community. . . . In my journey I
was to relive the experience of the travellers of old; at the same time I
should be faced with that moment, so crucial to modern thought, at which a
community, which had thought itself complete, perfected, and self-sufficient,
is made to realise that it is nothing of the kind. . . . The counter-revelation
in short: the fact that it is not alone in the world, that it is but part of a
vast human ensemble, and that to know itself it must first look at the unrec-
ognisable image of itself in that mirror of which one long-forgotten splinter
was about to give out, for myself alone, its first and last reflection.

With such great expectations it came then as a distinct disappointment that rather than providing a purified vision of primitivity these ultimate savages proved intellectually inaccessible, beyond his grasp. He,
quite literally, could not communicate with them.

I had wanted to pursue "the Primitive" to its furthest point. Surely my wish
has been gratified by these delightful people whom no white man had seen
before me, and none would ever see again? My journey had been enthralling
and, at the end of it, I had come upon "my" savages. But alas—they were
all too savage. . . . There they were, all ready to teach me their customs
and beliefs and I knew nothing of their language. They were as close to me
as an image seen in a looking-glass. I could touch, but not understand them.
I had at one and the same time my reward and my punishment, for did not
my mistake, and that of my profession, lie in the belief that men are not always men? That some are more deserving of our interest and our attention
because there is something astonishing to us in their manners. . . . No
sooner are such people known, or guessed at, than their strangeness drops
away, and one might as well have stayed in one's own village. Or if, as in
the present case, their strangeness remained intact, then it was no good to
me, for I could not even begin to analyse it. Between these two extremes,
what are the equivocal cases which afford us [anthropologists] the excuses

by which we live? Who is, in the end, the one most defrauded by the disquiet we arouse in the reader? Our remarks must be pushed a certain distance if we are to make them intelligible, and yet they must be cut off halfway, since the people whom they astonish are very like those for whom the customs in question are a matter of course. Is it the reader who is deceived by his belief in us? Or ourselves, who have not the right to be satisfied before we have completely dissolved that residuum which gave our vanity its pretext?

At the end of the Quest there waited thus not a revelation but a riddle. The anthropologist seems condemned either to journey among men whom he can understand precisely because his own culture has already contaminated them, covered them with "the filth, *our* filth, that we have thrown in the face of humanity," or among those who, not so contaminated, are for that reason largely unintelligible to him. Either he is a wanderer among true savages (of whom there are precious few left in any case) whose very otherness isolates his life from theirs or he is a nostalgic tourist "hastening in search of a vanished reality . . . an archaeologist of space, trying in vain to repiece together the idea of the exotic with the help of a particle here and a fragment of debris there." Confronted with looking-glass men he can touch but not grasp, and with half-ruined men "pulverised by the development of Western civilisation," Lévi-Strauss compares himself to the Indian in the legend who had been to the world's end and there asked questions of peoples and things and was disappointed in what he heard. "I am the victim of a double infirmity: what I see is an affliction to me; what I do not see a reproach."

Must the anthropologist therefore despair? Are we never to know savages at all? No, because there is another avenue of approach to their world than personal involvement in it—namely, the construction out of the particles and fragments of debris it is still possible to collect (or which have already been collected) of a theoretical model of society which, though it corresponds to none which can be observed in reality will nonetheless help us towards an understanding of the basic foundations of human existence. And this is possible because despite the surface strangeness of primitive men and their societies they are, at a deeper level, a psychological level, not alien at all. The mind of man is, at bottom, everywhere the same: so that what could not be accomplished by a drawing near, by an attempt to enter bodily into the world of particular savage tribes, can be accomplished instead by a standing back, by the development of a general, closed, abstract, formalistic science of thought, a universal grammar of the intellect. It is not by storming the citadels of savage life directly, seeking to penetrate their mental life phenomenologically (a sheer impossibility) that a valid anthropology can be written. It is by intellectually reconstituting the shape of that life out of its filth-covered "archaeological" remains, reconstructing the conceptual systems that, from deep beneath its surface, animated it and gave it form.

What a journey to the heart of darkness could not produce, an immersion in structural linguistics, communication theory, cybernetics, and mathematical logic can. Out of the disappointed romanticism of *Tristes Tropiques* arose the exultant sciencism of Lévi-Strauss' other major work, *La Pensée Sauvage* (1962).[2]

II

La Pensée Sauvage actually departs from an idea first set forth in *Tristes Tropiques* with respect to the Caduveo and their sociological tattoos: namely, that the totality of a people's customs always forms an ordered whole, a system. The number of these systems is limited. Human societies, like individual human beings, never create out of whole cloth but merely choose certain combinations from a repertoire of ideas anteriorly available to them. Stock themes are endlessly arranged and rearranged into different patterns: variant expressions of an underlying ideational structure which it should be possible, given enough ingenuity, to reconstitute. The job of the ethnologist is to describe the surface patterns as best he can, to reconstitute the deeper structures out of which they are built, and to classify those structures, once reconstituted, into an analytical scheme—rather like Mendeleev's periodic table of the elements. After that "all that would remain for us to do would be to re-

[2] An English translation (also not integral) has appeared as *The Savage Mind* (London, 1966). However, the translation (mercifully unattributed) is, unlike Russell's sensitive rendering of *Tristes Tropiques,* execrable, and I have for the most part made my own English versions rather than quote from it. Lévi-Strauss' collection of essays, *Anthropologie Structurale,* in which many of the themes of his more recent work first appeared, has been translated as *Structural Anthropology* (New York, 1963); his *Le Totémisme Aujourd'hui* (Paris, 1962), a sort of dry run for *La Pensée Sauvage,* as *Totemism* (Boston, 1963).

cognise those [structures] which [particular] societies had in fact adopted." Anthropology is only apparently the study of customs, beliefs, or institutions. Fundamentally it is the study of thought.

In *La Pensée Sauvage* this governing notion—that the universe of conceptual tools available to the savage is closed and he must make do with it to build whatever cultural forms he builds—reappears in the guise of what Lévi-Strauss calls "the science of the concrete." Savages build models of reality—of the natural world, of the self, of society. But they do so not as modern scientists do by integrating abstract propositions into a framework of formal theory, sacrificing the vividness of perceived particulars for the explanatory power of generalized conceptual systems, but by ordering perceived particulars into immediately intelligible wholes. The science of the concrete arranges directly sensed realities—the unmistakable differences between kangaroos and ostriches, the seasonal advance and retreat of flood waters, the progress of the sun or the phases of the moon. These become structural models representing the underlying order of reality as it were analogically. "Savage thought extends its grasp by means of *imagines mundi*. It fashions mental constructions which render the world intelligible to the degree that they contrive to resemble it."

This uncanonical science ("which we prefer to call 'primary' rather than 'primitive' ") puts a philosophy of finitude into practice. The elements of the conceptual world are given, prefabricated as it were, and thinking consists in fiddling with the elements. Savage logic works like a kaleidoscope whose chips can fall into a variety of patterns while remaining unchanged in quantity, form, or color. The number of patterns producible in this way may be large if the chips are numerous and varied enough, but it is not infinite. The patterns consist in the disposition of the chips vis-à-vis one another (that is, they are a function of the relationships among the chips rather than their individual properties considered separately). And their range of possible transformations is strictly determined by the construction of the kaleidoscope, the inner law which governs its operation. And so it is too with savage thought. Both anecdotal and geometric, it builds coherent structures out of "the odds and ends left over from psychological or historical process."

These odds and ends, the chips of the kaleidoscope, are images drawn from myth, ritual, magic, and empirical lore. (How, precisely, they have come into being in the first place is one of the points on which Lévi-Strauss is not too explicit, referring to them vaguely as the "residue of events . . . fossil remains of the history of an individual or a society.") Such images are inevitably embodied in larger structures—in myths, ceremonies, folk taxonomies, and so on—for, as in a kaleidoscope, one always sees the chips distributed in *some* pattern, however ill-formed or irregular. But, as in a kaleidoscope, they are detachable from these structures and arrangeable into different ones of a similar sort. Quoting Franz Boas that "it would seem that mythological worlds have been built up, only to be shattered again, and that new worlds were built from the fragments," Lévi-Strauss generalizes this permutational view of thinking to savage thought in general. It is all a matter of shuffling discrete (and concrete) images—totem animals, sacred colors, wind directions, sun deities, or whatever—so as to produce symbolic structures capable of formulating and communicating objective (which is not to say accurate) analyses of the social and physical worlds.

Consider totemism. Long regarded as an autonomous, unitary institution, a kind of primitive nature worship to be explained in terms of mechanical theories of one sort or another—evolutionist, functionalist, psychoanalytic, utilitarian—it is for Lévi-Strauss only a special case of this overall tendency to build conceptual schemes out of particular images.

In totemism, a logical parallel is (quite subconsciously) postulated between two series, one natural and one cultural. The order of differences between the terms on one side of the parallel is isomorphic with the order of differences between the terms on the other side. In the simplest case, the apparent physical differences between animal species—bear, eagle, turtle, and so forth—are put into correspondence with the sociological differences between social groups—clans *A, B, C,* and so on. It is not the specific characteristics of bear, eagle, and turtle as such which are critical—fox, rabbit, and crow would have served as well—but the sensible contrast between any pair of them. It is upon this that the savage seizes to represent intellectually to himself and to others the structure of his clan system. When he says that the members of his clan are descended from bear but those of his neighbor's from eagle, he is not giving forth with a bit of illiterate biology. He is saying, in a concrete metaphorical way, that the relationship between his clan and his neighbors is analogous to the perceived relationship between species. Considered term by term, totemic beliefs are simply arbitrary. "History" has cast them up and "history" may ultimately destroy them, alter their role, or replace them with others. But seen as an ordered set they become coherent, for they are able then to represent symbolically another sort of set similarly ordered: allied, exogamous, patrilineal clans. And the point is general. The relationship between a symbolic structure and its referent, the basis of its *meaning,* is fundamentally "logical," a coincidence of form—not affective, not historical, not functional. Savage thought is frozen reason and anthropology is, like music and mathematics, "one of the few true vocations."

Or like linguistics. For in language too the constituent units— phonemes, morphemes, words—are, from a semantic point of view, arbitrary. Why the French call a certain kind of animal *"chien"* and the English call it "dog," or why English forms its plurals by adding "s" and Malay forms its by doubling roots are not the sorts of questions linguists—structural linguists, at any rate—any longer consider it profitable to ask except in historical terms. It is only when language is ordered, by the rules of grammar and syntax, into utterances—strings of speech embodying propositions—that significance emerges and communication is possible. And in language too this guiding order, this *ur*-system of forms in terms of which discrete units are shuffled in such a way as to turn sound into speech, is subconscious. It is a deep structure which a linguist reconstitutes from its surface manifestations. One can become conscious of one's grammatical categories by reading linguistic treatises just as one can become conscious of one's cultural categories by reading ethnological ones. But, as acts, both speaking and behaving are spontaneous performances fed from underground springs. Finally, and most important, linguistic study (and, along with it, information theory and class logic) also defines its basic units, its constituent elements, not in terms of their common properties but their differences, that is, by contrasting them in pairs. Binary opposition—that dialectical chasm between plus and minus which computer technology has rendered the *lingua franca* of modern science—forms the basis of savage thought as it does of language. And indeed it is this which makes them essentially variant forms of the same thing: communications systems.

With this door open all things are possible. Not just the logic of totemic classifications but of any classificatory scheme at all—plant taxonomies, personal names, sacred geographies, cosmologies, hair styles among the Omaha Indians, or design motifs on Australian bull-roarers —can, *en principe,* be exposed. For they always trace down to an underlying opposition of paired terms—high and low, right and left, peace and war, and so on—expressed in concrete images, palpable concepts, "beyond which it is, for intrinsic reasons, both useless and impossible to go." Further, once certain of these schemas, or structures, are determined, they can then be related to one another—that is, reduced to a more general, and "deeper," structure embracing them both. They are shown to be mutually derivable from each other by logical operations —inversion, transposition, substitution: all sorts of systematic permutations—just as one transforms an English sentence into the dots and dashes of Morse code or turns a mathematical expression into its complement by changing all the signs. One can even move between different levels of social reality—the exchange of women in marriage, the exchange of gifts in trade, the exchange of symbols in ritual—by demonstrating that the logical structures of these various institutions are, when considered as communication schemes, isomorphic.

Some of these essays in "socio-logic" are, like the analysis of totemism, persuasive and enlightening as far as they go. (Inasmuch as any metaphysical content or affective aura these beliefs may have is vigorously excluded from attention, this is not really so very far.) Others, like the attempt to show that totemism and caste are capable ("by means of a very simple transformation") of being reduced to variant expressions of the same general underlying structure are at least intriguing if not precisely convincing. And others, like the attempts to show that the different ways in which horses, dogs, birds, and cattle are named form a coherent three-dimensional system of complementary images cross-cut by relations of inverted symmetry, are triumphs of self-parody. They are exercises in "depth interpretation" farfetched enough to make even a psychoanalyst blush. It is all terribly ingenious. If a model of society which is "eternal and universal" can be built up out of the debris of dead and dying societies—a model which reflects neither time, nor place, nor circumstance but (this from *Totemism*) "a direct expression of the structure of the mind (and behind the mind, probably of the brain)"—then this may well be the way to build it.

III

For what Lévi-Strauss has made for himself is an infernal culture machine. It annuls history, reduces sentiment to a shadow of the intellect, and replaces the particular minds of particular savages in particular jungles with the Savage Mind immanent in us all. It has made it possible

for him to circumvent the impasse to which his Brazilian expedition led
—physical closeness and intellectual distance—by what perhaps he always really wanted—intellectual closeness and physical distance. "I
stood out against the new tendencies in metaphysical thinking which
were then [i.e., in 1934] beginning to take shape," he wrote in *Tristes
Tropiques,* explaining his dissatisfaction with academic philosophy and
his turn towards anthropology.

Phenomenology I found unacceptable, in so far as it postulated a continuity
between experience and reality. That one enveloped and explained the other
I was quite willing to agree, but I had learnt . . . that there is no continuity
in the passage between the two and that to reach reality we must first repu-
diate experience, even though we may later reintegrate it into an objective
synthesis in which sentimentality plays no part.

As for the trend of thought which was to find fulfilment in existentialism,
it seemed to me to be the exact opposite of true thought, by reason of its in-
dulgent attitude toward the illusions of subjectivity. To promote private
preoccupations to the rank of philosophical problems is dangerous . . . ex-
cusable as an element in teaching procedure, but perilous in the extreme if
it leads the philosopher to turn his back on his mission. That mission (he
holds it only until science is strong enough to take over from philosophy) is
to understand Being in relation to itself, and not in relation to oneself.

The High Science of *La Pensée Sauvage* and the Heroic Quest of
Tristes Tropiques are, at base, but "very simple transformations" of one
another. They are variant expressions of the same deep underlying
structure: the universal rationalism of the French Enlightenment. For
all the apostrophes to structural linguistics, information theory, class
logic, cybernetics, game theory, and other advanced doctrines, it is not
de Saussure, or Shannon, or Boole, or Weiner, or von Neumann who is
Lévi-Strauss' real *guru* (nor, despite the ritual invocation of them for
dramatic effect, Marx or Buddha)—but Rousseau.

Rousseau is our master and our brother. . . . For there is only one way in
which we can escape the contradiction inherent in the notion of the position of the anthropologist, and that is by reformulating, on our own account, the intellectual procedures which allowed Rousseau to move forward
from the ruins left by the *Discours sur l'Origine de l'Inégalité* to the ample
design of the *Social Contract,* of which *Emile* reveals the secret. He it is
who showed us how, after we have destroyed every existing order, we can
still discover the principles which allow us to erect a new order in their
stead.

Like Rousseau, Lévi-Strauss' search is not after all for men, whom he
doesn't much care for, but for Man, with whom he is enthralled. It is,

as much in *La Pensée Sauvage* as in *Tristes Tropiques,* the jewel in the lotus he is after. The "unshakable basis of human society" is not really social at all but psychological—a rational, universal, eternal, and thus (in the great tradition of French moralism) virtuous mind.

Rousseau ("of all the *philosophes* the nearest to being an anthropologist") demonstrates the method by which the paradox of the anthropological traveler—who comes either too late to find savagery or too early to appreciate it—can at last be solved. We must, as he did, develop the ability to penetrate the savage mind by employing (to provide Lévi-Strauss with what he perhaps least needs, another *expression*) what might be called epistemological empathy. The bridge between our world and that of our subjects (extinct, opaque, or merely tattered) lies not in personal confrontation—which, so far as it occurs, corrupts both them and us. It lies in a kind of experimental mind reading. And Rousseau, "trying on [himself] modes of thought taken from elsewhere or merely imagined" (in order to demonstrate "that every human mind is a locus of virtual experience where what goes on in the minds of men, however remote they may be, can be investigated"), was the first to undertake it. One understands the thought of savages neither by mere introspection nor by mere observation, but by attempting to think as they think and with their materials. What one needs, aside from obsessively detailed ethnography, is a neolithic intelligence.

The philosophical conclusions which for Lévi-Strauss follow from this postulate—that savages can only be understood by reenacting their thought processes with the debris of their cultures—add up, in turn, to a technically reconditioned version of Rousseauian moralism.

Savage ("wild," "undomesticated") modes of thought are primary in human mentality. They are what we all have in common. The civilized ("tamed," "domesticated") thought patterns of modern science and scholarship are specialized productions of our own society. They are secondary, derived, and, though not unuseful, artificial. Although these primary modes of thought (and thus the foundations of human social life) are "undomesticated" like the "wild pansy"—that spectacularly untranslatable pun which gives *La Pensée Sauvage* its title—they are essentially intellectual, rational, logical, not emotional, instinctive, or mystical. The best—but in no sense perfect—time for man was the neolithic (i.e., postagricultural, preurban) age: what Rousseau (who, contrary to the usual stereotype of him, was not a primitivist) called *société naissante*. For it was then that this mentality flourished, producing, out of its "science of the concrete," those arts of civilization—

agriculture, animal husbandry, pottery, weaving, food conservation and preparation, and so on—which still provide the foundations of our existence.

It would have been better for man had he kept to this "middle ground between the indolence of the primitive state and the questing activity to which we are prompted by our *armour propre"*—instead of abandoning it, by some unhappy chance, for the restless ambitiousness, the pride and egoism, of mechanical civilization. But he *has* left it. The task of social reform consists in turning us again toward that middle state, not by drawing us back into the neolithic but by presenting us with compelling reminders of its human achievements, its sociological grace, so as to draw us forward into a rational future where its ideals —the balancing of self-regard with general sympathy—will be even more fully realized. And it is a scientifically enriched anthropology ("legitimizing the principles of savage thought and restoring them to their rightful place") which is the appropriate agency of such reform. Progress toward humanness—that gradual unfolding of the higher intellectual faculties Rousseau called *perfectibilité*—was destroyed by cultural parochialism, armed with a half-grown science. Cultural universalism, armed with a mature science, will once more set it in motion.

If [the human] race has so far concentrated on one task, and one alone— that of building a society in which Man can live—then the sources of strength on which our remote ancestors drew are present also in ourselves. All the stakes are still on the board, and we can take them up at any time we please. Whatever was done, and done badly, can be begun all over again: "The golden age [wrote Rousseau] which blind superstition situated behind or ahead of us is *in us.*" Human brotherhood acquires a palpable significance when we find our image of it confirmed in the poorest of tribes, and when that tribe offers us an experience which, when joined with many hundreds of others, has a lesson to teach us.

IV

But perhaps more interesting than this modernized profession of a classical faith in (to use Hooker's phrase) "the perpetual and general voice of men" is what the fate of such an attempt to set King Reason back upon his throne in the guise of the Cerebral Savage will be in today's world. However much it is set round with symbolic logic, matrix algebra, or structural linguistics, can we—after all that has happened since 1762—still believe in the sovereignty of the intellect?

After a century-and-a-half of investigations into the depths of human consciousness which have uncovered vested interests, infantile emotions, or a chaos of animal appetites, we now have one which finds there the pure light of natural wisdom that shines in all alike. It will doubtless be greeted, in some quarters, with a degree of welcome, not to say relief. Yet that such an investigation should have been launched from an anthropological base seems distinctly surprising. For anthropologists are forever being tempted—as Lévi-Strauss himself once was—out of libraries and lecture halls, where it is hard to remember that the mind of man is no dry light, into "the field," where it is impossible to forget it. Even if there are not many "true savages" out there any more, there are enough vividly peculiar human individuals around to make any doctrine of man which sees him as the bearer of changeless truths of reason—an "original logic" proceeding from "the structure of the mind"—seem merely quaint, an academic curiosity.

That Lévi-Strauss should have been able to transmute the romantic passion of *Tristes Tropiques* into the hypermodern intellectualism of *La Pensée Sauvage* is surely a startling achievement. But there remain the questions one cannot help but ask. Is this transmutation science or alchemy? Is the "very simple transformation" which produced a general theory out of a personal disappointment real or a sleight of hand? Is it a genuine demolition of the walls which seem to separate mind from mind by showing that the walls are surface structures only, or is it an elaborately disguised evasion necessitated by a failure to breach them when they were directly encountered? Is Lévi-Strauss writing, as he seems to be claiming in the confident pages of *La Pensée Sauvage,* a prolegomenon to all future anthropology? Or is he, like some uprooted neolithic intelligence cast away on a reservation, shuffling the debris of old traditions in a vain attempt to revivify a primitive faith whose moral beauty is still apparent but from which both relevance and credibility have long since departed?

Chapter 14 / Person, Time, and Conduct in Bali

The Social Nature of Thought

Human thought is consummately social: social in its origins, social in its functions, social in its forms, social in its applications. At base, thinking is a public activity—its natural habitat is the houseyard, the marketplace, and the town square. The implications of this fact for the anthropological analysis of culture, my concern here, are enormous, subtle, and insufficiently appreciated.

I want to draw out some of these implications by means of what might seem at first glance an excessively special, even a somewhat esoteric inquiry: an examination of the cultural apparatus in terms of which the people of Bali define, perceive, and react to—that is, think about—individual persons. Such an investigation is, however, special and esoteric only in the descriptive sense. The facts, as facts, are of little immediate interest beyond the confines of ethnography, and I shall summarize them as briefly as I can. But when seen against the background of a general theoretical aim—to determine what follows for the analysis of culture from the proposition that human thinking is essentially a social activity—the Balinese data take on a peculiar importance.

Not only are Balinese ideas in this area unusually well developed, but they are, from a Western perspective, odd enough to bring to light some

general relationships between different orders of cultural conceptualization that are hidden from us when we look only at our own
all-too-familiar framework for the identification, classification, and handling of human and quasi-human individuals. In particular, they point
up some unobvious connections between the way in which a people perceive themselves and others, the way in which they experience time, and
the affective tone of their collective life—connections that have an import not just for the understanding of Balinese society but human society generally.

The Study of Culture

A great deal of recent social scientific theorizing has turned upon an
attempt to distinguish and specify two major analytical concepts: culture
and social structure.[1] The impetus for this effort has sprung from a desire to take account of ideational factors in social processes without succumbing to either the Hegelian or the Marxist forms of reductionism. In
order to avoid having to regard ideas, concepts, values, and expressive
forms either as shadows cast by the organization of society upon the
hard surfaces of history or as the soul of history whose progress is but a
working out of their internal dialectic, it has proved necessary to regard
them as independent but not self-sufficient forces—as acting and having
their impact only within specific social contexts to which they adapt, by
which they are stimulated, but upon which they have, to a greater or
lesser degree, a determining influence. "Do you really expect," Marc
Bloch wrote in his little book on *The Historian's Craft,* "to know the
great merchants of Renaissance Europe, vendors of cloth or spices, mo-
nopolists in copper, mercury or alum, bankers of Kings and the Em-

[1] The most systematic and extensive discussions are to be found in T. Parsons
and E. Shils, eds., *Toward a General Theory of Action* (Cambridge, Mass., 1959);
and T. Parsons, *The Social System* (Glencoe, Ill., 1951). Within anthropology,
some of the more notable treatments, not all of them in agreement, include: S. F.
Nadel, *Theory of Social Structure* (Glencoe, Ill., 1957); E. Leach, *Political Systems of Highland Burma* (Cambridge, Mass., 1954); E. E. Evans-Pritchard, *Social Anthropology* (Glencoe, Ill., 1951); R. Redfield, *The Primitive World and Its
Transformations* (Ithaca, 1953); C. Lévi-Strauss, "Social Structure," in his *Structural Anthropology* (New York, 1963), pp. 277–323; R. Firth, *Elements of Social
Organization* (New York, 1951); and M. Singer, "Culture," in *International
Encyclopedia of the Social Sciences,* vol. 3 (New York, 1968), p. 527.

peror, by knowing their merchandise alone? Bear in mind that they were painted by Holbein, that they read Erasmus and Luther. To understand the attitude of the medieval vassal to his seigneur you must inform yourself about his attitude to his God as well." Both the organization of social activity, its institutional forms, and the systems of ideas which animate it must be understood, as must the nature of the relations obtaining between them. It is to this end that the attempt to clarify the concepts of social structure and of culture has been directed.

There is little doubt, however, that within this two-sided development it has been the cultural side which has proved the more refractory and remains the more retarded. In the very nature of the case, ideas are more difficult to handle scientifically than the economic, political, and social relations among individuals and groups which those ideas inform. And this is all the more true when the ideas involved are not the explicit doctrines of a Luther or an Erasmus, or the articulate images of a Holbein, but the half-formed, taken-for-granted, indifferently systematized notions that guide the normal activities of ordinary men in everyday life. If the scientific study of culture has lagged, bogged down most often in mere descriptivism, it has been in large part because its very subject matter is elusive. The initial problem of any science—defining its object of study in such a manner as to render it susceptible of analysis—has here turned out to be unusually hard to solve.

It is at this point that the conception of thinking as basically a social act, taking place in the same public world in which other social acts occur, can play its most constructive role. The view that thought does not consist of mysterious processes located in what Gilbert Ryle has called a secret grotto in the head but of a traffic in significant symbols —objects in experience (rituals and tools; graven idols and water holes; gestures, markings, images, and sounds) upon which men have impressed meaning—makes of the study of culture a positive science like any other.[2] The meanings that symbols, the material vehicles of thought, embody are often elusive, vague, fluctuating, and convoluted, but they are, in principle, as capable of being discovered through systematic empirical investigation—especially if the people who perceive them will

---

[2] G. Ryle, *The Concept of Mind* (New York, 1949). I have dealt with some of the philosophical issues, here passed over in silence, raised by the "extrinsic theory of thought," above, Chapter 3, pp. 55–61, and need now only re-emphasize that this theory does not involve a commitment to behaviorism, in either its methodological or epistemological forms; nor yet again to any disputation of the brute fact that it is individuals, not collectivities, who think.

cooperate a little—as the atomic weight of hydrogen or the function of the adrenal glands. It is through culture patterns, ordered clusters of significant symbols, that man makes sense of the events through which he lives. The study of culture, the accumulated totality of such patterns, is thus the study of the machinery individuals and groups of individuals employ to orient themselves in a world otherwise opaque.

In any particular society, the number of generally accepted and frequently used culture patterns is extremely large, so that sorting out even the most important ones and tracing whatever relationships they might have to one another is a staggering analytical task. The task is somewhat lightened, however, by the fact that certain sorts of patterns and certain sorts of relationships among patterns recur from society to society, for the simple reason that the orientational requirements they serve are generically human. The problems, being existential, are universal; their solutions, being human, are diverse. It is, however, through the circumstantial understanding of these unique solutions, and in my opinion only in that way, that the nature of the underlying problems to which they are a comparable response can be truly comprehended. Here, as in so many branches of knowledge, the road to the grand abstractions of science winds through a thicket of singular facts.

One of these pervasive orientational necessities is surely the characterization of individual human beings. Peoples everywhere have developed symbolic structures in terms of which persons are perceived not baldly as such, as mere unadorned members of the human race, but as representatives of certain distinct categories of persons, specific sorts of individuals. In any given case, there are inevitably a plurality of such structures. Some, for example kinship terminologies, are ego-centered: that is, they define the status of an individual in terms of his relationship to a specific social actor. Others are centered on one or another subsystem or aspect of society and are invariant with respect to the perspectives of individual actors: noble ranks, age-group statuses, occupational categories. Some—personal names and sobriquets—are informal and particularizing; others—bureaucratic titles and caste designations—are formal and standardizing. The everyday world in which the members of any community move, their taken-for-granted field of social action, is populated not by anybodies, faceless men without qualities, but by somebodies, concrete classes of determinate persons positively characterized and appropriately labeled. And the symbol systems which define these classes are not given in the nature of things

—they are historically constructed, socially maintained, and individually applied.

Even a reduction of the task of cultural analysis to a concern only with those patterns having something to do with the characterization of individual persons renders it only slightly less formidable, however. This is because there does not yet exist a perfected theoretical framework within which to carry it out. What is called structural analysis in sociology and social anthropology can ferret out the functional implications for a society of a particular system of person-categories, and at times even predict how such a system might change under the impact of certain social processes; but only if the system—the categories, their meanings, and their logical relationships—can be taken as already known. Personality theory in social-psychology can uncover the motivational dynamics underlying the formation and the use of such systems and can assess their effect upon the character structures of individuals actually employing them; but also only if, in a sense, they are already given, if how the individuals in question see themselves and others has been somehow determined. What is needed is some systematic, rather than merely literary or impressionistic, way to discover what *is* given, what the conceptual structure embodied in the symbolic forms through which persons are perceived actually is. What we want and do not yet have is a developed method of describing and analyzing the meaningful structure of experience (here, the experience of persons) as it is apprehended by representative members of a particular society at a particular point in time—in a word, a scientific phenomenology of culture.

Predecessors, Contemporaries, Consociates, and Successors

There have been, however, a few scattered and rather abstract ventures in cultural analysis thus conceived, from the results of which it is possible to draw some useful leads into our more focused inquiry. Among the more interesting of such forays are those which were carried out by the late philosopher-cum-sociologist Alfred Schutz, whose work represents a somewhat heroic, yet not unsuccessful, attempt to fuse influences stemming from Scheler, Weber, and Husserl on the one side with ones stemming from James, Mead, and Dewey on the other.[3] Schutz covered a multitude of topics—almost none of them in terms of any extended or systematic consideration of specific social processes—seeking always to uncover the meaningful structure of what he regarded as "the paramount reality" in human experience: the world of daily life as men confront it, act in it, and live through it. For our own purposes, one of his exercises in speculative social phenomenology—the disaggregation of the blanket notion of "fellowmen" into "predecessors," "contemporaries," "consociates," and "successors"—provides an especially valuable starting point. Viewing the cluster of culture patterns Balinese use to characterize individuals in terms of this breakdown brings out, in a most suggestive way, the relationships between conceptions of personal identity, conceptions of temporal order, and conceptions of behavioral style which, as we shall see, are implicit in them.

The distinctions themselves are not abstruse, but the fact that the classes they define overlap and interpenetrate makes it difficult to formulate them with the decisive sharpness analytical categories demand. "Consociates" are individuals who actually meet, persons who encounter one another somewhere in the course of daily life. They thus share, however briefly or superficially, not only a community of time but also of space. They are "involved in one another's biography" at least minimally; they "grow older together" at least momentarily, interacting directly and personally as egos, subjects, selves. Lovers, so long as love lasts, are consociates, as are spouses until they separate or friends until they fall out. So also are members of orchestras, players at games, strangers chatting on a train, hagglers in a market, or inhabitants of a village: any set of persons who have an immediate, face-to-face relationship. It is, however, persons having such relations more or less continuously and to some enduring purpose, rather than merely sporadically or incidentally, who form the heart of the category. The others shade over into being the second sort of fellowmen: "contemporaries."

Contemporaries are persons who share a community of time but not of space: they live at (more or less) the same period of history and have, often very attenuated, social relationships with one another, but they do not—at least in the normal course of things—meet. They are linked not by direct social interaction but through a generalized set of symbolically formulated (that is, cultural) assumptions about each oth-

[3] For an introduction to Schutz's work in this field, see his *The Problem of Social Reality*, Collected Papers, 1, ed. M. Natanson (The Hague, 1962).

er's typical modes of behavior. Further, the level of generalization involved is a matter of degree, so that the graduation of personal involvement in consociate relations from lovers through chance acquaintances
—relations also culturally governed, of course—here continues until
social ties slip off into a thoroughgoing anonymity, standardization, and
interchangeability:

Thinking of my absent friend A., I form an ideal type of his personality and
behavior based on my past experience of A. as my consociate. Putting a letter in a mailbox, I expect that unknown people, called postmen, will act in a
typical way, not quite intelligible to me, with the result that my letter will
reach the addressee within typically reasonable time. Without ever having
met a Frenchman or a German, I understand "Why France fears the rear-
mament of Germany." Complying with a rule of English grammar, I follow
[in my writings] a socially-approved behavior pattern of contemporary English-speaking fellow-men to which I have to adjust to make myself under-
standable. And, finally, any artifact or utensil refers to the anonymous fel-
low-man who produced it to be used by other anonymous fellow-men for
attaining typical goals by typical means. These are just a few of the examples but they are arranged according to the degree of increasing anonymity
involved and therewith of the construct needed to grasp the Other and his
behavior.[4]

Finally, "predecessors" and "successors" are individuals who do not
share even a community of time and so, by definition, cannot interact;
and, as such, they form something of a single class over against both
consociates and contemporaries, who can and do. But from the point of
view of any particular actor they do not have quite the same significance. Predecessors, having already lived, can be known or, more accurately, known about, and their accomplished acts can have an influence
upon the lives of those for whom they are predecessors (that is, their
successors), though the reverse is, in the nature of the case, not possible. Successors, on the other hand, cannot be known, or even known
about, for they are the unborn occupants of an unarrived future; and
though their lives can be influenced by the accomplished acts of those
whose successors they are (that is, their predecessors), the reverse is
again not possible.[5]

[4] Ibid., pp. 17–18. Brackets added, paragraphing altered.
[5] Where "ancestor worship" on the one side or "ghost beliefs" on the other are
present, successors may be regarded as (ritually) capable of interacting with their
predecessors, or predecessors of (mystically) interacting with their successors. But
in such cases the "persons" involved are, while the interaction is conceived to be
occurring, phenomenologically not predecessors and successors, but contemporaries, or even consociates. It should be kept clearly in mind that, both here and
in the discussion to follow, distinctions are formulated from the actor's point of

For empirical purposes, however, it is more useful to formulate these distinctions less strictly also, and to emphasize that, like those setting off consociates from contemporaries, they are relative and far from clear-cut in everyday experience. With some exceptions, our older consociates and contemporaries do not drop suddenly into the past, but fade more or less gradually into being our predecessors as they age and die, during which period of apprentice ancestorhood we may have some effect upon them, as children so often shape the closing phases of their parents' lives. And our younger consociates and contemporaries grow gradually into becoming our successors, so that those of us who live long enough often have the dubious privilege of knowing who is to replace us and even occasionally having some glancing influence upon the direction of his growth. "Consociates," "contemporaries," "predecessors," and "successors" are best seen not as pigeonholes into which individuals distribute one another for classificatory purposes, but as indicating certain general and not altogether distinct, matter-of-fact relationships which individuals conceive to obtain between themselves and others.

But again, these relationships are not perceived purely as such; they are grasped only through the agency of cultural formulations of them. And, being culturally formulated, their precise character differs from society to society as the inventory of available culture patterns differs; from situation to situation within a single society as different patterns among the plurality of those which are available are deemed appropriate for application; and from actor to actor within similar situations as idiosyncratic habits, preferences, and interpretations come into play. There are, at least beyond infancy, no neat social experiences of any importance in human life. Everything is tinged with imposed significance, and fellowmen, like social groups, moral obligations, political institutions, or ecological conditions are apprehended only through a screen of significant symbols which are the vehicles of their objectification, a screen that is therefore very far from being neutral with respect to their "real" nature. Consociates, contemporaries, predecessors, and successors are as much made as born.[6]

---

view, not from that of an outside, third-person observer. For the place of actor-oriented (sometimes miscalled "subjective") constructs in the social sciences, see, T. Parsons, *The Structure of Social Action* (Glencoe, Ill., 1937), especially the chapters on Max Weber's methodological writings.

[6] It is in this regard that the consociate-contemporary-predecessor-successor formulation differs critically from at least some versions of the *umwelt-mitwelt-vorwelt-vogelwelt* formulation from which it derives, for there is no question here

Balinese Orders of Person-Definition

In Bali,[7] there are six sorts of labels which one person can apply to another in order to identify him as a unique individual and which I want to consider against this general conceptual background: (1) personal names; (2) birth order names; (3) kinship terms; (4) teknonyms; (5) status titles (usually called "caste names" in the literature on Bali); and (6) public titles, by which I mean quasi-occupational titles borne by chiefs, rulers, priests, and gods. These various labels are not, in most cases, employed simultaneously, but alternatively, depending upon the situation and sometimes the individual. They are not, also, all the sorts of such labels ever used; but they are the only ones which are generally recognized and regularly applied. And as each sort consists not of a mere collection of useful tags but of a distinct and bounded terminological system, I shall refer to them as "symbolic orders of person-definition" and consider them first serially, only later as a more or less coherent cluster.

PERSONAL NAMES

The symbolic order defined by personal names is the simplest to describe because it is in formal terms the least complex and in social ones the least important. All Balinese have personal names, but they

---

of apodictic deliverances of "transcendental subjectivity" à la Husserl but rather of socio-psychologically developed and historically transmitted "forms of understanding" à la Weber. For an extended, if somewhat indecisive, discussion of this contrast, see M. Merleau-Ponty, "Phenomenology and the Sciences of Man," in his *The Primacy of Perception* (Evanston, 1964), pp. 43–55.

[7] In the following discussion, I shall be forced to schematize Balinese practices severely and to represent them as being much more homogeneous and rather more consistent than they really are. In particular, categorical statements, of either a positive or negative variety ("All Balinese . . ."; "No Balinese . . ."), must be read as having attached to them the implicit qualification ". . . so far as my knowledge goes," and even sometimes as riding roughshod over exceptions deemed to be "abnormal." Ethnographically fuller presentations of some of the data here summarized can be found in H. and C. Geertz, "Teknonymy in Bali: Parenthood, Age-Grading, and Genealogical Amnesia," *Journal of the Royal Anthropological Institute* 94 (part 2) (1964):94–108; C. Geertz, "Tihingan: A Balinese Village," *Bijdragen tot de taal-, land- en volkenkunde,* 120 (1964):1–33; and C. Geertz, "Form and Variation in Balinese Village Structure," *American Anthropologist* 61 (1959):991–1012.

rarely use them, either to refer to themselves or others or in addressing anyone. (With respect to one's forebears, including one's parents, it is in fact sacrilegious to use them.) Children are more often referred to and on occasion even addressed by their personal names. Such names are therefore sometimes called "child" or "little" names, though once they are ritually bestowed 105 days after birth, they are maintained unchanged through the whole course of a man's life. In general, personal names are seldom heard and play very little public role.

Yet, despite this social marginality, the personal-naming system has some characteristics which, in a rather left-handed way, are extremely significant for an understanding of Balinese ideas of personhood. First, personal names are, at least among the commoners (some 90 percent of the population), arbitrarily coined nonsense syllables. They are not drawn from any established pool of names which might lend to them any secondary significance as being "common" or "unusual," as reflecting someone's being named "after" someone—an ancestor, a friend of the parents, a famous personage—or as being propitious, suitable, characteristic of a group or region, indicating a kinship relation, and so forth.[8] Second, the duplication of personal names within a single community—that is, a politically unified, nucleated settlement—is studiously avoided. Such a settlement (called a *bandjar,* or "hamlet") is the primary face-to-face group outside the purely domestic realm of the family, and in some respects is even more intimate. Usually highly endogamous and always highly corporate, the hamlet is the Balinese world of consociates par excellence; and, within it, every person possesses, however unstressed on the social level, at least the rudiments of a completely unique cultural identity. Third, personal names are monomials, and so do not indicate familial connections, or in fact membership in any sort of group whatsoever. And, finally, there are (a few rare, and in any case only partial, exceptions aside) no nicknames, no epithets of the "Richard-the-Lion-Hearted" or "Ivan-the-Terrible" sort among the no-

[8] While personal names of commoners are mere inventions, meaningless in themselves, those of the gentry are often drawn from Sanskrit sources and "mean" something, usually something rather high-flown, like "virtuous warrior" or "courageous scholar." But this meaning is ornamental rather than denotative, and in most cases what the meaning of the name is (as opposed to the simple fact that it has one) is not actually known. This contrast between mere babble among the peasantry and empty grandiloquence among the gentry is not without cultural significance, but its significance lies mainly in the area of the expression and perception of social inequality, not of personal identity.

bility, not even any diminutives for children or pet names for lovers, spouses, and so on.

Thus, whatever role the symbolic order of person-definition marked out by the personal-naming system plays in setting Balinese off from one another or in ordering Balinese social relations is essentially residual in nature. One's name is what remains to one when all the other socially much more salient cultural labels attached to one's person are removed. As the virtually religious avoidance of its direct use indicates, a personal name is an intensely private matter. Indeed, toward the end of a man's life, when he is but a step away from being the deity he will become after his death and cremation, only he (or he and a few equally aged friends) may any longer know what in fact it is; when he disappears it disappears with him. In the well-lit world of everyday life, the purely personal part of an individual's cultural definition, that which in the context of the immediate consociate community is most fully and completely his, and his alone, is highly muted. And with it are muted the more idiosyncratic, merely biographical, and, consequently, transient aspects of his existence as a human being (what, in our more egoistic framework, we call his "personality") in favor of some rather more typical, highly conventionalized, and, consequently, enduring ones.

BIRTH ORDER NAMES

The most elementary of such more standardized labels are those automatically bestowed upon a child, even a stillborn one, at the instant of its birth, according to whether it is the first, second, third, fourth, etc., member of a sibling set. There is some local and status-group variation in usage here, but the most common system is to use *Wayan* for the first child, *Njoman* for the second, *Made* (or *Nengah*) for the third, and *Ktut* for the fourth, beginning the cycle over again with Wayan for the fifth, Njoman for the sixth, and so on.

These birth order names are the most frequently used terms of both address and reference within the hamlet for children and for young men and women who have not yet produced offspring. Vocatively, they are almost always used simply, that is, without the addition of the personal name: "Wayan, give me the hoe," and so forth. Referentially, they may be supplemented by the personal name, especially when no other way is convenient to get across which of the dozens of Wayans or Njomans in the hamlet is meant: "No, not Wayan Rugrug, Wayan Kepig," and so on. Parents address their own children and childless siblings address one another almost exclusively by these names, rather than by either personal names or kin terms. For persons who have had children, however, they are never used either inside the family or out, teknonyms being employed, as we shall see, instead, so that, *in cultural terms,* Balinese who grow to maturity without producing children (a small minority) remain themselves children—that is, are symbolically pictured as such—a fact commonly of great shame to them and embarrassment to their consociates, who often attempt to avoid having to use vocatives to them altogether.[9]

The birth order system of person-definition represents, therefore, a kind of *plus ça change* approach to the denomination of individuals. It distinguishes them according to four completely contentless appellations, which neither define genuine classes (for there is no conceptual or social reality whatsoever to the class of all Wayans or all Ktuts in a community), nor express any concrete characteristics of the individuals to whom they are applied (for there is no notion that Wayans have any special psychological or spiritual traits in common against Njomans or Ktuts). These names, which have no literal meaning in themselves (they are not numerals or derivatives of numerals) do not, in fact, even indicate sibling position or rank in any realistic or reliable way.[10] A Wayan may be a fifth (or ninth!) child as well as a first; and, given a traditional peasant demographic structure—great fertility plus a high rate of still-births and deaths in infancy and childhood—a Made or a Ktut may actually be the oldest of a long string of siblings and a Wayan the youngest. What they do suggest is that, for all procreating couples, births form a circular succession of Wayans, Njomans, Mades, Ktuts, and once again Wayans, an endless four-stage replication of an imperishable form. Physically men come and go as the ephemerae they are,

[9] This is, of course, not to say that such people are reduced in *sociological* (much less psychological) terms to playing the role of a child, for they are accepted as adults, if incomplete ones, by their consociates. The failure to have children is, however, a distinct handicap for anyone desiring much local power or prestige, and I have for my part never known a childless man who carried much weight in hamlet councils, or for that matter who was not socially marginal in general.

[10] From a merely etymological point of view, they do have a certain aura of meaning, for they derive from obsolete roots indicating "leading," "medial," and "following"; but these gossamery meanings have no genuine everyday currency and are, if at all, but very peripherally perceived.

but socially the *dramatis personae* remain eternally the same as new Wayans and Ktuts emerge from the timeless world of the gods (for infants, too, are but a step away from divinity) to replace those who dissolve once more into it.

KINSHIP TERMS

Formally, Balinese kinship terminology is quite simple in type, being of the variety known technically as "Hawaiian" or "Generational." In this sort of system, an individual classifies his relatives primarily according to the generation they occupy with respect to his own. That is to say, siblings, half-siblings, and cousins (and their spouses' siblings, and so forth) are grouped together under the same term; all uncles and aunts on either side are terminologically classed with mother and father; all children of brothers, sisters, cousins, and so on (that is, nephews of one sort or another) are identified with own children; and so on, downward through the grandchild, great-grandchild, etc., generations, and upward through the grandparent, great-grandparent, etc., ones. For any given actor, the general picture is a layer-cake arrangement of relatives, each layer consisting of a different generation of kin—that of actor's parents or his children, of his grandparents or his grandchildren, and so on, with his own layer, the one from which the calculations are made, located exactly halfway up the cake.[11]

Given the existence of this sort of system, the most significant (and rather unusual) fact about the way it operates in Bali is that the terms it contains are almost never used vocatively, but only referentially, and then not very frequently. With rare exceptions, one does not actually call one's father (or uncle) "father," one's child (or nephew/niece) "child," one's brother (or cousin) "brother," and so on. For relatives genealogically junior to oneself vocative forms do not even exist; for relatives senior they exist but, as with personal names, it is felt to demonstrate a lack of respect for one's elders to use them. In fact, even the referential forms are used only when specifically needed to convey some kinship information as such, almost never as general means of identifying people.

[11] In point of fact, the Balinese system (or, in all probability, any other system) is not purely generational; but the intent here is merely to convey the general form of the system, not its precise structure. For the full terminological system, see H. and C. Geertz, "Teknonymy in Bali."

Kinship terms appear in public discourse only in response to some question, or in describing some event which has taken place or is expected to take place, with respect to which the existence of the kin tie is felt to be a relevant piece of information. ("Are you going to Father-of-Regreg's tooth-filing?" "Yes, he is my 'brother.' ") Thus, too, modes of address and reference within the family are no more (or not much more) intimate or expressive of kin ties in quality than those within the hamlet generally. As soon as a child is old enough to be capable of doing so (say, six years, though this naturally varies) he calls his mother and father by the same term—a teknonym, status group title, or public title—that everyone else who is acquainted with them uses toward them, and is called in turn Wayan, Ktut, or whatever, by them. And, with even more certainty, he will refer to them, whether in their hearing or outside of it, by this popular, extradomestic term as well.

In short, the Balinese system of kinship terminology defines individuals in a primarily taxonomic, not a face-to-face idiom, as occupants of regions in a social field, not partners in social interaction. It functions almost entirely as a cultural map upon which certain persons can be located and certain others, not features of the landscape mapped, cannot. Of course, some notions of appropriate interpersonal behavior follow once such determinations are made, once a person's place in the structure is ascertained. But the critical point is that, in concrete practice, kin terminology is employed virtually exclusively in service of ascertainment, not behavior, with respect to whose patterning other symbolic appliances are dominant.[12] The social norms associated with kinship, though real enough, are habitually overridden, even within kinship-type groups themselves (families, households, lineages) by culturally better armed norms associated with religion, politics, and, most fundamentally of all, social stratification.

Yet in spite of the rather secondary role it plays in shaping the moment-to-moment flow of social intercourse, the system of kinship terminology, like the personal-naming system, contributes importantly, if indirectly, to the Balinese notion of personhood. For, as a system of significant symbols, it too embodies a conceptual structure under whose agency individuals, one's self as well as others, are apprehended; a conceptual structure which is, moreover, in striking congruence with those

---

[12] For a distinction, similar to the one drawn here, between the "ordering" and the "role-designating" aspects of kin terminologies, see D. Schneider and G. Homans, "Kinship Terminology and the American Kinship System," *American Anthropologist* 57 (1955):1195–1208.

embodied in the other, differently constructed and variantly oriented, orders of person-definition. Here, also, the leading motif is the immobilization of time through the iteration of form.

This iteration is accomplished by a feature of Balinese kin terminology I have yet to mention: in the third generation above and below the actor's own, terms become completely reciprocal. That is to say, the term for "great-grandparent" and "great-grandchild" is the same: *kumpi*. The two generations, and the individuals who comprise them, are culturally identified. Symbolically, a man is equated upwardly with the most distant ascendant, downwardly with the most distant descendant, he is ever likely to interact with as a living person.

Actually, this sort of reciprocal terminology proceeds on through the fourth generation, and even beyond. But as it is only extremely rarely that the lives of a man and his great-great-grandparent (or great-great-grandchild) overlap, this continuation is of only theoretical interest, and most people don't even know the terms involved. It is the four-generation span (i.e., the actor's own, plus three ascending or descending) which is considered the attainable ideal, the image, like our three-score-and-ten, of a fully completed life, and around which the kumpi-kumpi terminology puts, as it were, an emphatic cultural parenthesis.

This parenthesis is accentuated further by the rituals surrounding death. At a person's funeral, all his relatives who are generationally junior to him must make homage to his lingering spirit in the Hindu palms-to-forehead fashion, both before his bier and, later, at the graveside. But this virtually absolute obligation, the sacramental heart of the funeral ceremony, stops short with the third descending generation, that of his "grandchildren." His "great-grandchildren" are his kumpi, as he is theirs, and so, the Balinese say, they are not really junior to him at all but rather "the same age." As such, they are not only not required to show homage to his spirit, but they are expressly forbidden to do so. A man prays only to the gods and, what is the same thing, his seniors, not to his equals or juniors.[13]

Balinese kinship terminology thus not only divides human beings into generational layers with respect to a given actor, it bends these layers into a continuous surface which joins the "lowest" with the "highest" so that, rather than a layer-cake image, a cylinder marked off into six parallel bands called "own," "parent," "grandparent," "kumpi," "grand-

---

[13] Old men of the same generation as the deceased do not pray to him either, of course, for the same reason.

child," and "child" is perhaps more exact.[14] What at first glance seems a very diachronic formulation, stressing the ceaseless progression of generations is, in fact, an assertion of the essential unreality—or anyway the unimportance—of such a progression. The sense of sequence, of sets of collaterals following one another through time, is an illusion generated by looking at the terminological system as though it were used to formulate the changing quality of face-to-face interactions between a man and his kinsmen as he ages and dies—as indeed many, if not most such systems are used. When one looks at it, as the Balinese primarily do, as a common-sense taxonomy of the possible types of familial relationships human beings may have, a classification of kinsmen into natural groups, it is clear that what the bands on the cylinder are used to represent is the genealogical order of seniority among living people and nothing more. They depict the spiritual (and what is the same thing, structural) relations among coexisting generations, not the location of successive generations in an unrepeating historical process.

TEKNONYMS

If personal names are treated as though they were military secrets, birth order names applied mainly to children and young adolescents, and kinship terms invoked at best sporadically, and then only for purposes of secondary specification, how, then, do most Balinese address and refer to one another? For the great mass of the peasantry, the answer is: by teknonyms.[15]

As soon as a couple's first child is named, people begin to address and

[14] It might seem that the continuation of terms beyond the kumpi level would argue against this view. But in fact it supports it. For, in the rare case where a man has a ("real" or "classificatory") great-great-grandchild (*kelab*) old enough to worship him at his death, the child is, again, forbidden to do so. But here not because he is "the same age" as the deceased but because he is "(a generation) older"—i.e., equivalent to the dead man's "father." Similarly, an old man who lives long enough to have a great-great-grandchild kelab who has passed infancy and then died will worship—alone—at the child's grave, for the child is (one generation) senior to him. In principle, the same pattern holds in more distant generations, when, as the Balinese do not use kin terms to refer to the dead or the unborn, the problem becomes entirely theoretical: "That's what we'd call them and how we would treat them if we had any, which we never do."

[15] Personal pronouns are another possibility and might indeed be considered as a separate symbolic order of person-definition. But, in fact, their use also tends to be avoided whenever possible, often at the expense of some awkwardness of expression.

refer to them as "Father-of" and "Mother-of" Regreg, Pula, or whatever the child's name happens to be. They will continue to be so called (and to call themselves) until their first grandchild is born, at which time they will begin to be addressed and referred to as "Grandfather-of" and "Grandmother-of" Suda, Lilir, or whomever; and a similar transition occurs if they live to see their first great-grandchild.[16] Thus, over the "natural" four-generation kumpi-to-kumpi life span, the term by which an individual is known will change three times, as first he, then at least one of his children, and finally at least one of his grandchildren produce offspring.

Of course, many if not most people neither live so long nor prove so fortunate in the fertility of their descendants. Also, a wide variety of other factors enter in to complicate this simplified picture. But, subtleties aside, the point is that we have here a culturally exceptionally well developed and socially exceptionally influential system of teknonymy. What impact does it have upon the individual Balinese's perceptions of himself and his acquaintances?

Its first effect is to identify the husband and wife pair, rather as the bride's taking on of her husband's surname does in our society; except that here it is not the act of marriage which brings about the identification but of procreation. Symbolically, the link between husband and wife is expressed in terms of their common relation to their children, grandchildren, or great-grandchildren, not in terms of the wife's incorporation into her husband's "family" (which, as marriage is highly endogamous, she usually belongs to anyway).

This husband-wife—or, more accurately, father-mother—pair has very great economic, political, and spiritual importance. It is, in fact, the fundamental social building block. Single men cannot participate in the hamlet council, where seats are awarded by married couple; and,

---

[16] This use of a descendant's personal name as part of a teknonym in no way contradicts my earlier statements about the lack of public currency of such names. The "name" here is part of the appellation of the person bearing the teknonym, not, even derivatively, of the eponymous child, whose name is taken purely as a reference point and is without—so far as I can tell—any independent symbolic value at all. If the child dies, even in infancy, the teknonym is usually maintained unchanged; the eponymous child addresses and refers to his father and mother by the teknonym which includes his own name quite unself-consciously; there is no notion that the child whose name is embraced in his parents', grandparents', or great-grandparents' teknonyms is, on that account, any way different from or privileged over his siblings whose names are not; there is no shifting of teknonyms to include the names of favored or more able offspring, and so on.

with rare exceptions, only men with children carry any weight there. (In fact, in some hamlets men are not even awarded seats until they have a child.) The same is true for descent groups, voluntary organizations, irrigation societies, temple congregations, and so on. In virtually all local activities, from the religious to the agricultural, the parental couple participates as a unit, the male performing certain tasks, the female certain complementary ones. By linking a man and a wife through an incorporation of the name of one of their direct descendants into their own, teknonymy underscores both the importance of the marital pair in local society and the enormous value which is placed upon procreation.[17]

This value also appears, in a more explicit way, in the second cultural consequence of the pervasive use of teknonyms: the classification of individuals into what, for want of a better term, may be called procreational strata. From the point of view of any actor, his hamletmates are divided into childless people, called Wayan, Made, and so on; people with children, called "Father (Mother)-of"; people with grandchildren, called "Grandfather (Grandmother)-of"; and people with greatgrandchildren, called "Great-grandparent-of." And to this ranking is attached a general image of the nature of social hierarchy: childless people are dependent minors; fathers-of are active citizens directing community life; grandfathers-of are respected elders giving sage advice from behind the scenes; and great-grandfathers-of are senior dependents, already half-returned to the world of the gods. In any given case, various mechanisms have to be employed to adjust this rather too-schematic formula to practical realities in such a way as to allow it to mark out a workable social ladder. But, with these adjustments, it does, indeed, mark one out, and as a result a man's "procreative status" is a major element in his social identity, both in his own eyes and those of everyone else. In Bali, the stages of human life are not conceived in terms of the processes of biological aging, to which little cultural attention is given, but of those of social regenesis.

Thus, it is not sheer reproductive power as such, how many children one can oneself produce, that is critical. A couple with ten children is no more honored than a couple with five; and a couple with but a single child who has in turn but a single child outranks them both.

[17] It also underscores another theme which runs through all the orders of person-definition discussed here: the minimization of the difference between the sexes which are represented as being virtually interchangeable so far as most social roles are concerned. For an intriguing discussion of this theme, see J. Belo, *Rangda and Barong* (Locust Valley, N.Y., 1949).

What counts is reproductive continuity, the preservation of the community's ability to perpetuate itself just as it is, a fact which the third result of teknonymy, the designation of procreative chains, brings out most clearly.

The way in which Balinese teknonymy outlines such chains can be seen from the model diagram (Figure 1). For simplicity, I have shown only the male teknonyms and have used English names for the referent generation. I have also arranged the model so as to stress the fact that teknonymous usage reflects the absolute age not the genealogical order (or the sex) of the eponymous descendants.

As Figure 1 indicates, teknonymy outlines not only procreative sta-

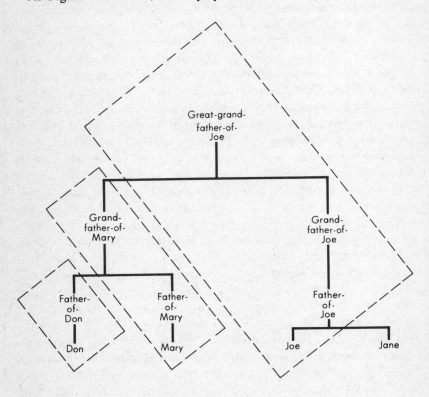

FIGURE 1

Balinese Teknonymy

NOTE: Mary is older than Don; Joe is older than Mary, Jane, and Don. The relative ages of all other people, save of course as they are ascendants and descendants, are irrelevant so far as teknonymy is concerned.

tuses but specific sequences of such statuses, two, three, or four (very, very occasionally, five) generations deep. Which particular sequences are marked out is largely accidental: had Mary been born before Joe, or Don before Mary, the whole alignment would have been altered. But though the particular individuals who are taken as referents, and hence the particular sequences of filiation which receive symbolic recognition, is an arbitrary and not very consequential matter, the fact that such sequences are marked out stresses an important fact about personal identity among the Balinese: an individual is not perceived in the context of who his ancestors were (*that,* given the cultural veil which slips over the dead, is not even known), but rather in the context of whom he is ancestral to. One is not defined, as in so many societies of the world, in terms of who produced one, some more or less distant, more or less grand founder of one's line, but in terms of whom one has produced, a specific, in most cases still living, half-formed individual who is one's child, grandchild, or great-grandchild, and to whom one traces one's connection through a particular set of procreative links.[18] What links "Great-grandfather-of-Joe," "Grandfather-of-Joe," and "Father-of-Joe" is the fact that, in a sense, they have cooperated to produce Joe—that is, to sustain the social metabolism of the Balinese people in general and their hamlet in particular. Again, what looks like a celebration of a temporal process is in fact a celebration of the maintenance of what, borrowing a term from physics, Gregory Bateson has aptly called a "steady state."[19] In this sort of teknonymous regime, the entire population is classified in terms of its relation to and representation in that subclass of the population in whose hands social regenesis now most instantly lies—the oncoming cohort of prospective parents. Under its aspect even that most time-saturated of human conditions, great-grandparenthood, appears as but an ingredient in an unperishing present.

[18] In this sense, birth order terms could, in a more elegant analysis, be defined as "zero teknonyms" and included in this symbolic order: a person called Wayan, Njoman, etc., is a person who has produced no one, who has, as yet anyway, no descendants.

[19] G. Bateson, "Bali: The Value System of a Steady State," in M. Fortes, ed., *Social Structure: Studies Presented to Radcliffe-Brown* (New York, 1963), pp. 35–53. Bateson was the first to point out, if somewhat obliquely, the peculiar achronic nature of Balinese thought, and my more narrowly focused analysis has been much stimulated by his general views. See also his "An Old Temple and a New Myth," *Djawa* (Jogjakarta) 17 (1937):219–307. [These have now been reprinted in J. Belo, ed., *Traditional Balinese Culture* (New York, 1970), pp. 384–402; 111–136.]

STATUS TITLES

In theory, everyone (or nearly everyone) in Bali bears one or another title—*Ida Bagus, Gusti, Pasek, Dauh,* and so forth—which places him on a particular rung in an all-Bali status ladder; each title represents a specific degree of cultural superiority or inferiority with respect to each and every other one, so that the whole population is sorted out into a set of uniformly graded castes. In fact, as those who have tried to analyze the system in such terms have discovered, the situation is much more complex.

It is not simply that a few low-ranking villagers claim that they (or their parents) have somehow "forgotten" what their titles are; nor that there are marked inconsistencies in the ranking of titles from place to place, at times even from informant to informant; nor that, in spite of their hereditary basis, there are nevertheless ways to change titles. These are but (not uninteresting) details concerning the day-to-day working of the system. What is critical is that status titles are not attached to groups at all, but only to individuals.[20]

Status in Bali, or at least that sort determined by titles, is a personal characteristic; it is independent of any social structural factors whatsoever. It has, of course, important practical consequences, and those consequences are shaped by and expressed through a wide variety of social arrangements, from kinship groups to governmental institutions. But to be a *Dewa,* a *Pulosari,* a *Pring,* or a *Maspadan* is at base only to have inherited the right to bear that title and to demand the public tokens of deference associated with it. It is not to play any particular role, to belong to any particular group, or to occupy any particular economic, political, or sacerdotal position.

The status title system is a pure prestige system. From a man's title you know, given your own title, exactly what demeanor you ought to display toward him and he toward you in practically every context of public life, irrespective of whatever other social ties obtain between you

[20] Neither how many different titles are found in Bali (though there must be well over a hundred) nor how many individuals bear each title is known, for there has never been a census taken in these terms. In four hamlets I studied intensively in southeastern Bali a total of thirty-two different titles were represented, the largest of which was carried by nearly two hundred and fifty individuals, the smallest by one, with the modal figure running around fifty or sixty. See C. Geertz, "Tihingan: A Balinese Village."

and whatever you may happen to think of him as a man. Balinese politesse is very highly developed and it rigorously controls the outer surface of social behavior over virtually the entire range of daily life.
Speech style, posture, dress, eating, marriage, even house-construction,
place of burial, and mode of cremation are patterned in terms of a precise code of manners which grows less out of a passion for social grace
as such as out of some rather far-reaching metaphysical considerations.

The sort of human inequality embodied in the status title system and
the system of etiquette which expresses it is neither moral, nor economic, nor political—it is religious. It is the reflection in everyday interaction of the divine order upon which such interaction, from this
point of view a form of ritual, is supposed to be modeled. A man's title
does not signal his wealth, his power, or even his moral reputation, it
signals his spiritual composition; and the incongruity between this and
his secular position may be enormous. Some of the greatest movers and
shakers in Bali are the most rudely approached, some of the most delicately handled the least respected. It would be difficult to conceive of
anything further from the Balinese spirit than Machiavelli's comment
that titles do not reflect honor upon men, but rather men upon their titles.

In theory, Balinese theory, all titles come from the gods. Each has
been passed along, not always without alteration, from father to child,
like some sacred heirloom, the difference in prestige value of the different titles being an outcome of the varying degree to which the men who
have had care of them have observed the spiritual stipulations embodied
in them. To bear a title is to agree, implicitly at least, to meet divine
standards of action, or at least approach them, and not all men have
been able to do this to the same extent. The result is the existing discrepancy in the rank of titles and of those who bear them. Cultural status, as opposed to social position, is here once again a reflection of distance from divinity.

Associated with virtually every title there are one or a series of
legendary events, very concrete in nature, involving some spiritually significant misstep by one or another holder of the title. These offenses—
one can hardly call them sins—are regarded as specifying the degree to
which the title has declined in value, the distance which it has fallen
from a fully transcendent status, and thus as fixing, in a general way at
least, its position in the overall scale of prestige. Particular (if mythic)
geographical migrations, cross-title marriages, military failures, breaches

of mourning etiquette, ritual lapses, and the like are regarded as having debased the title to a greater or lesser extent: greater for the lower titles, lesser for the higher.

Yet, despite appearances, this uneven deterioration is, in its essence, neither a moral nor an historical phenomenon. It is not moral because the incidents conceived to have occasioned it are not, for the most part, those against which negative ethical judgments would, in Bali any more than elsewhere, ordinarily be brought, while genuine moral faults (cruelty, treachery, dishonesty, profligacy) damage only reputations, which pass from the scene with their owners, not titles which remain. It is not historical because these incidents, disjunct occurrences in a once-upon-a-time, are not invoked as the causes of present realities but as statements of their nature. The important fact about title-debasing events is not that they happened in the past, or even that they happened at all, but that they are debasing. They are formulations not of the processes which have brought the existing state of affairs into being, nor yet of moral judgments upon it (in neither of which intellectual exercises the Balinese show much interest): they are images of the underlying relationship between the form of human society and the divine pattern of which it is, in the nature of things, an imperfect expression—more imperfect at some points than at others.

But if, after all that has been said about the autonomy of the title system, such a relationship between cosmic patterns and social forms is conceived to exist, exactly how is it understood? How is the title system, based solely on religious conceptions, on theories of inherent differences in spiritual worth among individual men, connected up with what, looking at the society from the outside, we would call the "realities" of power, influence, wealth, reputation, and so on, implicit in the social division of labor? How, in short, is the actual order of social command fitted into a system of prestige ranking wholly independent of it so as to account for and, indeed, sustain the loose and general correlation between them which in fact obtains? The answer is: through performing, quite ingeniously, a kind of hat trick, a certain sleight of hand, with a famous cultural institution imported from India and adapted to local tastes—the Varna System. By means of the Varna System the Balinese inform a very disorderly collection of status pigeonholes with a simple shape which is represented as growing naturally out of it but which in fact is arbitrarily imposed upon it.

As in India, the Varna System consists of four gross categories—

Brahmana, Satria, Wesia, and *Sudra*—ranked in descending order of prestige, and with the first three (called in Bali, *Triwangsa*—"the three peoples") defining a spiritual patriciate over against the plebeian fourth. But in Bali the Varna System is not in itself a cultural device for making status discriminations but for correlating those already made by the title system. It summarizes the literally countless fine comparisons implicit in that system in a neat (from some points of view all-too-neat) separation of sheep from goats, and first-quality sheep from second, second from third.[21] Men do not perceive one another as Satrias or Sudras but as, say, Dewas or Kebun Tubuhs, merely using the Satria-Sudra distinction to express generally, and for social organizational purposes, the order of contrast which is involved by identifying Dewa as a Satria title and Kebun Tubuh as a Sudra one. Varna categories are labels applied not to men, but to the titles they bear—they formulate the structure of the prestige system; titles, on the other hand, are labels applied to individual men—they place persons within that structure. To the degree that the Varna classification of titles is congruent with the actual distribution of power, wealth, and esteem in the society—that is, with the system of social stratification—the society is considered to be well ordered. The right sort of men are in the right sort of places: spiritual worth and social standing coincide.

This difference in function between title and Varna is clear from the way in which the symbolic forms associated with them are actually used. Among the Triwangsa gentry, where, some exceptions aside, teknonymy is not employed, an individual's title is used as his or her main term of address and reference. One calls a man *Ida Bagus, Njakan,* or *Gusi* (*not* Brahmana, Satria, or Wesia) and refers to him by the same terms, sometimes adding a birth order name for more exact specification (Ida Bagus Made, Njakan Njoman, and so forth). Among the Sudras, titles are used only referentially, never in address, and then mainly with respect to members of other hamlets than one's own, where the person's teknonym may not be known, or, if known, considered to be too familiar in tone to be used for someone not a hamletmate. Within the hamlet, the referential use of Sudra titles occurs only when prestige status information is considered relevant ("Father-of-Joe is a *Kedisan,* and

[21] Varna categories are often subdivided, especially by high-status persons, into three ranked classes—superior (*utama*), medium (*madia*), and inferior (*nista*)—the various titles in the overall category being appropriately subgrouped. A full analysis of the Balinese system of social stratification—as much Polynesian as Indian in type—cannot be given here.

thus 'lower' than we *Pande,*" and so on), while address is, of course, in terms of teknonyms. Across hamlet lines, where, except between close friends, teknonyms fall aside, the most common term of address is *Djero*. Literally, this means "inside" or "insider," thus a member of the Triwangsa, who are considered to be "inside," as against the Sudras, who are "outside" (*Djaba*); but in this context it has the effect of saying, "In order to be polite, I am addressing you as though you were a Triwangsa, which you are not (if you were, I would call you by your proper title), and I expect the same pretense from you in return." As for Varna terms, they are used, by Triwangsa and Sudra alike, only in conceptualizing the overall prestige hierarchy in general terms, a need which usually appears in connection with transhamlet political, sacerdotal, or stratificatory matters: "The kings of Klungkung are Satrias, but those of Tabanan only Wesias," or "There are lots of rich Brahmanas in Sanur, which is why the Sudras there have so little to say about hamlet affairs," and so on.

The Varna System thus does two things. It connects up a series of what appear to be ad hoc and arbitrary prestige distinctions, the titles, with Hinduism, or the Balinese version of Hinduism, thus rooting them in a general world view. And it interprets the implications of that world view, and therefore the titles, for social organization: the prestige gradients implicit in the title system ought to be reflected in the actual distribution of wealth, power, and esteem in society, and, in fact, be completely coincident with it. The degree to which this coincidence actually obtains is, of course, moderate at best. But, however many exceptions there may be to the rule—Sudras with enormous power, Satrias working as tenant farmers, Brahmanas neither esteemed nor estimable—it is the rule and not the exceptions that the Balinese regard as truly illuminating the human condition. The Varna System orders the title system in such a way as to make it possible to view social life under the aspect of a general set of cosmological notions: notions in which the diversity of human talent and the workings of historical process are regarded as superficial phenomena when compared with the location of persons in a system of standardized status categories, as blind to individual character as they are immortal.

PUBLIC TITLES

This final symbolic order of person-definition is, on the surface, the most reminiscent of one of the more prominent of our own ways of identifying and characterizing individuals.[22] We, too, often (all too often, perhaps) see people through a screen of occupational categories —as not just practicing this vocation or that, but as almost physically infused with the quality of being a postman, teamster, politician, or salesman. Social function serves as the symbolic vehicle through which personal identity is perceived; men are what they do.

The resemblance is only apparent, however. Set amid a different cluster of ideas about what selfhood consists in, placed against a different religio-philosophical conception of what the world consists in, and expressed in terms of a different set of cultural devices—public titles —for portraying it, the Balinese view of the relation between social role and personal identity gives a quite different slant to the ideographic significance of what we call occupation but the Balinese call *linggih*— "seat," "place," "berth."

This notion of "seat" rests on the existence in Balinese thought and practice of an extremely sharp distinction between the civic and domestic sectors of society. The boundary between the public and private domains of life is very clearly drawn both conceptually and institutionally. At every level, from the hamlet to the royal palace, matters of general concern are sharply distinguished and carefully insulated from matters of individual or familial concern, rather than being allowed to interpenetrate as they do in so many other societies. The Balinese sense of the public as a corporate body, having interests and purposes of its own, is very highly developed. To be charged, at any level, with special responsibilities with respect to those interests and purposes is to be set aside from the run of one's fellowmen who are not so charged, and it is this special status that public titles express.

At the same time, though the Balinese conceive the public sector of society as bounded and autonomous, they do not look upon it as form-

[22] The existence of one other order, that having to do with sex markers (*Ni* for women, *I* for men) ought at least to be mentioned. In ordinary life, these titles are affixed only to personal names (most of which are themselves sexually neutral) or to personal names plus birth order name, and then only infrequently. As a result, they are, from the point of view of person-definition, of but incidental importance, and I have felt justified in omitting explicit consideration of them.

ing a seamless whole, or even a whole at all. Rather they see it as consisting of a number of separate, discontinuous, and at times even competitive realms, each self-sufficient, self-contained, jealous of its rights, and based on its own principles of organization. The most salient of such realms include: the hamlet as a corporate political community; the local temple as a corporate religious body, a congregation; the irrigation society as a corporate agricultural body; and, above these, the structures of regional—that is, suprahamlet—government and worship, centering on the nobility and the high priesthood.

A description of these various public realms or sectors would involve an extensive analysis of Balinese social structure inappropriate in the present context.[23] The point to be made here is that, associated with each of them, there are responsible officers—stewards is perhaps a better term—who as a result bear particular titles: *Klian, Perbekel, Pekaseh, Pemangku, Anak Agung, Tjakorda, Dewa Agung, Pedanda,* and so on up to perhaps a half a hundred or more. And these men (a very small proportion of the total population) are addressed and referred to by these official titles—sometimes in combination with birth order names, status titles, or, in the case of Sudras, teknonyms for purposes of secondary specification.[24] The various "village chiefs" and "folk priests" on the Sudra level, and, on the Triwangsa, the host of "kings," "princes," "lords," and "high priests" do not merely occupy a role. They become, in the eyes of themselves and those around them, absorbed into it. They are truly public men, men for whom other aspects of personhood—individual character, birth order, kinship relations, procreative status, and prestige rank take, symbolically at least, a secondary position. We, focusing upon psychological traits as the heart of personal identity, would say they have sacrificed their true selves to their role; they, focusing on social position, say that their role is of the essence of their true selves.

Access to these public-title-bearing roles is closely connected with the system of status titles and its organization into Varna categories, a connection effected by what may be called "the doctrine of spiritual eli-

[23] For an essay in this direction, see C. Geertz, "Form and Variation in Balinese Village Structure."

[24] Place names associated with the function the title expresses are perhaps even more common as secondary specification: "Klian Pau," "Pau" being the name of the hamlet of which the person is klian (chief, elder); "Anak Agung Kaleran," "Kaleran"—literally "north" or "northern"—being the name (and the location) of the lord's palace.

gibility." This doctrine asserts that political and religious "seats" of translocal—regional or Bali-wide—significance are to be manned only by Triwangsas, while those of local significance ought properly to be in the hands of Sudras. At the upper levels the doctrine is strict: only Satrias—that is, men bearing titles deemed of Satria rank—may be kings or paramount princes, only Wesias or Satrias lords or lesser princes, only Brahmanas high priests, and so on. At the lower levels, it is less strict; but the sense that hamlet chiefs, irrigation society heads, and folk priests should be Sudras, that Triwangsas should keep their place, is quite strong. In either case, however, the overwhelming majority of persons bearing status titles of the Varna category or categories theoretically eligible for the stewardship roles to which the public titles are attached do not have such roles and are not likely to get them. On the Triwangsa level, access is largely hereditary, primogenitural even, and a sharp distinction is made between that handful of individuals who "own power" and the vast remainder of the gentry who do not. On the Sudra level, access to public office is more often elective, but the number of men who have the opportunity to serve is still fairly limited. Prestige status decides what sort of public role one can presume to occupy; whether or not one occupies such a role is another question altogether.

Yet, because of the general correlation between prestige status and public office the doctrine of spiritual eligibility brings about, the order of political and ecclesiastical authority in the society is hooked in with the general notion that social order reflects dimly, and ought to reflect clearly, metaphysical order; and, beyond that, that personal identity is to be defined not in terms of such superficial, because merely human, matters as age, sex, talent, temperament, or achievement—that is, biographically, but in terms of location in a general spiritual hierarchy—that is, typologically. Like all the other symbolic orders of person-definition, that stemming from public titles consists of a formulation, with respect to different social contexts, of an underlying assumption: it is not what a man is as a man (as we would phrase it) that matters, but where he fits in a set of cultural categories which not only do not change but, being transhuman, cannot.

And, here too, these categories ascend toward divinity (or with equal accuracy, descend from it), their power to submerge character and nullify time increasing as they go. Not only do the higher level public titles borne by human beings blend gradually into those borne by the gods,

becoming at the apex identical with them, but at the level of the gods
there is literally nothing left of identity but the title itself. All gods and
goddesses are addressed and referred to either as *Dewa* (f. *Dewi*) or, for
the higher ranking ones, *Betara* (f. *Betari*). In a few cases, these general
appellations are followed by particularizing ones: Betara Guru, Dewi
Sri, and so forth. But even such specifically named divinities are not
conceived as possessing distinctive personalities: they are merely
thought to be administratively responsible, so to speak, for regulating
certain matters of cosmic significance: fertility, power, knowledge,
death, and so on. In most cases, Balinese do not know, and do not want
to know, which gods and goddesses are those worshipped in their various temples (there is always a pair, one male, one female), but merely
call them *"Dewa (Dewi) Pura* Such-and-Such"—god (goddess) of temple such-and-such. Unlike the ancient Greeks and Romans, the average
Balinese shows little interest in the detailed doings of particular gods,
nor in their motivations, their personalities, or their individual histories.
The same circumspection and propriety is maintained with respect to
such matters as is maintained with respect to similar matters concerning
elders and superiors generally.[25]

The world of the gods is, in short, but another public realm, transcending all the others and imbued with an ethos which those others
seek, so far as they are able, to embody in themselves. The concerns of
this realm lie on the cosmic level rather than the political, the economic, or the ceremonial (that is, the human) and its stewards are men
without features, individuals with respect to whom the usual indices of
perishing humanity have no significance. The nearly faceless, thoroughly
conventionalized, never-changing icons by which nameless gods known
only by their public titles are, year after year, represented in the thousands of temple festivals across the island comprise the purest expres-

[25] Traditional texts, some of them fairly extensive, relating certain activities of
the gods, do exist and fragments of the stories are known. But not only do these
myths also reflect the typological view of personhood, the static view of time, and
the ceremonialized style of interaction I am seeking to characterize, but the general reticence to discuss or think about the divine means that the stories they relate enter but slightly into Balinese attempts to understand and adapt to "the
world." The difference between the Greeks and the Balinese lies not so much in
the sort of lives their gods lead, scandalous in both cases, as in their attitude toward those lives. For the Greeks, the private doings of Zeus and his associates
were conceived to illuminate the all-too-similar doings of men, and so gossip
about them had philosophical import. For the Balinese, the private lives of Betara Guru and his associates are just that, private, and gossip about them is
unmannerly—even, given their place in the prestige hierarchy, impertinent.

sion of the Balinese concept of personhood. Genuflecting to them (or, more precisely, to the gods for the moment resident in them) the Balinese are not just acknowledging divine power. They are also confronting the image of what they consider themselves at bottom to be; an image which the biological, psychological, and sociological concomitants of being alive, the mere materialities of historical time, tend only to obscure from sight.

A Cultural Triangle of Forces

There are many ways in which men are made aware, or rather make themselves aware, of the passage of time—by marking the changing of the seasons, the alterations of the moon, or the progress of plant life; by the measured cycling of rites, or agricultural work, or household activities; by the preparation and scheduling of projected acts and the memory and assessment of accomplished ones; by the preservation of genealogies, the recital of legends, or the framing of prophecies. But surely among the most important is by the recognition in oneself and in one's fellowmen of the process of biological aging, the appearance, maturation, decay, and disappearance of concrete individuals. How one views this process affects, therefore, and affects profoundly, how one experiences time. Between a people's conception of what it is to be a person and their conception of the structure of history there is an unbreakable internal link.

Now, as I have been stressing, the most striking thing about the culture patterns in which Balinese notions of personal identity are embodied is the degree to which they depict virtually everyone—friends, relatives, neighbors, and strangers; elders and youths; superiors and inferiors; men and women; chiefs, kings, priests, and gods; even the dead and the unborn—as stereotyped contemporaries, abstract and anonymous fellowmen. Each of the symbolic orders of person-definition, from concealed names to flaunted titles, acts to stress and strengthen the standardization, idealization, and generalization implicit in the relation between individuals whose main connection consists in the accident of their being alive at the same time and to mute or gloss over those implicit in the relation between consociates, men intimately

involved in one another's biographies, or between predecessors and successors, men who stand to one another as blind testator and unwitting
heir. Of course, people in Bali *are* directly, and sometimes deeply, involved in one another's lives; they *do* feel their world to have been shaped
by the actions of those who came before them and orient their actions
toward shaping the world of those who will come after them. But it is
not these aspects of their existence as persons—their immediacy and individuality, or their special, never-to-be-repeated, impact upon the
stream of historical events—which are culturally played up, symbolically emphasized: it is their social placement, their particular location
within a persisting, indeed an eternal, metaphysical order.[26] The illuminating paradox of Balinese formulations of personhood is that they are
—in our terms anyway—depersonalizing.

In this way, the Balinese blunt, though of course they cannot efface,
three of the most important sources of a sense of temporality: the apprehension of one's comrades (and thus oneself with them) as perpetually perishing; the awareness of the heaviness with which the completed
lives of the dead weigh upon the uncompleted lives of the living; and
the appreciation of the potential impact upon the unborn of actions just
now being undertaken.

Consociates, as they meet, confront and grasp one another in an immediate present, a synoptic "now"; and in so doing they experience the
elusiveness and ephemerality of such a now as it slips by in the ongoing
stream of face-to-face interaction. "For each partner [in a consociate
relationship] the other's body, his gestures, his gait and facial expressions, are immediately observable, not merely as things or events of the
outer world but in their physiognomical significance, that is as [expres-
sions] of the other's thoughts. . . . Each partner participates in the on-
rolling life of the other, can grasp in a vivid present the other's thoughts
as they are built up step by step. They may thus share one another's an-

[26] It is the overall order which is conceived to be fixed, not the individual's
location within it, which is movable, though more along certain axes than others.
(Along some, e.g., birth order, it is not movable at all.) But the point is that this
movement is not, or anyway not primarily, conceived in what we would regard
to be temporal terms: when a "father-of" becomes a "grandfather-of," the alteration is perceived as being less one of aging than a change in social (and what is
here the same thing, cosmic) coordinates, a directed movement through a particular sort of unchanging attribute, space. Also, within some symbolic orders of person-definition, location is not conceived as an absolute quality because coordinates are origin-dependent: in Bali, as elsewhere, one man's brother is another
man's uncle.

ticipations of the future as plans, or hopes, or anxieties. . . . [They] are mutually involved in one another's biography; they are growing older together. . . ." [27] As for predecessors and successors, separated by a material gulf, they perceive one another in terms of origins and outcomes, and in so doing experience the inherent chronologicality of events, the linear progress of standard, transpersonal time—the sort whose passage can be measured with clocks and calendars.[28]

In minimizing, *culturally,* all three of these experiences—that of the evanescing present consociate intimacy evokes; that of the determining past contemplation of predecessors evokes; and that of the moldable future anticipation of successors evokes—in favor of the sense of pure simultaneity generated by the anonymized encounter of sheer contemporaries, the Balinese produce yet a second paradox. Linked to their depersonalizing conception of personhood is a detemporalizing (again from our point of view) conception of time.

TAXONOMIC CALENDARS AND PUNCTUAL TIME

Balinese calendrical notions—their cultural machinery for demarcating temporal units—reflect this clearly; for they are largely used not to measure the elapse of time, nor yet to accent the uniqueness and irrecoverability of the passing moment, but to mark and classify the qualitative modalities in terms of which time manifests itself in human experience. The Balinese calendar (or, rather, calendars; as we shall see there are two of them) cuts time up into bounded units not in order to count and total them but to describe and characterize them, to formulate their differential social, intellectual, and religious significance.[29]

[27] Schutz, *The Problem of Social Reality,* pp. 16–17. Brackets added.
[28] Ibid., pp. 221–222.
[29] As a preface to the following, and an appendix to the preceding, discussion, it should be remarked that, just as the Balinese do have consociate relations with one another and do have some sense of the material connection between ancestors and descendants, so too they do have some, as we would put it, "true" calendrical concepts—absolute dates in the so-called Caka system, Hinduistic notions of successive epochs, as well as, indeed, access to the Gregorian calendar. But these are (ca. 1958) unstressed and of distinctly secondary importance in the ordinary course of everyday life; variant patterns applied in restricted contexts for specific purposes by certain sorts of persons on sporadic occasions. A complete analysis of Balinese culture—so far as such a thing is possible—would indeed have to take account of them; and from certain points of view they are not without theoretical significance. The point, here and elsewhere, in this quite in-

The two calendars which the Balinese employ are a lunar-solar one and one built around the interaction of independent cycles of day-names, which I shall call "permutational." The permutational calendar is by far the most important. It consists of ten different cycles of day-names. These cycles are of varying lengths. The longest contains ten day-names, following one another in a fixed order, after which the first day-name reappears and the cycle starts over. Similarly, there are nine, eight, seven, six, five, four, three, two, and even—the ultimate of a "contemporized" view of time—one day-name cycles. The names in each cycle are also different, and the cycles run concurrently. That is to say, any given day has, at least in theory, ten different names simultaneously applied to it, one from each of the ten cycles. Of the ten cycles only those containing five, six, and seven day-names are of major cultural significance, however, although the three-name cycle is used to define the market week and plays a role in fixing certain minor rituals, such as the personal-naming ceremony referred to earlier.

Now, the interaction of these three main cycles—the five, the six, and the seven—means that a given trinomially designated day (that is, one with a particular combination of names from all three cycles) will appear once in every two hundred and ten days, the simple product of five, six, and seven. Similar interactions between the five- and seven-name cycles produce binomially designated days which turn up every thirty-five days, between the six- and seven-name cycles binomially designated days which occur every forty-two days, and between the five- and six-name cycles binomially designated days appearing at thirty-day intervals. The conjunctions that each of these four periodicities, super-cycles as it were, define (*but not the periodicities themselves*) are considered not only to be socially significant but to reflect, in one fashion or another, the very structure of reality.

The outcome of all this wheels-within-wheels computation is a view of time as consisting of ordered sets of thirty, thirty-five, forty-two, or two hundred and ten quantum units ("days"), each of which units has a particular qualitative significance of some sort indexed by its trinomial or binomial name: rather like our notion of the unluckiness of

---

complete analysis, however, is not that the Balinese are, as the Hungarians are reputed to be, immigrants from another planet entirely unlike ourselves, but merely that the major thrust of their thought concerning certain matters of critical social importance lies, at least for the moment, in a markedly different direction from ours.

Friday-the-Thirteenth. To identify a day in the forty-two-day set—and thus assess its practical and/or religious significance—one needs to determine its place, that is, its name, in the six-name cycle (say, *Ariang*) and in the seven- (say, *Boda*): the day is *Boda-Ariang,* and one shapes one's actions accordingly. To identify a day in the thirty-five-day set, one needs its place and name in the five-name cycle (for example, *Klion*) and in the seven-: for example, *Boda-Klion*—this is *rainan,* the day on which one must set out small offerings at various points to "feed" the gods. For the two hundred and ten-day set, unique determination demands names from all three weeks: for example, *Boda-Ariang-Klion,* which, it so happens, is the day on which the most important Balinese holiday, Galungan, is celebrated.[30]

Details aside, the nature of time-reckoning this sort of calendar facilitates is clearly not durational but punctual. That is, it is not used (and could only with much awkwardness and the addition of some ancillary devices be used) to measure the rate at which time passes, the amount which has passed since the occurrence of some event, or the amount which remains within which to complete some project: it is adapted to and used for distinguishing and classifying discrete, self-subsistent particles of time—"days." The cycles and supercycles are endless, unanchored, uncountable, and, as their internal order has no significance, without climax. They do not accumulate, they do not build, and they are not consumed. They don't tell you what time it is; they tell you what kind of time it is.[31]

[30] Because the thirty-seven-name cycles (*uku*) which make up the two hundred and ten-day supercycle are also named, they can be, and commonly are, used in conjunction with five- and seven-day names, so eliminating the need to invoke names from the six-name cycle. But this is merely a notational matter: the result is exactly the same, though the days of the thirty- and forty-two-day supercycles are thus obscured. Balinese devices—charts, lists, numerical calculation, mnemonics—for making calendrical determinations and assessing their meaning are both complex and various, and there are differences in technique and interpretation between individuals, villages, and regions of the island. Printed calendars in Bali (a still not very widespread innovation) contrive to show at once the uku; the day in each of the ten permutating cycles (including the one that never changes!); the day and month in the lunar-solar system; the day, the month, and year in the Gregorian and Islamic calendars; and the day, month, year, and year-name in the Chinese calendar—complete with notations of all the important holidays from Christmas to Galungan these various systems define. For fuller discussions of Balinese calendrical ideas and their socioreligious meaning, see R. Goris, "Holidays and Holy Days," in J. L. Swellengrebel, ed., *Bali* (The Hague, 1960), pp. 115–129, together with the references cited there.

[31] More accurately: the *days* they define tell you what kind of time it is. Though the cycles and supercycles, being cycles, are recurrent, it is not this fact about them which is attended to or to which significance is attached. The thirty-,

The uses of the permutational calendar extend to virtually all aspects of Balinese life. In the first instance, it determines (with one exception) all the holidays—that is, general community celebrations—of which Goris lists some thirty-two in all, or on the average about one day out of every seven.[32] These do not appear, however, in any discernible overall rhythm. If we begin, arbitrarily, with *Radité-Tungleh-Paing* as "one," holidays appear on days numbering: 1, 2, 3, 4, 14, 15, 24, 49, 51, 68, 69, 71, 72, 73, 74, 77, 78, 79, 81, 83, 84, 85, 109, 119, 125, 154, 183, 189, 193, 196, 205, 210.[33] The result of this sort of spasmodic occurrence of festivals, large and small, is a perception of time—that is, of days—as falling broadly into two very general varieties, "full" and "empty": days on which something of importance goes on and others on which nothing, or at least nothing much, goes on, the former often being called "times" or "junctures" and the latter "holes." All of the other applications of the calendar merely reinforce and refine this general perception.

Of these other applications, the most important is the determination

---

thirty-five-, forty-two-, and two hundred and ten-day periodicities, and thus the intervals they demarcate, are not, or are only very peripherally, perceived as such; nor are the intervals implicit in the elementary periodicities, the cycles proper, which generate them—a fact which has sometimes been obscured by calling the former "months" and "years" and the latter "weeks." It is—one cannot stress it too strongly—only the "days" which really matter, and the Balinese sense of time is not much more cyclical than it is durative: it is particulate. Within individual days there is a certain amount of short-range, not very carefully calibrated, durative measurement, by the public beating of slit-gongs at various points (morning, midday, sundown, and so on) of the diurnal cycle, and for certain collective labor tasks where individual contributions have to be roughly balanced, by water-clocks. But even this is of little importance: in contrast to their calendrical apparatus, Balinese horological concepts and devices are very undeveloped.

[32] Goris, "Holidays and Holy Days," p. 121. Not all of these holidays are major, of course. Many of them are celebrated simply within the family and quite routinely. What makes them holidays is that they are identical for all Balinese, something not the case for other sorts of celebrations.

[33] Ibid. There are, of course, subrhythms resulting from the workings of the cycles: thus every thirty-fifth day is a holiday because it is determined by the interaction of the five- and seven-name cycles, but in terms of the sheer succession of days there is none, though there is some clustering here and there. Goris regards Radité-Tungleh-Paing as the "first day of the . . . Balinese [permutational] year" (and thus those days as the first days of their respective cycles); but though there may (or may not: Goris doesn't say) be some textual basis for this, I could find no evidence that the Balinese in fact so perceive it. In fact, if any day is regarded as something of what we would regard as a temporal milestone it would be Galungan (number seventy-four in the above reckoning). But even this idea is very weakly developed at best; like other holidays, Galungan merely happens. To present the Balinese calendar, even partially, in terms of Western flow-of-time ideas is, in my opinion, inevitably to misrender it phenomenologically.

of temple celebrations. No one knows how many temples there are on Bali, though Swellengrebel has estimated that there are more than 20,-000.[34] Each of these temples—family temples, descent-group temples, agricultural temples, death temples, settlement temples, associational temples, "caste" temples, state temples, and so on—has its own day of celebration, called *odalan,* a term which though commonly, and misleadingly, translated as "birthday" or, worse yet, "anniversary," literally means "coming out," "emergence," "appearance"—that is, not the day on which the temple was built but the day on which it is (and since it has been in existence always has been) "activated," on which the gods come down from the heavens to inhabit it. In between odalans it is quiescent, uninhabited, empty; and, aside from a few offerings prepared by its priest on certain days, nothing happens there.

For the great majority of the temples, the odalan is determined according to the permutational calendar (for the remainder, odalans are determined by the lunar-solar calendar, which as we shall see, comes to about the same thing so far as modes of time-perception are concerned), again in terms of the interaction of the five-, six-, and seven-name cycles. What this means is that temple ceremonies—which range from the incredibly elaborate to the almost invisibly simple—are of, to put it mildly, frequent occurrence in Bali, though here too there are certain days on which many such celebrations fall and others on which, for essentially metaphysical reasons, none do.[35]

Balinese life is thus not only irregularly punctuated by frequent holidays, which everyone celebrates, but by even more frequent temple celebrations which involve only those who are, usually by birth, members of the temple. As most Balinese belong to a half-dozen temples or more, this makes for a fairly busy, not to say frenetic, ritual life, though again one which alternates, unrhythmically, between hyperactivity and quiescence.

In addition to these more religious matters of holidays and temple festivals, the permutational calendar invades and encompasses the more

[34] Swellengrebel, *Bali,* p. 12. These temples are of all sizes and degrees of significance, and Swellengrebel notes that the Bureau of Religious Affairs on Bali gave a (suspiciously precise) figure, ca. 1953, of 4,661 "large and important" temples for the island, which, it should be remembered, is, at 2,170 square miles, about the size of Delaware.

[35] For a description of a full-blown odalan (most of which last three days rather than just one), see J. Belo, *Balinese Temple Festival* (Locust Valley, N.Y., 1953). Again, odalans are most commonly computed by the use of the *uku* rather than the six-name cycle, together with the five and seven-name cycles. See note 30.

secular ones of everyday life as well.[36] There are good and bad days on which to build a house, launch a business enterprise, change residence, go on a trip, harvest crops, sharpen cock spurs, hold a puppet show, or (in the old days) start a war, or conclude a peace. The day on which one was born, which again is not a birthday in our sense (when you ask a Balinese when he was born his reply comes to the equivalent of "Thursday, the ninth," which is not of much help in determining his age) but his odalan, is conceived to control or, more accurately, to indicate much of his destiny.[37] Men born on this day are liable to suicide, on that to become thieves, on this to be rich, on that to be poor; on this to be well, or long-lived, or happy, on that to be sickly, or short-lived, or unhappy. Temperament is similarly assessed, and so is talent. The diagnosis and treatment of disease is complexly integrated with calendrical determinations, which may involve the odalans of both the patient and the curer, the day on which he fell ill, as well as days metaphysically associated with the symptoms and with the medicine. Before marriages are contracted, the odalans of the individuals are compared to see if their conjunction is auspicious, and if not there will be—at least if the parties, as is almost always the case, are prudent—no marriage. There is a time to bury and a time to cremate, a time to marry and a time to divorce, a time—to shift from the Hebraic to the Balinese idiom—for the mountain top and a time for the market, for social withdrawal and social participation. Meetings of village council, irrigation societies, voluntary associations are all fixed in terms of the permutational (or, more rarely, the lunar-solar) calendar; and so are periods for sitting quietly at home and trying to keep out of trouble.

The lunar-solar calendar, though constructed on a different basis, actually embodies the same punctual conception of time as the permutational. Its main distinction and, for certain purposes, advantage is that it is more or less anchored; it does not drift with respect to the seasons. This calendar consists of twelve numbered months which run from

[36] There are also various metaphysical conceptions associated with days bearing different names—constellations of gods, demons, natural objects (trees, birds, beasts), virtues and vices (love, hate . . .), and so on—which explain "why" it has the character it has—but these need not be pursued here. In this area, as well as in the associated "fortune telling" operations described in the text, theories and interpretations are less standardized and computation is not confined to the five-, six-, and seven-name cycles, but extended to various permutations of the others, a fact which makes the possibilities virtually limitless.

[37] With respect to individuals the term applied is more often *otonan* than odalan, but the root meaning is just the same: "emerging," "appearance," "coming out."

new moon to new moon.[38] These months are then divided into two sorts of (also numbered) days: lunar (*tithi*) and solar (*diwasa*). There are always thirty lunar days in a month, but, given the discrepancy between the lunar and solar years, there are sometimes thirty solar days in a month and sometimes twenty-nine. In the latter case, two lunar days are considered to fall on one solar day—that is, one lunar day is skipped. This occurs every sixty-three days; but, although this calculation is astronomically quite accurate, the actual determination is not made on the basis of astronomical observation and theory, for which the Balinese do not have the necessary cultural equipment (to say nothing of the interest); it is determined by the use of the permutational calendar. The calculation was of course originally arrived at astronomically; but it was arrived at by the Hindus from whom the Balinese, in the most distant past, imported the calendar. For the Balinese, the double lunar day— the day on which it is two days at once—is just one more special kind of day thrown up by the workings of the cycles and supercycles of the permutational calendar—a priori, not a posteriori, knowledge.

In any case, this correction still leaves a nine–eleven-day deviation from the true solar year, and this is compensated for by the interpolation of a leap-month every thirty months, an operation which though again originally a result of Hindu astronomical observation and calculation is here simply mechanical. Despite the fact that the lunar-solar calendar *looks* astronomical, and thus *seems* to be based on some perceptions of natural temporal processes, celestial clocks, this is an illusion arising from attending to its origins rather than its uses. Its uses are as divorced from observation of the heavens—or from any other experience of passing time—as are those of the permutational calendar by which it is so rigorously paced. As with the permutational calendar, it is the system, automatic, particulate, fundamentally not metrical but classificatory, which tells you what day (or what kind of day) it is, not the appearance of the moon, which, as one looks casually up at it, is experienced not as a determinant of the calendar but as a reflex of it. What is "really real" is the name—or, in this case, the (two-place) number—of the day, its place in the transempirical taxonomy of days, not its epiphenomenal reflection in the sky.[39]

[38] The names of the last two months—borrowed from Sanskrit—are not strictly speaking numbers as are those of the other ten; but in terms of Balinese perceptions they "mean" eleventh and twelfth.

[39] In fact, as another Indic borrowing, the years are numbered too, but— outside of priestly circles where familiarity with it is more a matter of scholarly

In practice, the lunar-solar calendar is used in the same way for the same sorts of things as the permutational. The fact that it is (loosely) anchored makes it rather more handy in agricultural contexts, so that planting, weeding, harvesting, and the like are usually regulated in terms of it, and some temples having a symbolic connection with agriculture or fertility celebrate their reception of the gods according to it. This means that such receptions appear only about every 355 (in leap years, about 385) rather than 210 days. But otherwise the pattern is unchanged.

In addition, there is one major holiday, *Njepi* ("to make quiet"), which is celebrated according to the lunar-solar calendar. Often called, by Western scholars, "the Balinese New Year," even though it falls at the beginning (that is, the new moon) of not the first but the tenth month and is concerned not with renewal or rededication but with an accentuated fear of demons and an attempt to render one's emotions tranquil. Njepi is observed by an eerie day of silence: no one goes out on the streets, no work is conducted, no light or fire is lit, while conversation even within houseyards is muted. The lunar-solar system is not much used for "fortune telling" purposes, though the new moon and full moon days are considered to have certain qualitative characteristics, sinister in the first case, auspicious in the second. In general, the lunar-solar calendar is more a supplement to the permutational than an alternative to it. It makes possible the employment of a classificatory, full-and-empty, "detemporalized" conception of time in contexts where the fact that natural conditions vary periodically has to be at least minimally acknowledged.

CEREMONY, STAGE FRIGHT, AND ABSENCE OF CLIMAX

The anonymization of persons and the immobilization of time are thus but two sides of the same cultural process: the symbolic de-emphasis, in the everyday life of the Balinese, of the perception of fellowmen

---

prestige, a cultural ornament, than anything else—year enumeration plays virtually no role in the actual use of the calendar, and lunar-solar dates are almost always given without the year, which is, with the rarest of exceptions, neither known nor cared about. Ancient texts and inscriptions sometimes indicate the year, but in the ordinary course of life the Balinese never "date" anything, in our sense of the term, except perhaps to say that some event—a volcanic eruption, a war, and so forth—happened "when I was small," "when the Dutch were here," or, the Balinese *illo tempore*, "in Madjapahit times," and so on.

as consociates, successors, or predecessors in favor of the perception of them as contemporaries. As the various symbolic orders of person-definition conceal the biological, psychological, and historical foundation of that changing pattern of gifts and inclinations we call personality behind a dense screen of ready-made identities, iconic selves, so the calendar, or rather the application of the calendar, blunts the sense of dissolving days and evaporating years that those foundations and that pattern inevitably suggest by pulverizing the flow of time into disconnected, dimensionless, motionless particles. A sheer contemporary needs an absolute present in which to live; an absolute present can be inhabited only by a contemporized man. Yet, there is a third side to this same process which transforms it from a pair of complementary prepossessions into a triangle of mutually reinforcing cultural forces: the ceremonialization of social intercourse.

To maintain the (relative) anonymization of individuals with whom one is in daily contact, to dampen the intimacy implicit in face-to-face relationships—in a word, to render consociates contemporaries—it is necessary to formalize relations with them to a fairly high degree, to confront them in a sociological middle distance where they are close enough to be identified but not so close as to be grasped: quasi strangers, quasi friends. The ceremoniousness of so much of Balinese daily life, the extent (and the intensity) to which interpersonal relations are controlled by a developed system of conventions and proprieties, is thus a logical correlate of a thoroughgoing attempt to block the more creatural aspects of the human condition—individuality, spontaneity, perishability, emotionality, vulnerability—from sight. This attempt is, like its counterparts, only very partially successful, and the ceremonialization of Balinese social interaction is no closer to being complete than is the anonymization of persons or the immobilization of time. But the degree to which its success is wished for, the degree to which it is an obsessing ideal, accounts for the degree to which the ceremonialization obtains, for the fact that in Bali manners are not a mere matter of practical convenience or incidental decoration but are of deep spiritual concern. Calculated politesse, outward form pure and simple, has there a normative value that we, who regard it as pretentious or comic when we don't regard it as hypocritical, can scarcely, now that Jane Austen is about as far from us as Bali, any longer appreciate.

Such an appreciation is rendered even more difficult by the presence within this industrious polishing of the surfaces of social life of a peculiar note, a stylistic nuance, we would not, I think, expect to be there. Being stylistic and being a nuance (though an altogether pervasive one), it is very difficult to communicate to someone who has not himself experienced it. "Playful theatricality" perhaps hits near it, if it is understood that the playfulness is not lighthearted but almost grave and the theatricality not spontaneous but almost forced. Balinese social relations are at once a solemn game and a studied drama.

This is most clearly seen in their ritual and (what is the same thing) artistic life, much of which is in fact but a portrait of and a mold for their social life. Daily interaction is so ritualistic and religious activity so civic that it is difficult to tell where the one leaves off and the other begins; and both are but expressions of what is justly Bali's most famous cultural attribute: her artistic genius. The elaborate temple pageants; the grandiloquent operas, equilibristic ballets, and stilted shadow plays; the circuitous speech and apologetic gestures—all these are of a piece. Etiquette is a kind of dance, dance a kind of ritual, and worship a form of etiquette. Art, religion, and politesse all exalt the outward, the contrived, the well-wrought appearance of things. They celebrate the forms; and it is the tireless manipulation of these forms—what they call "playing"—that gives to Balinese life its settled haze of ceremony.

The mannered cast of Balinese interpersonal relations, the fusion of rite, craft, and courtesy, thus leads into a recognition of the most fundamental and most distinctive quality of their particular brand of sociality: its radical aestheticism. Social acts, all social acts, are first and foremost designed to please—to please the gods, to please the audience, to please the other, to please the self; but to please as beauty pleases, not as virtue pleases. Like temple offerings or gamelan concerts, acts of courtesy are works of art, and as such they demonstrate, and are meant to demonstrate, not rectitude (or what we would call rectitude) but sensibility.

Now, from all this—that daily life is markedly ceremonious; that this ceremoniousness takes the form of an earnest, even sedulous, kind of "playing" with public forms; that religion, art, and etiquette are then but differently directed manifestations of an overall cultural fascination with the worked-up semblance of things; and that morality here is consequently aesthetic at base—it is possible to attain a more exact understanding of two of the most marked (and most remarked) features of the affective tone of Balinese life: the importance of the emotion of what has been (wrongly) called "shame" in interpersonal relations, and the failure of collective activity—religious, artistic, political, economic—to build toward the definable consummations, what has been (acutely) called its "absence of climax."[40] One of these themes, the first, leads directly back toward conceptions of personhood, the other, no less directly, toward conceptions of time, so securing the vertices of our metaphorical triangle connecting the Balinese behavioral style with the ideational environment in which it moves.

The concept of "shame," together with its moral and emotional cousin "guilt," has been much discussed in the literature, entire cultures sometimes being designated as "shame cultures" because of the presumed prominence in them of an intense concern with "honor," "reputation," and the like, at the expense of a concern, conceived to be dominant in "guilt cultures," with "sin," "inner worth," and so forth.[41] The usefulness of such an overall categorization and the complex problems of comparative psychological dynamics involved aside, it has proven difficult in such studies to divest the term "shame" of what is after all its most common meaning in English—"consciousness of guilt"—and so to disconnect it very completely from guilt as such—"the fact or feeling of having done something reprehensible." Usually, the contrast has been turned upon the fact that "shame" tends to be applied (although, actually, far from exclusively) to situations in which wrongdoing is publicly exposed, and "guilt" (though equally far from exclusively) to situations in which it is not. Shame is the feeling of disgrace and humiliation which follows upon a transgression found out; guilt is the feeling of secret badness attendant upon one not, or not yet, found out. Thus, though shame and guilt are not precisely the same thing in our ethical and psychological vocabulary, they are of the same family; the one is a surfacing of the other, the other a concealment of the one.

But Balinese "shame," or what has been translated as such (*lek*), has nothing to do with transgressions, exposed or unexposed, acknowledged or hidden, merely imagined or actually performed. This is not to say that Balinese feel neither guilt nor shame, are without either conscience or pride, anymore than they are unaware that time passes or that men are unique individuals. It is to say that neither guilt nor shame is of cardinal importance as affective regulators of their interpersonal conduct,

[40] On the "shame" theme in Balinese culture, see M. Covarrubias, *The Island of Bali* (New York, 1956); on "absence of climax," G. Bateson and M. Mead, *Balinese Character* (New York, 1942).

[41] For a comprehensive critical review, see G. Piers and M. Singer, *Shame and Guilt* (Springfield, Ill., 1953).

and that *lek,* which is far and away the most important of such regulators, culturally the most intensely emphasized, ought therefore not to be translated as "shame," but rather, to follow out our theatrical image, as "stage fright." It is neither the sense that one has transgressed nor the sense of humiliation that follows upon some uncovered transgression, both rather lightly felt and quickly effaced in Bali, that is the controlling emotion in Balinese face-to-face encounters. It is, on the contrary, a diffuse, usually mild, though in certain situations virtually paralyzing, nervousness before the prospect (and the fact) of social interaction, a chronic, mostly low-grade worry that one will not be able to bring it off with the required finesse.[42]

Whatever its deeper causes, stage fright consists in a fear that, for want of skill or self-control, or perhaps by mere accident, an aesthetic illusion will not be maintained, that the actor will show through his part and the part thus dissolve into the actor. Aesthetic distance collapses, the audience (and the actor) loses sight of Hamlet and gains it, uncomfortably for all concerned, of bumbling John Smith painfully miscast as the Prince of Denmark. In Bali, the case is the same, if the drama more humble. What is feared—mildly in most cases, intensely in a few—is that the public performance that is etiquette will be botched, that the social distance etiquette maintains will consequently collapse, and that the personality of the individual will then break through to dissolve his standardized public identity. When this occurs, as it sometimes does, our triangle falls apart: ceremony evaporates, the immediacy of the moment is felt with an excruciating intensity, and men become unwilling consociates locked in mutual embarrassment, as though they had inadvertently intruded upon one another's privacy. *Lek* is at once the awareness of the ever-present possibility of such an interpersonal disaster and, like stage fright, a motivating force toward avoiding it. It is the fear of *faux pas*—rendered only that much more probable by an elaborated politesse—that keeps social intercourse on its deliberately narrowed rails. It is *lek,* more than anything else, that protects Balinese

---

[42] Again, I am concerned here with cultural phenomenology, not psychological dynamics. It is, of course, quite possible, though I do not think the evidence is available either to prove or disprove it, that Balinese "stage fright" is connected with unconscious guilt feelings of some sort or another. My only point is that to translate *lek* as either "guilt" or "shame" is, given the usual sense of these terms in English, to misrender it, and that our word "stage fright"—"nervousness felt at appearing before an audience," to resort to *Webster's* again—gives a much better, if still imperfect, idea of what the Balinese are in fact talking about when they speak, as they do almost constantly, of *lek.*

concepts of personhood from the individualizing force of face-to-face encounters.

"Absence of climax," the other outstanding quality of Balinese social behavior, is so peculiarly distinctive and so distinctively odd that only extended description of concrete events could properly evoke it. It amounts to the fact that social activities do not build, or are not permitted to build, toward definitive consummations. Quarrels appear and disappear, on occasion they even persist, but they hardly ever come to a head. Issues are not sharpened for decision, they are blunted and softened in the hope that the mere evolution of circumstances will resolve them, or better yet, that they will simply evaporate. Daily life consists of self-contained, monadic encounters in which something either happens or does not—an intention is realized or it is not, a task accomplished or not. When the thing doesn't happen—the intention is frustrated, the task unaccomplished—the effort may be made again from the beginning at some other time; or it may simply be abandoned. Artistic performances start, go on (often for very extended periods when one does not attend continually but drifts away and back, chatters for a while, sleeps for a while, watches rapt for a while), and stop; they are as uncentered as a parade, as directionless as a pageant. Ritual often seems, as in the temple celebrations, to consist largely of getting ready and cleaning up. The heart of the ceremony, the obeisance to the gods come down onto their altars, is deliberately muted to the point where it sometimes seems almost an afterthought, a glancing, hesitant confrontation of anonymous persons brought physically very close and kept socially very distant. It is all welcoming and bidding farewell, foretaste and aftertaste, with but the most ceremonially buffered, ritually insulated sort of actual encounter with the sacred presences themselves. Even in such a dramatically more heightened ceremony as the Rangda-Barong, fearful witch and foolish dragon combat ends in a state of complete irresolution, a mystical, metaphysical, and moral standoff leaving everything precisely as it was, and the observer—or anyway the foreign observer—with the feeling that something decisive was on the verge of happening but never quite did.[43]

In short, events happen like holidays. They appear, vanish, and reappear—each discrete, sufficient unto itself, a particular manifesta-

[43] For a description of the Rangda–Barong combat, see J. Belo, *Rangda and Barong;* for a brilliant evocation of its mood, G. Bateson and M. Mead, *Balinese Character.* See also above, pp. 114–118.

tion of the fixed order of things. Social activities are separate performances; they do not march toward some destination, gather toward some denouement. As time is punctual, so life is. Not orderless, but qualitatively ordered, like the days themselves, into a limited number of established kinds. Balinese social life lacks climax because it takes place in a motionless present, a vectorless now. Or, equally true, Balinese time lacks motion because Balinese social life lacks climax. The two imply one another, and both together imply and are implied by the Balinese contemporization of persons. The perception of fellowmen, the experience of history, and the temper of collective life—what has sometimes been called ethos—are hooked together by a definable logic. But the logic is not syllogistic; it is social.

Cultural Integration, Cultural Conflict, Cultural Change

Referring as it does both to formal principles of reasoning and to rational connections among facts and events, "logic" is a treacherous word; and nowhere more so than in the analysis of culture. When one deals with meaningful forms, the temptation to see the relationship among them as immanent, as consisting of some sort of intrinsic affinity (or disaffinity) they bear for one another, is virtually overwhelming. And so we hear cultural integration spoken of as a harmony of meaning, cultural change as an instability of meaning, and cultural conflict as an incongruity of meaning, with the implication that the harmony, the instability, or the incongruity are properties of meaning itself, as, say, sweetness is a property of sugar or brittleness of glass.

Yet, when we try to treat these properties as we would sweetness or brittleness, they fail to behave, "logically," in the expected way. When we look for the constituents of the harmony, the instability, or the incongruity, we are unable to find them resident in that of which they are presumably properties. One cannot run symbolic forms through some sort of cultural assay to discover their harmony content, their stability ratio, or their index of incongruity; one can only look and see if the forms in question are in fact coexisting, changing, or interfering with one another in some way or other, which is like tasting sugar to see if it is sweet or dropping a glass to see if it is brittle, not like investigating the chemical composition of sugar or the physical structure of glass. The reason for this is, of course, that meaning is not intrinsic in the objects, acts, processes, and so on, which bear it, but—as Durkheim, Weber, and so many others have emphasized—imposed upon them; and the explanation of its properties must therefore be sought in that which does the imposing—men living in society. The study of thought is, to borrow a phrase from Joseph Levenson, the study of men thinking; [44] and as they think not in some special place of their own, but in the same place—the social world—that they do everything else, the nature of cultural integration, cultural change, or cultural conflict is to be probed for there: in the experiences of individuals and groups of individuals as, under the guidance of symbols, they perceive, feel, reason, judge, and act.

To say this is, however, not to yield to psychologism, which along with logicism is the other great saboteur of cultural analysis; for human experience—the actual living through of events—is not mere sentience, but, from the most immediate perception to the most mediated judgment, significant sentience—sentience interpreted, sentience grasped. For human beings, with the possible exception of neonates, who except for their physical structure are human only *in posse* anyway, all experience is construed experience, and the symbolic forms in terms of which it is construed thus determine—in conjunction with a wide variety of other factors ranging from the cellular geometry of the retina to the endogenous stages of psychological maturation—its intrinsic texture. To abandon the hope of finding the "logic" of cultural organization in some Pythagorean "realm of meaning" is not to abandon the hope of finding it at all. It is to turn our attention toward that which gives symbols their life: their use. [45]

What binds Balinese symbolic structures for defining persons (names,

[44] J. Levenson, *Modern China and Its Confucian Past* (Garden City, 1964), p. 212. Here, as elsewhere, I use "thinking" to refer not just to deliberate reflection but intelligent activity of any sort, and "meaning" to refer not just to abstract "concepts" but significance of any sort. This is perhaps somewhat arbitrary, and a little loose, but one must have general terms to talk about general subjects, even if what falls under such subjects is very far from being homogeneous.

[45] "Every sign *by itself* seems dead. *What* gives it life?—in use it is *alive*. Is life breathed into it there?—Or is its *use* its life?" L. Wittgenstein, *Philosophical Investigations* (New York, 1953), p. 128e. Italics in original.

kin terms, teknonyms, titles, and so on) to their symbolic structures for characterizing time (permutational calendars, and so forth), and both of these to their symbolic structures for ordering interpersonal behavior (art, ritual, politesse, and so on), is the interaction of the effects each of these structures has upon the perceptions of those who use them, the way in which their experiential impacts play into and reinforce one another. A penchant for "contemporizing" fellowmen blunts the sense of biological aging; a blunted sense of biological aging removes one of the main sources of a sense of temporal flow; a reduced sense of temporal flow gives to interpersonal events an episodic quality. Ceremonialized interaction supports standardized perceptions of others; standardized perceptions of others support a "steady-state" conception of society; a steady-state conception of society supports a taxonomic perception of time. And so on: one could begin with conceptions of time and go around, in either direction, the same circle. The circle, though continuous, is not in a strict sense closed, because none of these modes of experience is more than a dominant tendency, a cultural emphasis, and their subdued opposites, equally well-rooted in the general conditions of human existence and not without some cultural expression of their own, coexist with them, and indeed act against them. Yet, they *are* dominant; they *do* reinforce one another; and they *are* persisting. And it is to this state of affairs, neither permanent nor perfect, that the concept "cultural integration"—what Weber called *"Sinnzusammenhang"*—can be legitimately applied.

In this view, cultural integration is no longer taken to be a *sui generis* phenomenon locked away from the common life of man in a logical world of its own. Perhaps even more important, however, it is also not taken to be an all-embracing, completely pervasive, unbounded one. In the first place, as just noted, patterns counteractive to the primary ones exist as subdominant but nonetheless important themes in, so far as we can tell, any culture. In an ordinary, quite un-Hegelian way, the elements of a culture's own negation are, with greater or lesser force, included within it. With respect to the Balinese, for example, an investigation of their witch beliefs (or, to speak phenomenologically, witch experiences) as inverses of what might be called their person beliefs, or of their trance behavior as an inverse of their etiquette, would be most enlightening in this respect and would add both depth and complexity to the present analysis. Some of the more famous attacks upon received cultural characterizations—revelations of suspicion and factionalism among the "harmony-loving" Pueblans, or of an "amiable side" to the rivalrous Kwakiutl—consist essentially in a pointing out of the existence, and the importance, of such themes.[46]

But beyond this sort of natural counterpoint there are also simple, unbridged discontinuities between certain major themes themselves. Not everything is connected to everything else with equal directness; not everything plays immediately into or against everything else. At the very least such universal primary interconnection has to be empirically demonstrated, not just, as so often has been the case, axiomatically assumed.

Cultural discontinuity, and the social disorganization which, even in highly stable societies, can result from it, is as real as cultural integration. The notion, still quite widespread in anthropology, that culture is a seamless web is no less a *petitio principii* than the older view that culture is a thing of shreds and patches which, with a certain excess of enthusiasm, it replaced after the Malinowskian revolution of the early thirties. Systems need not be exhaustively interconnected to be systems. They may be densely interconnected or poorly, but which they are— how rightly integrated they are—is an empirical matter. To assert connections among modes of experiencing, as among any variables, it is necessary to find them (and find ways of finding them), not simply assume them. And as there are some rather compelling theoretical reasons for believing that a system which is both complex, as any culture is, and fully joined cannot function, the problem of cultural analysis is as much a matter of determining independencies as interconnections, gulfs as well as bridges.[47] The appropriate image, if one must have images, of cultural organization, is neither the spider web nor the pile of sand. It is

[46] Li An-che, "Zuñi: Some Observations and Queries," *American Anthropologist* 39 (1937):62–76; H. Codere, "The Amiable Side of Kwakiutl Life," *American Anthropologist* 58 (1956):334–351. Which of two antithetical patterns or clusters of patterns, if either, is in fact primary, is of course an empirical problem, but not, particularly if some thought is given to what "primacy" means in this connection, an insoluble one.

[47] "It has thus been shown that, for adaptations to accumulate, there must *not* be channels . . . from some variables . . . to others. . . . The idea so often implicit in physiological writings that all will be well if only sufficient cross-connections are available is . . . quite wrong." W. R. Ashby, *Design for a Brain*, 2nd ed. rev. (New York, 1960), p. 155. Italics in original. Of course, the reference here is to direct connections—what Ashby calls "primary joins." Any variable with no relations whatsoever to other variables in the system would simply not be part of it. For a discussion of the nest of theoretical problems involved here, see Ashby, pp. 171–183, 205–218. For an argument that cultural discontinuity may not only be compatible with the effective functioning of the social systems they govern but even supportive of such functioning, see J. W. Fernandez, "Symbolic Consensus in a Fang Reformative Cult," *American Anthropologist* 67 (1965):902–929.

rather more the octopus, whose tentacles are in large part separately integrated, neurally quite poorly connected with one another and with what in the octopus passes for a brain, and yet who nonetheless manages both to get around and to preserve himself, for a while anyway, as a viable if somewhat ungainly entity.

The close and immediate interdependency between conceptions of person, time, and conduct which has been proposed in this essay is, so I would argue, a general phenomenon, even if the particular Balinese form of it is peculiar to a degree, because such an interdependency is inherent in the way in which human experience is organized, a necessary effect of the conditions under which human life is led. But it is only one of a vast and unknown number of such general interdependencies, to some of which it is more or less directly connected, to others only very indirectly, to others for all practical purposes virtually not at all.

The analysis of culture comes down therefore not to an heroic "holistic" assault upon "the basic configurations of the culture," an overarching "order of orders" from which more limited configurations can be seen as mere deductions, but to a searching out of significant symbols, clusters of significant symbols, and clusters of clusters of significant symbols—the material vehicles of perception, emotion, and understanding—and the statement of the underlying regularities of human experience implicit in their formation. A workable theory of culture is to be achieved, if it is to be achieved, by building up from directly observable modes of thought, first to determinate families of them and then to more variable, less tightly coherent, but nonetheless ordered "octopoid" systems of them, confluences of partial integrations, partial incongruencies, and partial independencies.

Culture moves rather like an octopus too—not all at once in a smoothly coordinated synergy of parts, a massive coaction of the whole, but by disjointed movements of this part, then that, and now the other which somehow cumulate to directional change. Where, leaving cephalopods behind, in any given culture the first impulses toward progression will appear, and how and to what degree they will spread through the system, is, at this stage of our understanding, if not wholly unpredictable, very largely so. Yet that if such impulses appear within some rather closely interconnected and socially consequential part of the system, their driving force will most likely be high, does not appear to be too unreasonable a supposition.

Any development which would effectively attack Balinese person-perceptions, Balinese experiences of time, or Balinese notions of propriety would seem to be laden with potentialities for transforming the greater part of Balinese culture. These are not the only points at which such revolutionary developments might appear (anything which attacked Balinese notions of prestige and its bases would seem at least equally portentous), but surely they are among the most important. If the Balinese develop a less anonymized view of one another, or a more dynamic sense of time, or a more informal style of social interaction, a very great deal indeed—not everything, but a very great deal—would have to change in Balinese life, if only because any one of these changes would imply, immediately and directly, the others and all three of them play, in different ways and in different contexts, a crucial role in shaping that life.

Such cultural changes could, in theory, come from within Balinese society or from without; but considering the fact that Bali is now part of a developing national state whose center of gravity is elsewhere—in the great cities of Java and Sumatra—it would seem most likely to come from without.

The emergence for almost the first time in Indonesian history of a political leader who is human, all-too-human, not merely in fact but in appearance would seem to imply something of a challenge to traditional Balinese personhood conceptions. Not only is Sukarno a unique, vivid, and intensely intimate personality in the eyes of the Balinese, he is also, so to speak, aging in public. Despite the fact that they do not engage in face-to-face interaction with him, he is phenomenologically much more their consociate than their contemporary, and his unparalleled success in achieving this kind of relationship—not only in Bali, but in Indonesia quite generally—is the secret of a good deal of his hold on, his fascination for, the population. As with all truly charismatic figures his power comes in great part from the fact that he does not fit traditional cultural categories but bursts them open by celebrating his own distinctiveness. The same is true, in reduced intensity, for the lesser leaders of the New Indonesia, down to those small-frog Sukarnos (with whom the population *does* have face-to-face relations) now beginning to appear in Bali itself.[48] The sort of individualism which Burckhardt saw the Re-

[48] It is perhaps suggestive that the only Balinese of much importance in the central Indonesian government during the early years of the Republic—he was foreign minister for a while—was the Satria paramount prince of Gianjar, one of

naissance princes bringing, through sheer force of character, to Italy, and bringing with it the modern Western consciousness, may be in the process of being brought, in rather different form, to Bali by the new populist princes of Indonesia.

Similarly, the politics of continuing crisis on which the national state has embarked, a passion for pushing events toward their climaxes rather than away from them, would seem to pose the same sort of challenge to Balinese conceptions of time. And when such politics are placed, as they are increasingly being placed, in the historical framework so characteristic of New Nation nationalism almost everywhere—original greatness, foreign oppression, extended struggle, sacrifice and self-liberation, impending modernization—the whole conception of the relation of what is now happening to what has happened and what is going to happen is altered.

And finally, the new informality of urban life and of the pan-Indonesian culture which dominates it—the growth in importance of youth and youth culture with the consequent narrowing, sometimes even the reversal, of the social distance between generations; the sentimental comradeship of fellow revolutionaries; the populist equalitarianism of political ideology, Marxist and non-Marxist alike—appears to contain a similar threat to the third, the ethos or behavioral style, side of the Balinese triangle.

All this is admittedly mere speculation (though, given the events of the fifteen years of Independence, not wholly groundless speculation) and when, how, how fast, and in what order Balinese perceptions of person, time, and conduct will change is, if not wholly unpredictable in general, largely so in detail. But as they do change—which seems to me certain, and in fact already to have well begun[49]—the sort of analysis here developed of cultural concepts as active forces, of thought as a

---

the traditional Balinese kingdoms, who bore the marvellously Balinese "name" of Anak Agung Gde Agung. "Anak Agung" is the public title borne by the members of the ruling house of Gianjar, Gde is a birth order title (the Triwangsa equivalent of Wayan), and Agung though a personal name is in fact just an echo of the public title. As "gde" and "agung" both mean "big," and "anak" means man, the whole name comes to something like "Big, Big, Big Man"—as indeed he was, until he fell from Sukarno's favor. More recent political leaders in Bali have taken to the use of their more individualized personal names in the Sukarno fashion and to the dropping of titles, birth order names, teknonyms, and so on, as "feudal" or "old-fashioned."

[49] This was written in early 1965; for the dramatic changes that, in fact, occurred later that year, see pp. 282–283 and Chapter 11.

public phenomenon with effects like other public phenomena, should aid us in discovering its outlines, its dynamics, and, even more important, its social implications. Nor, in other forms and with other results, should it be less useful elsewhere.

Chapter 15 / Deep Play:
Notes on the
Balinese Cockfight

The Raid

Early in April of 1958, my wife and I arrived, malarial and diffident, in a Balinese village we intended, as anthropologists, to study. A small place, about five hundred people, and relatively remote, it was its own world. We were intruders, professional ones, and the villagers dealt with us as Balinese seem always to deal with people not part of their life who yet press themselves upon them: as though we were not there. For them, and to a degree for ourselves, we were nonpersons, specters, invisible men.

We moved into an extended family compound (that had been arranged before through the provincial government) belonging to one of the four major factions in village life. But except for our landlord and the village chief, whose cousin and brother-in-law he was, everyone ignored us in a way only a Balinese can do. As we wandered around, uncertain, wistful, eager to please, people seemed to look right through us with a gaze focused several yards behind us on some more actual stone or tree. Almost nobody greeted us; but nobody scowled or said anything unpleasant to us either, which would have been almost as satisfactory.

If we ventured to approach someone (something one is powerfully, inhibited from doing in such an atmosphere), he moved, negligently but definitely, away. If, seated or leaning against a wall, we had him trapped, he said nothing at all, or mumbled what for the Balinese is the ultimate nonword—"yes." The indifference, of course, was studied; the villagers were watching every move we made, and they had an enormous amount of quite accurate information about who we were and what we were going to be doing. But they acted as if we simply did not exist, which, in fact, as this behavior was designed to inform us, we did not, or anyway not yet.

This is, as I say, general in Bali. Everywhere else I have been in Indonesia, and more latterly in Morocco, when I have gone into a new village, people have poured out from all sides to take a very close look at me, and, often an all-too-probing feel as well. In Balinese villages, at least those away from the tourist circuit, nothing happens at all. People go on pounding, chatting, making offerings, staring into space, carrying baskets about while one drifts around feeling vaguely disembodied. And the same thing is true on the individual level. When you first meet a Balinese, he seems virtually not to relate to you at all: he is, in the term Gregory Bateson and Margaret Mead made famous, "away." [1] Then—in a day, a week, a month (with some people the magic moment never comes)—he decides, for reasons I have never quite been able to fathom, that you *are* real, and then he becomes a warm, gay, sensitive, sympathetic, though, being Balinese, always precisely controlled, person. You have crossed, somehow, some moral or metaphysical shadow line. Though you are not exactly taken as a Balinese (one has to be born to that), you are at least regarded as a human being rather than a cloud or a gust of wind. The whole complexion of your relationship dramatically changes to, in the majority of cases, a gentle, almost affectionate one—a low-keyed, rather playful, rather mannered, rather bemused geniality.

My wife and I were still very much in the gust-of-wind stage, a most frustrating, and even, as you soon begin to doubt whether you are really real after all, unnerving one, when, ten days or so after our arrival, a large cockfight was held in the public square to raise money for a new school.

Now, a few special occasions aside, cockfights are illegal in Bali

[1] G. Bateson and M. Mead, *Balinese Character: A Photographic Analysis* (New York, 1942), p. 68.

under the Republic (as, for not altogether unrelated reasons, they were under the Dutch), largely as a result of the pretensions to puritanism radical nationalism tends to bring with it. The elite, which is not itself so very puritan, worries about the poor, ignorant peasant gambling all his money away, about what foreigners will think, about the waste of time better devoted to building up the country. It sees cockfighting as "primitive," "backward," "unprogressive," and generally unbecoming an ambitious nation. And, as with those other embarrassments—opium smoking, begging, or uncovered breasts—it seeks, rather unsystematically, to put a stop to it.

Of course, like drinking during Prohibition or, today, smoking marihuana, cockfights, being a part of "The Balinese Way of Life," nonetheless go on happening, and with extraordinary frequency. And, as with Prohibition or marihuana, from time to time the police (who, in 1958 at least, were almost all not Balinese but Javanese) feel called upon to make a raid, confiscate the cocks and spurs, fine a few people, and even now and then expose some of them in the tropical sun for a day as object lessons which never, somehow, get learned, even though occasionally, quite occasionally, the object dies.

As a result, the fights are usually held in a secluded corner of a village in semisecrecy, a fact which tends to slow the action a little—not very much, but the Balinese do not care to have it slowed at all. In this case, however, perhaps because they were raising money for a school that the government was unable to give them, perhaps because raids had been few recently, perhaps, as I gathered from subsequent discussion, there was a notion that the necessary bribes had been paid, they thought they could take a chance on the central square and draw a larger and more enthusiastic crowd without attracting the attention of the law.

They were wrong. In the midst of the third match, with hundreds of people, including, still transparent, myself and my wife, fused into a single body around the ring, a superorganism in the literal sense, a truck full of policemen armed with machine guns roared up. Amid great screeching cries of "pulisi! pulisi!" from the crowd, the policemen jumped out, and, springing into the center of the ring, began to swing their guns around like gangsters in a motion picture, though not going so far as actually to fire them. The superorganism came instantly apart as its components scattered in all directions. People raced down the road, disappeared headfirst over walls, scrambled under platforms, folded themselves behind wicker screens, scuttled up coconut trees.

Cocks armed with steel spurs sharp enough to cut off a finger or run a hole through a foot were running wildly around. Everything was dust and panic.

On the established anthropological principle, "When in Rome," my wife and I decided, only slightly less instantaneously than everyone else, that the thing to do was run too. We ran down the main village street, northward, away from where we were living, for we were on that side of the ring. About halfway down another fugitive ducked suddenly into a compound—his own, it turned out—and we, seeing nothing ahead of us but rice fields, open country, and a very high volcano, followed him. As the three of us came tumbling into the courtyard, his wife, who had apparently been through this sort of thing before, whipped out a table, a tablecloth, three chairs, and three cups of tea, and we all, without any explicit communication whatsoever, sat down, commenced to sip tea, and sought to compose ourselves.

A few moments later, one of the policemen marched importantly into the yard, looking for the village chief. (The chief had not only been at the fight, he had arranged it. When the truck drove up he ran to the river, stripped off his sarong, and plunged in so he could say, when at length they found him sitting there pouring water over his head, that he had been away bathing when the whole affair had occurred and was ignorant of it. They did not believe him and fined him three hundred rupiah, which the village raised collectively.) Seeing me and my wife, "White Men," there in the yard, the policeman performed a classic double take. When he found his voice again he asked, approximately, what in the devil did we think we were doing there. Our host of five minutes leaped instantly to our defense, producing an impassioned description of who and what we were, so detailed and so accurate that it was my turn, having barely communicated with a living human being save my landlord and the village chief for more than a week, to be astonished. We had a perfect right to be there, he said, looking the Javanese upstart in the eye. We were American professors; the government had cleared us; we were there to study culture; we were going to write a book to tell Americans about Bali. And we had all been there drinking tea and talking about cultural matters all afternoon and did not know anything about any cockfight. Moreover, we had not seen the village chief all day; he must have gone to town. The policeman retreated in rather total disarray. And, after a decent interval, bewildered but relieved to have survived and stayed out of jail, so did we.

The next morning the village was a completely different world for us. Not only were we no longer invisible, we were suddenly the center of all attention, the object of a great outpouring of warmth, interest, and most especially, amusement. Everyone in the village knew we had fled like everyone else. They asked us about it again and again (I must have told the story, small detail by small detail, fifty times by the end of the day), gently, affectionately, but quite insistently teasing us: "Why didn't you just stand there and tell the police who you were?" "Why didn't you just say you were only watching and not betting?" "Were you really afraid of those little guns?" As always, kinesthetically minded and, even when fleeing for their lives (or, as happened eight years later, surrendering them), the world's most poised people, they gleefully mimicked, also over and over again, our graceless style of running and what they claimed were our panic-stricken facial expressions. But above all, everyone was extremely pleased and even more surprised that we had not simply "pulled out our papers" (they knew about those too) and asserted our Distinguished Visitor status, but had instead demonstrated our solidarity with what were now our covillagers. (What we had actually demonstrated was our cowardice, but there is fellowship in that too.) Even the Brahmana priest, an old, grave, halfway-to-heaven type who because of its associations with the underworld would never be involved, even distantly, in a cockfight, and was difficult to approach even to other Balinese, had us called into his courtyard to ask us about what had happened, chuckling happily at the sheer extraordinariness of it all.

In Bali, to be teased is to be accepted. It was the turning point so far as our relationship to the community was concerned, and we were quite literally "in." The whole village opened up to us, probably more than it ever would have otherwise (I might actually never have gotten to that priest, and our accidental host became one of my best informants), and certainly very much faster. Getting caught, or almost caught, in a vice raid is perhaps not a very generalizable recipe for achieving that mysterious necessity of anthropological field work, rapport, but for me it worked very well. It led to a sudden and unusually complete acceptance into a society extremely difficult for outsiders to penetrate. It gave me the kind of immediate, inside-view grasp of an aspect of "peasant mentality" that anthropologists not fortunate enough to flee headlong with their subjects from armed authorities normally do not get. And, perhaps most important of all, for the other things might have come in other ways, it put me very quickly on to a combination emotional explosion, status war, and philosophical drama of central significance to the society whose inner nature I desired to understand. By the time I left I had spent about as much time looking into cockfights as into witchcraft, irrigation, caste, or marriage.

Of Cocks and Men

Bali, mainly because it is Bali, is a well-studied place. Its mythology, art, ritual, social organization, patterns of child rearing, forms of law, even styles of trance, have all been microscopically examined for traces of that elusive substance Jane Belo called "The Balinese Temper." [2] But, aside from a few passing remarks, the cockfight has barely been noticed, although as a popular obsession of consuming power it is at least as important a revelation of what being a Balinese "is really like" as these more celebrated phenomena.[3] As much of America surfaces in a ball park, on a golf links, at a race track, or around a poker table, much of Bali surfaces in a cock ring. For it is only apparently cocks that are fighting there. Actually, it is men.

To anyone who has been in Bali any length of time, the deep psychological identification of Balinese men with their cocks is unmistakable. The double entendre here is deliberate. It works in exactly the same way in Balinese as it does in English, even to producing the same tired jokes, strained puns, and uninventive obscenities. Bateson and Mead have even suggested that, in line with the Balinese conception of the body as a set of separately animated parts, cocks are viewed as detachable, self-operating penises, ambulant genitals with a life of their own.[4]

---

[2] J. Belo, "The Balinese Temper," in *Traditional Balinese Culture*, ed. J. Belo (New York, 1970) (originally published in 1935), pp. 85–110.

[3] The best discussion of cockfighting is again Bateson and Mead's *Balinese Character*, pp. 24–25, 140; but it, too, is general and abbreviated.

[4] Ibid., pp. 25–26. The cockfight is unusual within Balinese culture in being a single-sex public activity from which the other sex is totally and expressly excluded. Sexual differentiation is culturally extremely played down in Bali and most activities, formal and informal, involve the participation of men and women on equal ground, commonly as linked couples. From religion, to politics, to economics, to kinship, to dress, Bali is a rather "unisex" society, a fact both its customs and its symbolism clearly express. Even in contexts where women do not in fact play much of a role—music, painting, certain agricultural activities—their absence, which is only relative in any case, is more a mere matter of fact than

And while I do not have the kind of unconscious material either to confirm or disconfirm this intriguing notion, the fact that they are mascu-
line symbols par excellence is about as indubitable, and to the Balinese
about as evident, as the fact that water runs downhill.

The language of everyday moralism is shot through, on the male side
of it, with roosterish imagery. *Sabung,* the word for cock (and one
which appears in inscriptions as early as A.D. 922), is used metaphorically to mean "hero," "warrior," "champion," "man of parts," "political candidate," "bachelor," "dandy," "lady-killer," or "tough guy." A
pompous man whose behavior presumes above his station is compared
to a tailless cock who struts about as though he had a large, spectacular
one. A desperate man who makes a last, irrational effort to extricate
himself from an impossible situation is likened to a dying cock who
makes one final lunge at his tormentor to drag him along to a common
destruction. A stingy man, who promises much, gives little, and be-
grudges that, is compared to a cock which, held by the tail, leaps at another without in fact engaging him. A marriageable young man still shy
with the opposite sex or someone in a new job anxious to make a good
impression is called "a fighting cock caged for the first time." [5] Court
trials, wars, political contests, inheritance disputes, and street arguments
are all compared to cockfights.[6] Even the very island itself is perceived
from its shape as a small, proud cock, poised, neck extended, back taut,
tail raised, in eternal challenge to large, feckless, shapeless Java.[7]

But the intimacy of men with their cocks is more than metaphorical.
Balinese men, or anyway a large majority of Balinese men, spend an
enormous amount of time with their favorites, grooming them, feeding
them, discussing them, trying them out against one another, or just gaz-

---

socially enforced. To this general pattern, the cockfight, entirely of, by, and for
men (women—at least *Balinese* women—do not even watch), is the most striking
exception.

[5] C. Hooykaas, *The Lay of the Jaya Prana* (London, 1958), p. 39. The lay has
a stanza (no. 17) with the reluctant bridegroom use. Jaya Prana, the subject of a
Balinese Uriah myth, responds to the lord who has offered him the loveliest of
six hundred servant girls: "Godly King, my Lord and Master / I beg you, give me
leave to go / such things are not yet in my mind; / like a fighting cock encaged /
indeed I am on my mettle / I am alone / as yet the flame has not been fanned."

[6] For these, see V. E. Korn, *Het Adatrecht van Bali,* 2d ed. (The Hague, 1932),
index under *toh.*

[7] There is indeed a legend to the effect that the separation of Java and Bali is
due to the action of a powerful Javanese religious figure who wished to protect
himself against a Balinese culture hero (the ancestor of two Ksatria castes) who
was a passionate cockfighting gambler. See C. Hooykaas, *Agama Tirtha* (Amsterdam, 1964), p. 184.

ing at them with a mixture of rapt admiration and dreamy self-absorption. Whenever you see a group of Balinese men squatting idly in the council shed or along the road in their hips down, shoulders forward, knees up fashion, half or more of them will have a rooster in his hands, holding it between his thighs, bouncing it gently up and down to strengthen its legs, ruffling its feathers with abstract sensuality, pushing it out against a neighbor's rooster to rouse its spirit, withdrawing it toward his loins to calm it again. Now and then, to get a feel for another bird, a man will fiddle this way with someone else's cock for a while, but usually by moving around to squat in place behind it, rather than just having it passed across to him as though it were merely an animal.

In the houseyard, the high-walled enclosures where the people live, fighting cocks are kept in wicker cages, moved frequently about so as to maintain the optimum balance of sun and shade. They are fed a special diet, which varies somewhat according to individual theories but which is mostly maize, sifted for impurities with far more care than it is when mere humans are going to eat it, and offered to the animal kernel by kernel. Red pepper is stuffed down their beaks and up their anuses to give them spirit. They are bathed in the same ceremonial preparation of tepid water, medicinal herbs, flowers, and onions in which infants are bathed, and for a prize cock just about as often. Their combs are cropped, their plumage dressed, their spurs trimmed, and their legs massaged, and they are inspected for flaws with the squinted concentration of a diamond merchant. A man who has a passion for cocks, an enthusiast in the literal sense of the term, can spend most of his life with them, and even those, the overwhelming majority, whose passion though intense has not entirely run away with them, can and do spend what seems not only to an outsider, but also to themselves, an inordinate amount of time with them. "I am cock crazy," my landlord, a quite ordinary *afficionado* by Balinese standards, used to moan as he went to move another cage, give another bath, or conduct another feeding. "We're all cock crazy."

The madness has some less visible dimensions, however, because although it is true that cocks are symbolic expressions or magnifications of their owner's self, the narcissistic male ego writ out in Aesopian terms, they are also expressions—and rather more immediate ones—of what the Balinese regard as the direct inversion, aesthetically, morally, and metaphysically, of human status: animality.

The Balinese revulsion against any behavior regarded as animal-like can hardly be overstressed. Babies are not allowed to crawl for that reason. Incest, though hardly approved, is a much less horrifying crime than bestiality. (The appropriate punishment for the second is death by drowning, for the first being forced to live like an animal.) [8] Most demons are represented—in sculpture, dance, ritual, myth—in some real or fantastic animal form. The main puberty rite consists in filing the child's teeth so they will not look like animal fangs. Not only defecation but eating is regarded as a disgusting, almost obscene activity, to be conducted hurriedly and privately, because of its association with animality. Even falling down or any form of clumsiness is considered to be bad for these reasons. Aside from cocks and a few domestic animals— oxen, ducks—of no emotional significance, the Balinese are aversive to animals and treat their large number of dogs not merely callously but with a phobic cruelty. In identifying with his cock, the Balinese man is identifying not just with his ideal self, or even his penis, but also, and at the same time, with what he most fears, hates, and ambivalence being what it is, is fascinated by—"The Powers of Darkness."

The connection of cocks and cockfighting with such Powers, with the animalistic demons that threaten constantly to invade the small, cleared-off space in which the Balinese have so carefully built their lives and devour its inhabitants, is quite explicit. A cockfight, any cockfight, is in the first instance a blood sacrifice offered, with the appropriate chants and oblations, to the demons in order to pacify their ravenous, cannibal hunger. No temple festival should be conducted until one is made. (If it is omitted, someone will inevitably fall into a trance and command with the voice of an angered spirit that the oversight be immediately corrected.) Collective responses to natural evils—illness, crop failure, volcanic eruptions—almost always involve them. And that famous holiday in Bali, "The Day of Silence" (*Njepi*), when everyone sits silent and immobile all day long in order to avoid contact with a sudden influx of demons chased momentarily out of hell, is preceded the previous day by large-scale cockfights (in this case legal) in almost every village on the island.

In the cockfight, man and beast, good and evil, ego and id, the creative power of aroused masculinity and the destructive power of loosened an-

---

[8] An incestuous couple is forced to wear pig yokes over their necks and crawl to a pig trough and eat with their mouths there. On this, see J. Belo, "Customs Pertaining to Twins in Bali," in *Traditional Balinese Culture*, ed. J. Belo, p. 49; on the abhorrence of animality generally, Bateson and Mead, *Balinese Character*, p. 22.

imality fuse in a bloody drama of hatred, cruelty, violence, and death. It is little wonder that when, as is the invariable rule, the owner of the winning cock takes the carcass of the loser—often torn limb from limb by its enraged owner—home to eat, he does so with a mixture of social embarrassment, moral satisfaction, aesthetic disgust, and cannibal joy. Or that a man who has lost an important fight is sometimes driven to wreck his family shrines and curse the gods, an act of metaphysical (and social) suicide. Or that in seeking earthly analogues for heaven and hell the Balinese compare the former to the mood of a man whose cock has just won, the latter to that of a man whose cock has just lost.

The Fight

Cockfights (*tetadjen; sabungan*) are held in a ring about fifty feet square. Usually they begin toward late afternoon and run three or four hours until sunset. About nine or ten separate matches (*sehet*) comprise a program. Each match is precisely like the others in general pattern: there is no main match, no connection between individual matches, no variation in their format, and each is arranged on a completely ad hoc basis. After a fight has ended and the emotional debris is cleaned away—the bets have been paid, the curses cursed, the carcasses possessed—seven, eight, perhaps even a dozen men slip negligently into the ring with a cock and seek to find there a logical opponent for it. This process, which rarely takes less than ten minutes, and often a good deal longer, is conducted in a very subdued, oblique, even dissembling manner. Those not immediately involved give it at best but disguised, sidelong attention; those who, embarrassedly, are, attempt to pretend somehow that the whole thing is not really happening.

A match made, the other hopefuls retire with the same deliberate indifference, and the selected cocks have their spurs (*tadji*) affixed—razor-sharp, pointed steel swords, four or five inches long. This is a delicate job which only a small proportion of men, a half-dozen or so in most villages, know how to do properly. The man who attaches the spurs also provides them, and if the rooster he assists wins, its owner awards him the spur-leg of the victim. The spurs are affixed by winding a long length of string around the foot of the spur and the leg of the cock. For reasons I shall come to presently, it is done somewhat differently from case to case, and is an obsessively deliberate affair. The lore about spurs is extensive—they are sharpened only at eclipses and the dark of the moon, should be kept out of the sight of women, and so forth. And they are handled, both in use and out, with the same curious combination of fussiness and sensuality the Balinese direct toward ritual objects generally.

The spurs affixed, the two cocks are placed by their handlers (who may or may not be their owners) facing one another in the center of the ring.[9] A coconut pierced with a small hole is placed in a pail of water, in which it takes about twenty-one seconds to sink, a period known as a *tjeng* and marked at beginning and end by the beating of a slit gong. During these twenty-one seconds the handlers (*pengangkeb*) are not permitted to touch their roosters. If, as sometimes happens, the animals have not fought during this time, they are picked up, fluffed, pulled, prodded, and otherwise insulted, and put back in the center of the ring and the process begins again. Sometimes they refuse to fight at all, or one keeps running away, in which case they are imprisoned together under a wicker cage, which usually gets them engaged.

Most of the time, in any case, the cocks fly almost immediately at one another in a wing-beating, head-thrusting, leg-kicking explosion of animal fury so pure, so absolute, and in its own way so beautiful, as to be almost abstract, a Platonic concept of hate. Within moments one or the other drives home a solid blow with his spur. The handler whose cock has delivered the blow immediately picks it up so that it will not get a return blow, for if he does not the match is likely to end in a mutually mortal tie as the two birds wildly hack each other to pieces. This is particularly true if, as often happens, the spur sticks in its victim's body, for then the aggressor is at the mercy of his wounded foe.

With the birds again in the hands of their handlers, the coconut is now sunk three times after which the cock which has landed the blow

[9] Except for unimportant, small-bet fights (on the question of fight "importance," see below) spur affixing is usually done by someone other than the owner. Whether the owner handles his own cock or not more or less depends on how skilled he is at it, a consideration whose importance is again relative to the importance of the fight. When spur affixers and cock handlers are someone other than the owner, they are almost always a quite close relative—a brother or cousin—or a very intimate friend of his. They are thus almost extensions of his personality, as the fact that all three will refer to the cock as "mine," say "I" fought So-and-So, and so on, demonstrates. Also, owner-handler-affixer triads tend to be fairly fixed, though individuals may participate in several and often exchange roles within a given one.

must be set down to show that he is firm, a fact he demonstrates by wandering idly around the ring for a coconut sink. The coconut is then sunk twice more and the fight must recommence.

During this interval, slightly over two minutes, the handler of the wounded cock has been working frantically over it, like a trainer patching a mauled boxer between rounds, to get it in shape for a last, desperate try for victory. He blows in its mouth, putting the whole chicken head in his own mouth and sucking and blowing, fluffs it, stuffs its wounds with various sorts of medicines, and generally tries anything he can think of to arouse the last ounce of spirit which may be hidden somewhere within it. By the time he is forced to put it back down he is usually drenched in chicken blood, but, as in prize fighting, a good handler is worth his weight in gold. Some of them can virtually make the dead walk, at least long enough for the second and final round.

In the climactic battle (if there is one; sometimes the wounded cock simply expires in the handler's hands or immediately as it is placed down again), the cock who landed the first blow usually proceeds to finish off his weakened opponent. But this is far from an inevitable outcome, for if a cock can walk, he can fight, and if he can fight, he can kill, and what counts is which cock expires first. If the wounded one can get a stab in and stagger on until the other drops, he is the official winner, even if he himself topples over an instant later.

Surrounding all this melodrama—which the crowd packed tight around the ring follows in near silence, moving their bodies in kinesthetic sympathy with the movement of the animals, cheering their champions on with wordless hand motions, shiftings of the shoulders, turnings of the head, falling back en masse as the cock with the murderous spurs careens toward one side of the ring (it is said that spectators sometimes lose eyes and fingers from being too attentive), surging forward again as they glance off toward another—is a vast body of extraordinarily elaborate and precisely detailed rules.

These rules, together with the developed lore of cocks and cockfighting which accompanies them, are written down in palm-leaf manuscripts (*lontar; rontal*) passed on from generation to generation as part of the general legal and cultural tradition of the villages. At a fight, the umpire (*saja komong; djuru kembar*)—the man who manages the coconut —is in charge of their application and his authority is absolute. I have never seen an umpire's judgment questioned on any subject, even by the more despondent losers, nor have I ever heard, even in private, a charge of unfairness directed against one, or, for that matter, complaints about umpires in general. Only exceptionally well trusted, solid, and, given the complexity of the code, knowledgeable citizens perform this job, and in fact men will bring their cocks only to fights presided over by such men. It is also the umpire to whom accusations of cheating, which, though rare in the extreme, occasionally arise, are referred; and it is he who in the not infrequent cases where the cocks expire virtually together decides which (if either, for, though the Balinese do not care for such an outcome, there can be ties) went first. Likened to a judge, a king, a priest, and a policeman, he is all of these, and under his assured direction the animal passion of the fight proceeds within the civic certainty of the law. In the dozens of cockfights I saw in Bali, I never once saw an altercation about rules. Indeed, I never saw an open altercation, other than those between cocks, at all.

This crosswise doubleness of an event which, taken as a fact of nature, is rage untrammeled and, taken as a fact of culture, is form perfected, defines the cockfight as a sociological entity. A cockfight is what, searching for a name for something not vertebrate enough to be called a group and not structureless enough to be called a crowd, Erving Goffman has called a "focused gathering"—a set of persons engrossed in a common flow of activity and relating to one another in terms of that flow.[10] Such gatherings meet and disperse; the participants in them fluctuate; the activity that focuses them is discrete—a particulate process that reoccurs rather than a continuous one that endures. They take their form from the situation that evokes them, the floor on which they are placed, as Goffman puts it; but it is a form, and an articulate one, nonetheless. For the situation, the floor is itself created, in jury deliberations, surgical operations, block meetings, sit-ins, cockfights, by the cultural preoccupations—here, as we shall see, the celebration of status rivalry —which not only specify the focus but, assembling actors and arranging scenery, bring it actually into being.

In classical times (that is to say, prior to the Dutch invasion of 1908), when there were no bureaucrats around to improve popular morality, the staging of a cockfight was an explicitly societal matter. Bringing a cock to an important fight was, for an adult male, a compulsory duty of citizenship; taxation of fights, which were usually held on market day, was a major source of public revenue; patronage of the art was

[10] E. Goffman, *Encounters: Two Studies in the Sociology of Interaction* (Indianapolis, 1961), pp. 9–10.

a stated responsibility of princes; and the cock ring, or *wantilan,* stood in the center of the village near those other monuments of Balinese civility—the council house, the origin temple, the marketplace, the signal tower, and the banyan tree. Today, a few special occasions aside, the newer rectitude makes so open a statement of the connection between the excitements of collective life and those of blood sport impossible, but, less directly expressed, the connection itself remains intimate and intact. To expose it, however, it is necessary to turn to the aspect of cockfighting around which all the others pivot, and through which they exercise their force, an aspect I have thus far studiously ignored. I mean, of course, the gambling.

Odds and Even Money

The Balinese never do anything in a simple way that they can contrive to do in a complicated one, and to this generalization cockfight wagering is no exception.

In the first place, there are two sorts of bets, or *toh.*[11] There is the single axial bet in the center between the principals (*toh ketengah*), and there is the cloud of peripheral ones around the ring between members of the audience (*toh kesasi*). The first is typically large; the second typically small. The first is collective, involving coalitions of bettors clustering around the owner; the second is individual, man to man. The first is a matter of deliberate, very quiet, almost furtive arrangement by the coalition members and the umpire huddled like conspirators in the center of the ring; the second is a matter of impulsive shouting, public offers, and public acceptances by the excited throng around its edges. And most curiously, and as we shall see most revealingly, *where the first is always, without exception, even money, the second, equally without ex-*

[11] This word, which literally means an indelible stain or mark, as in a birthmark or a vein in a stone, is used as well for a deposit in a court case, for a pawn, for security offered in a loan, for a stand-in for someone else in a legal or ceremonial context, for an earnest advanced in a business deal, for a sign placed in a field to indicate its ownership is in dispute, and for the status of an unfaithful wife from whose lover her husband must gain satisfaction or surrender her to him. See Korn, *Het Adatrecht van Bali;* Th. Pigeaud, *Javaans-Nederlands Handwoordenboek* (Groningen, 1938); H. H. Juynboll, *Oudjavaansche-Nederlandsche Woordenlijst* (Leiden, 1923).

ception, is never such. What is a fair coin in the center is a biased one on the side.

The center bet is the official one, hedged in again with a webwork of rules, and is made between the two cock owners, with the umpire as overseer and public witness.[12] This bet, which, as I say, is always relatively and sometimes very large, is never raised simply by the owner in whose name it is made, but by him together with four or five, sometimes seven or eight, allies—kin, village mates, neighbors, close friends. He may, if he is not especially well-to-do, not even be the major contributor; though, if only to show that he is not involved in any chicanery, he must be a significant one.

Of the fifty-seven matches for which I have exact and reliable data on the center bet, the range is from fifteen ringgits to five hundred, with a mean at eighty-five and with the distribution being rather noticeably trimodal: small fights (15 ringgits either side of 35) accounting for about 45 percent of the total number; medium ones (20 ringgits either side of 70) for about 25 percent; and large (75 ringgits either side of 175) for about 20 percent, with a few very small and very large ones out at the extremes. In a society where the normal daily wage of a manual laborer —a brickmaker, an ordinary farmworker, a market porter—was about three ringgits a day, and considering the fact that fights were held on the average about every two-and-a-half days in the immediate area I studied, this is clearly serious gambling, even if the bets are pooled rather than individual efforts.

The side bets are, however, something else altogether. Rather than the solemn, legalistic pactmaking of the center, wagering takes place rather in the fashion in which the stock exchange used to work when it was out on the curb. There is a fixed and known odds paradigm which runs in a continuous series from ten-to-nine at the short end to two-to-one at the long: 10–9, 9–8, 8–7, 7–6, 6–5, 5–4, 4–3, 3–2, 2–1. The man who wishes to back the *underdog cock* (leaving aside how favorites, *kebut,* and underdogs, *ngai,* are established for the moment) shouts the short-side number indicating the odds he wants *to be given.* That is, if he shouts *gasal,* "five," he wants the underdog at five-to-four (or, for

---

[12] The center bet must be advanced in cash by both parties prior to the actual fight. The umpire holds the stakes until the decision is rendered and then awards them to the winner, avoiding, among other things, the intense embarrassment both winner and loser would feel if the latter had to pay off personally following his defeat. About 10 percent of the winner's receipts are subtracted for the umpire's share and that of the fight sponsors.

him, four-to-five); if he shouts "four," he wants it at four-to-three (again, he putting up the "three"); if "nine," at nine-to-eight, and so on. A man backing the favorite, and thus considering giving odds if he can get them short enough, indicates the fact by crying out the color-type of that cock—"brown," "speckled," or whatever.[13]

As odds-takers (backers of the underdog) and odds-givers (backers of the favorite) sweep the crowd with their shouts, they begin to focus in on one another as potential betting pairs, often from far across the ring. The taker tries to shout the giver into longer odds, the giver to shout the taker into shorter ones.[14] The taker, who is the wooer in this situation, will signal how large a bet he wishes to make at the odds he is shouting by holding a number of fingers up in front of his face and vigorously waving them. If the giver, the wooed, replies in kind, the bet is made; if he does not, they unlock gazes and the search goes on.

The side betting, which takes place after the center bet has been made and its size announced, consists then in a rising crescendo of

[13] Actually, the typing of cocks, which is extremely elaborate (I have collected more than twenty classes, certainly not a complete list), is not based on color alone, but on a series of independent, interacting, dimensions, which include—besides color—size, bone thickness, plumage, and temperament. (But *not* pedigree. The Balinese do not breed cocks to any significant extent, nor, so far as I have been able to discover, have they ever done so. The *asil,* or jungle cock, which is the basic fighting strain everywhere the sport is found, is native to southern Asia, and one can buy a good example in the chicken section of almost any Balinese market for anywhere from four or five ringgits up to fifty or more.) The color element is merely the one normally used as the type name, except when the two cocks of different types—as on principle they must be—have the same color, in which case a secondary indication from one of the other dimensions ("large speckled" v. "small speckled," etc.) is added. The types are coordinated with various cosmological ideas which help shape the making of matches, so that, for example, you fight a small, headstrong, speckled brown-on-white cock with flat-lying feathers and thin legs from the east side of the ring on a certain day of the complex Balinese calendar, and a large, cautious, all-black cock with tufted feathers and stubby legs from the north side on another day, and so on. All this is again recorded in palm-leaf manuscripts and endlessly discussed by the Balinese (who do not all have identical systems), and a full-scale componential-cum-symbolic analysis of cock classifications would be extremely valuable both as an adjunct to the description of the cockfight and in itself. But my data on the subject, though extensive and varied, do not seem to be complete and systematic enough to attempt such an analysis here. For Balinese cosmological ideas more generally see Belo, ed., *Traditional Balinese Culture,* and J. L. Swellengrebel, ed., *Bali: Studies in Life, Thought, and Ritual* (The Hague, 1960).

[14] For purposes of ethnographic completeness, it should be noted that it is possible for the man backing the favorite—the odds-giver—to make a bet in which he wins if his cock wins or there is a tie, a slight shortening of the odds (I do not have enough cases to be exact, but ties seem to occur about once every fifteen or twenty matches). He indicates his wish to do this by shouting *sapih* ("tie") rather than the cock-type, but such bets are in fact infrequent.

shouts as backers of the underdog offer their propositions to anyone who will accept them, while those who are backing the favorite but do not like the price being offered, shout equally frenetically the color of the cock to show they too are desperate to bet but want shorter odds.

Almost always odds-calling, which tends to be very consensual in that at any one time almost all callers are calling the same thing, starts off toward the long end of the range—five-to-four or four-to-three—and then moves, also consensually, toward the short end with greater or lesser speed and to a greater or lesser degree. Men crying "five" and finding themselves answered only with cries of "brown" start crying "six," either drawing the other callers fairly quickly with them or retiring from the scene as their too-generous offers are snapped up. If the change is made and partners are still scarce, the procedure is repeated in a move to "seven," and so on, only rarely, and in the very largest fights, reaching the ultimate "nine" or "ten" levels. Occasionally, if the cocks are clearly mismatched, there may be no upward movement at all, or even a movement down the scale to four-to-three, three-to-two, very, very rarely two-to-one, a shift which is accompanied by a declining number of bets as a shift upward is accompanied by an increasing number. But the general pattern is for the betting to move a shorter or longer distance up the scale toward the, for sidebets, nonexistent pole of even money, with the overwhelming majority of bets falling in the four-to-three to eight-to-seven range.[15]

As the moment for the release of the cocks by the handlers approaches, the screaming, at least in a match where the center bet is large, reaches almost frenzied proportions as the remaining unfulfilled bettors try desperately to find a last-minute partner at a price they can live with. (Where the center bet is small, the opposite tends to occur:

[15] The precise dynamics of the movement of the betting is one of the most intriguing, most complicated, and, given the hectic conditions under which it occurs, most difficult to study, aspects of the fight. Motion picture recording plus multiple observers would probably be necessary to deal with it effectively. Even impressionistically—the only approach open to a lone ethnographer caught in the middle of all this—it is clear that certain men lead both in determining the favorite (that is, making the opening cock-type calls which always initiate the process) and in directing the movement of the odds, these "opinion leaders" being the more accomplished cockfighters-cum-solid-citizens to be discussed below. If these men begin to change their calls, others follow; if they begin to make bets, so do others and—though there are always a large number of frustrated bettors crying for shorter or longer odds to the end—the movement more or less ceases. But a detailed understanding of the whole process awaits what, alas, it is not very likely ever to get: a decision theorist armed with precise observations of individual behavior.

betting dies off, trailing into silence, as odds lengthen and people lose interest.) In a large-bet, well-made match—the kind of match the Balinese regard as "real cockfighting"—the mob scene quality, the sense that sheer chaos is about to break loose, with all those waving, shouting, pushing, clambering men is quite strong, an effect which is only heightened by the intense stillness that falls with instant suddenness, rather as if someone had turned off the current, when the slit gong sounds, the cocks are put down, and the battle begins.

When it ends, anywhere from fifteen seconds to five minutes later, *all bets are immediately paid*. There are absolutely no IOUs, at least to a betting opponent. One may, of course, borrow from a friend before offering or accepting a wager, but to offer or accept it you must have the money already in hand and, if you lose, you must pay it on the spot, before the next match begins. This is an iron rule, and as I have never heard of a disputed umpire's decision (though doubtless there must sometimes be some), I have also never heard of a welshed bet, perhaps because in a worked-up cockfight crowd the consequences might be, as they are reported to be sometimes for cheaters, drastic and immediate.

It is, in any case, this formal asymmetry between balanced center bets and unbalanced side ones that poses the critical analytical problem for a theory which sees cockfight wagering as the link connecting the fight to the wider world of Balinese culture. It also suggests the way to go about solving it and demonstrating the link.

The first point that needs to be made in this connection is that the higher the center bet, the more likely the match will in actual fact be an even one. Simple considerations of rationality suggest that. If you are betting fifteen ringgits on a cock, you might be willing to go along with even money even if you feel your animal somewhat the less promising. But if you are betting five hundred you are very, very likely to be loathe to do so. Thus, in large-bet fights, which of course involve the better animals, tremendous care is taken to see that the cocks are about as evenly matched as to size, general condition, pugnacity, and so on as is humanly possible. The different ways of adjusting the spurs of the animals are often employed to secure this. If one cock seems stronger, an agreement will be made to position his spur at a slightly less advantageous angle—a kind of handicapping, at which spur affixers are, so it is said, extremely skilled. More care will be taken, too, to employ skillful handlers and to match them exactly as to abilities.

In short, in a large-bet fight the pressure to make the match a genuinely fifty-fifty proposition is enormous, and is consciously felt as such. For medium fights the pressure is somewhat less, and for small ones less yet, though there is always an effort to make things at least approximately equal, for even at fifteen ringgits (five days' work) no one wants to make an even money bet in a clearly unfavorable situation. And, again, what statistics I have tend to bear this out. In my fifty-seven matches, the favorite won thirty-three times overall, the underdog twenty-four, a 1.4 : 1 ratio. But if one splits the figures at sixty ringgits center bets, the ratios turn out to be 1.1 : 1 (twelve favorites, eleven underdogs) for those above this line, and 1.6 : 1 (twenty-one and thirteen) for those below it. Or, if you take the extremes, for very large fights, those with center bets over a hundred ringgits the ratio is 1 : 1 (seven and seven); for very small fights, those under forty ringgits, it is 1.9 : 1 (nineteen and ten).[16]

Now, from this proposition—that the higher the center bet the more exactly a fifty-fifty proposition the cockfight is—two things more or less immediately follow: (1) the higher the center bet is, the greater the pull on the side betting toward the short-odds end of the wagering spectrum, and vice versa; (2) the higher the center bet is, the greater the volume of side betting, and vice versa.

The logic is similar in both cases. The closer the fight is in fact to even money, the less attractive the long end of the odds will appear and, therefore, the shorter it must be if there are to be takers. That this is the case is apparent from mere inspection, from the Balinese's own analysis of the matter, and from what more systematic observations I was able to collect. Given the difficulty of making precise and complete recordings of side betting, this argument is hard to cast in numerical form, but in all my cases the odds-giver, odds-taker consensual point, a quite pronounced mini-max saddle where the bulk (at a guess, two-thirds to three-quarters in most cases) of the bets are actually made, was three or four points further along the scale toward the shorter end for

---

[16] Assuming only binomial variability, the departure from a fifty-fifty expectation in the sixty-ringgits-and-below case is 1.38 standard deviations, or (in a one direction test) an eight in one hundred possibility by chance alone; for the below-forty-ringgits case it is 1.65 standard deviations, or about five in one hundred. The fact that these departures though real are not extreme merely indicates, again, that even in the smaller fights the tendency to match cocks at least reasonably evenly persists. It is a matter of relative relaxation of the pressures toward equalization, not their elimination. The tendency for high-bet contests to be coin-flip propositions is, of course, even more striking, and suggests the Balinese know quite well what they are about.

the large-center-bet fights than for the small ones, with medium ones generally in between. In detail, the fit is not, of course, exact, but the general pattern is quite consistent: the power of the center bet to pull the side bets toward its own even-money pattern is directly proportional to its size, because its size is directly proportional to the degree to which the cocks are in fact evenly matched. As for the volume question, total wagering is greater in large-center-bet fights because such fights are considered more "interesting," not only in the sense that they are less predictable, but, more crucially, that more is at stake in them—in terms of money, in terms of the quality of the cocks, and consequently, as we shall see, in terms of social prestige.[17]

The paradox of fair coin in the middle, biased coin on the outside is thus a merely apparent one. The two betting systems, though formally incongruent, are not really contradictory to one another, but are part of a single larger system in which the center bet is, so to speak, the "center of gravity," drawing, the larger it is the more so, the outside bets toward the short-odds end of the scale. The center bet thus "makes the game," or perhaps better, defines it, signals what, following a notion of Jeremy Bentham's, I am going to call its "depth."

The Balinese attempt to create an interesting, if you will, "deep," match by making the center bet as large as possible so that the cocks matched will be as equal and as fine as possible, and the outcome, thus, as unpredictable as possible. They do not always succeed. Nearly half the matches are relatively trivial, relatively uninteresting—in my borrowed terminology, "shallow"—affairs. But that fact no more argues against my interpretation than the fact that most painters, poets, and playwrights are mediocre argues against the view that artistic effort is

[17] The reduction in wagering in smaller fights (which, of course, feeds on itself; one of the reasons people find small fights uninteresting is that there is less wagering in them, and contrariwise for large ones) takes place in three mutually reinforcing ways. First, there is a simple withdrawal of interest as people wander off to have a cup of coffee or chat with a friend. Second, the Balinese do not mathematically reduce odds, but bet directly in terms of stated odds as such. Thus, for a nine-to-eight bet, one man wagers nine ringgits, the other eight; for five-to-four, one wagers five, the other four. For any given currency unit, like the ringgit, therefore, 6.3 times as much money is involved in a ten-to-nine bet as in a two-to-one bet, for example, and, as noted, in small fights betting settles toward the longer end. Finally, the bets which are made tend to be one- rather than two-, three-, or in some of the very largest fights, four- or five-finger ones. (The fingers indicate the *multiples* of the stated bet odds at issue, not absolute figures. Two fingers in a six-to-five situation means a man wants to wager ten ringgits on the underdog against twelve, three in an eight-to-seven situation, twenty-one against twenty-four, and so on.)

directed toward profundity and, with a certain frequency, approximates it. The image of artistic technique is indeed exact: the center bet is a means, a device, for creating "interesting," "deep" matches, *not* the reason, or at least not the main reason, *why* they are interesting, the source of their fascination, the substance of their depth. The question of why such matches are interesting—indeed, for the Balinese, exquisitely absorbing—takes us out of the realm of formal concerns into more broadly sociological and social-psychological ones, and to a less purely economic idea of what "depth" in gaming amounts to.[18]

Playing with Fire

Bentham's concept of "deep play" is found in his *The Theory of Legislation*.[19] By it he means play in which the stakes are so high that it is, from his utilitarian standpoint, irrational for men to engage in it at all. If a man whose fortune is a thousand pounds (or ringgits) wages five

---

[18] Besides wagering there are other economic aspects of the cockfight, especially its very close connection with the local market system which, though secondary both to its motivation and to its function, are not without importance. Cockfights are open events to which anyone who wishes may come, sometimes from quite distant areas, but well over 90 percent, probably over 95, are very local affairs, and the locality concerned is defined not by the village, nor even by the administrative district, but by the rural market system. Bali has a three-day market week with the familiar "solar-system"-type rotation. Though the markets themselves have never been very highly developed, small morning affairs in a village square, it is the microregion such rotation rather generally marks out—ten or twenty square miles, seven or eight neighboring villages (which in contemporary Bali is usually going to mean anywhere from five to ten or eleven thousand people) from which the core of any cockfight audience, indeed virtually all of it, will come. Most of the fights are in fact organized and sponsored by small combines of petty rural merchants under the general premise, very strongly held by them and indeed by all Balinese, that cockfights are good for trade because "they get money out of the house, they make it circulate." Stalls selling various sorts of things as well as assorted sheer-chance gambling games (see below) are set up around the edge of the area so that this even takes on the quality of a small fair. This connection of cockfighting with markets and market sellers is very old, as, among other things, their conjunction in inscriptions [R. Goris, *Prasasti Bali,* 2 vols. (Bandung, 1954)] indicates. Trade has followed the cock for centuries in rural Bali, and the sport has been one of the main agencies of the island's monetization.

[19] The phrase is found in the Hildreth translation, International Library of Psychology (1931), note to p. 106; see L. L. Fuller, *The Morality of Law* (New Haven, 1964), p. 6 ff.

hundred of it on an even bet, the marginal utility of the pound he stands to win is clearly less than the marginal disutility of the one he stands to lose. In genuine deep play, this is the case for both parties. They are both in over their heads. Having come together in search of pleasure they have entered into a relationship which will bring the participants, considered collectively, net pain rather than net pleasure. Bentham's conclusion was, therefore, that deep play was immoral from first principles and, a typical step for him, should be prevented legally.

But more interesting than the ethical problem, at least for our concerns here, is that despite the logical force of Bentham's analysis men do engage in such play, both passionately and often, and even in the face of law's revenge. For Bentham and those who think as he does (nowadays mainly lawyers, economists, and a few psychiatrists), the explanation is, as I have said, that such men are irrational—addicts, fetishists, children, fools, savages, who need only to be protected against themselves. But for the Balinese, though naturally they do not formulate it in so many words, the explanation lies in the fact that in such play, money is less a measure of utility, had or expected, than it is a symbol of moral import, perceived or imposed.

It is, in fact, in shallow games, ones in which smaller amounts of money are involved, that increments and decrements of cash are more nearly synonyms for utility and disutility, in the ordinary, unexpanded sense—for pleasure and pain, happiness and unhappiness. In deep ones, where the amounts of money are great, much more is at stake than material gain: namely, esteem, honor, dignity, respect—in a word, though in Bali a profoundly freighted word, status.[20] It is at stake symbolically, for (a few cases of ruined addict gamblers aside) no one's status is actually altered by the outcome of a cockfight; it is only, and that momentarily, affirmed or insulted. But for the Balinese, for whom nothing is more pleasurable than an affront obliquely delivered or more painful than one obliquely received—particularly when mutual acquaintances, undeceived by surfaces, are watching—such appraisive drama is deep indeed.

This, I must stress immediately, is *not* to say that the money does not matter, or that the Balinese is no more concerned about losing five

---

[20] Of course, even in Bentham, utility is not normally confined as a concept to monetary losses and gains, and my argument here might be more carefully put in terms of a denial that for the Balinese, as for any people, utility (pleasure, happiness . . .) is merely identifiable with wealth. But such terminological problems are in any case secondary to the essential point: the cockfight is not roulette.

hundred ringgits than fifteen. Such a conclusion would be absurd. It is because money *does,* in this hardly unmaterialistic society, matter and matter very much that the more of it one risks, the more of a lot of other things, such as one's pride, one's poise, one's dispassion, one's masculinity, one also risks, again only momentarily but again very publicly as well. In deep cockfights an owner and his collaborators, and, as we shall see, to a lesser but still quite real extent also their backers on the outside, put their money where their status is.

It is in large part *because* the marginal disutility of loss is so great at the higher levels of betting that to engage in such betting is to lay one's public self, allusively and metaphorically, through the medium of one's cock, on the line. And though to a Benthamite this might seem merely to increase the irrationality of the enterprise that much further, to the Balinese what it mainly increases is the meaningfulness of it all. And as (to follow Weber rather than Bentham) the imposition of meaning on life is the major end and primary condition of human existence, that access of significance more than compensates for the economic costs involved.[21] Actually, given the even-money quality of the larger matches, important changes in material fortune among those who regularly participate in them seem virtually nonexistent, because matters more or less even out over the long run. It is, actually, in the smaller, shallow fights, where one finds the handful of more pure, addict-type gamblers involved—those who *are* in it mainly for the money—that "real" changes in social position, largely downward, are affected. Men of this sort, plungers, are highly dispraised by "true cockfighters" as fools who do not understand what the sport is all about, vulgarians who simply miss the point of it all. They are, these addicts, regarded as fair game for the genuine enthusiasts, those who do understand, to take a little money away from—something that is easy enough to do by luring them, through the force of their greed, into irrational bets on mismatched cocks. Most of them do indeed manage to ruin themselves in a

[21] M. Weber, *The Sociology of Religion* (Boston, 1963). There is nothing specifically Balinese, of course, about deepening significance with money, as Whyte's description of corner boys in a working-class district of Boston demonstrates: "Gambling plays an important role in the lives of Cornerville people. Whatever game the corner boys play, they nearly always bet on the outcome. When there is nothing at stake, the game is not considered a real contest. This does not mean that the financial element is all-important. I have frequently heard men say that the honor of winning was much more important than the money at stake. The corner boys consider playing for money the real test of skill and, unless a man performs well when money is at stake, he is not considered a good competitor." W. F. Whyte, *Street Corner Society,* 2d ed. (Chicago, 1955), p. 140.

remarkably short time, but there always seems to be one or two of them around, pawning their land and selling their clothes in order to bet, at any particular time.[22]

This graduated correlation of "status gambling" with deeper fights and, inversely, "money gambling" with shallower ones is in fact quite general. Bettors themselves form a sociomoral hierarchy in these terms. As noted earlier, at most cockfights there are, around the very edges of the cockfight area, a large number of mindless, sheer-chance-type gambling games (roulette, dice throw, coin-spin, pea-under-the-shell) operated by concessionaires. Only women, children, adolescents, and various other sorts of people who do not (or not yet) fight cocks—the extremely poor, the socially despised, the personally idiosyncratic—play at these games, at, of course, penny ante levels. Cockfighting men would be ashamed to go anywhere near them. Slightly above these people in standing are those who though they do not themselves fight cocks, bet on the smaller matches around the edges. Next, there are those who fight cocks in small, or occasionally medium matches, but have not the status to join in the large ones, though they may bet from time to time on the side in those. And finally, there are those, the really substantial members of the community, the solid citizenry around whom local life revolves, who fight in the larger fights and bet on them around the side. The focusing element in these focused gatherings, these men generally dominate and define the sport as they dominate and define the society. When a Balinese male talks, in that almost venerative way, about "the true cockfighter," the *bebatoh* ("bettor") or *djuru kurung* ("cage keeper"), it is this sort of person, not those who bring the mentality of the pea-and-shell game into the quite different, inappropriate context of the cockfight, the driven gambler (*potét,* a word which has the secondary meaning of thief or reprobate), and the wistful hanger-on, that they

---

[22] The extremes to which this madness is conceived on occasion to go—and the fact that it is considered madness—is demonstrated by the Balinese folk tale *I Tuhung Kuning.* A gambler becomes so deranged by his passion that, leaving on a trip, he orders his pregnant wife to take care of the prospective newborn if it is a boy but to feed it as meat to his fighting cocks if it is a girl. The mother gives birth to a girl, but rather than giving the child to the cocks she gives them a large rat and conceals the girl with her own mother. When the husband returns, the cocks, crowing a jingle, inform him of the deception and, furious, he sets out to kill the child. A goddess descends from heaven and takes the girl up to the skies with her. The cocks die from the food given them, the owner's sanity is restored, the goddess brings the girl back to the father, who reunites him with his wife. The story is given as "Geel Komkommertje" in J. Hooykaas-van Leeuwen Boomkamp, *Sprookjes en Verhalen van Bali* (The Hague, 1956), pp. 19–25.

mean. For such a man, what is really going on in a match is something rather closer to an *affaire d'honneur* (though, with the Balinese talent for practical fantasy, the blood that is spilled is only figuratively human) than to the stupid, mechanical crank of a slot machine.

What makes Balinese cockfighting deep is thus not money in itself, but what, the more of it that is involved the more so, money causes to happen: the migration of the Balinese status hierarchy into the body of the cockfight. Psychologically an Aesopian representation of the ideal/demonic, rather narcissistic, male self, sociologically it is an equally Aesopian representation of the complex fields of tension set up by the controlled, muted, ceremonial, but for all that deeply felt, interaction of those selves in the context of everyday life. The cocks may be surrogates for their owners' personalities, animal mirrors of psychic form, but the cockfight is—or more exactly, deliberately is made to be —a simulation of the social matrix, the involved system of cross-cutting, overlapping, highly corporate groups—villages, kingroups, irrigation societies, temple congregations, "castes"—in which its devotees live.[23] And as prestige, the necessity to affirm it, defend it, celebrate it, justify it, and just plain bask in it (but not, given the strongly ascriptive character of Balinese stratification, to seek it), is perhaps the central driving force in the society, so also—ambulant penises, blood sacrifices, and monetary exchanges aside—is it of the cockfight. This apparent amusement and seeming sport is, to take another phrase from Erving Goffman, "a status bloodbath." [24]

The easiest way to make this clear, and at least to some degree to demonstrate it, is to invoke the village whose cockfighting activities I observed the closest—the one in which the raid occurred and from which my statistical data are taken.

Like all Balinese villages, this one—Tihingan, in the Klungkung region of southeast Bali—is intricately organized, a labyrinth of alliances and oppositions. But, unlike many, two sorts of corporate groups, which are also status groups, particularly stand out, and we may concentrate on them, in a part-for-whole way, without undue distortion.

[23] For a fuller description of Balinese rural social structure, see C. Geertz, "Form and Variation in Balinese Village Structure," *American Anthropologist* 61 (1959): pp. 94–108; "Tihingan, A Balinese Village," in R. M. Koentjaraningrat, *Villages in Indonesia* (Ithaca, 1967), pp. 210–243; and, though it is a bit off the norm as Balinese villages go, V. E. Korn, *De Dorpsrepubliek tnganan Pagringsingan* (Santpoort, Netherlands, 1933).

[24] Goffman, *Encounters*, p. 78.

First, the village is dominated by four large, patrilineal, partly endogamous descent groups which are constantly vying with one another and form the major factions in the village. Sometimes they group two and two, or rather the two larger ones versus the two smaller ones plus all the unaffiliated people; sometimes they operate independently. There are also subfactions within them, subfactions within the subfactions, and so on to rather fine levels of distinction. And second, there is the village itself, almost entirely endogamous, which is opposed to all the other villages round about in its cockfight circuit (which, as explained, is the market region), but which also forms alliances with certain of these neighbors against certain others in various supravillage political and social contexts. The exact situation is thus, as everywhere in Bali, quite distinctive; but the general pattern of a tiered hierarchy of status rivalries between highly corporate but various based groupings (and, thus, between the members of them) is entirely general.

Consider, then, as support of the general thesis that the cockfight, and especially the deep cockfight, is fundamentally a dramatization of status concerns, the following facts, which to avoid extended ethnographic description I shall simply pronounce to be facts—though the concrete evidence, examples, statements, and numbers that could be brought to bear in support of them, is both extensive and unmistakable:

1. A man virtually never bets against a cock owned by a member of his own kingroup. Usually he will feel obliged to bet for it, the more so the closer the kin tie and the deeper the fight. If he is certain in his mind that it will not win, he may just not bet at all, particularly if it is only a second cousin's bird or if the fight is a shallow one. But as a rule he will feel he must support it and, in deep games, nearly always does. Thus the great majority of the people calling "five" or "speckled" so demonstratively are expressing their allegiance to their kinsman, not their evaluation of his bird, their understanding of probability theory, or even their hopes of unearned income.

2. This principle is extended logically. If your kingroup is not involved you will support an allied kingroup against an unallied one in the same way, and so on through the very involved networks of alliances which, as I say, make up this, as any other, Balinese village.

3. So, too, for the village as a whole. If an outsider cock is fighting any cock from your village, you will tend to support the local one. If, what is a rarer circumstance but occurs every now and then, a cock

from outside your cockfight circuit is fighting one inside it, you will also tend to support the "home bird."

4. Cocks which come from any distance are almost always favorites, for the theory is the man would not have dared to bring it if it was not a good cock, the more so the further he has come. His followers are, of course, obliged to support him, and when the more grand-scale legal cockfights are held (on holidays, and so on) the people of the village take what they regard to be the best cocks in the village, regardless of ownership, and go off to support them, although they will almost certainly have to give odds on them and to make large bets to show that they are not a cheapskate village. Actually, such "away games," though infrequent, tend to mend the ruptures between village members that the constantly occurring "home games," where village factions are opposed rather than united, exacerbate.

5. Almost all matches are sociologically relevant. You seldom get two outsider cocks fighting, or two cocks with no particular group backing, or with group backing which is mutually unrelated in any clear way. When you do get them, the game is very shallow, betting very slow, and the whole thing very dull, with no one save the immediate principals and an addict gambler or two at all interested.

6. By the same token, you rarely get two cocks from the same group, even more rarely from the same subfaction, and virtually never from the same sub-subfaction (which would be in most cases one extended family) fighting. Similarly, in outside village fights two members of the village will rarely fight against one another, even though, as bitter rivals, they would do so with enthusiasm on their home grounds.

7. On the individual level, people involved in an institutionalized hostility relationship, called *puik,* in which they do not speak or otherwise have anything to do with each other (the causes of this formal breaking of relations are many: wife-capture, inheritance arguments, political differences) will bet very heavily, sometimes almost maniacally, against one another in what is a frank and direct attack on the very masculinity, the ultimate ground of his status, of the opponent.

8. The center bet coalition is, in all but the shallowest games, *always* made up by structural allies—no "outside money" is involved. What is "outside" depends upon the context, of course, but given it, no outside money is mixed in with the main bet; if the principals cannot raise it, it is not made. The center bet, again especially in deeper games, is thus the most direct and open expression of social opposition, which is one

of the reasons why both it and matchmaking are surrounded by such an air of unease, furtiveness, embarrassment, and so on.

9. The rule about borrowing money—that you may borrow *for* a bet but not *in* one—stems (and the Balinese are quite conscious of this) from similar considerations: you are never at the *economic* mercy of your enemy that way. Gambling debts, which can get quite large on a rather short-term basis, are always to friends, never to enemies, structurally speaking.

10. When two cocks are structurally irrelevant or neutral so far as *you* are concerned (though, as mentioned, they almost never are to each other) you do not even ask a relative or a friend whom he is betting on, because if you know how he is betting and he knows you know, and you go the other way, it will lead to strain. This rule is explicit and rigid; fairly elaborate, even rather artificial precautions are taken to avoid breaking it. At the very least you must pretend not to notice what he is doing, and he what you are doing.

11. There is a special word for betting against the grain, which is also the word for "pardon me" (*mpura*). It is considered a bad thing to do, though if the center bet is small it is sometimes all right as long as you do not do it too often. But the larger the bet and the more frequently you do it, the more the "pardon me" tack will lead to social disruption.

12. In fact, the institutionalized hostility relation, *puik,* is often formally initiated (though its causes always lie elsewhere) by such a "pardon me" bet in a deep fight, putting the symbolic fat in the fire. Similarly, the end of such a relationship and resumption of normal social intercourse is often signalized (but, again, not actually brought about) by one or the other of the enemies supporting the other's bird.

13. In sticky, cross-loyalty situations, of which in this extraordinarily complex social system there are of course many, where a man is caught between two more or less equally balanced loyalties, he tends to wander off for a cup of coffee or something to avoid having to bet, a form of behavior reminiscent of that of American voters in similar situations.[25]

14. The people involved in the center bet are, especially in deep fights, virtually always leading members of their group—kinship, village, or whatever. Further, those who bet on the side (including these

[25] B. R. Berelson, P. F. Lazersfeld, and W. N. McPhee, *Voting: A Study of Opinion Formation in a Presidential Campaign* (Chicago, 1954).

people) are, as I have already remarked, the more established members of the village—the solid citizens. Cockfighting is for those who are involved in the everyday politics of prestige as well, not for youth, women, subordinates, and so forth.

15. So far as money is concerned, the explicitly expressed attitude toward it is that it is a secondary matter. It is not, as I have said, of no importance; Balinese are no happier to lose several weeks' income than anyone else. But they mainly look on the monetary aspects of the cockfight as self-balancing, a matter of just moving money around, circulating it among a fairly well-defined group of serious cockfighters. The really important wins and losses are seen mostly in other terms, and the general attitude toward wagering is not any hope of cleaning up, of making a killing (addict gamblers again excepted), but that of the horseplayer's prayer: "Oh, God, please let me break even." In prestige terms, however, you do not want to break even, but, in a momentary, punctuate sort of way, win utterly. The talk (which goes on all the time) is about fights against such-and-such a cock of So-and-So which your cock demolished, not on how much you won, a fact people, even for large bets, rarely remember for any length of time, though they will remember the day they did in Pan Loh's finest cock for years.

16. You must bet on cocks of your own group aside from mere loyalty considerations, for if you do not people generally will say, "What! Is he too proud for the likes of us? Does he have to go to Java or Den Pasar [the capital town] to bet, he is such an important man?" Thus there is a general pressure to bet not only to show that you are important locally, but that you are not so important that you look down on everyone else as unfit even to be rivals. Similarly, home team people must bet against outside cocks or the outsiders will accuse them—a serious charge—of just collecting entry fees and not really being interested in cockfighting, as well as again being arrogant and insulting.

17. Finally, the Balinese peasants themselves are quite aware of all this and can and, at least to an ethnographer, do state most of it in approximately the same terms as I have. Fighting cocks, almost every Balinese I have ever discussed the subject with has said, is like playing with fire only not getting burned. You activate village and kingroup rivalries and hostilities, but in "play" form, coming dangerously and entrancingly close to the expression of open and direct interpersonal and intergroup aggression (something which, again, almost never happens in the normal course of ordinary life), but not quite, because, after all, it is "only a cockfight."

More observations of this sort could be advanced, but perhaps the general point is, if not made, at least well-delineated, and the whole argument thus far can be usefully summarized in a formal paradigm:

THE MORE A MATCH IS . . .

1. Between near status equals (and/or personal enemies)
2. Between high status individuals

THE DEEPER THE MATCH.

THE DEEPER THE MATCH . . .

1. The closer the identification of cock and man (or, more properly, the deeper the match the more the man will advance his best, most closely-identified-with cock).
2. The finer the cocks involved and the more exactly they will be matched.
3. The greater the emotion that will be involved and the more the general absorption in the match.
4. The higher the individual bets center and outside, the shorter the outside bet odds will tend to be, and the more betting there will be overall.
5. The less an "economic" and the more a "status" view of gaming will be involved, and the "solider" the citizens who will be gaming.[26]

Inverse arguments hold for the shallower the fight, culminating, in a reversed-signs sense, in the coin-spinning and dice-throwing amusements. For deep fights there are no absolute upper limits, though there are of course practical ones, and there are a great many legendlike tales of great Duel-in-the-Sun combats between lords and princes in classical times (for cockfighting has always been as much an elite concern as a popular one), far deeper than anything anyone, even aristocrats, could produce today anywhere in Bali.

Indeed, one of the great culture heroes of Bali is a prince, called after his passion for the sport, "The Cockfighter," who happened to be away at a very deep cockfight with a neighboring prince when the whole of his family—father, brothers, wives, sisters—were assassinated by

---

[26] As this is a formal paradigm, it is intended to display the logical, not the causal, structure of cockfighting. Just which of these considerations leads to which, in what order, and by what mechanisms, is another matter—one I have attempted to shed some light on in the general discussion.

commoner usurpers. Thus spared, he returned to dispatch the upstart, regain the throne, reconstitute the Balinese high tradition, and build its most powerful, glorious, and prosperous state. Along with everything else that the Balinese see in fighting cocks—themselves, their social order, abstract hatred, masculinity, demonic power—they also see the archetype of status virtue, the arrogant, resolute, honor-mad player with real fire, the ksatria prince.[27]

[27] In another of Hooykaas-van Leeuwen Boomkamp's folk tales ("De Gast," *Sprookjes en Verhalen van Bali,* pp. 172–180), a low caste *Sudra,* a generous, pious, and carefree man who is also an accomplished cockfighter, loses, despite his accomplishment, fight after fight until he is not only out of money but down to his last cock. He does not despair, however—"I bet," he says, "upon the Unseen World."

His wife, a good and hard-working woman, knowing how much he enjoys cockfighting, gives him her last "rainy day" money to go and bet. But, filled with misgivings due to his run of ill luck, he leaves his own cock at home and bets merely on the side. He soon loses all but a coin or two and repairs to a food stand for a snack, where he meets a decrepit, odorous, and generally unappetizing old beggar leaning on a staff. The old man asks for food, and the hero spends his last coins to buy him some. The old man then asks to pass the night with the hero, which the hero gladly invites him to do. As there is no food in the house, however, the hero tells his wife to kill the last cock for dinner. When the old man discovers this fact, he tells the hero he has three cocks in his own mountain hut and says the hero may have one of them for fighting. He also asks for the hero's son to accompany him as a servant, and, after the son agrees, this is done.

The old man turns out to be Siva and, thus, to live in a great palace in the sky, though the hero does not know this. In time, the hero decides to visit his son and collect the promised cock. Lifted up into Siva's presence, he is given the choice of three cocks. The first crows: "I have beaten fifteen opponents." The second crows, "I have beaten twenty-five opponents." The third crows, "I have beaten the king." "That one, the third, is my choice," says the hero, and returns with it to earth.

When he arrives at the cockfight, he is asked for an entry fee and replies, "I have no money; I will pay after my cock has won." As he is known never to win, he is let in because the king, who is there fighting, dislikes him and hopes to enslave him when he loses and cannot pay off. In order to insure that this happens, the king matches his finest cock against the hero's. When the cocks are placed down, the hero's flees, and the crowd, led by the arrogant king, hoots in laughter. The hero's cock then flies at the king himself, killing him with a spur stab in the throat. The hero flees. His house is encircled by the king's men. The cock changes into a Garuda, the great mythic bird of Indic legend, and carries the hero and his wife to safety in the heavens.

When the people see this, they make the hero king and his wife queen and they return as such to earth. Later their son, released by Siva, also returns and the hero-king announces his intention to enter a hermitage. ("I will fight no more cockfights. I have bet on the Unseen and won.") He enters the hermitage and his son becomes king.

Feathers, Blood, Crowds, and Money

"Poetry makes nothing happen," Auden says in his elegy of Yeats, "it survives in the valley of its saying . . . a way of happening, a mouth." The cockfight too, in this colloquial sense, makes nothing happen. Men go on allegorically humiliating one another and being allegorically humiliated by one another, day after day, glorying quietly in the experience if they have triumphed, crushed only slightly more openly by it if they have not. *But no one's status really changes.* You cannot ascend the status ladder by winning cockfights; you cannot, as an individual, really ascend it at all. Nor can you descend it that way.[28] All you can do is enjoy and savor, or suffer and withstand, the concocted sensation of drastic and momentary movement along an aesthetic semblance of that ladder, a kind of behind-the-mirror status jump which has the look of mobility without its actuality.

Like any art form—for that, finally, is what we are dealing with— the cockfight renders ordinary, everyday experience comprehensible by presenting it in terms of acts and objects which have had their practical consequences removed and been reduced (or, if you prefer, raised) to the level of sheer appearances, where their meaning can be more powerfully articulated and more exactly perceived. The cockfight is "really real" only to the cocks—it does not kill anyone, castrate anyone, reduce anyone to animal status, alter the hierarchical relations among people, or refashion the hierarchy; it does not even redistribute income in any significant way. What it does is what, for other peoples with other temperaments and other conventions, *Lear* and *Crime and Punishment* do; it catches up these themes—death, masculinity, rage, pride, loss, beneficence, chance—and, ordering them into an encompassing structure, presents them in such a way as to throw into relief a particular view of their essential nature. It puts a construction on them, makes them, to

---

[28] Addict gamblers are really less declassed (for their status is, as everyone else's, inherited) than merely impoverished and personally disgraced. The most prominent addict gambler in my cockfight circuit was actually a very high caste *satria* who sold off most of his considerable lands to support his habit. Though everyone privately regarded him as a fool and worse (some, more charitable, regarded him as sick), he was publicly treated with the elaborate deference and politeness due his rank. On the independence of personal reputation and public status in Bali, see above, Chapter 14.

those historically positioned to appreciate the construction, meaningful
—visible, tangible, graspable—"real," in an ideational sense. An
image, fiction, a model, a metaphor, the cockfight is a means of expression; its function is neither to assuage social passions nor to heighten
them (though, in its playing-with-fire way it does a bit of both), but, in
a medium of feathers, blood, crowds, and money, to display them.

The question of how it is that we perceive qualities in things—
paintings, books, melodies, plays—that we do not feel we can assert literally to be there has come, in recent years, into the very center of aesthetic theory.[29] Neither the sentiments of the artist, which remain his,
nor those of the audience, which remain theirs, can account for the agitation of one painting or the serenity of another. We attribute grandeur,
wit, despair, exuberance to strings of sounds; lightness, energy, violence, fluidity to blocks of stone. Novels are said to have strength,
buildings eloquence, plays momentum, ballets repose. In this realm of
eccentric predicates, to say that the cockfight, in its perfected cases at
least, is "disquietful" does not seem at all unnatural, merely, as I have
just denied it practical consequence, somewhat puzzling.

The disquietfulness arises, "somehow," out of a conjunction of three
attributes of the fight: its immediate dramatic shape; its metaphoric content; and its social context. A cultural figure against a social ground, the
fight is at once a convulsive surge of animal hatred, a mock war of sym-
bolical selves, and a formal simulation of status tensions, and its aesthetic power derives from its capacity to force together these diverse
realities. The reason it is disquietful is not that it has material effects (it
has some, but they are minor); the reason that it is disquietful is that,
joining pride to selfhood, selfhood to cocks, and cocks to destruction, it
brings to imaginative realization a dimension of Balinese experience
normally well-obscured from view. The transfer of a sense of gravity
into what is in itself a rather blank and unvarious spectacle, a commotion of beating wings and throbbing legs, is effected by interpreting it as
expressive of something unsettling in the way its authors and audience
live, or, even more ominously, what they are.

As a dramatic shape, the fight displays a characteristic that does not
seem so remarkable until one realizes that it does not have to be there:

[29] For four, somewhat variant, treatments, see S. Langer, *Feeling and Form*
(New York, 1953); R. Wollheim, *Art and Its Objects* (New York, 1968);
N. Goodman, *Languages of Art* (Indianapolis, 1968); M. Merleau-Ponty, "The Eye
and the Mind," in his *The Primacy of Perception* (Evanston, Ill., 1964), pp.
159–190.

a radically atomistical structure.[30] Each match is a world unto itself, a particulate burst of form. There is the matchmaking, there is the betting, there is the fight, there is the result—utter triumph and utter defeat—and there is the hurried, embarrassed passing of money. The loser is not consoled. People drift away from him, look around him, leave him to assimilate his momentary descent into nonbeing, reset his face, and return, scarless and intact, to the fray. Nor are winners congratulated, or events rehashed; once a match is ended the crowd's attention turns totally to the next, with no looking back. A shadow of the experience no doubt remains with the principals, perhaps even with some of the witnesses of a deep fight, as it remains with us when we leave the theater after seeing a powerful play well-performed; but it quite soon fades to become at most a schematic memory—a diffuse glow or an abstract shudder—and usually not even that. Any expressive form lives only in its own present—the one it itself creates. But, here, that present is severed into a string of flashes, some more bright than others, but all of them disconnected, aesthetic quanta. Whatever the cockfight says, it says in spurts.

But, as I have argued lengthily elsewhere, the Balinese live in spurts.[31] Their life, as they arrange it and perceive it, is less a flow, a directional movement out of the past, through the present, toward the future than an on-off pulsation of meaning and vacuity, an arhythmic alternation of short periods when "something" (that is, something significant) is happening, and equally short ones where "nothing" (that is, nothing much) is—between what they themselves call "full" and "empty" times, or, in another idiom, "junctures" and "holes." In focusing activity down to a burning-glass dot, the cockfight is merely being Balinese in the same way in which everything from the monadic en-

---

[30] British cockfights (the sport was banned there in 1840) indeed seem to have lacked it, and to have generated, therefore, a quite different family of shapes. Most British fights were "mains," in which a preagreed number of cocks were aligned into two teams and fought serially. Score was kept and wagering took place both on the individual matches and on the main as a whole. There were also "battle Royales," both in England and on the Continent, in which a large number of cocks were let loose at once with the one left standing at the end the victor. And in Wales, the so-called Welsh main followed an elimination pattern, along the lines of a present-day tennis tournament, winners proceeding to the next round. As a genre, the cock fight has perhaps less compositional flexibility than, say, Latin comedy, but it is not entirely without any. On cockfighting more generally, see A. Ruport, *The Art of Cockfighting* (New York, 1949); G. R. Scott, *History of Cockfighting* (London, 1957); and L. Fitz-Barnard, *Fighting Sports* (London, 1921).

[31] Above, pp. 391–398.

counters of everyday life, through the clanging pointillism of *gamelan* music, to the visiting-day-of-the-gods temple celebrations are. It is not an imitation of the punctuateness of Balinese social life, nor a depiction of it, nor even an expression of it; it is an example of it, carefully prepared.[32]

If one dimension of the cockfight's structure, its lack of temporal directionality, makes it seem a typical segment of the general social life, however, the other, its flat-out, head-to-head (or spur-to-spur) aggressiveness, makes it seem a contradiction, a reversal, even a subversion of it. In the normal course of things, the Balinese are shy to the point of obsessiveness of open conflict. Oblique, cautious, ·subdued, controlled, masters of indirection and dissimulation—what they call *alus,* "polished," "smooth"—they rarely face what they can turn away from, rarely resist what they can evade. But here they portray themselves as wild and murderous, with manic explosions of instinctual cruelty. A powerful rendering of life as the Balinese most deeply do not want it (to adapt a phrase Frye has used of Gloucester's blinding) is set in the context of a sample of it as they do in fact have it.[33] And, because the context suggests that the rendering, if less than a straightforward description, is nonetheless more than an idle fancy; it is here that the disquietfulness—the disquietfulness of the *fight,* not (or, anyway, not necessarily) its patrons, who seem in fact rather thoroughly to enjoy it —emerges. The slaughter in the cock ring is not a depiction of how things literally are among men, but, what is almost worse, of how, from a particular angle, they imaginatively are.[34]

---

[32] For the necessity of distinguishing among "description," "representation," "exemplification," and "expression" (and the irrelevance of "imitation" to all of them) as modes of symbolic reference, see Goodman, *Languages of Art,* pp. 61–110, 45–91, 225–241.

[33] N. Frye, *The Educated Imagination* (Bloomington, Ind., 1964), p. 99.

[34] There are two other Balinese values and disvalues which, connected with punctuate temporality on the one hand and unbridled aggressiveness on the other, reinforce the sense that the cockfight is at once continuous with ordinary social life and a direct negation of it: what the Balinese call *ramé,* and what they call *paling. Ramé* means crowded, noisy, and active, and is a highly sought-after social state: crowded markets, mass festivals, busy streets are all *ramé,* as, of course, is, in the extreme, a cockfight. *Ramé* is what happens in the "full" times (its opposite, *sepi,* "quiet," is what happens in the "empty" ones). *Paling* is social vertigo, the dizzy, disoriented, lost, turned-around feeling one gets when one's place in the coordinates of social space is not clear, and it is a tremendously disfavored, immensely anxiety-producing state. Balinese regard the exact maintenance of spatial orientation ("not to know where north is" is to be crazy), balance, decorum, status relationships, and so forth, as fundamental to ordered life (*krama*) and *paling,* the sort of whirling con-

The angle, of course, is stratificatory. What, as we have already seen, the cockfight talks most forcibly about is status relationships, and what it says about them is that they are matters of life and death. That prestige is a profoundly serious business is apparent everywhere one looks in Bali—in the village, the family, the economy, the state. A peculiar fusion of Polynesian title ranks and Hindu castes, the hierarchy of pride is the moral backbone of the society. But only in the cockfight are the sentiments upon which that hierarchy rests revealed in their natural colors. Enveloped elsewhere in a haze of etiquette, a thick cloud of euphemism and ceremony, gesture and allusion, they are here expressed in only the thinnest disguise of an animal mask, a mask which in fact demonstrates them far more effectively than it conceals them. Jealousy is as much a part of Bali as poise, envy as grace, brutality as charm; but without the cockfight the Balinese would have a much less certain understanding of them, which is, presumably, why they value it so highly.

Any expressive form works (when it works) by disarranging semantic contexts in such a way that properties conventionally ascribed to certain things are unconventionally ascribed to others, which are then seen actually to possess them. To call the wind a cripple, as Stevens does, to fix tone and manipulate timbre, as Schoenberg does, or, closer to our case, to picture an art critic as a dissolute bear, as Hogarth does, is to cross conceptual wires; the established conjunctions between objects and their qualities are altered, and phenomena—fall weather, melodic shape, or cultural journalism—are clothed in signifiers which normally point to other referents.[35] Similarly, to connect—and connect, and connect—the collision of roosters with the divisiveness of status is to invite a transfer

fusion of position the scrambling cocks exemplify as its profoundest enemy and contradiction. On *ramé*, see Bateson and Mead, *Balinese Character*, pp. 3, 64; on *paling*, ibid., p. 11, and Belo, ed., *Traditional Balinese Culture*, p. 90 ff.

[35] The Stevens reference is to his "The Motive for Metaphor" ("You like it under the trees in autumn,/Because everything is half dead./The wind moves like a cripple among the leaves/And repeats words without meaning") [Copyright 1947 by Wallace Stevens, reprinted from *The Collected Poems of Wallace Stevens* by permission of Alfred A. Knopf, Inc., and Faber and Faber Ltd.]; the Schoenberg reference is to the third of his *Five Orchestral Pieces* (Opus 16), and is borrowed from H. H. Drager, "The Concept of 'Tonal Body,'" in *Reflections on Art*, ed. S. Langer (New York, 1961), p. 174. On Hogarth, and on this whole problem—there called "multiple matrix matching"—see E. H. Gombrich, "The Use of Art for the Study of Symbols," in *Psychology and the Visual Arts*, ed. J. Hogg (Baltimore, 1969), pp. 149–170. The more usual term for this sort of semantic alchemy is "metaphorical transfer," and good technical discussions of it can be found in M. Black, *Models and Metaphors* (Ithaca, N.Y., 1962), p. 25 ff; Goodman, *Language as Art*, p. 44 ff; and W. Percy, "Metaphor as Mistake," *Sewanee Review* 66 (1958): 78–99.

of perceptions from the former to the latter, a transfer which is at once a description and a judgment. (Logically, the transfer could, of course, as well go the other way; but, like most of the rest of us, the Balinese are a great deal more interested in understanding men than they are in understanding cocks.)

What sets the cockfight apart from the ordinary course of life, lifts it from the realm of everyday practical affairs, and surrounds it with an aura of enlarged importance is not, as functionalist sociology would have it, that it reinforces status discriminations (such reinforcement is hardly necessary in a society where every act proclaims them), but that it provides a metasocial commentary upon the whole matter of assorting human beings into fixed hierarchical ranks and then organizing the major part of collective existence around that assortment. Its function, if you want to call it that, is interpretive: it is a Balinese reading of Balinese experience, a story they tell themselves about themselves.

Saying Something of Something

To put the matter this way is to engage in a bit of metaphorical refocusing of one's own, for it shifts the analysis of cultural forms from an endeavor in general parallel to dissecting an organism, diagnosing a symptom, deciphering a code, or ordering a system—the dominant analogies in contemporary anthropology—to one in general parallel with penetrating a literary text. If one takes the cockfight, or any other collectively sustained symbolic structure, as a means of "saying something of something" (to invoke a famous Aristotelian tag), then one is faced with a problem not in social mechanics but social semantics.[36] For the anthropologist, whose concern is with formulating sociological principles, not with promoting or appreciating cockfights, the question is, what does one learn about such principles from examining culture as an assemblage of texts?

Such an extension of the notion of a text beyond written material,

[36] The tag is from the second book of the *Organon, On Interpretation*. For a discussion of it, and for the whole argument for freeing "the notion of text . . . from the notion of scripture or writing" and constructing, thus, a general hermeneutics, see P. Ricoeur, *Freud and Philosophy* (New Haven, 1970), p. 20 ff.

and even beyond verbal, is, though metaphorical, not, of course, all that novel. The *interpretatio naturae* tradition of the middle ages, which, culminating in Spinoza, attempted to read nature as Scripture, the Nietszchean effort to treat value systems as glosses on the will to power (or the Marxian one to treat them as glosses on property relations), and the Freudian replacement of the enigmatic text of the manifest dream with the plain one of the latent, all offer precedents, if not equally recommendable ones.[37] But the idea remains theoretically undeveloped; and the more profound corollary, so far as anthropology is concerned, that cultural forms can be treated as texts, as imaginative works built out of social materials, has yet to be systematically exploited.[38]

In the case at hand, to treat the cockfight as a text is to bring out a feature of it (in my opinion, the central feature of it) that treating it as a rite or a pastime, the two most obvious alternatives, would tend to obscure: its use of emotion for cognitive ends. What the cockfight says it says in a vocabulary of sentiment—the thrill of risk, the despair of loss, the pleasure of triumph. Yet what it says is not merely that risk is exciting, loss depressing, or triumph gratifying, banal tautologies of affect, but that it is of these emotions, thus exampled, that society is built and individuals are put together. Attending cockfights and participating in them is, for the Balinese, a kind of sentimental education. What he learns there is what his culture's ethos and his private sensibility (or, anyway, certain aspects of them) look like when spelled out externally in a collective text; that the two are near enough alike to be articulated in the symbolics of a single such text; and—the disquieting part—that the text in which this revelation is accomplished consists of a chicken hacking another mindlessly to bits.

Every people, the proverb has it, loves its own form of violence. The cockfight is the Balinese reflection on theirs: on its look, its uses, its force, its fascination. Drawing on almost every level of Balinese experience, it brings together themes—animal savagery, male narcissism, opponent gambling, status rivalry, mass excitement, blood sacrifice—

[37] Ibid.

[38] Lévi-Strauss' "structuralism" might seem an exception. But it is only an apparent one, for, rather than taking myths, totem rites, marriage rules, or whatever as texts to interpret, Lévi-Strauss takes them as ciphers to solve, which is very much not the same thing. He does not seek to understand symbolic forms in terms of how they function in concrete situations to organize perceptions (meanings, emotions, concepts, attitudes); he seeks to understand them entirely in terms of their internal structure, *independent de tout sujet, de tout objet, et de toute contexte.* See above, Chapter 13.

whose main connection is their involvement with rage and the fear of
rage, and, binding them into a set of rules which at once contains them
and allows them play, builds a symbolic structure in which, over and
over again, the reality of their inner affiliation can be intelligibly felt.
If, to quote Northrop Frye again, we go to see *Macbeth* to learn what a
man feels like after he has gained a kingdom and lost his soul, Balinese
go to cockfights to find out what a man, usually composed, aloof, almost
obsessively self-absorbed, a kind of moral autocosm, feels like when, attacked, tormented, challenged, insulted, and driven in result to the extremes of fury, he has totally triumphed or been brought totally low.
The whole passage, as it takes us back to Aristotle (though to the *Poet-
ics* rather than the *Hermeneutics*), is worth quotation:

> But the poet [as opposed to the historian], Aristotle says, never makes any
> real statements at all, certainly no particular or specific ones. The poet's job
> is not to tell you what happened, but what happens: not what did take
> place, but the kind of thing that always does take place. He gives you the
> typical, recurring, or what Aristotle calls universal event. You wouldn't go
> to *Macbeth* to learn about the history of Scotland—you go to it to learn
> what a man feels like after he's gained a kingdom and lost his soul. When
> you meet such a character as Micawber in Dickens, you don't feel that there
> must have been a man Dickens knew who was exactly like this: you feel
> that there's a bit of Micawber in almost everybody you know, including
> yourself. Our impressions of human life are picked up one by one, and re-
> main for most of us loose and disorganized. But we constantly find things in
> literature that suddenly coordinate and bring into focus a great many such
> impressions, and this is part of what Aristotle means by the typical or uni-
> versal human event.[39]

It is this kind of bringing of assorted experiences of everyday life to
focus that the cockfight, set aside from that life as "only a game" and
reconnected to it as "more than a game," accomplishes, and so creates
what, better than typical or universal, could be called a paradigmatic
human event—that is, one that tells us less what happens than the kind
of thing that would happen if, as is not the case, life were art and could
be as freely shaped by styles of feeling as *Macbeth* and *David Copper-
field* are.

Enacted and re-enacted, so far without end, the cockfight enables the
Balinese, as, read and reread, *Macbeth* enables us, to see a dimension
of his own subjectivity. As he watches fight after fight, with the active
watching of an owner and a bettor (for cockfighting has no more inter-

[39] Frye, *The Educated Imagination*, pp. 63–64.

est as a pure spectator sport than does croquet or dog racing), he grows familiar with it and what it has to say to him, much as the attentive listener to string quartets or the absorbed viewer of still life grows slowly more familiar with them in a way which opens his subjectivity to himself.[40]

Yet, because—in another of those paradoxes, along with painted feelings and unconsequenced acts, which haunt aesthetics—that subjectivity does not properly exist until it is thus organized, art forms generate and regenerate the very subjectivity they pretend only to display. Quartets, still lifes, and cockfights are not merely reflections of a pre-existing sensibility analogically represented; they are positive agents in the creation and maintenance of such a sensibility. If we see ourselves as a pack of Micawbers, it is from reading too much Dickens (if we see ourselves as unillusioned realists, it is from reading too little); and similarly for Balinese, cocks, and cockfights. It is in such a way, coloring experience with the light they cast it in, rather than through whatever material effects they may have, that the arts play their role, as arts, in social life.[41]

In the cockfight, then, the Balinese forms and discovers his temperament and his society's temper at the same time. Or, more exactly, he forms and discovers a particular facet of them. Not only are there a great many other cultural texts providing commentaries on status hier-

[40] The use of the, to Europeans, "natural" visual idiom for perception—"see," "watches," and so forth—is more than usually misleading here, for the fact that, as mentioned earlier, Balinese follow the progress of the fight as much (perhaps, as fighting cocks are actually rather hard to see except as blurs of motion, more) with their bodies as with their eyes, moving their limbs, heads, and trunks in gestural mimicry of the cocks' maneuvers, means that much of the individual's experience of the fight is kinesthetic rather than visual. If ever there was an example of Kenneth Burke's definition of a symbolic act as "the dancing of an attitude" [*The Philosophy of Literary Form*, rev. ed. (New York, 1957), p. 9] the cockfight is it. On the enormous role of kinesthetic perception in Balinese life, Bateson and Mead, *Balinese Character*, pp. 84–88; on the active nature of aesthetic perception in general, Goodman. *Language of Art*, pp. 241–244.

[41] All this coupling of the occidental great with the oriental lowly will doubtless disturb certain sorts of aestheticians as the earlier efforts of anthropologists to speak of Christianity and totemism in the same breath disturbed certain sorts of theologians. But as ontological questions are (or should be) bracketed in the sociology of religion, judgmental ones are (or should be) bracketed in the sociology of art. In any case, the attempt to deprovincialize the concept of art is but part of the general anthropological conspiracy to deprovincialize all important social concepts—marriage, religion, law, rationality—and though this is a threat to aesthetic theories which regard certain works of art as beyond the reach of sociological analysis, it is no threat to the conviction, for which Robert Graves claims to have been reprimanded at his Cambridge tripos, that some poems are better than others.

archy and self-regard in Bali, but there are a great many other critical sectors of Balinese life besides the stratificatory and the agonistic that receive such commentary. The ceremony consecrating a Brahmana priest, a matter of breath control, postural immobility, and vacant concentration upon the depths of being, displays a radically different, but to the Balinese equally real, property of social hierarchy—its reach toward the numinous transcendent. Set not in the matrix of the kinetic emotionality of animals, but in that of the static passionlessness of divine mentality, it expresses tranquillity not disquiet. The mass festivals at the village temples, which mobilize the whole local population in elaborate hostings of visiting gods—songs, dances, compliments, gifts —assert the spiritual unity of village mates against their status inequality and project a mood of amity and trust.[42] The cockfight is not the master key to Balinese life, any more than bullfighting is to Spanish. What it says about that life is not unqualified nor even unchallenged by what other equally eloquent cultural statements say about it. But there is nothing more surprising in this than in the fact that Racine and Molière were contemporaries, or that the same people who arrange chrysanthemums cast swords.[43]

The culture of a people is an ensemble of texts, themselves ensembles, which the anthropologist strains to read over the shoulders of those to whom they properly belong. There are enormous difficulties in such an enterprise, methodological pitfalls to make a Freudian quake,

[42] For the consecration ceremony, see V. E. Korn, "The Consecration of the Priest," in Swellengrebel, ed., Bali: Studies, pp. 131–154; for (somewhat exaggerated) village communion, R. Goris, "The Religious Character of the Balinese Village," ibid., pp. 79–100.

[43] That what the cockfight has to say about Bali is not altogether without perception and the disquiet it expresses about the general pattern of Balinese life is not wholly without reason is attested by the fact that in two weeks of December 1965, during the upheavals following the unsuccessful coup in Djakarta, between forty and eighty thousand Balinese (in a population of about two million) were killed, largely by one another—the worst outburst in the country. [J. Hughes, Indonesian Upheaval (New York, 1967), pp. 173–183. Hughes' figures are, of course, rather casual estimates, but they are not the most extreme.] This is not to say, of course, that the killings were caused by the cockfight, could have been predicted on the basis of it, or were some sort of enlarged version of it with real people in the place of the cocks—all of which is nonsense. It is merely to say that if one looks at Bali not just through the medium of its dances, its shadowplays, its sculpture, and its girls, but—as the Balinese themselves do—also through the medium of its cockfight, the fact that the massacre occurred seems, if no less appalling, less like a contradiction to the laws of nature. As more than one real Gloucester has discovered, sometimes people actually get life precisely as they most deeply do not want it.

and some moral perplexities as well. Nor is it the only way that symbolic forms can be sociologically handled. Functionalism lives, and so does psychologism. But to regard such forms as "saying something of something," and saying it to somebody, is at least to open up the possibility of an analysis which attends to their substance rather than to reductive formulas professing to account for them.

As in more familiar exercises in close reading, one can start anywhere in a culture's repertoire of forms and end up anywhere else. One can stay, as I have here, within a single, more or less bounded form, and circle steadily within it. One can move between forms in search of broader unities or informing contrasts. One can even compare forms from different cultures to define their character in reciprocal relief. But whatever the level at which one operates, and however intricately, the guiding principle is the same: societies, like lives, contain their own interpretations. One has only to learn how to gain access to them.

Acknowledgments

"The Impact of the Concept of Culture on the Concept of Man," in *New Views of the Nature of Man,* ed. J. Platt (Chicago: University of Chicago Press, 1966), pp. 93–118. Reprinted by permission of The University of Chicago Press and © 1966 by The University of Chicago.

"The Growth of Culture and the Evolution of Mind." Reprinted with permission of Macmillan Publishing Co., Inc., from *Theories of the Mind,* edited by J. Scher, pp. 713–740. Copyright © The Free Press of Glencoe, a Division of The Macmillan Company, 1962.

"Religion as a Cultural System," in *Anthropological Approaches to the Study of Religion,* ed. M. Banton (London: Tavistock Publications Ltd, 1966), pp. 1–46. Reprinted by permission.

"Ethos, World View and the Analysis of Sacred Symbols." Copyright © 1957 by The Antioch Review, Inc. First published in *The Antioch Review,* Vol. 17, No. 4; reprinted by permission of the editors.

"Ritual and Social Change: A Javanese Example," in *American Anthropologist* 61 (1959): 991–1012. Reprinted by permission.

" 'Internal Conversion' in Contemporary Bali," in *Malayan and Indonesian Studies presented to Sir Richard Winstedt,* eds. J. Bastin and R. Roolvink (Oxford: Oxford University Press, 1964), pp. 282–302. Reprinted by permission of The Clarendon Press, Oxford, England.

"Ideology as a Cultural System." Reprinted with permission of Macmillan Publishing Co., Inc., from *Ideology and Discontent,* edited by D. Apter, pp. 47–56. Copyright © 1964 by The Free Press of Glencoe, a Division of The Macmillan Company.

Index